Indians,
Merchants,
and Markets

Jeremy   Baskes

Indians, Merchants, and Markets

A REINTERPRETATION
OF THE *Repartimiento* AND
SPANISH-INDIAN ECONOMIC
RELATIONS IN COLONIAL
OAXACA, 1750–1821

Stanford University Press
Stanford, California

Stanford University Press
Stanford, California
© 2000 by the Board of Trustees of the Leland Stanford Junior University

Printed in the United States of America
On acid-free, archival-quality paper

Library of Congress Cataloging-in-Publication Data
Baskes, Jeremy
    Indians, merchants, and markets : reinterpretation of the repartimiento and Spanish-Indian economic relations in colonial Oaxaca, 1750–1821 / Jeremy Baskes.
        p.   cm.
    Includes bibliographical references and index.
    ISBN 0-8047-3512-3 (alk. paper)
        1. Indians of Mexico — Agriculture — Mexico — Oaxaca.   2. Indians of Mexico — Commerce — Mexico — Oaxaca.   3. Indians of Mexico — Mexico — Oaxaca — Economic conditions.   4. Agricultural credit — Mexico — Oaxaca — History.   5. Cochineal — Mexico — Oaxaca — Marketing — History.   6. Dye industry — Mexico — Oaxaca — History.   7. Colonial administrators — Mexico — Oaxaca — History.   8. Spain — Colonies — America — Administration.   I. Title.
    F1219.1.O11 B29 2000
    338.4'766726 — dc21   00-039489

Designed by Janet Wood
Typeset by Keystone Typesetting, Inc., in 10/13 Sabon

Original Printing 2000

Last figure below indicates year of this printing:
09   08   07   07   06   05   04   03   02   01   00

For my parents, Roger and Julie Baskes

and my wife, Jane Erickson

Contents

Contents

Tables

Illustrations

Acknowledgments

In the nearly ten years that I have worked on this project, I have benefited from the tremendous generosity of numerous persons and institutions. The University of Chicago Center for Latin American Studies provided travel funds to Oaxaca which allowed me to conduct preliminary doctoral research. A Fulbright Grant from the Institute of International Education in 1991 helped fund a year's dissertation research in the archives of Oaxaca and Mexico City. I returned to Mexico in the summer of 1994 with a Thomas E. Winslow Grant from Ohio Wesleyan University. In 1997 I received a Fulbright from the Council for International Exchange which financed six months at the *Archivo General de Indias* in Seville, Spain. This Fulbright was supplemented by another Thomas E. Winslow Grant from Ohio Wesleyan University. Without all of this support, this book would have taken much longer to finish.

This project began as my dissertation at the University of Chicago. Numerous professors, friends, and colleagues there read portions of the manuscript or lent their moral and intellectual support. I am especially grateful to Kate Bjork, Robin Derby, Peter Guardino, Richard Warren, and Eric Zolov. I also thank my dissertation committee, Ralph Austen, Friedrich Katz, and John Coatsworth. Throughout the process, John Coatsworth's penetrating comments and insightful advice have helped to shape and strengthen this manuscript. My debt to him is enormous.

Three other scholars read the entire manuscript and gave me invaluable and deeply appreciated input. Ken Andrien forced me to widen my perspective and better situate my research in the broader colonial historiography. More generally, he has provided friendship and has become one of my closest colleagues. Nils Jacobsen provided advice, ideas, and support from the very beginning of this project. Richard Salvucci's lengthy and detailed comments helped me to bolster many of my arguments and recast a few.

Acknowledgments

In Mexico and Spain, I also benefited from the input and support of friends and scholars. I first met Pat McNamara in the Notarial Archive of Oaxaca, and he fast became a close friend and valued colleague with whom I have frequently discussed my research. Leticia Reina kindly helped me get oriented in Oaxaca and gave me considerable assistance. In Mexico City, Carlos Marichal provided me with guidance and encouragement. In Seville, Jason Lemon and Georgina Moreno Coello imparted friendship and advice. I also profited from my discussions with Arij Ouweneel.

Current and past colleagues at Ohio Wesleyan University have generously helped in a variety of ways. I thank Peter Alexander, Carol Doubikin, Mark Gingerich, Bob Gitter, Will Pyle, Deborah Van Broekhoven, and William Walker. Other scholars who have commented on portions of this manuscript at various stages include David Galenson, John Kicza, Robert Patch, Vicente Pinilla, Alfonso Quiroz, Steve Stern, Enrique Tandeter, and Gail Triner.

At Stanford University Press, I thank Norris Pope, Stacey Lynn, and Ruth Steinberg, as well as the anonymous reviewer whose comments helped me in the final push to finish the book. The editor of the Series on Social Science History, Steve Haber, also provided valuable comments and gave me encouragement for several years before the manuscript was even submitted to Stanford University Press. I am also grateful to the editors of the *Journal of Latin American Studies* for permission to reprint in chapter four of this book materials that first appeared in that journal. In the process of publishing the *JLAS* article, I also profited from the comments of the anonymous reviewers.

Among the many to whom I owe gratitude, three people stand out, my parents, Roger and Julie Baskes, and my wife, Jane Erickson. My parents provided me with love and a childhood environment which encouraged me to pursue intellectual endeavors. My wife, Jane, more than any other person, has endured the enjoyment and the hardships of writing this book. She has twice uprooted herself to accompany me abroad, and without her love, encouragement, and companionship, I cannot imagine having finished this book. My parents and wife have also served as my "editorial staff," reading, editing, and commenting on numerous drafts of the work. Jane even accompanied me to the Mexican archives as my research assistant. For all of their help, love, and support, I dedicate this book to them.

J.B.

Note on Abbreviations and Conventions

The following abbreviations and conventions are used in the text.

Abbreviations

AFY	Archivo de la Familia Yraeta
AGEO	Archivo General del Estado de Oaxaca
AGI	Archivo General de Indias
AGN	Archivo General de la Nación
AGNO	Archivo General de Notarias de Oaxaca
AHMO	Archivo Histórico Municipal de Oaxaca
AJT	Archivo Judicial de Teposcolula
AJVA	Archivo Judicial de Villa Alta
BMLT	Biblioteca Miguel Lerdo de Tejada de la Secretaría de Hacienda y Crédito Público
BNM	Biblioteca Nacional de México

Currency

1 peso = 8 reales de plata (pieces of eight)
1 peso = 20 reales de vellón
1 real de plata = 12 granos

Weights

1 arroba = 25 pounds = 11.325 kilograms
1 pound = 16 ounces = .453 kilograms
1 quintal = 4 arrobas = a hundredweight = 100 pounds

Volumes

A zurrón and a sobornal were large sacks containing from 7 to 9 arrobas of cochineal.

Indians,
Merchants,
and Markets

Chapter One

Introduction

T his is a study of the *repartimiento* and market participation of indigenous peasants in late-colonial Oaxaca, Mexico. Like peasants in other
regions of Mexico, indigenous Oaxacans produced staple crops destined
primarily for their own personal consumption. But Oaxacan peasants
were also deeply engaged in the production for export of a crimson-
colored dye called *grana cochinilla*. Produced in small backyard cactus
groves, cochineal earned considerable income for peasant households and
became a critical component of their survival strategies.

Extensive participation in the market economy, either as producers of
cochineal or consumers of commodities, required that peasants have access to credit. Credit, however, was not widely available in remote rural
regions, largely owing to the limits of market integration in rural colonial
Mexico. Only one source of financing was widely available to peasants;
this credit system, called the *repartimiento*, was operated by the Crown's
district magistrates, the *alcaldes mayores*.[1]

The Crown appointed the *alcaldes mayores* to serve in indigenous regions of Spanish America and granted them broad responsibilities, which
included the collection of Indian tribute and the administration of justice.
While these local officials were theoretically prohibited by the Law of
Indies from trading with their charges, such restrictions were regularly
violated, and such violations were, until 1786, tolerated or even sanctioned by the Crown. The majority of their trade was conducted through
the *repartimiento* system, by which *alcaldes mayores* supplied peasants
with goods or cash on credit.

The *repartimiento* occupies an especially prominent role in the historiography of colonial Spanish America. In nearly all scholarly works (and
in college courses on colonial Spanish America) the *repartimiento* is identified as the example par excellence of a barbarous, late-colonial, coercive
institution designed by the state to extract wealth from the Indian popula-

tion. For their role in the *repartimiento*, the *alcaldes mayores* are most often portrayed as sadistic villains, the very embodiment of the Black Legend.[2] In this traditional historiography, the *repartimiento* is depicted as a system in which regional officials used violence and intimidation to compel reluctant indigenous communities to participate in the market as consumers and producers at exceedingly unfavorable prices.

This book rejects the conventional portrayal of the *repartimiento*. Despite the prominence of the *repartimiento* in the literature, historians have never closely examined how the system actually functioned at the local level. As Lockhart and Schwartz note, "The topic has generated an entrenched mythology, but what is known about the actual operation of *repartos* is actually very little."[3] By examining the system in great detail and employing microeconomic analysis, this book seeks to rectify these past shortcomings and, in the process, construct a revisionist depiction of the system of *repartimiento*. It shows that the *repartimiento* was an institution designed to provide producer and consumer credit to indigenous peasants under conditions of tremendous risk and imperfect markets, and that peasants participated in the *repartimiento* voluntarily because through the system they obtained valued goods and needed income, unobtainable from other sources. Without the *repartimiento*, peasants would not have had regular access to the credit which enabled them to engage in more lucrative activities and purchase higher-priced commodities. While at times the *repartimiento*, and market participation in general, yielded undesired hardships, more often indigenous peasants benefited from economic exchange.

During the past several decades, the *repartimiento* has attracted significant attention in the historiography of colonial Spanish America. In general, the *repartimiento* has been approached from two very different angles. Scholars interested in the late-colonial Bourbon Reforms have examined the *repartimiento* because it was selected as a main target of reform. These important studies have been predominantly institutional and political histories, focusing closely on the late-eighteenth-century debates over the *repartimiento*, the difficulty of prohibiting it, and general attempts to introduce the Intendancy system into Spain's colonies.[4] Other studies have reviewed the *repartimiento* in an effort to elucidate issues such as indigenous rebellion or the structures of Indian communities.[5] While these latter works have sometimes yielded interesting observations, none has gone far enough in explaining how the *repartimiento* worked and few have questioned its conventional interpretation.

Ironically, in the colonial era itself there was more extensive and more varied debate about the nature of the *repartimiento* than exists in most modern scholarship. Over the course of the second half of the eighteenth century, the *repartimiento* occupied increasingly more and more of the attention of Mexico's colonial elite. Extensive investigations into the *repartimiento* were carried out by Crown officials, often prompted by passionate defenses or condemnations of the system by merchants or clerics, respectively. Such testimonies provide scholars with considerable perspective on the role of coercion in the *repartimiento*, and the image that emerges is far more nuanced and complex than the one conventionally found in modern scholarship.[6] In modern colonial monographs, few scholars move beyond one-dimensional depictions, in which the *alcalde mayor*'s unbridled force drives peasants unwillingly into the market.

Several notable exceptions exist to the traditional depictions of the *repartimiento*. A careful reading of the classic works of Brian R. Hamnett and David Brading suggests that these scholars attempted to avoid taking a position on whether or not *repartimientos* were forced. Given the wide acceptance of the traditional view, however, such neutrality has gone unnoticed; in fact, Hamnett's work, especially, is often cited in reference to forced *repartimientos*.[7] Two other historians, Horst Pietschmann and María de los Angeles Romero Frizzi, have actually proposed that the *repartimiento* was less coerced than universally believed. While suggestive, these brief studies are more reflective than based on extensive research, and, more important, neither begins to develop alternative interpretations of the *repartimiento*.[8]

The only significant exception to the traditional depiction is Arij Ouweneel's recent work on Central Mexico. Ouweneel rejects the notion that peasants were forced to accept *repartimientos*; he argues that the *repartimiento* was a form of "private tribute" (evolved from preconquest tribute) granted by the Indians to the *alcalde mayor* as compensation for his just rule, what Ouweneel calls "*buen gobierno*." It was thus a system of reciprocity in which the *alcalde* received tribute (his *repartimiento* profits) in exchange for governing justly: "Such taxes were obligatory — like modern forms of tax — and were universally accepted as long as the *alcalde mayor* observed the familiar rules of '*buen gobierno*.' "[9] While Ouweneel moves well beyond the one-dimensional depictions found elsewhere, his interpretation still leaves considerable doubt that peasants desired or needed the *repartimiento*, despite his repeated assertion that they did. He states that the *repartimiento* was an "obligatory" tax, yet he also argues

3

that Indians "generally cooperated with this trade on a voluntary basis, sometimes on their own initiative, and in any case were usually motivated by economic considerations."[10] While much of the information in Ouweneel's book supports his contention that *repartimientos* were not forced, his contention that the system evolved from preconquest practices of reciprocity is less convincing. While his arguments are provocative, he does not provide a solid explanation for why the *repartimiento* existed or why peasants would pay this tax "on their own initiative."[11]

This book builds on the rich historiography that exists for the colonial province of Oaxaca.[12] William B. Taylor's study of colonial Oaxacan landholdings revealed that, unlike the northern regions of colonial Mexico where large *haciendas* dominated, in Oaxaca land was overwhelmingly controlled by small peasant landholders. *Haciendas* did exist, but they were neither dominant nor particularly profitable. Oaxaca, in short, was a region of indigenous peasants who throughout the colonial era retained access to land which they worked in small peasant plots.[13] The inability of Spanish *haciendas* to thrive in this southern province did not mean that the region was poor. In fact, Oaxaca was one of colonial Mexico's wealthiest provinces. The greatest wealth to be obtained in Oaxaca, however, was in commerce, not through extensive control over land. Indians produced numerous commodities highly marketable in Mexico and beyond, the most important of these being *grana cochinilla*, Mexico's second most important export product for most of the colonial period.

Most wealthy Oaxacans were involved to some degree in the dye trade, although the greatest beneficiaries of the trade were the wealthy merchants of Mexico City's consulado. As Hamnett has demonstrated, Mexico's wealthiest and most powerful merchants came to control the valuable Oaxacan dye trade because they were able to forge alliances with the Oaxacan district magistrates, the *alcaldes mayores*, by providing the financial backing that these officials needed to assume office. The *alcaldes mayores*, in turn, served as commercial agents for these wealthy merchants, trading on their behalf with the Indians of Oaxaca by issuing *repartimientos*. Historians have argued that the *alcaldes mayores* were indispensable partners to these merchants because they forced reluctant Indians to produce large quantities of cochineal, an argument that this work challenges.[14] This study shows that the *alcaldes mayores* became the valued partners of the consulado merchants not because they forced peasants to produce cochineal in the first place, but because they could use their political power to collect debts. Without the political power to enforce contracts, private merchants would not assume the risks implicit in lending widely to the indigenous peasantry.

The implications of this revisionist depiction of the *repartimiento* system are profound for myriad issues central to an understanding of colonial society. In much of the historiography on colonial Spanish America, Indians are depicted as reluctant to engage in market activities, and when they do, their participation is coerced and usually has detrimental results. As this book argues, far from resisting the market, peasants were active, willing, and shrewd in their market engagement.

This revision of the *repartimiento* also contributes to current debates about the nature of colonial rule and Spanish colonialism. The traditional depiction of the *repartimiento* presupposes an enormously powerful state capable of penetrating indigenous society to a substantial degree. Many historians, however, are increasingly skeptical about the strength of the Crown, especially in the more remote corners of the empire.[15] The view of the *repartimiento* set forth in this book does not attribute to the state such tremendous coercive capacity; its functioning does not require an enormously powerful state apparatus. This revisionist portrayal of the *repartimiento* is more in line with notions of limited state hegemony. Put simply, the colonial state and its agents were not in the business of forcing peasants into the market through the *repartimiento* as has traditionally been believed.

This is not to suggest that the colonial state was inconsequential. In fact, the colonial state played an important, even critical, role in shaping and regulating the economic and business environment. In 1751 the Crown legalized the *repartimiento*, only to prohibit it again in 1786. The Crown's capricious and arbitrary implementation of policy had a profound impact on the colony's economy in general and on the cochineal industry specifically. In examining the politics surrounding the *repartimiento*, this study, then, sheds light on the influence of the Crown's involvement in the economy.[16]

This study also contributes to the vast literature that has demonstrated the active role that indigenous peasants have played in shaping their own destinies. In traditional depictions of the *repartimiento*, with the exception of rare displays of collective action, peasants are seen as passive victims of the avarice of the *alcaldes mayores*, virtually powerless to challenge what is, allegedly, an extremely exploitative and deeply resented system. The *alcaldes mayores* supposedly forced peasants to purchase unwanted goods at artificially high prices and to pay for them by producing cochineal, which they were then required to sell to the official at below-market value. Facing such an exploitative system, peasants nonetheless acted passively.

If historians of colonial Spanish America have reached any consensus in the past quarter century, it is that Indians were not passive victims, that they exercised an active and critical role in the shaping of the colonial society and economy. To even attempt to review the vast literature on "resistance" or "agency" would be both impossible and unnecessary. Suffice to say that peasants employed a vast arsenal to resist the depredations of colonialism and protect themselves from Spanish greed and corruption. Indians were adept, even brilliant, in their use of the Spanish colonial courts to fight off their political and economic aggressors.[17] Indians also employed violent rebellion to resist colonial pressures.[18] Few political, social, or economic arenas were free of conflict.

Despite the universal recognition of peasant "agency" in nearly all spheres of colonial society, Indians are still portrayed as passive victims when it comes to the *repartimiento*.[19] And the *repartimiento* was no small matter, for it directly impacted the most important facet of the peasants' lives, their material conditions. How could peasants so prone to resist every possible aspect of colonial society be so passive in the face of the *repartimiento*, an institution universally depicted as having utterly impoverished, cheated, and exploited them? The answer, of course, is that they were not passive. Indians fought for better terms, evaded repayment of debts, and generally attempted to manipulate the *repartimiento* to their advantage (at least given their much weaker economic position vis-à-vis the *alcalde mayor*). In short, this study integrates the *repartimiento*, arguably the most important institution of Spanish–Amerindian economic exchange, more closely into the existing literature and knowledge about colonial Spanish America. The *alcaldes mayores* were not capable of forcing indigenous peasants to participate in a system so totally contrary to their economic interests. In fact, as this book shows, the Spanish officials did not have to coerce the Indians to participate at all. Peasants partook of their own free will.

6   This study examines the nexus of political, social, and economic forces surrounding *repartimiento* production of cochineal in colonial Oaxaca. Chapter 2 examines the evolution of the cochineal industry and contextualizes it within the broader society and economy of Oaxaca during the eighteenth century. It also explores in detail the micro-level operation of the *repartimiento*, particularly its role in financing indigenous produc-

tion of cochineal. Finally, the chapter examines the variety of ways in which the *alcaldes mayores* financed their business dealings.

Chapter 3 considers the heated debates regarding the *repartimiento*, which were especially sparked by Visitor General José de Gálvez's proposed 1768 Plan de Intendencias. More specifically, it discusses the impact of Crown intervention in the economy, looking particularly at the 1751 legalization of the *repartimiento* and its subsequent abolition in 1786. The chapter emphasizes the influential, yet ultimately destructive, intervention of the Crown into the colonial economy.

Chapter 4 challenges past interpretations of the role that coercion played in bringing peasants into the market as producers and consumers, and provides a revisionist interpretation of the *repartimiento*. This discussion entails the detailed examination of much of the evidence and logic employed by modern scholars to condemn the *repartimiento*. The chapter ends by arguing that the *repartimiento* was an institution designed to overcome the vast obstacles to trade on credit, obstacles which were inherent in the market imperfections and high-risk conditions that characterized colonial rural Spanish America.

Chapter 5 elaborates on the previous chapter by placing the *repartimiento* into the broader context of informal credit markets. By borrowing from the work of developmental economists, this chapter demonstrates that many of the obstacles faced by the *alcaldes mayores* in providing credit to peasants in eighteenth-century Oaxaca were similar to those faced by creditors in modern developing economies. Eighteenth-century creditors, like their modern counterparts in poorly integrated markets, were inhibited by poor access to information about peasants' creditworthiness, inadequate legal means to enforce contracts, and other barriers to trade. The Spanish-American trade was further hindered by the mistrust and uncertainty that inherently emerges in trade between peoples of different cultural backgrounds.[20] As the modern economic literature suggests and historians versed in the New Institutional Economics[21] are increasingly realizing, institutions are designed to overcome barriers to and reduce the costs of engaging in trade. This chapter shows how the institution of the *repartimiento* developed cost- and risk-reducing characteristics designed to mitigate the uncertainties and ambiguities of high-risk, cross-cultural credit transactions in the imperfectly integrated markets of colonial Spanish America.

Chapter 6 attempts to quantify the high levels of debtor default in *repartimiento* loans and to estimate the gross returns realized by one particular *alcalde mayor* from his *repartimiento* loans. The chapter argues that the high level of default and delay experienced by the *alcaldes mayores* dramatically eroded their profits, and that their actual returns were nowhere near as great as has been traditionally assumed.

Chapter 7 examines the marketing of cochineal by Indian producers outside of the *repartimiento* commercial circuit. Large amounts of cochineal were produced by peasants and sold on the "free market," either to traveling merchants, in local *tianguis*, or to the *alcalde mayor* himself. Evidence pointing to the emergence of wealthy peasant cochineal producers suggests socioeconomic differentiation in Oaxacan peasant communities, especially in the decades immediately prior to independence.

Chapter 8 traces the cochineal trade from the regions of production in rural Oaxaca to final markets in Northern Europe and examines the evolution of costs associated with the trade, including royal taxation, land and transatlantic transportation costs, and maritime insurance, among others. The chapter shows that growing fiscal pressures coupled with the post-1793, war-induced skyrocketing of transport and insurance costs, drove the profitability of the cochineal trade downward, thus explaining the depression that afflicted the trade in the mid-1790s.

The final chapter is a brief discussion of the severe decline of the cochineal industry after independence and speculates that Oaxaca's colonial prosperity might have been artificially produced by the Crown's intervention in the colonial economy.

Chapter Two

The *Repartimiento* and the Production of Cochineal

Long-distance trade was an integral aspect of Mexican civilizations for centuries before the arrival of Europeans. Tropical feathers, obsidian tools, jade, and cocoa beans were just a few of the items exchanged among distant regions. The Spanish conquest of Mexico expanded markets. Goods produced in Europe were introduced into the New World and American goods were shipped to European consumers. While the conquest altered the basket of marketed goods, economic exchange itself was nothing new to the Mexican people.

Indisputably, the American export most coveted in Europe was silver. The Andean mines of Potosí and the Mexican mines to the north of Mexico City produced tens of millions of pounds of silver, most of which was ultimately shipped to Spain and beyond. Throughout the colonial period, silver was the single most important Mexican export by value, exceeding in most years the value of all other exports combined. Unfortunately, silver bullion's dominance of the export trade has tended to eclipse in the historiography the study of other colonial products exported to Europe. While silver was important, other commodities were also exported in large quantities, especially indigenous dyestuffs such as blue indigo and red cochineal.

This study concentrates on the production and trade of cochineal dye, or simply, *grana*, as it was known in colonial Mexico. For much of the colonial period, cochineal was, after silver, Mexico's most valuable export, a commodity so highly in demand in Europe that it virtually guaranteed its seller a handsome profit, at least according to one seventeenth-century Spanish merchant.[1]

Crimson-colored cochineal dye comes from the dried bodies of *Dactylopius coccus*, an insect indigenous to southern Mexico. Parasitic to the *nopal* variety of cactus, cochineal, as the insect is commonly known, thrives when protected from its many natural predators. In the wild, cochineal insects neither reach the size nor the potency of domesticated insects.[2] The practice of producing dye from insects was not unique to America; even prior to the conquest Europeans had been producing red dye from an insect called *kermes* for more than a thousand years.[3] Mexican cochineal, however, revolutionized the dye business, for it was far more potent and its color more brilliant than that of the red dyes previously known in Europe.

Cochineal was distinguished from all other colonial exports, for its production was almost entirely carried out by Indians on small peasant plots. Labor demands in the production of *grana* were high. While not arduous, it was necessary to pay constant attention to the cochineal to protect it from its many predators, which included chickens, turkeys, lizards, and a number of insects.[4] Because *grana* production was labor intensive and there were no economies of scale, large-scale production based on wage labor proved uncompetitive.[5] While plantations did exist, they were few and their total output was small.[6]

The first step in the production of cochineal was the preparation of a *nopalera*, a *nopal* cactus patch. Peasants created a *nopalera* by digging small holes and then inserting a cactus leaf about halfway into each hole, leaving the rest of the leaf exposed. Placed in the earth in this way, the cactus would begin to grow and after a period of eighteen months to three years would be sufficiently mature to serve as host to the parasitic cochineal insect. A *nopalera* could be placed on virtually any plot of land, although well-irrigated land produced the best cacti.[7]

When a *nopalera* reached sufficient maturity, it was time to "seed" the cacti with cochineal insects. Producers attached *nidos* (nests filled with female insects) to the joints of each plant. While nests could be constructed of many different materials, palm leaves and corn husks were readily available, essentially free, and, thus, typically used. After the insects hatched, they emerged from the nests and spread themselves out across the cacti leaves, inserting their proboscises through the membranes of the cacti in order to feed on the plants' juices. The cochineal remained in this immobile state for three to four months, growing in size. During this period, it was necessary to guard the *grana* carefully, for numerous animals and insects preyed upon the cochineal. This process was very labor intensive, and involved literally purging every leaf of undesirable predators. Keeping the area in and around the *nopalera* well weeded also reduced the presence of predators. In addition, it was necessary to keep the cacti well pruned to prevent them from bearing fruit and flowers, both of which retarded the development of the cochineal. Finally, cochineal needed protection from extremes in weather. Excessive sunlight, wind, rain, or cold were sufficient to destroy the insects. As a result, *nopaleras* were sometimes protected from the elements with mud walls or primitive roofs. This stage of the cultivation process, then, demanded specialized skills and intensive labor.[8]

When the insects reached full size, producers carefully brushed them, still alive, from the leaf of the *nopal*, using either a specially designed stick or an animal tail. The final step was to kill and dry the insects, which was accomplished by a number of different processes, including immersion in boiling water, exposure to sun, heating on a skillet, and suffocation. Once dried, the insect resembled a seed, which is probably why the Spaniards called it *grana*, meaning grain. The red dye was contained inside the dried insect's body, which was marketed whole.[9]

Grana cochinilla was utilized in Mexico long before the arrival of Europeans. In his chronicle of the Mexican conquest, Bernal Diaz del Castillo reported that cochineal was abundant in the marketplace of Tenochtitlán.[10] According to Lee, cochineal was among the articles paid in tribute by conquered tribes to their Aztec rulers. In addition, the Indians of the Oaxacan region of the Mixteca dyed fabric, stone, and wood with cochineal dye, while Aztec women used it to color their bodies.[11] The greatest stimulus to its production, however, occurred only after the Spanish conquest of Mexico. Production expanded early in the colonial period, as Spanish merchants purchased *grana* for sale in the markets of Europe. By the late-1540s many Tlaxcalan Indians were producing it for export, and some had evidently grown wealthy.[12] By the end of the sixteenth century, Mexican cochineal was already widely traded in Europe, so much so that in 1589 the Amsterdam commodities exchange began recording its price.[13] Annual exports from Mexico before 1700 ranged from 5,000 to 14,000 arrobas of 25 pounds each, equal to 125,000 to 350,000 pounds.[14] In the eighteenth century, however, the cochineal industry reached maturity. By midcentury, annual production of *grana* surpassed in some years 1 million pounds. Output peaked in 1774, when more than 1.5 million pounds were produced.

While the Indians of Tlaxcala might have dominated the early-colonial production of cochineal, by the eighteenth century domesticated cochineal, *grana fina*, was produced exclusively in Oaxaca, with some minor spillover into towns bordering Oaxaca in the province of Puebla, portions of which pertain to the modern state of Guerrero. Inhabitants of several other regions of Spanish America, including Chiapas, Campeche, and parts of Peru, harvested small quantities of *grana silvestre*, wild cochineal, but neither the quality nor the quantity rivaled the *grana fina* of Oaxaca.[15]

Cochineal and the Population of Oaxaca in the Eighteenth Century

Even before the eighteenth century, the cochineal industry was of great importance to Oaxaca's economy. By midcentury, however, cochineal was indisputably the region's leading economic sector, excluding, perhaps, indigenous production of staple crops for consumption. A significant percentage of Oaxacan families were involved in some aspect of the cochineal industry, primarily as producers. In 1793, the Oaxacan Intendant Corregidor, Antonio de Mora y Peysal, estimated that the cochineal industry employed between 25,000 and 30,000 people in the province, a number representing around 8 percent of the population, but probably more than one-third of the households.[16] Because of its intensive demand for labor, the production of cochineal was virtually monopolized by indigenous peasants. A few Spanish *haciendas* in the central valleys of Oaxaca attempted to produce the dyestuff, but they were never capable of effectively competing with the peasant economy.[17] While not prominent in the production of cochineal, Europeans dominated the commercial end of the industry, trading the dyestuff from Oaxaca to Spain and beyond.

Indigenous control over the production of this highly marketable commodity had important consequences for Oaxaca's population and economy. In the northern regions of colonial Mexico, such as the Bajío, Spaniards came to control most of the productive landed resources, erecting large estates.[18] In most other regions, Indian village lands survived despite aggressive expansion and encroachment by non-Indian holdings.[19] In Oaxaca, in contrast, peasant landholding dominated, and *haciendas* were of extremely minor significance.[20] The retention of land that Oaxacan peasants enjoyed was a result of cochineal's importance. Ownership of Oaxacan land offered Spanish entrepreneurs few economic possibilities and certainly none which could rival the marketing of cochineal. As a result, Oaxaca's colonial elite concentrated on commerce, and the landed resources remained in the peasants' control.

Peasant control over the production of the province's key commodity also had a demographic impact. According to the census ordered by Viceroy Revillagigedo in the 1790s, Oaxaca's population remained overwhelmingly indigenous; 88.3 percent of the province's total population of 411,336 was categorized as Indian. Even more striking was the tremendous degree of segregation. Of the mere 6.3 percent of Oaxaca's total population listed as Spanish, 43 percent (10,970) resided in the city of Antequera de Oaxaca. The vast majority of Spaniards, 84 percent, lived in one of five towns—Antequera, Teposcolula, Juxtlahuaca, Xicayan, or Tehuantepec. Most of Oaxaca's other districts were virtually uninhabited by Spaniards. Villa Alta, the largest district, with a population of 58,280, was home to only 38 Spaniards. Spaniards barely reached 1.5 percent of the total population residing in the cochineal-rich regions of Miahuatlán, Nexapa, and the Chontales.[21]

While such demographic patterns are characteristic of much of colonial Spanish America, in no other province of New Spain was the Indian/Spanish ratio as skewed as it was in Oaxaca. Table 2.1 illustrates the percentages of the population categorized as Indian and Spanish for each of the provinces of Southern Mexico for which ethnic data were compiled in the 1790 census. Fortunately, we have data for Oaxaca, Puebla, México, Tlaxcala, and Mérida (Yucatán), arguably the most indigenous provinces of colonial Mexico. By a considerable margin, Oaxaca had both the highest percentage of Indians and the lowest percentage of Spaniards.

It seems likely that these demographic patterns were reinforced by the cochineal economy. All aspects of the production of cochineal remained in the hands of peasant producers. Indigenous peasants possessed the lands, planted the *nopal* cacti, introduced the bugs, collected the harvest, killed and dried the cochineal, and otherwise prepared it for market. The role of outsiders was indirect. Spaniards provided financing prior to the production process and were the primary consumers of the finished product. Their role, however, gave them little incentive to reside outside of the provincial towns. Similarly, the cochineal economy presented indigenous Oaxacans with little need to migrate either seasonally or permanently from their villages. Cochineal production remained a cottage industry, with most production occurring on small plots operated by individual households; the plots were no doubt often located merely a stone's throw away from the peasant producer's own house. Through the production of cochineal, Oaxacan peasants generated needed income. But unlike traditional sources of income garnered by colonial peasants, such as wage labor in *haciendas*, *obrajes*, or mines, cochineal production did not require permanent or even temporary migration. The result was that peasants were more likely to remain in their own villages, which, no doubt, strengthened community ties. In short, the organization of production in

TABLE 2.1

Race Distribution in Southern Mexican Provinces, 1790

Province	Total population	INDIANS		SPANIARDS		OTHER	
		Population	Percentage of total	Population	Percentage of total	Population	Percentage of total
Oaxaca	410,618	363,080	88%	25,809	6%	21,729	5%
Puebla	427,382	332,213	78%	38,677	9%	56,492	13%
Tlaxcala	58,848	43,378	74%	8,021	14%	7,449	13%
Yucatán (Mérida)[a]	364,022	264,955	73%	?	?	?	?
México	1,043,223	742,186	71%	134,965	13%	166,072	16%

SOURCE: *Primer censo de población de la Nueva España, 1790*, pp. 141–47.

NOTE: Percentages do not add up to 100% due to rounding.

[a]The census for Yucatan recorded "Spaniards and Mestizos" together; thus, the number of Spaniards alone is not discernable.

the cochineal industry exerted a profound impact on the demographic structure of Oaxaca. The industry served to reinforce traditional population dispersion in the region, which helps explain the strong survival of indigenous communities as well as the low percentage of non-Indians and their concentration in the provincial towns.

Social Geography of Oaxaca

Colonial racial categorizations, of course, cloaked an ethnic composition far more diverse and complex. The 1793 census might have classified as Indian 88.3 percent of the province's population, but this "Indian" population comprised numerous distinct cultural and linguistic groups. Within the province of Oaxaca, for example, there were speakers of at least fifteen different indigenous languages. By far the most widely spoken were Mixtec and Zapotec, the languages of the most successful imperial powers of preconquest Oaxaca.[22]

Mixtec was primarily spoken in the western third of Oaxaca in three distinct geographical regions actually named for the language itself (see Map 1). The Mixteca Alta is a region of high peaks and small valleys beginning some forty miles west of the city of Oaxaca along the Camino Real, New Spain's major north-south thoroughfare. The largest political jurisdiction within the boundaries of the Mixteca Alta was the important cochineal-producing *alcaldía mayor* of Teposcolula. Continuing northwest along the Camino Real one enters the Mixteca Baja, a region somewhat warmer, lower, and drier than the Mixteca Alta. While cochineal was produced in the Mixteca Baja, less was produced here than in the other Mixtec-speaking areas. The third region, the Mixteca de la Costa, rises from the Pacific Ocean into the more mountainous areas that border the Mixteca Alta and Mixteca Baja regions. The majority of the Mixteca de la Costa lay in the western half of the *alcaldía mayor* of Xicayan, another producer of large quantities of high-quality cochineal.

Oaxaca's Zapotec-speaking population inhabited the geographical center of the province, stretching south to the Pacific Ocean, north to the border of Veracruz, and east into the Isthmus of Tehuantepec. This vast region encompasses a broad variety of ecosystems and during the colonial era included a number of the wealthiest cochineal-producing districts in the province. The Sierra del Sur is the mountainous area between the coast to the south and the valleys of Oaxaca to the north. In this southern sierra were located the district of Miahuatlán and the western half of the district

MAP 1. Geographical Regions of Oaxaca

of Nexapa, both of which were prime cochineal-producing territories. The rugged mountains to the north of the Oaxacan valleys, known as the Sierra Zapoteca (now often called the Sierra de Juárez), were also inhabited by Zapotec-speaking populations. This large region incorporated a number of colonial districts, including Villa Alta, the district with the largest population in colonial Oaxaca and one in which the *repartimiento* operated extensively. Most of the Isthmus of Tehuantepec is tropical, yet this region did produce noteworthy amounts of *grana cochinilla*. While Zapotec was spoken over a broad area of Oaxaca, it is worth noting that there existed many different dialects of Zapotec, not all of which were mutually intelligible.

While Mixtec and Zapotec were by far the most extensively spoken indigenous languages in Oaxaca, there existed numerous additional languages. To identify but a few, Mixe was spoken in portions of Villa Alta, Nexapa, and, to a lesser extent, Tehuantepec. Chatino was spoken in the eastern half of Xicayan. Chontal was spoken in parts of the southern sierra and coast. And Zoque dominated in eastern Tehuantepec. In the districts of Teutila and Teotitlán del Camino, as well as the northern extremes of Teposcolula, all of which were located along the north-central

16

border with Puebla, the indigenous populations spoke Chocho, Chinantec, Mazatec, Cuicatec, Popoluca, Ixcateco, and Nahua.

Oaxaca's provincial capital was Antequera, which lay at the intersection of three valleys, the Valley of Etla, the Valley of Zimatlán, and the Valley of Tlacolula. The valleys of Etla and Zimatlán were carved up into numerous pieces, each of which belonged to a different political jurisdiction, either Oaxaca, Cuatro Villas del Marquesado, or Zimatlán. The Valley of Tlacolula pertained to the *alcaldía mayor* of Mitla y Tlacolula, more commonly referred to as the *alcaldía mayor* of Teotitlán del Valle, after the town in which the *alcalde mayor* resided. Within these three Oaxacan valleys, Spanish, Zapotec, Mixtec, and Nahua were all spoken to varying degrees during the colonial era.

Geographical Distribution of the Production of Cochineal

The colonial province of Oaxaca was subdivided into twenty-two distinct political jurisdictions (see Map 2), each called an *alcaldía mayor* before 1786 and a *subdelegación* after that year. Most districts in the province produced at least some cochineal. Table 2.2 shows the typical geographical distribution of production in the province, as well as the output-per-thousand Indians, estimated in the year 1793.[23]

No single region within the province of Oaxaca dominated production, although the districts in and around the central valley — the Marquesado, Oaxaca, Teotitlán del Valle, and Zimatlán — contributed 40 percent of the total. The jurisdictions of Xicayan and Miahuatlán were also among the largest *grana* producers, each with an estimated output of 2,600 arrobas. The *subdelegación* of Nexapa, which included both Nexapa and portions of the Chontales, was also a prime producer.[24] Overall, then, while some regions produced more than others, cochineal was produced in significant quantities throughout Oaxaca.

The last column in Table 2.2 lists the output of cochineal per thousand indigenous Oaxacans. Average production per thousand was 106 arrobas, but many regions deviated substantially from this average. The Indians of the Chontales produced the most *grana* per capita, 192 arrobas per thousand persons. The districts of Miahuatlán, Huamelula, Zimatlán, and Ixtepeji also produced large quantities per Indian inhabitant. While the town and *corregimiento* of Oaxaca produced more than most of the jurisdictions, production per Indian was well below average, obviously a re-

17

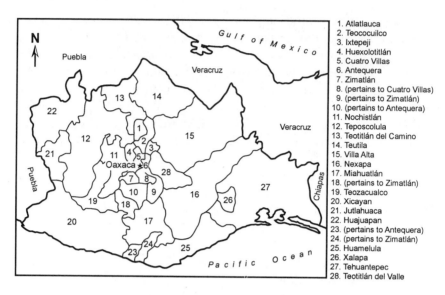

1. Atlatlauca
2. Teococuilco
3. Ixtepeji
4. Huexolotitlán
5. Cuatro Villas
6. Antequera
7. Zimatlán
8. (pertains to Cuatro Villas)
9. (pertains to Zimatlán)
10. (pertains to Antequera)
11. Nochistlán
12. Teposcolula
13. Teotitlán del Camino
14. Teutila
15. Villa Alta
16. Nexapa
17. Miahuatlán
18. (pertains to Zimatlán)
19. Teozacualco
20. Xicayan
21. Jutlahuaca
22. Huajuapan
23. (pertains to Antequera)
24. (pertains to Zimatlán)
25. Huamelula
26. Xalapa
27. Tehuantepec
28. Teotitlán del Valle

MAP 2. Political Districts of Oaxaca, 1786

flection of the high level of alternative opportunities available to Indians in the city. Villa Alta, the district with the largest population in the province of Oaxaca, produced the least amount of cochineal per person, but this is not entirely surprising. The Indians of Villa Alta were more occupied with their household production of *mantas*, high-quality cotton mantles.[25] Other districts in which *grana* was of lesser importance, though still very significant, included Teotitlán del Camino, Teposcolula, and Tehuantepec.[26]

The production of cochineal in all districts of Oaxaca reflected the dyestuff's importance in the local peasant economies as a highly valued commodity capable of producing money income. It was a supplement to more traditional crops but critical nonetheless. Income generated by the production and sale of cochineal was used by producers to meet the many necessary expenses they incurred, whether for tribute, religious services, communal events, or the purchase of items at a local store. In the words of don Joaquin Alvarez, the parish priest of Santa María Ozolotepec, Miahuatlán, cochineal "is the only commodity with which [the tributaries] maintain themselves and pay their debts."[27]

Grana cochinilla had many advantages as a supplement to traditional agriculture. First, *nopaleras*, the cactus groves in which the cochineal was produced and harvested, flourished almost anywhere, including on mar-

TABLE 2.2
Cochineal Output in Districts of Oaxaca (Estimated in 1793)

Jurisdiction	Arrobas produced	Percentage of total output	Indigenous population	Arrobas per thousand Indians
Oaxaca	2,500	10.59%	40,882	61
Nexapa	1,100	4.66%	12,885	85
Chontales	1,400	5.93%	7,283	192
Miahuatlán	2,600	11.02%	14,745	176
Huamelula	600	2.54%	3,250	185
Teotitlán del Valle	1,000	4.24%	12,159	82
Villa Alta	1,000	4.24%	58,088	17
Tehuantepec	1,000	4.24%	16,189	62
Teposcolula	1,300	5.51%	38,974	33
Zimatlán	2,700	11.44%	16,548	163
Nochistlán	200	0.85%	5,615	36
Ixtepeji	1,000	4.24%	5,469	183
Teococuilco	1,500	6.36%	12,792	117
Teotitlán del Camino	1,000	4.24%	18,506	54
Cuatro Villas–Marquesado	2,100	8.90%	17,249	122
Xicayan	2,600	11.02%	20,568	126
TOTALS	23,600	100.02%		

SOURCES: Reina, 188–90; AGN, Historia, vol. 75, exp. 8, p. 7.
NOTE: Percentages do not add up to 100% due to rounding.

ginal lands or small plots. As a result, peasants did not need to sacrifice valuable cropland for the production of cacti. Small backyard *nopaleras* were probably common. Second, while the production of cochineal was labor intensive, it was not physically demanding. Consequently, older family members or children could perform the bulk of the work. Further-more, since production was possible in the courtyard of a home, women could attend to the cochineal, as well as other domestic tasks, while men were away in the fields. In short, cochineal production efficiently utilized the available household labor pool.[28] Finally, in contrast to sources of income tapped by Indians in other parts of colonial Mexico, production of

19

cochineal did not require that individuals migrate. This was much more than just a convenience. The ability to remain at home allowed peasants to more easily balance the demands of cochineal production with the requirements of staple crop production. In addition, cottage production of dye was less disruptive to familial and communal life and explains, at least to some degree, the greater survival of peasant communities in Oaxaca than in most other Mexican regions.[29]

The Repartimiento

A salient feature of cochineal production was the heavy reliance of producers on external financing. The production of the dyestuff required a significant outlay of funds, particularly in the purchase of cochineal "seed," the pregnant females introduced into the *nopalera* at the start of the production cycle. In addition, months separated the introduction of the "seed" and the eventual harvesting of a marketable product. As a result, many producers sought to gain financing for their cochineal production and did so by contracting in advance to sell their output in exchange for immediate cash payments. Producers received money from Spaniards, promising to deliver to them at a later date some fixed amount of cochineal. Such transactions were called *repartimientos*.[30]

The origin of the *repartimiento* is not entirely clear. Certainly by the middle of the seventeenth century, the *repartimiento* was common in most indigenous regions of the Spanish colonies. Rodolfo Pastor speculates that the *repartimiento* in Mexico emerged during the half-century from 1580 to 1630, owing to a severe decline in indigenous consumption resulting from Indian depopulation. Spaniards responded to economic depression by forcing Indians to expand their consumption.[31] *Alcaldes mayores* in the Mixteca Alta were in the practice of giving indigenous silk producers cash advances against their production as early as the 1560s.[32] Rik Hoekstra and Arij Ouweneel suggest that the *repartimiento* had origins in the preconquest era, evolving from the tribute demands levied by local indigenous officials.[33] For the region of the Andes, one historian found that the *corregidores' repartimientos* were already well established by 1596.[34]

It is more likely that the *repartimiento* was an institution of European origin, although there is little doubt that elements of the system were uniquely adapted to the particular conditions existing in colonial Spanish America. In their study of the Spanish wool trade, Carla Rahn Phillips and William D. Phillips documented that as early as the mid–fifteenth century advance sales contracts existed between the merchants of Burgos and owners of sheep flocks, in which the former made cash advances to be repaid by the latter in wool at shearing time. This, however, was not the only similarity with the *repartimiento*. Like the *alcaldes mayores*, the Burgalese merchants also often faced difficulties collecting their debts and had to endure frequent and harsh criticism leveled by officials of the Church (both of these issues are discussed at length later in this book).[35] The *repartimiento* also resembled the *Verlagssystem* which developed in medieval Europe. This "putting-out" system entailed the advance of wages and raw materials to a network of largely peasant artisans, who were required to deliver a final manufactured product to the *Verleger*, the merchant-financier.[36] According to another scholar, "deferred payment for goods sold or advance payment for future delivery . . . was ubiquitous" in medieval and early-modern commerce.[37] In the colonial Latin American literature, one gets the notion that the *repartimiento* was a system uniquely devised by the district magistrates. While the origins of the *repartimiento* will remain somewhat uncertain, it is nonetheless important to recognize that similar institutions had long existed in Europe.

HOW THE *REPARTIMIENTO* OPERATED:
A MICRO-ECONOMIC VIEW

In Oaxaca the *repartimiento* generally worked in one of two ways. Most often, the *repartimiento* involved a cash disbursement made by the *alcalde mayor* to an Indian recipient, who, in turn, was obliged to repay the official at a later date in some specified product. Throughout Oaxaca cochineal dye was produced with *repartimiento* financing. In the *alcaldía mayor* of Villa Alta, the cash *repartimientos* also financed large volumes of *mantas*. Many other items were obtained on a smaller scale by the *alcaldes mayores* through *repartimiento* cash advances. *Huipiles* (loose-fitting blouses) were produced for both the *alcaldes mayores* of Teposcolula and Teotitlán del Camino Real, and the officials of Villa Alta financed the production of raw cotton. In a number of districts, even corn and wheat were acquired through *repartimiento* money advances to producers. In this first type of *repartimiento*, then, the *alcalde mayor* loaned money to peasant producers who repaid the *alcalde mayor* with whatever good was stipulated. The term of the loan, the length of time between the cash advance and the date payment in kind was due, differed from item to item. For *grana* cochineal loans, payment in cochineal was typically owed in six to eight months. Cash advances against the future delivery of goods were not unique to Oaxaca. The *repartimiento* system in Yucatán and

21

Guerrero usually operated in this "reverse" fashion.[38] In Puebla the *alcaldes mayores* obtained corn, wheat, chiles, nuts, cotton, cochineal, and other goods through *repartimientos* in coin.[39]

The second type of *repartimiento* that operated in Oaxaca is the one most widely reported for other areas of Spanish America, that is, the *repartimiento* of goods. In this practice, the *alcalde mayor* supplied items to the Indians of his district, who were then obliged to pay for them in the future. In Oaxaca, repayment was almost invariably made in cash, not kind. The most widely distributed items were *ganado mayor* (large livestock), especially oxen, bulls, and mules, and it was very unusual for any other item to be sold by the *alcalde mayor* through the *repartimiento*. Livestock was almost always advanced at the same terms: half-payment was expected in six months and the remainder was due at year's end.[40]

The *alcalde mayor* did not manage his *repartimientos* alone but was aided by several assistants, his *tenientes*, who helped him with all aspects of the transactions, from the distribution of goods and money, to the collection of debts. It was common for at least one of the *tenientes*, often the *teniente general*, to be appointed by the *aviador*, the *alcalde mayor's* merchant backer, and this helped ensure that the *alcalde mayor* was working in the merchant's best interests. Hamnett suggests that the *teniente general* shared in the profits of the *repartimientos*, but this seems to have been the exception. Most often, *tenientes* were paid an annual salary, ranging from three hundred to one thousand pesos plus living expenses.[41] The day-to-day operation of the *repartimiento* entailed traveling to the many Indian villages of the district and making *repartimiento* loans, either providing money or animals. *Repartimientos* in money were usually made at the beginning of a production cycle, September or October for cochineal. The *alcalde mayor* of Miahuatlán reported in 1752 that he always distributed pesos to the Indians of his district in September and October, contracting for them to pay him back at harvest time at the rate of one pound of *grana* cochineal for every twelve reales (1.5 pesos) that he advanced to them. A number of other officials and provincial priests signaled October and November as the most important months for extension of cochineal loans. As each noted, however, the *repartimientos* began as early as July and continued until as late as January.[42] Other items might follow different schedules, especially if they were not tied to production cycles. The *alcalde mayor* of Nexapa, for example, informed the Viceroy in 1752 that he and former *alcaldes mayores* of his district typically purchased mules for the *repartimiento* at the September fair in Puebla. These they brought to Nexapa, where they were sold on credit to the Indians of

TABLE 2.3

Summary Of Surviving *Repartimiento* Records

Year	Locale	Number of transactions	Pounds of grana due	Average pounds per transaction	To whom loaned
1765	Papalo, Teotitlán del Camino	791	4,991.53	6.31	individual
1765	Papalo, Teotitlán del Camino	9	184.63	20.51	community
1768	Huehuetla y Huautla	181	248.75	1.37	individual
1771	Coatlán, Miahuatlán	111	556.00	5.01	individual
1781–1785	Teposcolula	121	1,202.85	9.94	individual
1781–1785	Teposcolula	22	1,520.28	69.10	community
1811	Miahuatlán	111	534.56	4.82	individual
TOTALS		1,346	9,238.60	6.86	

SOURCES: AGN, Civil, vol. 302, *primera parte, cuaderno de las cuentas,* pp. 21–46; AGN, Civil, vol. 284, exp. 6, pp. 19v–24; AGN, Tierras, vol. 1038, exp. 1, pp. 212–13; AGN, Real Hacienda, Administración general de alcabalas, caja 43, pp. 1–37; AGEO, Real Intendencia de Oaxaca, legajo 40, exp. 24.

the region. *Repartimientos* were not made every year, according to the *alcalde mayor,* but only in the first three years of an official's tenure. After that, it was considered too risky to make such large loans, for collection was difficult. Whereas mules were financed for one year, with half due in six months, complete repayment often took much longer. This last point was echoed by all of the *alcaldes mayores,* who noted that collection of *repartimiento* debts was very difficult.[43]

While *repartimientos* were occasionally made to communities, they were far more commonly given directly to individuals. This conclusion is based on the interpretation of five surviving *libros de caja,* the actual ledgers showing the *repartimientos* of the *alcaldes mayores* for the production of cochineal dye in various regions of Oaxaca. The data, which come from diverse regions and time periods, are summarized in Table 2.3.[44]

The records show 1,346 separate transactions, in which a total of 9,239 pounds of cochineal were financed by *alcaldes mayores.* Of this total, *repartimientos* to individuals represented 82 percent, or 7,534 pounds, while only 18 percent of the *repartimientos,* by weight, were made to communities. Geographical analysis reveals that in Miahuatlán all *repartimientos* were made to individual households, whereas in Teposcolula communal *repartimientos,* which accounted for 56 percent, predominated slightly. In Papalo, Huehuetla, and Huautla, three regions pertaining to the *alcaldía mayor* of Teotitlán del Camino, *repartimientos* to communities existed in only Papalo and were rather unimportant relative to those received by individuals. Thus it was individual households that received the vast majority of *repartimientos.*[45]

Not surprisingly, average advances made to individuals were far smaller than those made to communities. The average *repartimiento* made to an individual was for the production of 5 pounds, 12 ounces of cochineal. In contrast, the communities of Teposcolula took average advances against 69 pounds, while those of Papalo contracted for 20.5 pounds. In some towns, both individuals and the community as a whole received *repartimientos.* For example, in San Juan Teposcolula the community received a *repartimiento* to produce 113 pounds, 3.5 ounces of cochineal. Apart from this communal *repartimiento,* four separate individuals from the same community took additional *repartimiento* loans to produce another 33.5 pounds.[46]

When individuals received *repartimiento* loans, they were personally responsible for repaying them, which they did by harvesting the cochineal insects produced in their *nopaleras,* often located in the patios of their homes or on a nearby plot of land. Thus, when an individual took a *repartimiento* in money from his or her *alcalde mayor,* he or she was personally responsible and accountable for producing the cochineal and repaying the official.

How communities organized production to repay contracted *repartimiento* debts is less clear. In the mid–eighteenth century, the community of San Juan Tabaa in the district of Villa Alta had small *nopaleras* worked by individual families as well as "two *nopaleras* administered directly by the community."[47] Presumably, these latter lands were worked communally to repay those *repartimiento* loans received by the community as a whole.

In other cases, the *alcalde mayor* loaned funds directly to the *principales,* the indigenous authorities, who subsequently spread the obligation among the individual families pertaining to the community.[48] Presumably, this was common when the community as a whole needed funds for some particular communal purpose. The rationale behind the authorities' subsequent allocation of this debt burden is difficult to discern, but

24

individual family resources and the ability of peasant producers to meet their obligations undoubtedly came into play. In any event, the same *principales* receiving the *repartimiento* were then held responsible for collecting the cochineal and repaying the *alcalde mayor.*

Making large loans directly to the Indian nobility worked to the benefit of the Spanish official in a number of ways. First, the official reduced his administrative costs by limiting the number of transactions, making one large rather than many small loans. Second, one would expect that the indigenous nobility could use their status within the communities to help collect the debts, and this would reduce the levels of default. Last, when individual peasants did default, the burden of paying the loan passed to the indigenous authorities.

Indian *alcaldes, gobernadores,* and other *principales* commonly received goods or money through the *repartimiento* for their personal use as well. Examining the same records employed above shows that twenty-one *repartimientos* were identified as having been made to a *gobernador, alcalde, principal,* or *cacique* for his personal use. In total, these indigenous authorities received *repartimientos* to produce slightly more than 120 pounds of cochineal, for an average of 5 pounds, 12 ounces per recipient, precisely the average for all individuals. It is doubtful that these 120 pounds represented the sum total taken by *principales.*[49] Quite likely, there were other native elites receiving *repartimientos* whose names appeared without their titles and who were thus unidentifiable as Indian officials. These figures reveal that indigenous authorities took *repartimientos* from the *alcalde mayor* but in amounts no larger than those taken by other villagers. It appears, then, that the Indian nobility did not always play an economic role different from other Indians. They, too, turned to the *alcalde mayor* for *repartimiento* loans, and based on the size of their loans, they do not appear to have been considered more creditworthy than others, at least when considered as individuals.

Regardless to whom the *repartimiento* was made, whether directly to an individual or to the community as a whole, the next step in the transaction involved the collection of the debts. In the case of cochineal, the *alcalde mayor* or his *teniente recaudador,* his debt collector, returned to the towns in which debtors lived in the late spring to collect the recently harvested cochineal. Debt collection, however, was difficult because debtors frequently proved unable or unwilling to repay their *repartimientos* promptly.[50] Often debtors were unable to meet their debt obligations, due, for example, to the loss of the harvest. This was particularly common for *grana* cochineal, which was unusually vulnerable to inclement weather.

25

When the item advanced by the *alcalde mayor* was a mule or an oxen, repayment was often delayed because debtors simply had not been able to save enough money. Farm animals were high-priced items for the average indigenous household, and making such large payments promptly was clearly difficult.[51] Inability to pay was probably the most common reason for delay or default, but other peasants simply evaded their debts or resisted repayment, dragging their feet as long as possible. Peasants who evaded contracted *repartimiento* debts reduced the economic pressures upon themselves, even if only temporarily, without increasing their debt burden because interest charges on *repartimiento* loans did not accrue but were fixed amounts independent of the length of time debts remained outstanding.

Alcaldes mayores who were unable to collect their *repartimiento* debts had several options available to them. First, they could simply permit the indebted peasant additional time to pay. In 1752 a number of provincial priests and *alcaldes mayores* suggested that this was often necessary. The *alcalde mayor* of Nexapa, for example, noted that few Indians entirely paid for their mules in one year as stipulated, but that most needed two to three years, and sometimes five. The official from Chichicapa-Zimatlán wrote that although total payment was due in one year, "one gives thanks to God when the money is collected in two years." Regarding the cochineal *repartimiento*, the *alcaldes mayores* and priests consulted generally agreed that when a debtor proved unable to repay, the *alcalde mayor* had to refinance the individual, hoping that the entire debt would be repaid in the following harvest.[52] The second option available to the *alcalde mayor* was to apply pressure to the debtor and his family or to imprison him. In fact, the *alcaldes mayores* often did resort to violent means to collect debts owed to them, especially when the Spanish official believed that the debtor was resisting repayment of a debt that he could in fact meet, or when the official feared that the debtor might attempt to flee the village without paying. Even if the debt still proved uncollectible, punishment of a recalcitrant debtor undoubtedly sent a powerful message to others to pay up promptly. This, at least, was the argument of the *alcalde mayor* of Zimatlán, Yldefonso María Sanchez Solache, who in 1784 stated that imprisoning debtors for short periods had "very favorable effects; being this a very powerful stimulus for the purpose of dedicating [the Indians] to their work."[53] Incarcerating an indigenous official was effective if the community as a whole owed the *alcalde mayor* funds, because the Indian authority served as a hostage to force the community to produce the outstanding debt. The final alternative open to the Spanish official was to embargo the personal belongings of the debtor and attempt to recover the value of the initial *repartimiento* with goods of equal worth. Needless to say, the average indigenous family in rural Oaxaca did not own many items valued by the *alcalde mayor*. When the debt originated from a *repartimiento* of a mule or oxen, the *alcalde mayor* could attempt to recover the animal. By then, however, the beast was older by a year or more and was, consequently, of lower worth.

Whether the *alcalde mayor* waited patiently, arrested and imprisoned the debtor, or confiscated his belongings, he incurred administrative costs which reduced the real value of the return he hoped to earn on his *repartimiento* loan. Not infrequently, all of the above collection methods failed. In such instances, the *alcalde mayor* had no choice but to simply write off the debts, entering *"incobrable"* (uncollectible), in his *repartimiento* ledger. The officials from Oaxacan districts all recognized that some level of total default was inevitable and that *repartimiento* loans, while providing potential for very high profitability, also placed principal at very substantial risk of loss.[54] That default was common is unquestionable; most of the judicial cases dealing with the *repartimiento* involve cases in which the *alcalde mayor* responded, often violently, to indebted peasants who failed to meet their obligations promptly.

The *repartimiento*, then, operated essentially in this fashion. The *alcalde mayor* supplied goods on credit to Indian consumers and made cash advances against the future output of indigenous producers. The recipient of a *repartimiento* was obliged to repay the debt within a pre-arranged time period. The *repartimiento* was thus a system of credit linking Indian production and consumption with the larger Spanish economy.

Finances of the Alcaldes Mayores

While the *alcalde mayor* provided credit to the Indians of his district, he too depended on credit. The *alcaldes mayores* were often individuals possessing little wealth of their own; many were either career bureaucrats or military men. Thus, before an official could make any loans to producers, he needed to obtain financing of his own. But obtaining money with which to trade was not the only reason why officials required funding. Even before assuming office, an entering official incurred significant expenses.

Until 1750 the position of *alcalde mayor* most often had to be purchased from the Crown. The Hapsburgs began selling the post of *alcalde mayor* in 1678, and this practice was continued by the Bourbons until

27

about 1750.[55] We have information on 147 different *alcaldes mayores* who served in thirteen different Oaxacan districts during the years 1695–1750. Of the total, 108 purchased their posts and 39 were granted them by the Crown as a reward for good services (see Appendix A). The latter tended to be either career bureaucrats or military men who were being rewarded for their service to the Crown. The social origins of the former are more difficult to assess. Many were associates of the merchants of Mexico City, who often served as the officials' bondsmen. Because of the potential profitability of operating *repartimientos*, many individuals were willing to pay for the privilege of serving as an *alcalde mayor*. The amounts paid to the Crown varied greatly, but the position of *alcalde mayor* in a cochineal-producing district of Oaxaca always fetched a significant amount. Joseph Hurtado y Benzal, for example, paid the substantial sum of 17,181 pesos to win the *alcaldía mayor* of the Pacific coastal district of Xicayan in 1748. During the entire eighteenth century, this post never sold for less than 6,000 pesos. Hurtado and others were no doubt attracted to Xicayan, owing to the potentially profitable trade in cochineal and cotton in which the district's population specialized.[56] The position of *alcalde mayor* of Nexapa, an eastern Oaxacan district rich in cochineal, was purchased in 1750 by Juan Joseph Martinez y Aguirre for 15,365 pesos.[57] Another highly prized district was Villa Alta in the Sierra Zapoteca, which always earned the Crown at least 5,000 pesos and which sold for its highest price of the century in 1747 to Miguel Joseph de Iturbide, who paid 8,625 pesos to assume the post. In Villa Alta, an *alcalde mayor* could profit greatly from the financing of peasant production of *mantas* as well as *grana* cochineal.[58] The Oaxacan posts were considered some of the most attractive in all of Mexico, but a number of posts in the Viceroyalty of Peru fetched sums comparable to the most expensive Oaxacan districts.[59]

The prices paid to purchase the offices of Xicayan, Nexapa, and Villa Alta were some of the highest paid for the entire district of Oaxaca, but to acquire any of the districts required a large outlay of funds. Theoretically, the price paid to obtain a specific office was a reflection of the perceived value of possessing that post, a function of its expected profitability. Naturally, if an individual hoped to win the post of Villa Alta, then he would have to make a large bid or risk being outbid by someone else. The bidding process encouraged aspirants to make ambitious proposals. Indeed, upon news of an impending vacancy, "public criers" announced the opening for nine consecutive days in the town where the vacancy was to occur and for thirty straight days in the provincial capital. Sealed bids were accepted during the entire "crying period," at the end of which the appointment was made by the Crown. Although the Crown retained the option of selecting a bid other than the highest one, the post usually went to the highest bidder.[60] To at least a limited degree, one would expect the prices paid to approach the perceived value of possessing the office, and thus by examining the evolution of these prices, one can analyze the perception of profitability over time.

While such an analysis is instructive, several factors nonetheless limit the usefulness of the findings. First, posts were frequently granted as rewards to individuals who had long served the Crown, especially in a military capacity. In such instances, we do not know how much the post would have fetched had it been auctioned. Second, positions were sold often a decade or more in advance of their vacancy. An individual purchased the future right to assume office at the completion of his predecessor's term. But often the purchase was made before the predecessor's tenure had even begun. As a result, purchase prices do not even reflect actual present value of the post, but rather perceived future value, discounted to the present. Payments were due immediately, so that the purchaser had to account for the fact that his capital (the purchase price) would not yield any return for years.[61] Nor could bidders predict when the position would actually become theirs. This is suggested by the fact that individuals sometimes bid for and received several posts, only to find out later that the terms overlapped. Consequently, many of the Crown grants listed several individuals who at the purchaser's discretion would serve as his substitutes in the event that he had died or for some other reason could not serve. It is likely that a bidder had at least a notion of when the post would vacate, and this also must have influenced his decision about how much to bid. All other things being equal, certainly an individual would pay more for a post that was likely to become his within a year than for one not likely to become his for ten years. This, too, makes a comparison of the prices paid misleading.

Many other peculiarities and exceptions make a precise analysis difficult. For example, purchases were sometimes bundled, as in the case of Juan Dongo who in 1716 purchased the posts of both Miahuatlán and Teotitlán del Valle (Mitla/Tlacolula) for a total of 5,400 pesos.[62] Since the contract does not indicate how much he paid for each individual post, it is impossible to know what he believed the value of each one to be. Another problem is that sometimes individuals who won the bidding process for one reason or another had to later make an additional contribution. This happened to Antonio de Silva, who paid 2,250 pesos for the post at Teposcolula in 1728, but was too sick to serve and had to pay an

29

additional 1,500 pesos in 1731, apparently to postpone his assumption of power.[63] In other cases, individuals made additional payments to move their assignments to more preferable posts. All of these changes and surplus contributions make the analysis more difficult still. Despite these obstacles, the data are presented in Appendix A.

As a quick glance at the data indicates, the purchase prices do not reveal any significant trends, beyond the more generalized conclusion that certain *alcaldías mayores* sold for higher prices than others. The three posts mentioned above, Xicayan, Villa Alta, and Nexapa, were the most highly prized in Oaxaca, with Miahuatlán and Zimatlán also fetching sizeable prices. By far the highest prices paid occurred in the late-1740s for several of the districts. It is at least possible that such high prices were a response to the expectation that the *repartimiento* would be legalized in 1751. The ability to openly trade with the Indians without fear of censure must have been worth a considerable sum. Peculiarly, prices were somewhat elevated in the late seventeenth century as well. One historian has speculated that such higher prices might have been the result of ignorance on the part of the bidders of the real value of posts, and that, over time, experience and greater knowledge revised the prices slightly downward.[64] One rather surprising conclusion is that despite a few notable exceptions, the prices paid were not particularly high. This would seem to indicate that either the posts were not highly sought, a conclusion that runs counter to everything we think we know about the Oaxacan posts, or that the bidding process was flawed (or at least not designed to maximize income). In all events, the purchase price data yield less than conclusive results.

Purchasing the post was not the only financial burden placed on an incoming official. Before an *alcalde mayor* was permitted to assume office, he was also required to provide a *fianza*, a financial guarantee that he would successfully collect and pay into the royal coffers whatever revenues were owed to the Crown, including Indian tribute, in the district to which he had received his appointment. This required officials to seek *fiadores*, financial guarantors willing to pay the Crown if the *alcalde mayor* failed to collect what was due.[65]

Most often, entering officials obtained *fianzas* from wealthy merchants of the Mexico City *consulado*, who demanded in exchange that the *alcaldes mayores* serve as their commercial agents. The merchants, often referred to as *aviadores*, supplied the *alcaldes mayores* with funds, called either an *avío* or a *habilitación*, which the *alcaldes* invested in partnership with the merchant, providing *repartimientos* to the indigenous populations in their respective districts. Merchants, thus, assumed the risks associated with the *fianza* because they expected to earn large profits through their trade with the Indians, and the *alcalde mayor* was an invaluable partner in such commerce, as he was able to use his judicial authority to enforce debts.[66]

Merchants and *alcaldes mayores* typically outlined their agreements in contracts which specified the requirements and obligations of each party. Several such contracts survive and offer important details about how the commercial alliances between *alcaldes mayores* and merchant-*aviadores* were structured. For example, don Manuel José Lopez, who was scheduled to take over the post of *alcalde mayor* of Teotitlán del Camino in northern Oaxaca, contracted in 1781 to receive from a wealthy merchant named don Juan Bautista Echarri fifty thousand pesos to finance the *repartimiento* in that district. The contract stipulated that Echarri would provide the funds, which he himself borrowed from the *cofradía* of Nuestra Señora del Rosario of the convent of Santo Domingo de México at an annual interest rate of 5 percent. Lopez, who put up no capital of his own, was responsible for the day-to-day management of the trade. He was to be aided by several *tenientes* selected by Echarri, each of whom were to be paid one thousand pesos annually plus food and the use of whatever beasts were needed in the daily operation of the cochineal trade. After first paying the interest due on the principal (50,000 pesos) and all salaries, the remaining profit from the trade was split between Echarri and Lopez, the former receiving 25 percent and the latter 75 percent.[67]

Another entering *alcalde mayor*, don Yldefonso María Sanchez Solache of the jurisdiction of Chichicapa-Zimatlán, received financing in 1782 from Mexico City merchant don Manuel Ramón de Goya. The merchant promised to provide 60,000–70,000 pesos to the *alcalde mayor* in the first year alone, followed by additional installments of 20,000–25,000 pesos per year until the termination of Sanchez's tenure. Like the prior contract, the merchant selected the *teniente general*. The "company" paid all salaries and covered the expenses of the *casa real* and all other administrative costs. The *alcalde mayor* was also to be reimbursed for all personal expenses not in excess of 1,500 pesos. Finally, the merchant agreed to pay into the royal treasury in three installments the annual tribute owed for the district. At the end of Sanchez's term in office, the profits from all trade were to be divided evenly between him and the merchant.[68]

In 1792 a similar contract was executed to finance the district of Miahuatlán. A Oaxacan merchant, don Simon Gutierrez de Villegas, promised to provide the *alcalde mayor*, don José María de Ceballos, with all of

31

the merchandise marketable in his district, as well as money to be loaned for the production of cochineal. As in each of the previous contracts, the merchant, Gutierrez, chose the *alcalde*'s assistants. The *alcalde mayor* of Miahuatlán received one-third of the total profits, after deduction of all costs, and the merchant kept the balance.[69]

It seems noteworthy that each of the Spanish officials received a differing percentage of profits, ranging from the one-third paid to the *alcalde mayor* of Miahuatlán to the 75 percent collected by the official of Teotitlán del Camino. Several elements may have contributed to these differences. Ceballos took over the post of *alcalde mayor* in 1792, a year when two factors combined to lower the attractiveness of investing capital into the operation of *repartimientos*. First, *repartimientos* had been explicitly prohibited by the Crown in 1786. While the ban was routinely disobeyed throughout Oaxaca and in other parts of the Spanish colonies, the risk of being discovered making illegal *repartimiento* loans to Indians existed and the consequence was the probable confiscation of capital. While never applied at this most rigorous level, the risk certainly scared away many merchants. In fact, don Juan Bautista Echarri, the financier of the *alcalde mayor* of Teotitlán del Camino, withdrew his capital in June 1787 for fear of repercussions.[70] While Gutierrez de Villegas was willing to risk getting caught, he may have been willing to do so only under the condition that he reap most of the profit. Ironically, Gutierrez was arrested in October 1792, accused of having conspired to evade the ban on *repartimientos*. Apparently, no further actions were taken in the case, and Gutierrez suffered no losses, for the "company" had yet to be initiated. A second possible reason for the lower percentage of profits reaped by Ceballos is related to the depressed price of cochineal. In 1793, the average price of cochineal in Oaxaca dipped to 13.5 reales per pound, the lowest average annual price for all prior years dating back to 1758, the first year for which data are available. Although the contract between Ceballos and his financier, Gutierrez de Villegas, was drafted sometime in 1792, the price may already have begun moving downward. News of war in Europe made investment in the production of an export commodity such as cochineal less than attractive. While shipping lanes remained open in 1792, a rational assessment of international affairs would have led any merchant to approach transatlantic trade cautiously. Perhaps Ceballos accepted a mere 33 percent of profits because he was unable to find other, more generous partners. Likewise, Gutierrez de Villegas may have concluded that investment in cochineal during a time of international instability was only warranted if the potential return was high.

The Lopez-Echarri contract, which gave Alcalde Lopez three-quarters of all profits also involved unusual circumstances. After stipulating all conditions of the contract, Echarri ceded his 25 percent to Lopez, stating that he wanted nothing to do with the business but only wanted to do what was good for his family members. Apparently, Lopez was related to Echarri and the latter helped him by obtaining a loan which the *alcalde mayor* could use to finance his *repartimientos*. What remains unexplained, however, was why the contract gave Echarri a portion of the profits in the first place.[71]

The final contract, between Alcalde Sanchez Colache and the merchant Manuel Ramón de Goya, was probably the most typical. One study found that in colonial Mexico City profits were divided equally in companies of this type, in which one party put up the capital and the other ran the day-to-day operations. While that study was looking at bakeries and tailors, it seems likely that companies generally would have been designed alike, regardless of their purpose.[72]

Hamnett's study suggests that merchant/*alcalde mayor* partnerships of the type described above were most common for the operation of the *repartimiento*. Nonetheless, other *alcaldes mayores* made different arrangements with their merchant-financiers. Asked by the Viceroy in 1752 about their finances, the Spanish officials in Oaxaca gave a variety of responses. The official from Teotitlán del Camino had received a loan from a merchant who charged him 8 percent, while the *alcalde mayor* of Miahuatlán had contracted with his financial backer to deliver whatever cochineal he could to the port of Veracruz, where he would be paid five pesos less than the prevailing Veracruz market price per arroba of twenty-five pounds. The five pesos, added the magistrate, worked out to be about 8 percent.[73]

Other *alcaldes mayores* turned to ecclesiastical sources of credit to finance their *repartimientos*. In 1752, the *alcaldes* of both Nexapa and Zimatlán-Chichicapa reported that they had secured loans on their own at interest rates of 5 percent per annum. Many years later, in 1798, don Juan José Ruiz, *subdelegado*[74] of the cochineal-rich district of Nexapa, requested a loan of sixty thousand pesos from the Bishopric of Oaxaca. While Ruiz received just sixteen thousand pesos at 5 percent from the Bishopric,[75] he obtained another thirty thousand pesos from the Renta del Colegio de Niñas Doncellas, in the city of Oaxaca.[76] A number of other *alcaldes mayores* received funds, either directly or indirectly, from religious sources and used them to finance *repartimientos* for cochineal production. Pablo de Ortega, *alcalde mayor* of Villa Alta, received twenty-five thousand pesos from the Colegio de Niñas Educadas in 1786. In the

33

same year, the Colegio de Niñas Educadas financed yet another *alcalde mayor*, the official of Teposcolula, Pedro de Quevedo, who received forty thousand pesos in two loans. In 1794, the *subdelegado* of Cuatro Villas del Marquesado borrowed sixty thousand pesos from yet a different religious institution.[77]

Borrowing money directly from the Church rather than from a private financial backer was advantageous to an *alcalde mayor*, since profits at the term's end belonged entirely to him. On the other hand, few people could obtain a large loan without first providing either significant collateral or a *fiador*. In addition, there were many risks involved in the cochineal trade, and borrowing large quantities left an individual financially exposed.[78]

The potential profitability of trading with the Indians, as well as the financial exigencies of assuming office, forced *alcaldes mayores* to seek financial backing. Many formed pacts with powerful merchants for the joint commercial exploitation of their districts, while others contracted loans directly. In either case, they used these funds to trade with the indigenous populations of their *alcaldías mayores*, employing their judicial authority to facilitate the collection of their *repartimiento* debts.

Indian Tribute and the Repartimiento

The financial relations between Spanish officials and indigenous peasants were not limited to the *repartimiento*. One of the primary responsibilities of the district magistrates was to collect Indian tribute on behalf of the Crown. Excluding exemptions, all Indian males between the ages of eighteen and fifty paid tribute to the Crown, at a rate which hovered around two pesos per tributary per year, but which varied from location to location. Traditionally, it was the indigenous officials who actually collected the tribute from community members and then delivered it to the *alcalde mayor*, in two or three annual installments.[79]

What interests us here are the potential links between the Indian tribute and the system of *repartimiento*. Intuitively, one would imagine that the intersection was substantial, since the *alcalde mayor* served as the local pinnacle of both systems. He and his *tenientes* simultaneously collected tribute and *repartimiento* debts, which at first glance suggests a conflict of interest. When a village owed money for both tribute and *repartimiento*, the *alcalde mayor* was likely to press harder for the latter and might be inclined to apply any payment to his *repartimiento* debts, even if the

Indians intended the payment to meet their tribute obligation. In 1790 the Intendant of Oaxaca, Antonio Mora y Peysal, accused the ex–*alcalde mayor* of Villa Alta, Pedro de Ortega, of this practice.[80] Even if true, the gravity of this apparent transgression is somewhat diminished by the fact that the *alcaldes mayores* provided *fianzas*, financial guarantees to the Crown that tribute and other taxes would be collected. The point is that in most circumstances, the *alcalde mayor* was liable to the Crown for tribute, even if he collected his *repartimiento* debts first. Occasionally, however, the Crown granted temporary exemptions from tribute in years when epidemics or famine produced crises within the indigenous communities. In those catastrophic years, the Spanish officials had very good reason to collect their *repartimiento* debts before collecting the tribute, since they too were relieved from financial responsibility for the tribute. In any event, *alcaldes mayores* must have served as the unexpected allies of Indians seeking the reduction of their tribute assessment. Tribute reduction, whether through a lower rate or a recount of tributaries, lessened the *alcaldes'* exposure as well. It also increased the Indians' disposable income, which might incline them to increase their business dealings with the *alcalde mayor*, or at least to repay their debts more promptly. Other studies have pointed to the practice of the district magistrates' deliberately undercounting the tributaries living in their districts.[81]

Once tribute was collected, the Spanish officials were responsible for depositing the Crown income into the royal treasury. In practice, it was not the *alcalde* himself who deposited the revenues, but his *aviador*, his financial backer, who delivered the tribute funds on the dates that they were due. Presumably, the main advantage of arranging the payment in this way was practical — to avoid transporting the wealth along Mexico's unguarded roads. There was another benefit to this practice as well: the officials and their *aviadores* could use the collected tribute monies in their own *repartimientos*, recycling the money without any delay. When a village paid its tribute, the *alcalde mayor* could immediately redistribute the funds as new *repartimiento* loans. Theoretically, the Crown forbade this practice, but in reality it could do little to prevent it. And, as long as the tribute was paid in a timely fashion, the Crown had little incentive to complain.[82] The benefit to the *alcalde mayor* and his commercial partners came from the fact that they had use of "free" funds for the period of time between collection of the tribute and its deposit in the royal treasury, what modern financial institutions refer to as the "float." These were funds which belonged to the Crown, yet they represented an interest-free loan during the interim.

35

In addition to these administrative issues, there was overlap between tribute and *repartimiento* at the micro-economic level. In the early-colonial period, all tribute was paid in kind; only gradually, at different times in different places, was this procedure commuted to tribute in coin. This occurred for several reasons. First, demanding that peasants pay their tribute in cash necessitated many to seek seasonal work for wages, and this helped to alleviate the chronic labor shortages faced by Spanish entrepreneurs. Second, tribute collectors, whether *encomenderos* or representatives of the Crown, faced the difficult and costly task of marketing the tribute in kind to convert it to silver. Requiring that tribute be paid in coin passed this burden to the Indians.

Conversion from tribute in kind to tribute in coin was already well advanced in the Valley of Mexico by the middle of the sixteenth century, yet, even in the late-colonial period, there were certain villages of New Spain, often the most remote, that still paid tribute, at least partially, in goods.[83] And the goods were often the very same ones that the *alcalde mayor* sought through the *repartimiento*.

In the Oaxacan district of Villa Alta, the Indians sometimes delivered their tribute in *mantas*, which, along with cochineal, was the main commodity that the *alcalde mayor* of Villa Alta purchased through *repartimiento* advances. This was an occasional source of tension, however, because it seems that the Indians might have preferred, at least at times, to pay in coin. In 1790, Bernardino Bonavia, the *alcalde mayor* of Villa Alta, complained in a letter to Viceroy Revillagigedo that some of the Indians insisted on meeting their tribute obligations in money rather than *mantas*, and that this had reduced the profitability of his post since he depended on the small profit that he earned from reselling the *mantas* in other parts of the colony. The issue resurfaced several years later when it was discovered that the new magistrate, don Bernardo Ruiz de Conejares, was also trying to collect tribute in *mantas*. In both cases, *bandos* were circulated advising the Indians that they were free to pay their tributes in either money or kind, whichever they preferred.[84] In each of these cases, it seems that the official was simply trying to collect tribute in typical *repartimiento* goods. At times, however, the overlap between tribute and *repartimiento* was more direct.

As a number of historians have suggested, the very participation of Indians in the *repartimiento* was often for the purpose of obtaining the funds they needed to pay their tribute to the Crown.[85] Eighteenth-century commentators often argued that this was a central reason why the *repartimiento* was valuable; it enabled peasants to meet their tribute obligations.[86] Certainly peasants sought *repartimiento* loans to pay their tribute, as was the case for Pedro de Vera, the Indian *alcalde* of San Andres de Teposcolula, who, along with other community members, contracted for a cochineal *repartimiento* of 2.5 arrobas (62.5 pounds) in October 1781 to pay their tribute.[87] The more intriguing question, however, is whether the tribute system "became merely a branch of the *repartimiento*," as Robert W. Patch has hypothesized for Yucatan and Guatemala.[88] Patch found that officials of these regions issued *repartimientos* twice each year and did so on the very same days that tribute payments were due; this led him to speculate that the Indians' "frequent inability to pay tribute was turned to the advantage of the entrepreneurs (*alcaldes mayores*), who could extend credit to Indians by paying their tribute debts in return for repayment in kind at a later date."[89] In other words, the officials paid the tribute and the peasants incurred a future obligation. What Patch describes is essentially a cash *repartimiento* in which no money exchanges hands, only a debt is incurred. How prevalent this practice was is difficult to assess; concrete evidence is lacking, but it seems likely that it occurred with regularity. A sizeable percentage of *repartimientos* was for very small amounts, just a peso or two, which could easily have been the tribute obligation of the recipient. Since the date on which the tribute was due might not correspond with the cochineal harvest, it seems likely that many peasants would have found themselves short on coin at tribute time and would have been forced to accept an additional *repartimiento* loan.

Perhaps lending additional credibility to this hypothesis, Daniele Dehouve found "a particular type of *repartimiento*" in Tlapa (modern-day Guerrero), in which the *alcalde mayor* purchased five thousand pesos' worth of cotton thread from the peasants, but rather than paying them in cash he merely applied the payment against an equivalent amount of their tribute obligation. According to Dehouve, this practice was nothing more than a disguised tribute. She is correct, unless, as seems likely, time elapsed between the date tribute was due and the date that the thread was delivered, in which case the *alcalde mayor* was advancing the peasants their tribute payments, perhaps because they did not have sufficient resources on the date the tribute was due, exactly what Patch hypothesizes. In short, it would have been a means for the peasants to meet their tribute on time without actually making any payments.[90]

37

The post of *alcalde mayor* was created to increase the Crown's control over its indigenous subjects. Vested with judicial authority, the *alcaldes mayores* were supposed to dispense justice, collect tribute and other taxes, and generally look after the Crown's interests. The actual activities of the Spanish officials, however, departed from this idealized role. The Crown proved unwilling to adequately compensate the officials, and before 1750 actually even required that the officials purchase their posts as well as expose themselves to financial risks in the form of the *fianza*. Faced with such significant economic burdens and wanting to enrich themselves rapidly, the *alcaldes mayores* forged alliances with the colony's mercantile interests and used the political power of their posts to advance their benefactors' and their own mutual commercial interests. The officials and their system of *repartimientos* became the financial nexus between the indigenous peasants' household economies and the wider colonial and international markets.

Chapter Three

The *Repartimiento* and Crown Politics

T he *repartimientos* of the *alcaldes mayores* were controversial and exposed the officials to significant criticism and often heated attacks. It is possible that no other issue in the eighteenth century captured the attention of the Crown and its agents more than the *repartimiento*. In part, the controversy lay in the fact that the *alcaldes mayores* ceased to be impartial colonial officials but, instead, more accurately resembled private merchants privileged with the use of judicial power to enforce debts owed to them. Furthermore, because the Spanish officials most often operated on behalf of the wealthy colonial merchants with whom they had made contracts, the Crown authority was, in effect, appropriated for the commercial use of wealthy merchants. The *alcaldes mayores'* primary loyalty was to the mercantile interests with whom they were allied, not the king.

For much of the colonial period, the Crown seemed content to ignore or even sanction the use in this manner of official authority, largely because the system of *repartimientos* did provide tangible benefits to the Crown. For one, the Crown received considerable income from the sale of these posts. As long as the Spanish Crown was content with selling its authority in exchange for a fixed income, this system operated well. The potential profits of trading with the Indians were substantial, and, consequently, aspirants were willing to pay handsomely for the job of *alcalde mayor*.[1]

The income earned by the Crown, however, was not the only benefit it obtained from the sale of the office of *alcalde mayor*. The ability to issue *repartimientos* also ensured that the *alcaldes mayores* would succeed in obtaining the required *fianza*. Wealthy merchants agreed to cover uncollected tax and tribute revenues precisely because this enabled them to form partnerships and benefit from the judicial power of the *alcalde mayor*, without which they dared not trade on credit with the Indians. The Crown, thus, gained greater financial security by selling its authority.

Merchants, *alcaldes mayores*, and the Crown, then, all benefited from the system of *repartimientos*. Merchants and *alcaldes mayores* contracted to jointly capitalize on the commercial possibilities of the Indian district, utilizing the *alcalde*'s judicial authority to enforce debts. The Crown, for its part, obtained officials who, instead of receiving a salary, actually paid the king for their positions. In addition, wealthy merchants guaranteed to the Crown that tribute and other revenues would be collected. What the king lost in direct control over his dominions was compensated by a guaranteed, hassle-free, fixed income.

Repartimiento *Financing and the* Production *of Cochineal*

The production of cochineal was directly dependent on the availability of credit, and credit depended largely on the legality of *repartimientos*. Without credit, many peasants could not produce a cash crop such as cochineal. Only when merchants had the ability to enforce the repayment of debts, however, did they feel sufficiently secure to loan funds to the peasant producers of cochineal.

For most of the eighteenth century, *repartimiento* financing was readily available and production of cochineal was abundant. Theoretically, *repartimientos* were illegal before 1751. But despite the fact that the Laws of the Indies expressly prohibited Spanish officials from conducting trade with the Indians under their charge, these restrictions were routinely ignored.[2] Not only did the Crown do little to enforce the restrictions, but the sale of offices essentially condoned the illegal practice.[3] The only reason why individuals paid large sums to receive office, after all, was to obtain the juridical authority without which they could not safely extend *repartimiento* loans. The royal position toward the *repartimiento*, however, underwent radical change over the second half of the eighteenth century. Legalized in 1751, the *repartimiento* was severely attacked by religious clerics and Bourbon reformers in the 1770s and 1780s, and was finally banned in 1786 by Article 12 of the Real Ordenanza de Intendentes.[4] When *repartimientos* were permitted, the production of cochineal was substantial. In contrast, the late-colonial abolition of the system of *repartimientos* coincided with a major decline in *grana* production.

In 1758 El Registro de Grana, a Oaxacan office established to guard against fraud in the cochineal business, began recording annually the levels

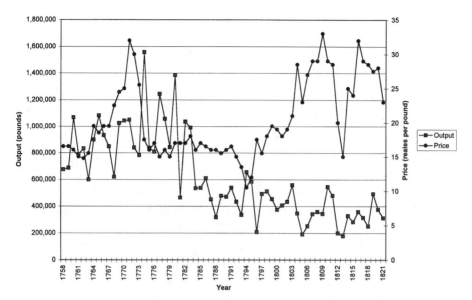

FIGURE 3.1. Price and output of cochineal in Oaxaca, 1758–1821. Data for all years except 1820 are adapted from "Memoria del gobierno del estado de Oaxaca," in the library of the AGEO, and the *Boletín de la sociedad Mexicana de geografía y estadística* 7 (1859). Sources: Appendix B; data for the year 1820 are adapted from Bustamante.

of grana cochinilla produced in the province.[5] By law, all merchants were required to submit their cochineal to this office, where it was weighed and checked for purity.[6] The Registry's figures for gross annual output survive and provide a good, though probably incomplete, record of total annual production of cochineal. These are presented in Appendix B.[7]

The annual output of cochineal registered, as well as the average price per pound in Oaxaca for the period 1758–1821 is displayed in Figure 3.1.[8] This figure demonstrates clearly the industry's late-colonial depression, related, in part, to the changing Crown position on the *repartimiento*. Registered output reached high levels for the first twenty-five years, averaging around 886,000 pounds annually, before dropping after 1783 by over half to an average near 402,000 pounds. With the exception of the six years from 1768 to 1773, prices hovered between 2.0 and 2.5 pesos until 1792, after which time they fell briefly, only to rise to very high levels for most of the remainder of the colonial period.

As far as the production of cochineal is concerned, the period 1750–

1821 can be divided into two roughly equal periods. During the first half, until the mid-1780s, cochineal production boomed, due both to the 1751 legalization of the *repartimiento* and to the healthy demand for the dye-stuff in Europe. The 1751 legislation legalized an already common practice but probably led to greater investment in the industry, since now the Spanish officials could trade more openly and legally with the Indians of their districts. In contrast, the 1786 implementation of the Real Ordenanza de Intendentes, an outgrowth of Visitor-General José de Gálvez's 1768 Plan de Intendencias, coincided with a severe depression in the dye trade. The intendancy system sought, among other things, to increase the Crown's control over local matters largely by reducing the autonomy of the *alcaldes mayores*. In certain ways, the Ordenanza was an attempt to undo the system that had previously dominated, in which the Crown tolerated the privatization of its power by the *alcaldes mayores*. Whereas earlier, the Spanish officials could make alliances with powerful merchants for the joint exploitation of a district's commerce, now the local-level officials were to be loyal and professional employees of the Crown. The cornerstone of reform was Article 12, which explicitly prohibited the provincial officials from providing *repartimiento* financing to the indigenous inhabitants of their districts. For the cochineal industry, the abolition of the *repartimiento* was devastating, for without the provision of credit, many Indians were unable to produce the dyestuff. This depression is clearly reflected in Figure 3.1. The production curve for the period 1786–1821 shows the considerable decay of the industry relative to the preceding decades. Production of cochineal depended greatly on the availability of *repartimiento* financing and was thus influenced by Crown policy toward the system, a policy that shifted fundamentally during the period after 1750.[9]

The 1751 Legalization of the Repartimiento

On 28 May 1751, the Crown by royal decree made legal the issuance of *repartimiento* loans. The *repartimiento* was not a new institution, having operated prior to 1751 semi-clandestinely. Officially illegal, the *repartimiento* was regularly tolerated.[10] Legalization was an attempt by the Crown to regulate the trade and to mitigate the potential for conflicts between the Spanish *alcaldes mayores* and the indigenous recipients of the *repartimiento* loans. The reformers further hoped that royal revenues would benefit from the system's legalization. As long as the *repartimiento* was illegal, the reformers postulated, then the *alcaldes mayores* would evade the taxes owed on their trade with the Indians.

To accomplish both these tasks, limiting abuses and increasing taxes, a royal *cédula* dated 15 June 1751 called upon all *alcaldes mayores* and parish priests to explain how the *repartimiento* system operated and what types and quantities of goods were involved. The royal government proposed the organization of a four-person *junta* to develop guidelines for the operation of the *repartimiento* trade, and an *arancel*, a list of typical quantities and values involved in the trade between the Spanish officials and the indigenous population.[11] The Spanish officials would then be required to abide by the rates stipulated by the *arancel*. It was hoped that with this approach the system could be better regulated and that the abuses inevitable in the *repartimiento* could be reduced.[12] While the 1751 legalization of the *repartimiento* went into effect, the *arancel* was never completed for Mexico.[13]

The language of the 15 June 1751 *cédula* reveals the position taken by the reformers which led to the *repartimiento*'s legalization. The policymakers recognized that normally only the Spanish officials provided goods on credit or extended loans to Indians because "neither a merchant nor any other person can risk making such loans, nor wait such long terms with a [debt] collection so difficult and costly."[14] Credit, however, was a necessity, for without it many Indians were unable to perform certain economic activities, cochineal production for one, or purchase certain high-priced goods. *Alcaldes mayores*, unlike other merchants, could make loans and collect debts because they controlled better resources to force debtors to repay. To explain why Indians were bad credit risks, the authors of the document resorted to the typical racist explanations upon which colonial society was predicated — Indians were lazy drunkards, resistant to hard work, and void of honor. Thus, the policymakers claimed, the stick of the *repartimiento* was necessary to ensure that Indians worked to repay their debts.

That Indians were likely candidates for default is unquestionable. Nearly all Spanish colonial commentators, whether they favored or opposed the *repartimiento*, recognized the propensity for peasants to repay their loans late. The innumerable colonial cases dealing with indigenous Mexicans who were delinquent in the payment of their debts further demonstrate this. Data presented in Chapter 6 indicate that in at least one case, the district of Teposcolula for the years 1781–1784, 70 percent of cochi-

43

neal *repartimiento* recipients delayed in repaying their debts to the *alcalde mayor*. What needs reevaluation, however, is the reason for default. The authors of the 1751 *cédula* fell back upon typical colonial Spanish depictions of the subject Indians. According to this ideology, Indians defaulted because they were lazy and resisted hard work.

In reality, of course, default had other causes. Frequently, debtors were unable to meet their obligations on time because of uncontrollable events — crop loss, for instance. In other cases, debtors simply were "dishonest," claiming that they were insolvent in order to stall debt repayments, or fleeing the village whenever the debt collector presented himself. To be certain, eighteenth-century Oaxacan peasants were poor credit risks, just as economic-development studies have repeatedly demonstrated modern-day peasants to be.[15]

Regardless of the reason, debt collection was difficult, and this necessitated the existence of an institution capable of operating under such high-risk conditions. As the policymakers realized, the *repartimiento* served such a purpose because the *alcalde mayor* could use judicial authority to enforce debt collection. Thus, the 1751 royal *cédula* accepted the necessity of the *repartimiento*. Without credit, Indians could not participate extensively in the market. Few merchants, however, would loan them funds, for the risk of default was high. Only the *alcalde mayor* was in a position to serve as creditor to the general indigenous population.

The responses to the royal *cédula* submitted by the *alcaldes mayores* and the parish priests revealed that by 1751 the *repartimiento* was already well established in the districts of Oaxaca.[16] This fact would seem to confirm that the 1751 legalization was merely the official sanctioning of an institution already widely practiced. There is no doubt that Indians were receiving *repartimiento* loans long before 1751, but what is difficult to assess is the extent of their expansion after 1751. Certainly the production of cochineal in Oaxaca rose sharply in the 1760s and 1770s (see Figure 3.1), but since the data only begin in 1758, we cannot be absolutely certain whether the boom years of the 1760s and 1770s were unique or whether previous booms had occurred. Regardless, it appears from the sharp increase in registered production after the 1750s that the legalization of the *repartimiento* encouraged the expansion of cochineal production as the *alcaldes mayores* responded to the added security of operating their *repartimientos* overtly by increasing their loans. They were doubtlessly aided by the provision of more generous *avios*, or financing, from their merchant allies.

The "Bourbon Reforms" and the
1786 Prohibition of Repartimientos

During the last decades of the eighteenth century, the Spanish royal government attempted to vastly reform its colonial possessions. The Bourbon Reforms, as they have been widely termed, encompassed a broad array of policies which generally sought to wrest control away from powerful interests.[17] No sector of colonial society remained untouched by the reformist Bourbon state. The highly independent Jesuit order was expelled from the Spanish colonies in 1767. Colonial defenses were reorganized and strengthened. Commercial privileges enjoyed by the *consulado* merchants of Spain and Mexico were attacked. Restrictions on trade were gradually lifted until finally the 1778 (1789 for Mexico) declaration of *comercio libre*, free trade, provided for freer commerce within the Spanish empire.

Administrative changes were also significant. In 1776 the Viceroyalty of Peru was divided, with the creation of the new Viceroyalty of Rio de la Plata with its capital at Buenos Aires. The culmination of the Crown's program for administrative reform, however, was the Real Ordenanza de Intendentes, introduced into Mexico in 1786, which attempted to increase the state's control over local affairs by completely overhauling the colonial bureaucracy.

The Real Ordenanza de Intendentes was the design of José de Gálvez, who, as Visitor-General, was sent to Mexico by the Crown in 1765.[18] In his Informe y Plan de Intendencias, the product of his *visita*, Gálvez outlined his proposals, which were later incorporated into the Ordenanza.[19] He equated the condition of Mexico to that of Spain upon the death in 1700 of Carlos II. Spain, according to Gálvez, had been resurrected by the introduction of *intendencias* in 1749. In a similarly deplorable state, Mexico needed similar reforms.[20] Gálvez was particularly critical of the "ruinous plague" of the *alcaldes mayores*, who "enrich themselves at the expense of the miserable Indians [and] the royal tribute, of which the king loses nearly half owing to the usurpations and illicit pacts of the *alcaldes* who entrusted with its collection decide how much of it they're entitled to as indemnification for their work, for the funds that they expend in their provisions, for the salaries they're not paid, and for the *fianzas* that they're charged."[21] The *alcaldes mayores* were supposed to facilitate the difficult job of the Viceroy, he argued, but instead, they created additional work. Meanwhile, the *audiencias* were swamped with the many suits brought by

45

Indians and others against the *alcaldes mayores*. In Gálvez's words: "A Viceroy lacking subordinate and capable magistrates in the vast provinces of an empire . . . could never, even if he were the greatest man in the world, govern [the empire] well, not to mention reestablish its ancient happiness and opulence. . . ."[22]

Gálvez's medicine for Mexico called for a total overhaul of the colonial system. His Plan de Intendencias was accepted by the Crown in August 1769 but was not immediately adopted, owing, in part, to the opposition of the entering Mexican Viceroy, Antonio María de Bucareli (1771–1779), who considered the proposed reforms costly and unnecessary. In Bucareli's view, Crown finances were healthy and the existing administrative system efficient.[23] And Bucareli was not the only person with a strong opinion about the Ordenanza; throughout the 1770s and early 1780s, testimonies were submitted to the Viceroys of Mexico and the Council of Indies both in support of and in opposition to Gálvez's proposed reforms.[24]

It was not until December 1786 that the system of *intendencias* was finally implemented in Mexico. It began with the partitioning of the colony into twelve districts, to each of which a new official, the *intendente corregidor*, was appointed. Gálvez had believed that the demands placed on the office of the Viceroy were too great for one individual to handle. This was to be rectified by the introduction of the *intendentes*, who were to report directly to the Viceroy and were to be powerful, local-level representatives of the Crown, administrative stages between the Viceroy and the provincial officials. The Ordenanza also provided for the replacement of *alcaldes mayores* with *subdelegados*, who while serving in the same districts as the *alcaldes mayores*, were to be subordinate to the *intendentes*. The *subdelegados*, unlike their predecessors, were to be paid, professional bureaucrats. Gálvez argued that the failure to adequately compensate the *alcaldes mayores* had been the reason why these officials had "indemnified themselves" by embezzling part of the royal tribute. Furthermore, these officials had fallen under the control of the consulado merchants precisely because they depended on the income which this alliance provided them. In an effort to remunerate the *subdelegados*, Article 132 of the Ordenanza de Intendentes provided for them to receive as salary 5 percent of the Indian tribute collected in their respective districts.[25] With honest, professional *subdelegados* in each of the districts where previously the *alcaldes mayores* had served, and with experienced *intendentes corregidores* at the helm of each of the newly created *intendencias*, the reformers believed that the Crown's authority would more

46

effectively reach the far corners of the Viceroyalty. The introduction of *intendentes*, then, was a reform designed to bridge the existing gap between the largely independent *alcaldes mayores* and the Viceroy—a reform, it was hoped, that would increase Crown control in remote regions of the Viceroyalty.

The central piece of legislation contained in the Real Ordenanza de Intendentes was Article 12, which banned the new *subdelegados* from making *repartimiento* loans to the Indians of their districts. Article 12 stated:

> Neither the *subdelegados* cited, nor the *alcaldes ordinarios*, nor the governors who still remain, nor any other person whatsoever may distribute (*repartir*) to Indians, Spaniards, mestizos, and the other castes, any personal property, produce, or any cattle, under the irremissable penalty of losing their value in favor of the Indians thus injured. . . . It is to be understood that the Indians and my other vassals of my dominions are free to trade wherever and with whomever it suits them, in order to provide themselves with everything they may need.[26]

It would be simplistic to identify any single reason for the Crown to halt the system of *repartimientos*. Gálvez characterized the *repartimiento* as a commercial monopoly in which the *alcalde mayor* sold goods to the Indians on credit "for excessive prices and exorbitant returns."[27] He further condemned the *alcaldes* because, he claimed, they evaded *alcabala* sales taxes that they should have been paying on their *repartimientos*.[28] Discussing Oaxaca specifically, Gálvez lamented:

> [As] this province is the richest and most opulent in all of New Spain, owing to the abundance of the exquisite product of *grana*, and the active trade in *mantas* and other manufactures, it causes much wonder and not a small amount of grief to see that the *Alcabalas* are in worse decay than even the Tributes, because the *alcaldes mayores*, who excessively enrich themselves with their monopolies and unjust transactions, evade this tax which they should satisfy on their purchases and sales.[29]

47

More generally, Article 12 was the natural outgrowth of the dominant free-trade ideology of the Bourbon reformers. Historians have noted that Gálvez surrounded himself with ideologues who were convinced that liberating trade would produce enormous benefits.[30] Policymakers viewed the *repartimiento* as an obstacle to free trade because the *alcaldes mayores* had employed it to maintain commercial monopolies. Freed from the control of the Spanish officials, Indians would benefit more from their own production and would consequently produce more. More production would lead to an expansion of colonial trade and would augment royal revenues, and these would be collected by the new, honest *subdelegados.* The market created by the end of *repartimientos,* according to Gálvez, would be filled by other merchants because "plentiful were the subjects dealing in the same goods and items as those that the *alcaldes mayores* provided."[31]

Finally, Article 12 signified a realization on the part of the Crown that increasing control over its colonies could only be accomplished through the replacement of its colonial officials with a more professional bureaucracy composed of career officials.[32] Under the old system, the allegiance of the *alcaldes mayores* naturally went to their *aviadores* rather than the Crown, because these merchants bankrolled both the Spanish officials and their business dealings. Not surprisingly, the *alcalde mayor* placed his own material well-being before the King's interests.

The *alcaldes'* ties to mercantile interests had been acceptable to the Crown as long as it was content to receive a fixed income from its colonial possessions. It was incompatible, however, with the activist, absolutist state that Gálvez and other Bourbon reformers envisioned. In order to recover authority in remote regions of its colonies, the Bourbon Crown had to cut the ties that its bureaucrats had with the powerful merchant houses, to recover the allegiance of the provincial officials. *Repartimientos* were the main target of reform because as long as they were permitted to continue, the loyalty and integrity of the Spanish officials were suspect. Merchants and *alcaldes mayores* made mutually beneficial contracts — merchants provided financing which the *alcaldes mayores* used in lucrative trade with the Indians. In replacing the *alcaldes mayores* with *subdelegados,* a new group of officials prohibited from trading with the Indians, the Bourbon state hoped to create a professional bureaucracy free of the corrupting influences of wealthy colonial interests.[33]

The prohibition of the *repartimiento* under Article 12 of the Real Ordenanza de Intendentes was arguably the most controversial piece of legislation passed by the Bourbon reformers. No other issue commanded the attention of Mexico's elites more than the question of the *repartimiento,* which sparked copious debate and discussion during the entire second half of the eighteenth century. Because the debates over the *repartimiento* have already been thoroughly explored, they are only summarized here.[34]

Even before the 1786 ban, passionate testimonies either in favor of or against the system were presented to the Crown and its officials. Supporters of *repartimiento* warned of the dire consequences that would result from Gálvez's proposed plan. They predicted economic depression, decimation of Crown finances, reduced quality of Crown officials, and the impoverishment of the Indians.[35] In contrast, the opponents of the *repartimiento*, led by the clergy, emphasized the suffering endured by the Indians as a result of the abusive practices of the *alcaldes mayores* and their often violent collection of debts. In addition, the *alcaldes mayores* were condemned as usurers and accused of obstructing the religious training of the Indians.[36]

The introduction of *intendencias* and the inclusion of the ban on *repartimientos* only intensified the debate. Proponents of the *repartimiento* identified a list of maladies which they argued were caused by its prohibition. Defenders of the system of *intendencias* countered with heated denials, pointing to alleged benefits resulting from the ban. Both Brading and MacLachlan have compared the eighteenth-century prohibition of *repartimientos* and the subsequent debates with the sixteenth-century struggles over the *encomienda*.[37] Both institutions came to obsess Crown officials and distract them from the reality of the colonies they were empowered to govern.

As Brian Hamnett clearly shows, the prohibition of the *repartimiento* created a number of problems. Without the possibility of trading with the Indians, few qualified Spaniards sought the post of *subdelegado*, for the position held few attractions on its own. In order for the Crown to attract qualified candidates, it would have been necessary to compensate them with generous salaries, for as long as salaries were insufficient remuneration on their own, either no one would serve or the ban on *repartimientos* would be ignored. While Article 132 of the Real Ordenanza did assign to the new officials a salary of 5 percent of all tribute collections made in a district, nowhere was this amount adequate compensation, and in most districts it failed even to cover the expenses of the office.[38]

Furthermore, the Crown declined to waive the requirement that the *subdelegados* provide *fianzas*, financial guarantees that all tribute and tax revenues would be collected. Before Article 12, merchant-financiers had gladly acted as *fiadores*, exposing themselves to significant risks because they expected to be rewarded with large trade profits. The abolition of *repartimientos* altered the equation. Once the allure of profit was removed, merchants lost interest in guaranteeing the revenue collections of the regional officials. The result was that several Oaxacan *subdelegados*

49

could not assume office for lack of a *fianza*. In order, then, for the Crown to attract interested and qualified candidates to the post of *subdelegado*, it was necessary, at the very least, to pay respectable salaries and to forgo the requirement that the officials provide financial guarantors. The Crown did neither.[39]

The situation was further complicated by the mounting evidence of economic decline in the old *alcaldías mayores*. In Oaxaca, the production of each of the two commodities long dependent on *repartimiento* financing, cotton mantles and cochineal dye, experienced steep declines in the mid-1780s. Most colonial observers attributed recession to the prohibition of *repartimientos*, arguing that Indians could no longer produce these commodities, which depended on *repartimiento* financing.

Indications of economic decline and the inability to find qualified candidates to serve as *subdelegados* sparked repeated official investigations into the *repartimiento* and the viability of the *intendencia* system during the 1790s.[40] Not surprisingly, opinions were diverse. On the one side, defenders of the new system vehemently opposed the return of the old practice of *repartimientos*. Led by officials such as the royalist Peninsular *intendente* of Oaxaca, Antonio de Mora y Peysal, they argued that the *repartimiento* was a corrupt system supported only by the ex–*alcaldes mayores* and their merchant backers. They argued that the *repartimiento* had led to great suffering on the part of Indians who had been forced to sell their output at prices below market value and who were subjected to the ruthless debt-collection techniques of the *alcaldes mayores*, which included imprisoning and beating those who did not pay promptly. With the end of the *repartimiento*, they argued, the indigenous population had benefited from increased competition, while trade had not suffered any significant decline. Instead, the system of *intendencias* had broken the monopolies and monopsonies of the *alcaldes mayores* to the benefit of the indigenous population and society as a whole.[41]

Supporters of the *repartimientos* painted a different picture. They argued that the end of the *repartimiento* system had contributed to general economic decline, especially in the largely rural and indigenous areas of the colony. Whereas before, Indians had received goods from the Spanish officials on credit, now they were forced to pay for goods up front. As a result, trade had declined, for few Indians could raise sufficient funds to purchase anything but low-cost items. Similarly, indigenous production of items requiring some level of investment capital had suffered because producers no longer received payment in advance but had somehow to

50

finance production themselves. Far from beneficial, then, the ban on *repartimientos* had been harmful to the Indians and had caused a great decline in the colony's economic welfare. Furthermore, without the income from the *repartimiento*, many Indians proved unable to pay their tribute and, consequently, royal revenues were adversely affected. In addition, opponents of Article 12 noted the increasing difficulty of obtaining *subdelegados* qualified to replace the old *alcaldes mayores*. Few individuals wanted the job, now that the opportunities for profit had disappeared. Those who did fill the posts were not performing their jobs and rarely ventured outside of the *cabeceras*, if they resided in the districts at all. This was in stark contrast to their predecessors, whose significant economic interests insured regular visits to even the most remote corners under their jurisdiction. Naturally, the solution to the problem, they argued, was to repeal the ban on *repartimientos*. With the abrogation of Article 12, there would be no shortage of capable individuals eager to serve well and able to provide the required *fianza*.[42]

The two sides of the debate emerged clearly in 1790 when the *intendente* of Oaxaca, José Antonio Mora y Peysal, and the new *subdelegado* of the Oaxacan district of Villa Alta, Bernardino Bonavia, each wrote a series of letters to the Viceroy, the Second Count Revillagigedo (1789–1794), to plead their respective positions regarding the *repartimiento*. In response to a request by the Viceroy for information about the effect of the ban on trade, Mora y Peysal wrote that despite the many predictions that the economy would collapse with the suspension of the *repartimiento*, trade and production were flourishing. In 1788, Mora noted, Indians had produced surplus corn which they had sold to the Oaxacan *alhondiga*, the public granary. More important, cochineal producers had obtained "seed" for their *nopaleras* despite the absence of *repartimiento* loans. This last point was crucial, for the Oaxacan economy was closely tied to the success of cochineal production, which, according to the supporters of the *repartimiento*, had traditionally depended on the advance payments made by the *alcaldes mayores*. Mora added that the 1789 dye harvest was considerable, and although the 1790 harvest had been disappointing, it was not due to the lack of credit, but to the year's high levels of precipitation, which had damaged the fragile cochineal insects. In effect, Mora ensured the Viceroy that the diminution of credit as a result of the abolition of *repartimientos* had not destroyed the rural economy, as Indians had found alternative means to fund their *grana* production.[43]

Bernardino Bonavia, the *subdelegado* of Villa Alta, outlined a different scenario in a September 1790 letter to the Viceroy. Bonavia began by

51

complaining that he was unable to support himself on the salary of 1,200 pesos that he received from his 5 percent of tributes collected. As it was, he noted, many towns were two years behind in their tribute payments, owing to the general economic stagnation that had resulted from the 1786 prohibition of *repartimientos*. According to Bonavia, before the ban, an *alcalde mayor* typically invested 100,000 pesos per year in the district, providing *repartimiento* loans to cochineal and cotton mantle producers. Now, 80,000 pesos per year were drained from Villa Alta in tribute payments, purchases of tobacco by inhabitants from the royal monopoly, and *beneficios* paid to the district's priests. With no additional capital infusions, the local economy was rapidly deteriorating. Bonavia added that he realized that the prohibition of *repartimientos* was intended to encourage greater competition, but he noted that no private merchants had filled the void because none would dare "expose their money with so many risks. . . . Nobody has wanted to get involved with loaning [the Indians] even a half *real*." Bonavia proposed the repeal of the ban, arguing that only the *subdelegado* would make loans, for only he could enforce contracts.[44]

Under the old system of *repartimientos*, claimed *subdelegado* Bonavia, the Indians had benefited from the trade in *mantas*. For each peso (8 reales) that the *alcalde mayor* advanced, an Indian weaver was required to deliver in the future one *manta*, which cost the producer approximately 2.5 reales to produce, thus yielding a profit to the producer of 5.5 reales per piece. In all, the *alcaldes mayores* typically contracted yearly for the production of eighty thousand *mantas*, which cost the Indians only 25,000 pesos to produce, resulting in 55,000 pesos worth of profit, out of which the Indians could pay their tribute and still have significant amounts left over for other expenses. With the end of the *repartimiento*, lamented Bonavia, the production of cotton mantles had sharply declined.[45]

Intendente Mora y Peysal responded to the claims made by Bonavia by arguing to the Viceroy that the *repartimiento* had instead been a burden on the cotton mantle weavers. Mora claimed that each mantle took a weaver at least ten days to produce, and that quite often producers proved unable to complete them on time and had to purchase them instead in the marketplace for ten reales, two reales more than they had received from the *alcalde mayor*. In addition to imprisoning debtors until their debts were repaid, the *alcalde mayor* subjected the Indians to many other abusive and extortionist practices. With the end of the *repartimiento*, Mora argued, the weavers sold their mantles for the full market price of ten reales, benefiting from the increased number of buyers. In short, argued Mora, Bonavia's testimony was simply a ruse intended to convince the

52

Viceroy to re-allow *repartimientos*. The end of *repartimientos* had not caused a collapse of the economy, as the Indians had been able and willing to finance their own production. Thus, the prohibition on *repartimientos* should remain.[46]

Undoubtedly, the truth lay somewhere between the testimonies of Bonavia and Mora, for both had good reasons to stretch the truth. One should be wary of Bonavia's expressed concern for the welfare of Villa Alta's Indians. He certainly exaggerated the profits realized by the indigenous population in order to emphasize the harm caused to the Indians by the prohibition of the *repartimiento*. As *subdelegado* of the largest district in Oaxaca, Bonavia had much to gain from the reversal of Article 12. In fact, he admitted as much, stating that the reason for his complaint was that he was unable to make enough money from his 5 percent share of tributes and that he desired to augment his earnings by trading in *mantas*. Yet despite the fact that Bonavia's testimony was far from disinterested, his claims cannot be dismissed. Much evidence, presented below, would seem to corroborate the *subdelegado*'s assertions.

Mora's testimony, however, was also self-interested. The Oaxacan *intendente* correctly condemned some of the worst abuses committed by the *alcaldes mayores* in the operation of their *repartimientos*, including the imprisonment of debtors. Mora, though, could not have taken any position other than the one he did, that the *repartimiento* was a source of suffering and an obstruction to economic growth. His selection as Oaxaca's first *intendente* was not coincidence but due to his unswerving commitment to Gálvez's system of *intendencias*, which had as its cornerstone reform the abolition of *repartimientos*. Because *repartimientos* were more important in Oaxaca than in any other Mexican province, the success or failure of the system of *intendencias* depended greatly on occurrences in Oaxaca. Thus, Mora could not possibly have assumed any stance other than a hard line against the *repartimiento*.

Article 12 became increasingly the central issue determining the success or failure of the Ordenanza's reforms. It became so pivotal and heated an issue that MacLachlan goes so far as to suggest that it became "an ideological test," a measure of one's doctrinal purity and commitment to the new system of *intendencias*. The Bourbon ideologues were so convinced that their policies were correct, designed as they were with enlightened scientific methods, that they proved unresponsive to the real conditions in the colony.[47] In this mold, the Oaxacan *intendente*, Mora y Peysal, was the quintessential Bourbon reformer.

As for the effect of the ban on the economy as a whole, strong evidence

53

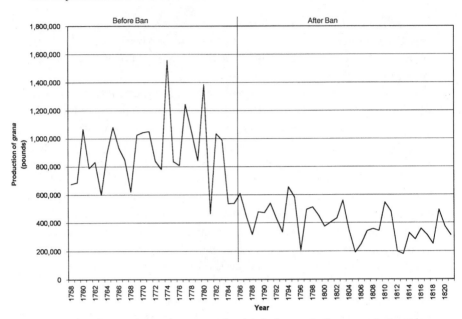

FIGURE 3.2. Comparison of *grana* production before and after *repartimiento* ban of 1786. Source: Appendix B.

refutes the position of Mora y Peysal and suggests instead a sharp decline in commerce in the mid-1780s. Using the massive statistical study of José María Murguía y Galardi, Hamnett found that the production of *mantas* from Villa Alta had fallen by 1828 to just 20 percent of the level produced before the ban. Figures provided in 1810 by the Bishop of Oaxaca, Antonio Bergoza y Jordán, showed a decline nearly as steep between 1787 and 1810.[48]

The evidence on the production of cochineal, displayed in Figure 3.2, is equally convincing. During the five years preceding the ban's implementation, from 1782 to 1786, the average cochineal production registered in Oaxaca was 742,040 pounds. In the five years after the ban, from 1787 to 1791, however, the average was only 451,342 pounds, a decline of 39 percent from the earlier period. Comparing the averages over ten years is even more persuasive. The average cochineal harvest registered in Oaxaca in the ten years before the prohibition was about double the amount registered in the subsequent ten years.

In his effort to defend the ban, Intendente Mora denied that the Oaxacan economy had suffered a serious downturn. There is no doubt, however, that the economy did enter into a significant depression. The production of cochineal and cotton mantles, the two products receiving the overwhelming majority of *repartimiento* financing in Oaxaca, had both experienced severe declines.

The Era of the Illegal Repartimiento

A number of historians have documented the clandestine reemergence of the *repartimiento* in the years following its prohibition.[49] Whether the *repartimiento* ever totally ceased, however, is doubtful. In Oaxaca, *subdelegados* were illegally making *repartimiento* loans at least as early as 1789. In that year, the *subdelegado* of Teotitlán del Valle was selling oxen teams on credit to the Indians of his district. In April, three Indians from the town of Macuilzóchitl in the jurisdiction of Teotitlán del Valle testified that they had agreed three months earlier to purchase oxen through the *repartimiento* of the *subdelegado*, Esteban Melgar, at twenty-six pesos per team of two. Melgar had recently confiscated these animals from another Indian who had had a long-outstanding debt from a *repartimiento* dating from the years before the ban. Thus, the *repartimiento* was not only operating in 1789, but the *subdelegado* had apparently continued to collect debts outstanding from the pre-ban era.[50]

Evasion of the ban was made possible, in part, by the inconsistency of authorities charged with enforcing the ban. The Oaxacan *intendente*, Mora y Peysal, was nearly alone in his attempts to implement Article 12 to the letter. Others, the Viceroys included, bent the rules or simply overlooked transgressions.

Not only did *subdelegados* face a regime only half-inclined to enforce the law, but policymakers nearly repealed Article 12. Faced with economic decline and the inability to find individuals willing to serve as *subdelegados*, the Junta Superior de Real Hacienda, the Superior Council on Royal Finances in Mexico City, recommended on 24 November 1794 to the new Viceroy, the Marques de Branciforte (1794–1798), that the ban be lifted and that the *subdelegados* be allowed to trade with the Indians. This merely made an already confused situation more uncertain, as some Crown officials in Spain and Mexico immediately began clamoring for the reversal of the Junta's decision, while others, including the Oaxacan *intendente*, Mora y Peysal, seemed bent on continuing to enforce the prohibition regardless. Viceroy Miguel José de Ananza (1798–1800), Viceroy Branciforte's successor, evaded the issue as best he could. When in 1798 the Council of the Indies demanded that he comment on the status of the

55

repartimiento, the Viceroy dodged the request, noting that he was awaiting special instructions from the Crown. Ex-Viceroy Branciforte, meanwhile, recommended to the king in 1800 the total repeal of Article 12. The
Council of Indies disagreed, however, which led, after much discussion, to
a total revision of the system of *intendencias* and the 1803 issuance of
the New Ordinance of Intendants.[51] Article 54 of the New Ordinance
once again ordered the prohibition of the *repartimiento*, arguing that the
subdelegados

> have caused so much damage to the honest administration of jus-
> tice, good government, happiness and greater development of those
> dominions: and not having even been enough to remedy this disor-
> der the severe prohibition made in the original Ordenanza de Inten-
> dentes, and repeated in subsequent royal orders; I declare again that
> neither *intendentes*, their aides, *subdelegados*, ministers, any other
> employee in the royal service, priests, miners, nor owners of *ha-
> ciendas* and *obrajes* . . . may distribute [*repartir*], directly or indi-
> rectly, to Indians or the other *castas*, products and goods from
> Spain or the Indies, or any other item, whether mules, or useful
> tools necessary for work in agriculture or mining, even if the [In-
> dians] ask for them or they're given as needed assistance for those
> lacking subsistence, clothes, or work; to obtain all of this [the In-
> dians] must remain absolutely free to trade and to agree upon the
> prices and terms that most benefit them.[52]

The new Ordenanza, however, was never introduced. In the following
year, the Crown reversed the Council's decree, noting financial exigencies. Thus, as Hamnett argued, despite the years of discussion, Article 12 "remained equivocal." As MacLachlan more accurately expressed
it, "the eighteenth-century ideology had reached a state of operational
paralysis."[53]

Oaxaca's Economy and the
Banning of the Repartimiento

56

While the opposing sides debated the future of the intendancy system and
the *repartimiento* in Mexico, the economy of Oaxaca languished. Colonial authorities may have been inclined to ignore *subdelegados* who disobeyed the ban on *repartimientos*, but it would be incorrect to conclude
that Article 12 had no effect on the Oaxacan economy. The *repartimiento*

did not cease, but the quantity and total value of funds loaned by the new officials decreased sharply. David Brading has suggested that the ban on *repartimientos* led the wealthiest merchants to abandon the cochineal trade. "Respectable merchants no longer cared to finance magistrates who wished to continue undercover trading."[54] The new officials proceeded to trade with the indigenous population, but they controlled far less capital than had their predecessors, the *alcaldes mayores*. As the flow of funds into rural areas decreased, the Oaxacan economy deteriorated.

The production of cochineal, long the jewel of the local economy, dropped sharply in the mid-1780s and for the rest of the colonial period remained at low levels in comparison to the earlier boom years. The production of cotton mantles in Villa Alta also plummeted. Indigenous production, however, was not the only sector of the economy to suffer. Historians have found that the collection of tithes in the bishopric of Oaxaca experienced violent fluctuations after 1790, suggesting instability in the overall economy. Since production by Indians of cochineal and other products was exempt from the tithe, the erratic level of collections in Oaxaca was not merely a reflection of the cochineal industry's depression.[55] Finally, William Taylor and Brian Hamnett documented the increasingly rapid turnover of property and high indebtedness of Oaxaca's small *hacendado* landowning class during the same period.[56]

Until his death in March 1808 Antonio de Mora y Peysal continued to support the ban and deny that it had caused economic deterioration. This position, however, was increasingly a minority one. Most observers linked the economic recession with the prohibition of the *repartimiento*. Even the Viceroys of Mexico came to attribute economic decline to the advent of Article 12.

When he took over as Viceroy of New Spain in 1789, Count Revillagigedo the Younger was convinced that with the passage of time the new system would ultimately bring greater prosperity to Mexico. His predecessor, Viceroy Manuel Antonio de Flores (1787–1789), was less confident. In his Instrucciones to the incoming Revillagigedo, Flores cautioned him about the dire consequences that many colonialists were predicting would result from the Intendancy system. Revillagigedo, however, chose to ignore these warnings, under the belief that more time was needed for the system to become established. Upon learning in 1790 that several *subdelegados* were illegally issuing *repartimientos*, Revillagigedo ordered their immediate and strict obedience to Article 12, stating that "free trade is the only means by which the Indies will prosper, the wealth of the treasury will increase, [and] justice will be administered."[57] By 1793, however, Revillagigedo was less confident. Commenting on the state of the economy and royal finances, the Viceroy admitted that one of the main reasons for the commercial downturn — stagnation, as he suggested — was the lack of *repartimientos*. According to the Viceroy, Indians proved unable to adjust to the end of the *repartimientos* because, he conjectured, they had grown accustomed to receiving payment for production in advance and obtaining merchandise on credit. As a result, Indians were without means to purchase inputs or livestock. The Viceroy added that the unavailability of credit to Indians was not due to a lack of private merchants who were willing to lend their capital, but, in the Viceroy's opinion, resulted from the general confusion over the meaning of Article 12, which many interpreted to mean that all credit transactions with Indians were illegal. Largely in contradiction to this assertion, he added that Indians were generally bad credit risks and that it was often necessary to coax them to repay with the *alcalde mayor*'s "stick" of judicial authority. With the end of *repartimiento* credit, the Viceroy suggested, the Indians had been unable to convert to a system that demanded payment for goods up front and receipt of payment only upon delivery of output. While his explanation of the difficult transition is clearly simplistic, based on the inability of the Indians to break with the custom of dealing in credit, his belief that the ban on the *repartimiento* was a prime cause for the depression was widely held.[58]

Alarming reports, from an increasingly wider sector of Spanish colonial society, were submitted to the Mexican Viceroys and the Council of Indies pointing to the failures resulting from the system of *intendencias* and the prohibition of *repartimientos*. Oaxacans were especially vocal because the economy of this southern province was so heavily dependent on goods produced with *repartimiento* financing, *grana* cochineal being the most important. In 1793 the Minister of the Royal Treasury in Oaxaca, don Francisco Antonio Villarrasa Rivera, wrote a long letter to Madrid alerting his superiors of the disasters which, he believed, had resulted from the suppression of *repartimientos*. According to Villarrasa, the rural economy of Oaxaca had rapidly deteriorated owing to Article 12, and this had had dire consequences for the royal finances that he oversaw. Crown revenues had decreased and Indians were having difficulty meeting their tribute obligations. Abrogation of Article 12, he argued, would remedy both problems.[59]

Asked in 1810 for their assessment of why the cochineal trade had experienced a severe decline, leading Oaxacan merchants, administrators, and clergymen all pointed to the ban on *repartimientos*. The bishop of

58

Oaxaca, Antonio Bergoza y Jordán (1800–1812), identified several factors including population decline, inflation, and war in Europe, but he singled out Article 12 as the main cause. Before the ban, argued the Bishop, Spanish officials had invested large sums to finance the production of the Indians, but now merchants limited their purchases to whatever they could buy at the Friday and Saturday markets. Repeating a commonly held opinion, Bergoza noted that no merchant would loan funds to the indigenous population without the *alcalde mayor* to help collect debts. The Bishop added that many Indians had used the ban on *repartimientos* as an excuse not to repay their debts, and this had further fueled resistance to risking funds. In short, production of cochineal would continue in its depressed state until the prohibition on *repartimientos* was lifted.[60]

The Oaxacan deputies of commerce, Francisco Antonio Goytia, Antonio Sánchez, Juan Francisco de la Vega, Josef Castañeda Zevallos, and Juan Carlos de Barberena, also blamed the decline in the production of *grana cochinilla* on the prohibition of the *repartimiento*. Indians could not produce cochineal, they argued, without the finances provided by merchants. For fear of losing their capital, however, merchants would not finance *grana* production without the mediation of the Spanish magistrates. The only reason production had not stopped altogether was that smaller merchants inhabiting cochineal-producing regions of Oaxaca continued to finance those producers whom they knew personally to be good credit risks.[61]

José Victoriano de Baños, the parish priest of the Oaxacan valley town of Tlalixtac, also testified, and he seemed almost exasperated by the question. As everybody knew, Baños wrote, the depression was due to the prohibition of *repartimientos*, for without funding the Indians could not produce cochineal, the production of which demanded the outlay of significant funds, especially in the purchase of "seed," the impregnated female cochineal insects placed on the nopal cactus at the start of the production cycle. Thus, the priest maintained, any program designed to resurrect the crippled industry had to also provide financing to indigenous producers. But, Baños cautioned, few merchants would advance funds to Indians for fear of losing their capital, since the repayment record of producers was poor. The *alcalde mayor*, in contrast, could collect loans that others could not, and thus he would extend funds more widely. The priest dismissed those who opposed the *repartimiento* on the grounds that profits were usurious. To such people, he argued, any profits were excessive. Besides, opponents rarely considered the numerous costs and risks experienced by the *alcaldes mayores*, costs such as freight, taxes, and sales

59

commissions, and risks such as uncollectible debts, delays in sales, and rapidly fluctuating prices due to war or peace.[62] Finally, the priest commented, the continued production of cochineal, albeit at low levels, was due to the fact that several *subdelegados* were disobeying the prohibition on *repartimientos* and were lending money to the indigenous cochineal producers illegally.[63]

Broad sectors of society attacked the prohibition of the *repartimiento* and blamed the economic downturn on the ban. Obviously, the termination of credit through the *repartimiento* had a negative impact on products dependent on such financing. Producers without credit had to cut back their production. However, there is also strong reason to believe that the depression would have occurred even without the prohibition, that the cochineal industry was entering into difficult times for reasons that had nothing to do with Article 12. Article 12 merely exacerbated the difficulties that the industry was already encountering. Returning to Figure 3.1, one sees that in 1784, two years before Article 12 became law, registered cochineal production suffered a steep decline, 46 percent relative to the previous year. Output then entered into a new plateau, at this lower level, which it maintained, more or less, for the rest of the colonial era. Since the downturn in the cochineal industry began *before* the ban on *repartimientos*, the ban could not have been the sole cause of the depression. Instead, as will be shown in Chapter 8, the slump resulted initially from a reduction in European demand for the dyestuff. When war erupted in 1793, trade interruptions and the rising cost of conducting transatlantic trade both ensured that the cochineal trade would remain depressed.

The ability of late-colonial policymakers to fully pursue their goals was limited. The system of *intendencias* was designed to centralize power, to increase the central government's control over local colonial affairs, and to reduce the autonomy of the district magistrates. In addition, the Bourbon reformers sought to liberate trade from the many powerful colonial groups which they believed constrained economic and fiscal growth. Not surprisingly, the *repartimiento* was targeted for reform. The *alcaldes mayores* of Mexico and their counterparts, the *corregidores* of the Viceroyalty of Peru, had long appropriated Crown authority for their own enrichment, employing state power in the collection of personal debts. Centralization of power by the Bourbon state required the cessation of such practices for, as long as they continued, the integrity and loyalty of the local officials were compromised. Furthermore, Gálvez and others were committed to lifting restrictions on trade. *Comercio libre* in the transatlantic imperial trade had its intracolonial counterpart in the prohibition of the *repartimiento*. In the eyes of these reformers, the *repartimiento* was a commercial monopoly (which to some extent it was) and its termination was deemed essential if the economy and royal finances were to expand.

Alcaldes mayores were replaced with *subdelegados*, who were forbidden to trade with the inhabitants of their districts. Crown authorities, however, were unwilling to sufficiently compensate the new officials, many of whom, like their predecessors, turned to the now illicit *repartimiento* trade. While many *subdelegados* continued to use state authority for their own business dealings, they controlled far fewer resources than had their predecessors. Wealthy merchants of Mexico City withdrew their funds from the *repartimiento* because they were uninterested in financing the trade now that it was illegal. The reduced levels of credit in the countryside after 1786 contributed to commercial depression.

The Bourbon reformers were mistaken to believe that the obstacles to free trade, which the *alcaldes mayores* represented, necessarily curtailed output. They were so certain that freer trade would yield increased trade that they failed to recognize that the *repartimiento* existed for rational economic reasons, that it promoted growth by facilitating the provision of credit to poor peasants. The reforms implemented by Gálvez and his cronies failed miserably. The system of *intendencias* severely injured the economy without fulfilling its primary goal, the creation of a disinterested, loyal bureaucracy.

John Coatsworth has argued that a major "obstacle to economic growth" in colonial Mexico was the "interventionist and pervasively arbitrary nature" of colonial policymakers.[64] The vacillating official position toward the *repartimiento* would tend to support this thesis. Just as the 1751 legalization of the *repartimiento* spurred the expansion of cochineal production, the 1786 prohibition contributed to the crippling of the colony's most profitable non-metal export. Reformers imbued with an ideology inconsistent with the status quo dismantled a political and economic system that had long functioned well. Their goal was commercial expansion, but at least in the case of the cochineal industry, depression occurred instead.

Chapter Four

Coerced or Voluntary?
Market Participation of Indians

Indians are capable of requesting the cargo of a flotilla, and
[so] it is a platitude (*vulgaridad*) and a misunderstanding
of the *repartimiento* to say that they are forced.[1]

Central to the eighteenth-century debates over the *repartimiento* was the question of whether or not the Indians needed or wanted the money and goods supplied by the *alcalde mayor*. Not surprisingly, opinions differed. Supporters of the system argued that the *repartimiento* provided credit to the Indians without which they could not consume or produce certain items. The detractors were a bit more diverse in their positions. While Gálvez depicted the *repartimiento* as a commercial monopoly which cheated the Indians with unfavorable prices, he explicitly recognized the Indians' need for credit. Others, such as Mora y Peysal, the *intendente* of Oaxaca, took stronger positions, arguing that the entire system was coercive and that the *alcaldes mayores* forced peasants to produce and consume goods totally against their wills.[2] While opinions were mixed during the colonial era, there has been little variance in the depictions of the *repartimiento* adopted by modern historians. In contemporary studies, the *repartimiento* has been universally depicted as a system of forced consumption and production. Ironically, the evils attributed to the *repartimiento* in many contemporary studies exceed even the harshest of criticisms leveled during the colonial period.[3] The nearly overwhelming consensus in the historiography is that the *repartimiento* was a coercive system in which the *alcalde mayor* served as a violent intermediary who, abusing the power of his position, threatened the Indians of his district with imprisonment, beatings, and sanctions if they refused to buy his stock of items or to produce for him output marketable in the Spanish economy. Prices were determined arbitrarily by the official and were so unfavorable to the Indians that one historian has claimed that the *alcalde*'s dealings "more nearly resembled robbery than commerce."[4] In such depictions, the official would simply present himself in an indigenous village and order the population to trade with him at whatever terms he stipulated. Thus the *repartimiento* is conventionally seen as the motor force driving Amerindians to participate in markets, a system created in response to a perceived unwillingness of Indians to produce and consume. This chapter takes a closer look at the operation of the *repartimiento*, addressing the issue of coercion, and will argue that the traditional historiographical depictions of the *repartimiento* need to be reevaluated. The argument presented here is that the *repartimiento* was not a system of forced production and consumption, but was an institution of credit which developed under colonial conditions of high risk. Peasants accepted *repartimientos* voluntarily because they provided peasants with valued goods and inputs and sorely needed income that was not readily available on credit or in advance from other sources. While at times the *repartimiento* resulted in undesired hardships to the peasants, including the unleashing of the *alcalde mayor*'s often violent debt collectors, more often indigenous peasants benefited from their market participation.

Traditional depictions of the *repartimiento* are overly simplistic. They suggest that Indians were reluctant to participate in the market, that they lived in closed, isolated, and self-sufficient communities, and that only the coercion of the *alcalde mayor* could induce them to trade. This picture contrasts sharply with the known trading activities of indigenous Mexicans, which even predated the arrival of Europeans. Long before the Spaniards arrived in America, central Mexican peasants marketed their output locally and elites consumed imported luxury goods. While the arrival of the Spanish may have partially changed the "basket of goods," there exists little doubt that Indians eagerly consumed the newly introduced items.[5]

Even more contradictory, this depiction suggests that Indians were powerless and passive in the face of an economic institution that was intensely exploitative. If historians of colonial Spanish America have reached any consensus, it is that indigenous peasants did not face exploitation passively. In the traditional portrayal of the *repartimiento*, however, Indians exhibit far too little resistance, given the degree of exploitation attributed to the system. This suggests that historians have either overlooked the agency of peasants or have misrepresented the *repartimiento*. In fact, they have done both.[6]

The traditional depictions also fail to illustrate convincingly how the *alcalde mayor* was able to force Indians to trade. The historiography accepts that the *alcalde mayor* used his judicial authority to coerce Indians to trade against their will and at exceedingly unfavorable terms. Such an argument, however, attributes to the state a level of coercive power in excess of its real capacity. As John Coatsworth has argued, the Crown

63

concentrated its resources in those colonial areas capable of producing the greatest royal revenues, such as the mines, ports, and urban areas. In remote rural regions, including most of Oaxaca, the state's authority was limited and the Crown was only able to dictate its will in extraordinary cases — when it sent in royal troops to contain rebellions, for example. In the day-to-day governing of indigenous society, the state's influence was limited.[7] Apart from the *alcalde mayor*, the state had no presence in the indigenous districts of Oaxaca. Priests and *hacendados* were the only other Spaniards who exerted even a modicum of power in the countryside, and they were more often the rivals of the Spanish officials than their helpful allies.[8] Thus, it is inconceivable that the Spanish colonial state forced Mexico's indigenous populations to participate in the market.[9] Furthermore, the mercantile activities of the *alcalde mayor*, his *repartimientos*, were his and his *aviador*'s private dealings, at times even prohibited by the Crown, as was the case before 1751 and after 1786. Hence, the *alcalde mayor* was on his own — he could not even count on the support of a weak and ineffective state. In short, the historiography suggests that the *alcalde mayor* and a couple of *tenientes* alone were capable of subjugating whole communities and forcing them to trade unwillingly; in fact, the *alcalde mayor* did not really have the power to coerce Indians to trade.

Some studies have argued that the *cacique* and other *principales* provided critical aid to the *alcalde mayor* and his system of *repartimiento*, serving as the quasi-ally and debt collector of the *alcalde mayor*, and sometimes even sharing in the profits.[10] John K. Chance even speculates that native elites of the Rincón, a region of Villa Alta, to a large extent owed their positions to the *alcaldes mayores*, who only supported the election of those Indians who helped in the operation of the *repartimientos*.[11] In contrast, María de los Angeles Romero Frizzi suggests that the role of the indigenous authorities in the operation of *repartimientos* has been exaggerated. Studying *repartimientos* in the Mixteca Alta until about 1725, she notes that villagers rarely accused their *principales* of cooperating with the *alcaldes mayores*. Instead, she found that Indian nobles were often the recipients of individual *repartimientos*, not the issuers, a status that appears to have continued in the eighteenth century.[12]

If indigenous leaders used the authority of their positions to reinforce the *repartimientos* of the Oaxacan Spanish *alcaldes mayores*, there survives little evidence. When an indigenous official became involved in litigation over the *repartimiento*, it was usually because he found himself incarcerated for non-payment of a debt, sometimes his own and sometimes one that he had contracted for the community as a whole. Far from the allies of the *alcalde mayor*, then, the indigenous authorities were the frequent targets of the sometimes harsh methods used in the collection of debts. If the indigenous elites had any political leverage, they failed to use it on behalf of the *alcalde mayor*.

Traditional portrayals of the *repartimiento* are also illogical and incomplete — they leave too many questions unanswered. If the *repartimiento* were truly nothing more than "robbery," in which the *alcalde mayor* forced Indians to do as he chose, then it is doubtful that he would have delivered to the Indians expensive and valued items such as livestock or money, and always on credit. A cash advance, from the perspective of the recipient, had the advantage of being easily fungible. While some portion of the loan was necessarily used to finance production, the remainder could be used however the recipient deemed desirable: to purchase needed commodities, to pay Crown tribute, to defray the costs of a village fiesta, or to meet whatever other expense the peasant might incur. The very fungibility of money, in contrast, was both a nuisance and a danger to the *alcalde mayor*. That the funds issued in the *repartimiento* could be used for other purposes meant that the *alcalde* and his *tenientes* had to guard against the total misuse of the funds. If the loan were not employed at least in part to finance production, then the debtor was almost certain to default. While certainly infrequent, the *alcalde mayor* also risked losing the entire loan if the debtor fled with the money. Thus, the *repartimiento* for the production of certain goods, cochineal included, was made in the form that most benefited the recipient and left the *alcalde mayor* most vulnerable to the loss of his principal, a highly implausible arrangement if the *alcalde mayor* truly exerted absolute control over the indigenous population as has been generally assumed. Instead, this suggests a less lopsided balance of power, one in which the *alcalde mayor* had to remain sensitive to the demands of the Indian consumers and producers of his district.

Similarly, goods distributed in the *repartimiento* were valuable and useful to the peasant economy. Mules, bulls, and oxen performed useful functions in the daily tasks of rural life, increasing productivity and facilitating the delivery of surplus production to regional markets. These animals, furnished by the *repartimiento* of the *alcalde mayor*, were the ones needed and demanded.[13] They were not the worthless items that some historians claim were sold through the *repartimiento*, such things as silk stockings, fur hats, or playing cards.[14] Rather, they were desirable yet expensive items that, without the extension of credit, were beyond the

65

means of most rural Oaxacans. Work animals helped pay for themselves by increasing productivity; peasants who received them in advance with no required down payment were more likely to produce the money to repay the *alcalde mayor*. Productivity increases resulting from the introduction of a farm animal probably compensated the peasant for the cost of the animal in the first year or two.[15]

Furthermore, many of the goods that the Spanish officials provided were a nuisance for them to obtain. Beasts of burden were often brought from distant regions, which entailed a substantial outlay for transport and fodder. In addition, such animals were highly vulnerable to death, illness, or loss. In 1772, for example, the *alcalde mayor* of Miahuatlán lost 12 of the 140 mules he brought to his district for sale in the *repartimiento*, nearly 10 percent.[16] The official of Villa Alta reported in 1776 that 6 of the 122 mules he received for a *repartimiento* in the village of San Francisco Cajonos were "useless" and had to be discarded.[17] That such troublesome goods were selected by the *alcalde mayor* for distribution, however, is not surprising; they served the needs of the peasantry and were, thus, in demand.

The decision to make *repartimientos* in cash against the future delivery of cochineal or other items was also a response to factors of supply and demand rather than some arbitrary decision on the part of government officials. Goods produced in exchange for *repartimiento* advances were normally items that had been traditionally produced by the indigenous economy. As Patch argued for Central America, "the commercial system run by the magistrates worked so well because it took advantage of an already existing sexual division of labor . . . [and] already existing structures of production."[18] Patch attributes this to the deliberate intentions of the *alcalde mayor*, but it seems equally plausible that the compatibility of the *repartimiento* with the peasant economy derived from a rational peasant strategy of economic adaptation; peasants discovered an economic niche and one in which they could obtain credit, and so they pursued it, producing goods that they had always produced and that utilized "marginal" or "surplus" resources. Cochineal exemplifies this notion nicely. Indians earned income from producing cochineal, for which they enjoyed a comparative advantage and could utilize primarily the labor of children and the elderly.

Historiographical portrayals of the *repartimiento* are simplistic. If the *alcalde mayor* could truly compel an Indian to purchase a sickly mule, then why did he not simply extort the money directly, giving nothing in exchange? Why did the *alcalde mayor* not simply confiscate indigenous

66

output or oblige Indians to produce cochineal, paying them nothing at all? Why not force worthless articles upon the Indians, rather than provide valuable livestock, obtained with such risk? The answers to such questions are obvious. The *alcalde mayor* could not merely steal from the Indians because he lacked the power to do so. Instead, he needed to provide them with goods and services not readily available. He did this by selling to them on credit goods that were useful and desired. He also became a banker to the Indians, lending them money.

Nobody else would supply the majority of the Indians with credit, because no one else had sufficient leverage to ensure that contracts and obligations were fulfilled, that debts were repaid. While the *alcalde mayor* had resources with which to try to enforce a willfully contracted debt, much more authority and control would have been needed to force an Indian into a contract against his will. Using force to collect a debt meant forcing one debtor to abide by the established rules of a contract entered into freely, rules that the rest of the indigenous population understood and accepted and had good reason to enforce, since future terms might depend on present levels of default.[19] It would have required much greater coercive capacity to force thousands of individuals to accept the rules in the first place, to agree to take unwanted *repartimiento* loans, and to fulfill the corresponding obligations.

In short, the traditional explanation for why the *repartimiento* existed is inadequate. To suggest that the *repartimiento* was created because only coercion could compel Indians to trade is false. Indians were not loathe to trade. To the contrary, commerce had flourished in Mesoamerica before the arrival of Europeans.[20] Moreover, the historiography on the *repartimiento* denies Indians much role in shaping or resisting a system that allegedly harmed them greatly. This contradicts the known agency of indigenous peasants during the colonial era. Finally, *alcaldes mayores* faced defined limits, beyond which they could not step for lack of coercive capacity. Operating without the backing of a strong state apparatus able to penetrate indigenous society, the Spanish officials lacked the resources necessary to install a regime sufficiently authoritarian to force the overwhelming Indian majority to produce and consume involuntarily.

Although the *alcalde mayor* lacked the power to force Indians against their will into the market as producers and consumers, the *repartimiento* did emerge in response to a limited participation in markets on the part of Indians, and the *repartimiento* was a motor force contributing to the greater integration of peasants into colonial markets. In order for the indigenous population to participate more extensively in the market, the extension of credit was essential. As most merchants and many colonial administrators realized, few Indians commanded sufficient economic resources to permit them to purchase that which they needed or desired. Similarly, most Indians lacked the finances to permit them to produce in bulk certain cash crops, cochineal for one. More generally, credit is an essential element of all agricultural economies; peasants and other agriculturists face production cycles which guarantee that certain times of the year will be lean and others more abundant. In addition, certain years produce bumper crops, while others yield scarcity. Credit helps smooth out the fluctuating income stream of agricultural producers and is often the primary reason why peasants need credit. The *repartimiento* expanded and deepened markets not because the *alcalde mayor* used force and coercion, but because the *repartimiento* provided the credit and financing without which many transactions would have been impossible.[21]

Cash *repartimientos* not only provided financing for production of cash crops like cochineal, but could also be partially used to meet other expenses such as tribute or religious fees. Peasants could also turn to the *repartimiento* for a loan when bad weather threatened their subsistence. The *repartimiento* system of credit, then, came to be an important outside source of funds for Oaxacan peasants to supplement the traditional rural economy. It became one weapon in their overall strategy of economic survival.[22]

It is important to note that peasants did have other sources of vital credit, but none of them was especially significant. Internal communal sources of credit existed, such as indigenous *cofradías* or *cajas de comunidad*, but about these we know very little and the paucity of references to them, relative to the *repartimiento*, indicates that they were of only minor importance.[23] Indians sometimes borrowed from one another as well. According to Bishop Ortigoza of Oaxaca, Indians sometimes loaned to each other small amounts at high rates of interest, rates the bishop condemned as usurious.[24] José Victoriano de Baños, the parish priest of the Oaxacan valley town of Tlalixtac, noted that in several villages which lacked *repartimientos*, the Indians borrowed from one another to produce cochineal at the exorbitant rate of one real per month for each peso loaned, or even one real per week for each peso. In either case, the rate of interest charged by these villagers far exceeded the rates customarily charged in the *repartimiento*.[25]

According to William B. Taylor, parish priests themselves sometimes disregarded Church doctrine to the contrary and engaged in trade with their parishioners, even issuing *repartimientos* to their Indian parishioners advancing mules and other goods to them.[26] This was the case in 1798 when don Joaquin de Urquijo, the parish priest of San Juan Ozolotepec in the Oaxacan district of Miahuatlán, was accused of assisting his brother, the merchant Manuel de Urquijo, in the operation of *repartimiento* loans to the local indigenous peasants.[27] Priests must have enjoyed certain leverage and respect within their parishes, which enabled them to more easily collect debts. Because they lived in the parish, it also seems likely that they possessed reliable information about which of the Indians were creditworthy.

Private merchants and local *hacendados* represented another source of funds and did sometimes loan money or sell goods on credit (i.e., provide *repartimientos*) to Indians, especially those they knew personally to be creditworthy. Even this, however, was a risky business.[28] Francisco Trujillo, a Spanish storekeeper and fair-sized trader who resided in his native Ixtlán, had extensive business dealings with the Indians of that district in the mid-1770s. An inventory of his belongings conducted upon his death revealed that he had frequently loaned money to peasants. For instance, Trujillo was owed 56 pesos by Ursula López for a loan he had made to her for "*grana* seed." At the time of his death, he was owed a total of 1,270 pesos and 6 reales, much of which represented debts owed for *grana*. Trujillo also had a large number of items in his possession which had been pawned by locals. Finally, twenty-four plots of land and a large number of animals were held by Trujillo as collateral against debts. As an established storekeeper and longtime resident of Ixtlán, Trujillo benefited from considerable experience with his neighbors, which provided valuable information about the creditworthiness of borrowers. Thus, Trujillo was probably able to more safely extend credit, as he could loan to the more dependable debtors. Furthermore, he could make continued access to credit contingent on the prompt payment of debts. In addition, Trujillo demanded collateral on at least some of his loans, and this also greatly reduced his risk. If a debt went unpaid, he could recoup his funds by liquidating the collateral security.[29] In contrast, peasants never provided collateral against the *repartimientos* of the *alcaldes mayores*. In rural economies, the ability to offer collateral against a loan is often the distinguishing factor between those who receive credit and those who are denied it. Economists who have examined rural credit have discovered that formal lenders "have had little success in reaching farmers without collateral or with below-average income."[30] For the same reason, Trujillo chose to make loans to certain peasants only when they guaranteed their loans with collateral. Poorer peasants without goods to pawn were probably excluded from borrowing from men like Trujillo.

Trujillo was certainly not the only private merchant who offered credit to peasants in Oaxaca's provinces. Other districts had local traders, storekeepers, or *hacendados* who provided credit to Indians whom they knew to be trustworthy or over whom they wielded leverage, such as *hacienda* workers.[31] In 1761 José de Bal, the owner of a shop in Villa Alta, accused the store manager, Francisco Herrera, of extending credit irresponsibly. Herrera responded that he had obeyed Bal's instructions of one year earlier and only extended credit to peasants who had been prompt in repaying previous loans. In essence, Herrera was collecting information about potential borrowers and using it to screen out the less creditworthy. This was possible because he managed a small shop with a regular clientele.[32]

For most merchants hoping to expand their business dealings into the indigenous districts of Mexico, however, the difficulty of assessing creditworthiness and collecting debts posed formidable obstacles, which they dared not recklessly ignore. The 1751 legalization of the *repartimiento* was justified on these grounds. As the Viceroy, the First Count Revillagigedo, noted in 1752: "No merchant, nor any other person, can expose [funds], nor wait terms so delayed and [face] so difficult and costly a collection" as can the *alcalde mayor*.[33] Most often, the value of a *repartimiento* was only several pesos, and even when farm animals were supplied on credit, the total amount of a transaction rarely exceeded fifty pesos. Given the low value of most credit transactions with Indians, trying to collect unpaid debts through legal means was too costly. Furthermore, legal procedures lasted months, sometimes years, and the outcome was far from certain.

The difficulty and high cost of collecting debts was the very consequence of the deficient Crown penetration of indigenous society. The *república de indios* retained its own political, social, and economic institutions over which the Crown had limited control. Spanish institutions, in this case legal tribunals, were insufficiently effective at the village level to enforce regularly and inexpensively debts owed by rural Oaxacans. The only representative of the Crown's authority at the local level was the *alcalde mayor*, and he was occupied with the operation of his own business dealings.

The economies of modern Western societies operate with highly developed institutions, institutions designed to reduce the uncertainties of trade and to ensure that contracts are easily enforceable at a reasonable cost.

Contracts specifically dictate the responsibilities of all parties, and when one party fails to abide by the stipulated terms of a contract, the other has recourse to institutions that either force the first to comply, penalize him, or, at the very least, ostracize him. In rural colonial Spanish America, such institutions essentially did not exist. The lack of developed institutions meant that the leverage available to most Spaniards to ensure repayment of debts and compliance with contracts was limited, at least at a reasonably low cost.[34] The *repartimiento* served as a substitute for the lack of more formal Spanish penetration because it was operated by the *alcalde mayor*, the one Spaniard possessing sufficient leverage to personally enforce contracts with the general population.[35] The *repartimiento*, then, served as a substitute for a more formal Spanish institutional presence.

Theoretically, the *alcalde mayor* could have employed the power of his office to collect the debts owed to private merchants as well, but this would have worked against the *alcalde mayor*'s own best interests; business the *alcalde mayor* facilitated for a competing merchant represented profits lost to him. At times the Crown ordered the *alcalde mayor* to help collect the debts of private merchants, but this only occurred in extreme cases. In general, the *alcalde mayor* was free from state supervision and could use his judicial authority however he chose. He was, consequently, reluctant to help his competition. Without greater security for their capital, merchants were unwilling to lend money to Indians they did not know personally to be trustworthy and solvent. This excluded most Indians.

The provision of credit was necessary to permit the expansion of markets. While few merchants were willing to risk their funds by lending them to the general indigenous population, the *repartimiento* was operated by the *alcalde mayor*, the one Spaniard personally possessing the Crown's authority to collect debts. The *repartimiento*, then, was a quasi-institution designed to operate in a colonial environment in which market imperfections effectively excluded private creditors. It reduced transaction and enforcement costs to a level where provision of credit became feasible and profitable.

Rebellions and Complaints against the Repartimiento

Two types of evidence have generally been presented by historians to argue that the *repartimiento* was a coercive system of forced production and consumption. First, scholars have attempted to identify the *reparti-*

miento as the catalyst for indigenous peasant rebellions. Second, the numerous complaints, by peasants and non-peasants alike, and official condemnations leveled against the *repartimiento* have been offered as proof that the *repartimiento* was coercive and involuntary.

REBELLIONS

Historians have identified the *repartimiento* as the cause of two widespread regional rebellions. First, the 1660 Rebellion of Tehuantepec has been attributed to the *repartimientos* of the *alcalde mayor* of Tehuantepec, who was murdered at the upheaval's start. Historians have not yet sufficiently investigated this movement, but Marcello Carmagnani, one of the few scholars who has even considered it, doubts that the rebels were driven by their opposition to the *repartimiento*. Instead, Carmagnani postulates that the rebellion was the outgrowth of a fierce political struggle within the Indian elite and between factions of this elite and the *alcalde mayor*.[36]

Much more fully documented is the 1780s Andean movement of Túpac Amaru, which Jürgen Golte has argued was primarily a rebellion against *repartimientos*. He found that the provinces most inclined to rebel were the very provinces in which the burden of *repartimiento* debt weighed most heavily.[37] Golte's thesis has subsequently been attacked by leading colonial Andean historians. Scarlett O'Phelan Godoy rejected Golte's theory as too deterministic, arguing instead that eighteenth-century Andean rebellions were caused by the mounting "competition between *hacendados, obrajes, corregidores* and priests for control over the local communities and their economic resources." According to O'Phelan, the *repartimiento* alone never provoked large-scale rebellions but merely local revolts.[38] Steve J. Stern also rejected Golte's "ingenious but flawed" study, arguing that the cause of the Túpac Amaru rebellion was more systemic, the result of a century-long depression of the colonial economy which contributed to growing exploitation of Andean communities and, consequently, to a deterioration of the Crown's perceived legitimacy.[39] Ward Stavig, too, attributed the rebellion to a breakdown of the legitimacy of Spanish rule in the eyes of indigenous communities.[40] Sinclair Thomson, discussing the related rebellion of Túpac Katari, suggested that this uprising occurred because "the great majority of *caciques*, including hereditary rulers, adopted a stance of collaboration" with the colonial rulers, leading to a "crisis of Andean rule."[41]

Certainly, it is beyond the scope of this study to address the causes of Túpac Amaru, let alone the broader issue of peasant rebellions. It is instructive to note, however, that Oaxaca experienced little unrest during the colonial period, despite the fact that the *repartimiento* was probably more important to the Oaxacan economy than to any other province in Mexico.[42] Far from rebellious, Oaxacans seemed prone *not* to rebel, as evidenced by the cool reception received by the insurgent priest José Morelos in 1812, despite his rebel army's call for the final termination of *repartimientos*. Morelos's army marched through the Mixteca en route to the occupation of the central Oaxacan valley, and in neither of these areas did villagers provide much support.[43]

When rebellions in colonial Spanish America did erupt, the earliest victims were often the local *alcaldes mayores*, as was the case in both the Tehuantepec and Túpac Amaru rebellions. This is hardly surprising. The *alcalde mayor* was at the crossroad between Indian and Spanish societies, an economic and, in part, cultural broker between the two worlds. He represented Spanish rule and the exploitation inherent in the colonial relationship between conqueror and conquered. As the main economic link with external markets, the Spanish *alcalde mayor* wielded considerable influence over the Indian society and economy. The *alcalde mayor* determined when credit was extended and who received it, and when local economic crises occurred, the *alcalde mayor* still demanded debt repayment. For all these reasons, the *alcalde mayor* was an obvious target for indigenous aggression. After all, popular uprisings are almost always directed at individuals easily identifiable as having contributed to the rebels' economic predicament.[44] Furthermore, the *repartimiento* itself was a conspicuous target, for it was most Indians' primary connection with the Spanish economy. When crops failed for lack of rain, the *alcalde mayor* unsympathetically demanded that his debts be paid anyway. In addition, the *alcaldes mayores* often employed great violence to collect their debts. They arrested and imprisoned debtors. They embargoed their belongings. At times, they even beat up debtors who failed to pay. Such injustices bred anger, and this rage erupted in revolts against the *alcalde mayor*'s authority and his system of credit. In short, it should not be surprising that peasants in rebellion pointed to the abuses of the *repartimiento*. It would be wrong, however, to conclude that the peasants did not need the credit or that their occasional outbursts directed against the system meant that their receipt of *repartimiento* credit was involuntary.

73

COMPLAINTS ABOUT THE *REPARTIMIENTO*

While rebellions are certainly the most striking evidence of peasant discontent, in the colonial period Indians far more commonly issued complaints through legal channels to gain redress for their grievances. Indians, however, were not the only ones inclined to complain about the *repartimientos* of the *alcalde mayor*. Protests were also issued by non-Indians who viewed the Spanish officials as their economic or political rivals. No matter who initiated the complaint, its receipt usually sparked a Crown investigation to see whether some crime or abuse had been committed by the magistrate. These investigations and the complaints that generated them offer a unique window into the inner workings of the *repartimiento* and provide testimonies from the actual recipients of *repartimientos*.

Grievances expressed against the *repartimiento* fall into four general categories, each of which is examined below. First, petitioners complained about the disparity between market and *repartimiento* prices. Second, the *alcaldes mayores* were accused of being monopolists, preventing competitors from operating freely in their districts. Third, the officials were denounced for the violent manner in which they attempted to collect debts. Last, plaintiffs charged that *repartimientos* were forced upon recipients.

REPARTIMIENTO PRICES

In several cases, complaints were made about the prices charged by the *alcalde mayor* for the merchandise he bought or sold through his *repartimientos*. Interestingly, the people most often issuing such complaints were not the recipients themselves but rival merchants or Crown administrators bent on prohibiting *repartimientos*.[45] The clergy, especially Bishop Ortigoza of Oaxaca (1775–1792), also condemned the *repartimiento* prices, accusing the *alcaldes mayores* of usury.[46] These arguments have been used by modern scholars in support of their assertions that the *repartimiento* was coerced. Prices, according to this argument, were unfavorable to Indians because they were dictated by the Spanish official who forced them upon indigenous producers and consumers.[47]

It is true that Indians paid more for goods obtained through the *repartimiento* than they would have had they purchased identical items in the marketplace. It is also clear that the *alcalde mayor* purchased output from Indian producers at below-market prices. A mule, for example, might be supplied to an Indian in the *repartimiento* for twenty-five pesos, when a similar mule might be bought at the marketplace for only fifteen pesos. Why, scholars have asked, would an Indian pay twenty-five pesos for a mule worth only fifteen? The usual answer is coercion. As Nancy Farriss expressed it, "The great discrepancy in prices, always in the Spaniard's favor, was of course one reason that the latter had to rely on force . . . in the first place."[48]

74

While it is perhaps true that an Indian could buy a mule in the market for only fifteen pesos, the mule provided by the Spanish official in the *repartimiento* was supplied on credit, and so it naturally had to be priced higher, because an interest charge was built into the final price, what economists call an implicit interest charge. The purchaser was not required to make any down payment, received immediate use of the animal, and did not have to pay anything for six months, at which time only half was due, and even this partial payment was often delayed.

To compare the market and *repartimiento* prices is misleading—the two transactions were distinct. When an Indian needed a mule and had at his disposal fifteen pesos, he could and did purchase the animal outright. As was frequently the case, however, the Indian was forced to turn to the Spanish official to purchase the mule, paying for it in installments. He received the animal on credit, and so he naturally paid a higher price for it, a price that included an implicit interest charge.[49]

As for the clergy's accusations that the *alcaldes mayores* were usurers, they were right. Among other things, usury laws prohibited a lender from charging more than 5 percent and, of course, the interest charges built into the *repartimiento* price (the implicit charge) always exceeded 5 percent.[50] Violation of the usury laws, however, did not mean that the *alcaldes'* transactions were forced upon the Indians. Instead, high interest rates reflected the high risk that these transactions entailed.[51]

Interest charges were included in the *repartimiento* price, rather than being charged explicitly (i.e., at a specified interest rate) for simplicity and to reduce transaction costs. The *alcalde mayor* issued hundreds of loans, the vast majority of which were only worth a few pesos. Calculating interest owed on so many small transactions would have been difficult and would have entailed substantial administrative costs. Consequently, the interest was simply incorporated into a *repartimiento* price that guaranteed a return to the *alcalde mayor* under most conditions. Furthermore, including the interest charge in the price probably helped the *alcaldes mayores* deflect some of the criticism emanating from the religious sectors bent on condemning the *repartimiento* as usurious. Had interest rates been explicitly stated, they would have been much easier targets for the clergy. Importantly, clerical condemnation of such transactions was far from new in eighteenth-century Oaxaca. Merchants had regularly faced such accusations for centuries.[52]

Repartimiento prices and market prices were different because the *repartimiento* was a fundamentally different type of transaction. In fact, the prices offered by private merchants were not better than those paid by the

75

alcalde mayor when the latter dealt *"al contado,"* in cash. The *alcalde mayor* not only acquired indigenous output by advancing funds through the *repartimiento*, he also bought large amounts outright, paying in cash and at market prices, the same prices paid by other merchants, powerful or weak.[53]

MONOPOLY AND MONOPSONY

Related to the issue of prices was a second type of complaint leveled against the *repartimiento*, which charged the Spanish officials with exercising a monopoly and preventing merchants from trading with the Indians. In 1774, for example, an itinerant merchant named Juan Fernando Herrera issued to the Viceroy a blanket complaint against the *alcaldes mayores* of the entire province of Oaxaca who, he claimed, had harmed his business of buying and selling cochineal by regularly interfering with his dealings with the Indians.[54]

Critics of the *repartimiento*, including Gálvez and his reformist colleagues, claimed that the *alcaldes mayores* excluded potential competition in order to enlarge their profits by forcing indigenous producers and consumers to deal only with them. It was necessary for the magistrate to exclude competitors, they argued, because competition would have provided Indians with more favorable terms. This argument was central to the 1786 abolition of the *repartimiento*, as proponents of free trade argued that commercial monopolies reduced the volume of trade and that the abolition of *repartimientos* would open and expand commerce, thereby benefiting smaller merchants and peddlers.[55]

While this explanation for the *repartimiento* is logical, it was probably not the entire story. There is little doubt that the *alcaldes mayores* did, at times, attempt to prevent competitors from trading with the Indians of their assigned districts, and this practice might have had the effect of moving prices slightly in the *alcaldes'* favor. It seems likely, however, that the magistrate's primary objective in limiting competition was for reasons other than hoping to benefit from monopoly or monopsony prices. In *repartimiento* transactions the officials did not need to exclude competition. They already possessed a virtual monopoly since only they could and did extend credit widely to the peasantry. The *alcaldes mayores* did not need to prohibit others from providing credit — few merchants would consider it, for they lacked the means to collect debts easily and cheaply.

Instead, the exclusionary practices of the Spanish officials were a rational defensive strategy designed to reduce the risk of *repartimiento* loans. When a propertyless, insolvent individual defaulted on a loan, the judicial authority of the Spanish official was largely worthless. It was impossible to collect a debt from a person with no assets. Consequently, the *alcalde mayor* had to reduce to the best of his ability the propensity of default. When an itinerant merchant entered a cochineal-producing village at harvest time, he offered to purchase the dyestuff from producers at market prices. Many of the producers, however, had already received advanced payments through the *repartimiento* and were thus obliged to deliver their cochineal to the *alcalde mayor*. If producers reneged on their contracts and sold their dyestuff to the traveling merchants, the *alcalde mayor* remained uncompensated for his loans and risked losing his funds entirely. Excluding other merchants from trading in his district, then, helped the *alcalde mayor* reduce the danger of default. The *alcaldes* did not fear that the traveling merchants would offer cheaper credit to the peasantry, but instead were concerned that the peddlers' mere presence would encourage the Indians to renege on their obligations.

This point was well illustrated by the *alcalde mayor* of Nexapa, who in 1752 observed that when market prices dropped he had no difficulty collecting the cochineal owed to him, but that when prices were high debtors sold their dyestuff to traveling merchants or in Antequera and later claimed to him that they had lost their harvests. The same was claimed by the *alcalde mayor* of Villa Alta, who in 1770 was unable to collect his cochineal debts from the Indians of his district because, as he testified to the Viceroy, the prevailing high prices had led debtors to renege on their contracted obligations and sell their output elsewhere. In 1784 the *alcalde mayor* of Zimatlán-Chichicapa also noted the propensity of Indians to abandon their obligations and sell elsewhere when prices rose. Arij Ouweneel noted that the Indians of Puebla also "developed a flair for the market" and bypassed their *repartimiento* debts to the official when market prices rose.[56]

In short, it is problematic to explain the exclusionary practices of the Spanish officials as an attempt to inflate the prices of goods sold to Indians and deflate the purchase prices of indigenous output. *Alcaldes mayores* enjoyed a near monopoly on credit transactions because they monopolized the judicial resources needed to enforce payment of debts. The competition which the traveling merchants represented would not have affected the credit terms, for these individuals were not normally in the business of providing credit. Instead, the *alcalde mayor* sought to limit the circulation of other merchants in an effort to lower his risk and reduce the potential for peasants to violate their contracts with him. Any monopoly benefit accruing to the *alcalde mayor* in the way of better prices for transactions outside of the *repartimiento* would have amounted to an added bonus, but in practice seldom materialized.

Finally, it is doubtful that the *alcalde mayor* often succeeded in excluding itinerant merchants, or that he even tried to do so in most years. The districts in which the *alcaldes mayores* served were geographically large, making virtually impossible the task of excluding competing merchants. Peddlers could have easily entered remote villages and traded with the inhabitants undetected by the *alcalde mayor* and his *tenientes*. The cost of limiting the circulation of such merchants would have been prohibitive, and the effort probably futile, given the inadequate manpower. Furthermore, in most years the need to reduce competition to avoid default was minimal. Only in years when cochineal prices rose to high levels need the *alcalde mayor* fear that peasants would evade repayment. In most years, the price differential was not large enough for peasants to risk unleashing the *alcalde mayor*'s wrath.

DEBT COLLECTION

The overwhelming majority of peasant complaints concerned the manner in which the *alcalde mayor* attempted to collect outstanding debts. As discussed in Chapter 2, when an *alcalde mayor* faced difficulties collecting his debts, there were several means at his disposal to aid him, some of which might lead a peasant to complain. First, he could imprison debtors in the hope that he could force them or their families to pay. Alternatively, the *alcalde mayor* could seize a debtor's meager belongings, hoping to recover the value of his loan. Finally, he might force a peasant to work off his debt in a neighboring *hacienda* or *obraje*, a rural workshop. O'Phelan has argued that in the Andes the *repartimiento* operated primarily as a "system of indebtedness" to supply labor to other colonial enterprises, especially *haciendas* and *obrajes*. For Oaxaca, however, the practice of recruiting labor by indebting peasants in the *repartimiento* was infrequent, if it occurred at all. Certainly, the sheer scale of *repartimiento* in Oaxaca suggests other reasons for its existence, especially given the paucity of Spanish-run economic enterprises in the region, which would have been competing for indigenous labor.[57] The families of debtors who were imprisoned or whose possessions were seized occasionally lodged complaints with authorities in Oaxaca or Mexico City. Generally, peasants begged for release from prison and return of their belongings, promising to repay their *repartimiento* debts at the next harvest or when their economic conditions improved. Such requests were usually granted, and the *alcalde mayor* was ordered to free the prisoner, refrain from harassing him, and wait patiently for the debtor to repay.

In five cases, accusations were made that the *alcalde mayor* had forced peasants to accept unwanted *repartimientos*. In one of the five, both indigenous recipients of the "forced" *repartimientos* and a local Spanish merchant accused the *alcalde mayor*. In three other cases, the claims were levied by indebted Indians alone, and in the last case, a Spanish functionary charged with investigating a peasant complaint denounced the *alcalde mayor*. Significantly, only four of the twenty-six complaints issued by peasants charged the *alcalde mayor* with having forced them to accept *repartimientos*. While these cases display compelling evidence of coercion, a case can also be made that such accusations were merely attempts by desperate peasants to resist repayment by denying the legitimacy of their debts. In each of the four cases, debtors responded to their imprisonment by claiming that they should not be held accountable for their debts because the *alcalde mayor* had forced them to take *repartimiento* loans they had not wanted. Charges of forced distribution always occurred many months and usually years after the loan was first extended. A typical complaint might follow this pattern: "Five years ago the *alcalde mayor* forced me to accept a *repartimiento* to produce cochineal, and now he's placed me in prison because I can't repay him." No documented protests were found that stated, "The *alcalde mayor* is trying to force me (or has just forced me) to accept funds to produce cochineal, but I don't want them." That is, accusations of force emerged only after the debtor was squeezed for repayment and claimed insolvency.[58] In addition, close scrutiny of the cases casts doubt on their authenticity.

In 1811, for example, several Indians from the northern valley town of Huitzo, pertaining to the district of Huexolotitlán, issued a complaint against their *subdelegado*,[59] don Juan Vicente Vidal, who had thrown them in jail for debt. They testified that in August 1810 they had received a *repartimiento* of money from Vidal to produce corn, agreeing to repay him in kind at harvest time at the rate of one fanega for each peso advanced. At harvest time, however, they resisted repayment because the market price was six to seven pesos per fanega and they had contracted for just one peso. As one debtor argued, "It wouldn't be sensible for us to pay."[60]

The recipient of the complaint, Antonio Izquierdo, the long-time advisor to the Oaxacan *intendente*, Mora y Peysal, one of the fiercest opponents of *repartimientos* in the colony, made his own conclusion; nobody

79

could be stupid enough to agree to the conditions of such a *repartimiento* unless forced.[61] Thus, he ordered all debtors released and prohibited Vidal from collecting any debts until an investigation had taken place. The subsequent inquiry, however, revealed a different situation. A peasant named Juan María Caballero, for instance, disclosed that Vidal had advanced him nine reales (1.125 pesos) to produce a fanega of corn. Despite the existing market price of 7.5 pesos per fanega, Caballero said he had accepted Vidal's offer, owing to his "urgency." Likewise, Bernarda Gonzalez, a widow, confessed that she had accepted Vidal's *repartimiento* of money for corn despite the unfavorable terms. As she testified: "Motivated by need . . . to support myself and my children, I asked him for six fanegas worth which he gladly gave me . . . giving me nine reales per fanega. . . . He didn't want to give me more [reales] but finding myself with no alternative, I had to take them."[62]

Izquierdo's assessment of the circumstance was incorrect. The *repartimientos* were not forcefully distributed. As the very debtors admitted, they accepted Vidal's *repartimientos* despite the rapacious terms because they had no real options — their material needs dictated that they accept the credit offered by the *alcalde mayor* even if it was at predatory rates. Obviously, they had no alternative creditor to whom to turn. Further testimony showed that the region was suffering from a drought and scarcity of corn and, undoubtedly, the small advance which the peasants took from Vidal allowed them to purchase enough corn to survive. Had their next harvests been abundant, they would have repaid their debts in corn worth far less than the going rate in 1811 of seven pesos per fanega, since the price of corn would have fallen. The drought, however, had continued, and when the debtors proved unable (or unwilling) to repay Vidal, they turned for help to the office of the Oaxacan *intendente*, who misinterpreted the evidence and wrongly accused the *alcalde mayor* of forcing the Indians to accept the credit.

Whether these particular debts were ever repaid is unclear. The long investigation into Vidal revealed that his poor management had contributed to the rise of intervillage conflicts in his district, conflicts not related to the *repartimiento*. Alluding to the approach of Morelos's rebel army, on 9 October 1812 Izquierdo recommended Vidal's removal. The danger of provoking discontent was clearly great at this time, and Vidal's continued presence was deemed a risk to stability.[63]

While the case at hand was extraordinary, owing to the insurgency of Morelos, the peasants of Huitzo who issued complaints would have gained considerably regardless. Their initial complaint won them their immediate release from jail and granted them temporary relief from fulfill-ing their debt obligations. This additional time allowed the debtors to concentrate on the new planting season without having to fear that the debt collectors would hassle them or confiscate their belongings. Release from prison and temporary suspension of debt obligations were so com-monly granted to indigenous complainants that it seems likely that peti-tions were sometimes made specifically with these ends in mind. Debtors were often even bolder, asking for debt payment moratoriums of two, three, or even five years, in the hope of giving themselves additional time to repay their debts.

In a different case, peasants from San Pablo Coatlán in the district of Miahuatlán issued a 1798 complaint against their *alcalde mayor*, don Fausto de Corres. Among other accusations, they claimed that don Fausto's *teniente* had forced them to accept *repartimientos* for cochineal and mules in 1797. The long investigation that followed was confusing. Most of the Indians interviewed denied that the *repartimientos* of Corres were forced, claiming instead that they were accepted willingly. Several other Indians came forth to claim that the parish priest, don Joaquin de Urquijo, was the real tyrant, demanding from them excessive *derramas*, unauthorized exactions. Corres himself brought suit against the priest, who he claimed had convinced several Indians to accuse him of forceful *repartimientos* in order to help the business dealings of the priest's brother, don Miguel de Urquijo, who was a merchant also trading in Miahuatlán. Joaquin de Urquijo, the priest, countered by accusing the *alcalde mayor* of defaming him unfairly. In fact, several Indians from San Juan Ozoltepec testified that they had heard that Corres had bribed individuals to make false accusations against their priest.

Accusations flew back and forth. At least some of them were made by individuals who had evidently been recruited by either Urquijo or Corres. The allegations on either side, however, must be interpreted cautiously. While it is true that several Indians accused *alcalde mayor* Corres of issu-ing forced *repartimientos*, most of the Indians, when asked to testify, defended Corres, stating that *repartimientos* were always received volun-tarily. In any event, the case was never resolved. Urquijo withdrew all complaints, as did Felipe Hernandez de la Peña, a spokesperson for sev-eral of the towns issuing complaints. Corres was forced to appear before the *intendente* in Oaxaca but was released without facing any charges of wrongdoing. The motives of the various parties are unclear, but what seems certain is that the *alcalde mayor* and the priest were at odds and the indigenous inhabitants of the district were drawn into the dispute. It appears likely, then, that accusations, true or false, were leveled in the midst of a larger power struggle between the *alcalde mayor* and the parish priest. Each party recruited indigenous allies to help him denounce his opponent. Accusing *subdelegado* Corres of forcefully issuing *repartimientos* was certainly an effective way for Urquijo to undermine Corres. Given the illegality of the *repartimiento* and the strong commitment displayed by the *intendente corregidor*, Mora y Peysal, to Article 12, such an accusation was guaranteed to raise red flags in Oaxaca and spark an investigation into Corres's activities. In fact, Corres was reprimanded by the *intendente*.[64] Such an interpretation is supported by Woodrow Borah, who found that peasant complaints against *alcaldes mayores* were far more likely to occur when the official and the parish priest were in conflict. In such cases, the priests often encouraged their parishioners to level complaints against the *alcalde mayor*, whether sincere or not. According to Borah, officials of the General Indian Court learned to determine the authenticity of the complaints in order to distinguish which ones were merely a reflection of struggles between Spaniards.[65] Taylor also noted the frequency of conflict between priests and Spanish officials.[66]

In at least one case, a debtor unable to meet his debts falsely accused his *alcalde mayor* of forcing him to accept the *repartimiento* in the first place. In 1788, Bernardo Antonio, an Indian cochineal producer from Santa María Tepoxco in the district of Teotitlán del Camino, issued a complaint to the *intendente corregidor* against his *alcalde mayor*, don Manuel Josef López. According to Antonio, he fled his village to seek help in Oaxaca when he learned that the *alcalde mayor* had ordered his arrest for debts he owed from the *repartimiento*. Antonio testified that five years earlier, upon his election to the post of village governor, *alcalde mayor* López had forced him to accept money to distribute to other community members to produce cochineal and *huipiles*. As a result, he came to owe *alcalde mayor* López eight arrobas (200 pounds) of cochineal and an unspecified number of *huipiles*.

Antonio's complaint sparked an investigation by Antonio de Mora y Peysal, the *intendente corregidor*, who ordered the *alcalde mayor* of Teotitlán del Camino to respond promptly to Antonio's charges. In his response, dated 23 May 1788, López admitted supplying Antonio with funds to produce not 200, but 155 pounds of cochineal and 546 *huipiles*. A ledger submitted by López revealed that Antonio had repaid all but 12 pounds, 12 ounces of cochineal and 14 *huipiles*. Repeated requests that the balance be paid had failed, leading López to order his *teniente* to arrest Antonio.

82

Facing imprisonment and loss of his few personal belongings, Bernardo Antonio eluded the *teniente* and escaped to Oaxaca to seek help. Antonio's main grievance, however, was apparently not the manner in which he had been allegedly forced to receive the money in the first place. The complaint occurred only after five years had passed and most of the debt had been repaid. Had this *repartimiento* been truly so onerous and unwanted, Antonio would have surely sought the aid of Oaxacan authorities much sooner. What had changed since the loan was initially made was the ability of Antonio to repay his debt. It was only the order for his arrest that prompted the complaint. The debtor came forward to deny the legitimacy of the debt only when pressure to pay became unbearable and incarceration seemed imminent.

This case, however, is extraordinary, because López was able to produce five letters, written to him in 1784 and 1785 by Antonio (or a scribe) and signed by Antonio himself, which both requested the *repartimiento* loans and acknowledged their receipt. López submitted these letters to disprove the claims against him. Antonio had requested the loans, not been forced to take them.[67] In this example, then, we see both an accusation of force and relatively conclusive proof that the allegation was untrue. Antonio was threatened with imprisonment and responded rationally by denying the legitimacy of his debts. Antonio undoubtedly hoped this approach would win him relief from his debt obligation, not unreasonable given the Crown's antagonism toward the *repartimiento* at that time, only two years after its official 1786 prohibition.[68]

Only five accusations of forced *repartimientos* in Oaxaca were found for the period 1750–1821, and there is sound reason to doubt the veracity of several of them.[69] Even if one were to accept accusations such as Bernardo Antonio's as true, the case in favor of the *repartimiento* being primarily a coercive system would be weak. The *repartimiento* was the major means through which Indians produced for and consumed goods originating in the non-Indian market. If the *repartimiento* were truly as coercive as many have argued, the incidence of complaints would surely have been much higher, despite the significant obstacles to lodging complaints.

Indians in Spanish America showed a remarkable penchant for utilizing the Spanish court systems. That so few archival examples were located indicates that claims of forced *repartimientos*, if they existed at all, must have been exceptional. Indians did issue complaints against the *repartimiento*, but the issues that they raised most often involved matters other than forced distribution. Indians turned to the courts to positively shape market exchanges and to manipulate the system to their benefit, not to

83

escape the *repartimiento* and trade altogether. While at times their petitions won them tangible benefits, more often their complaints merely handcuffed the *alcalde mayor* for awhile, and by doing so the Indians gained for themselves temporary relief from the debt collectors and additional time to comfortably repay the *alcalde*. Far from being passive victims of an exploitative system, the Oaxacan peasants actively used the courts, among other means, to increase the benefits they received (and to reduce the costs incurred) from their access to *repartimiento* credit. Vast research of the past several decades has shown conclusively that Indians were active agents in shaping colonial society. Thus, the fact that Indians turned to the legal system to manipulate the *repartimiento* should hardly be surprising. After all, the *repartimiento* was the main link that most peasants had with the broader European economy, and no issue could have been more vital to the peasants than their material interests.

The few accusations of force were far outnumbered by the numerous cases found in which the recipient of a *repartimiento* freely admitted that he or she had willingly accepted or requested a *repartimiento*. Several of these have already been mentioned. Most of the Indians of Miahuatlán claimed that they took *repartimientos* voluntarily from their *alcalde mayor*, don Fausto de Corres.[70] Likewise, the peasants from Huitzo admitted having requested *repartimientos* from their *alcalde mayor*, owing to their grave economic situation. The terms were poor, but the requests were not coerced.[71] Juan José Benítes, a native of San Mateo Sindihui in the jurisdiction of Teozacoalco, testified that in 1806, "seeing that my *alcalde mayor* was making *repartimientos* for cochineal as always has been the custom at the rate of twelve reales . . . I went to him to ask for twenty pounds worth." Benítes added that he later requested two additional cochineal *repartimientos*.[72]

Mateo Mendez of Santiago Matatlán, in the district of Teotitlán del Valle, noted that in 1792 he requested a *repartimiento* loan to produce twelve pounds of cochineal and to buy a team of oxen, but the *alcalde mayor* refused to make the loan until Mendez first paid off his debts from an earlier *repartimiento*. Other peasants from Teotitlán del Valle testified that the *alcalde mayor* only advanced money to cochineal producers who were "good payers."[73] In a similar vein, Ouweneel found that several villages of the Mexican district of Chalco, were not included in the *repartimientos* of 1721 and 1722 because they had not yet closed their debts from 1720.[74] To the degree that his knowledge of consumers permitted him, the *alcalde mayor* withheld *repartimiento* credit from peasants be-

84

lieved to be greater risks. Far from being forced, some peasants were denied *repartimientos*.

The community of Santo Tomas Mazaltepec, located in the district of Cuatro Villas del Marquesado del Valle, also sought oxen through the *repartimiento*. When in 1792 the inhabitants went to the town of Cuilapa to obtain *repartimiento* oxen, they rejected the beasts, complaining about their "fatal" condition. Only after the price was lowered and they were granted a longer-than-normal time to repay did they accept the animals. Not only did they freely accept them, but they bargained for a better price.[75]

Finally, in 1770 the *principales* of the town of Santiago Xilotepec in the jurisdiction of Nexapa submitted an urgent request to the *alcalde mayor* of Nexapa requesting a *repartimiento* of money to be repaid in cochineal, because, they claimed, they needed to pay their "offering, tribute and other things." Strapped for cash, the village elites turned to their *alcalde mayor* and his system of *repartimiento* and requested a loan. Economic need drove the Indians into the credit market. In this particular case, the *alcalde mayor* was unwilling to loan the funds, for his term in office was soon to expire and, he insisted, this would make it too difficult to collect the debt. Notifying his superiors, the *alcalde mayor* warned that economic conditions were so dire that not even the Indians' subsistence was guaranteed. If no additional *repartimiento* were made soon, he warned, the Indians might even rebel.[76]

The court cases cited in this chapter, of course, were unusual. These had been *repartimientos* that had required the involvement of parties normally extraneous to the process. During the period of this study, hundreds of thousands of *repartimientos* were made by the *alcaldes mayores* of Oaxaca, which were received and repaid without any dispute or resistance. These undocumented *repartimientos* were typical, not the ones that ended up in court.

Clerical Condemnations

Accusations by peasants of force in the distribution of *repartimientos* were uncommon. In contrast, colonial officials and clergy bent upon seeing the system banned often claimed that the *repartimientos* were unwillingly foisted upon Indians. However, even when one examines critically several of the most damning testimonies offered against the *repartimiento* in the early 1780s, testimonies that helped sway the Crown to ban the system, one uncovers additional, powerful evidence that the *repartimiento* was a system of credit, not coerced production and consumption.

For example, when in 1784 Bishop Ortigoza of Oaxaca submitted a strong condemnation of the *repartimiento* based on observations made during his 1776–1783 *visita* of the bishopric of Oaxaca, he attached the equally critical, but more informative, testimonies sent to him by two parish priests of Oaxaca, both of whom had considerable knowledge of the *repartimiento*. The first, authored by Manuel Eduardo Perez Bonilla, parish priest of Santo Tomás de Ixtlán, began by condemning the *alcaldes mayores* as usurers. The priest continued by noting the case of a number of peasants from his district who despite their protestations had been forced to take *repartimientos* of money, yielding profits to the *alcalde mayor* of fifteen thousand pesos.[77] He then, however, proceeded unwittingly to offer an alternative, more plausible explanation for the peasants' acceptance of the *repartimiento*:

> What grief, what misery, what extortions, what injustices, Illustrious Señor, have been seen and are seen every day in the villages, and especially in this *cabecera*, in order to collect and extract fifteen thousand pesos from hapless Indians [*infelices*], who having received or asked for money from the *teniente* in the down season [*tiempo muerto*] when it was least opportune to either plant corn or to seed *nopales*, later spent it unprofitably perhaps in eating, drinking or getting drunk as these hapless Indians are prone to do, and even more hapless for the thoughtlessness of having asked for money from usurers, who at debt collection time harass and oppress them.[78]

While the priest might have claimed that the *alcalde mayor* was forcing the Indians to accept the loans, he suggested otherwise in this passage. Instead, it appears that Indians took loans out of need, especially to smooth out consumption during the more difficult months of the agricultural cycle, not because they were forced. That the priest disapproved of the manner in which the peasants spent their money, if he was even correct, is immaterial.

86 In his continued description of the tactics of the *repartidores*, Perez accused the *alcalde*'s assistant, the *teniente*, of preying on poor Indians. Carrying with him a sack of money, Perez claimed, the *teniente* regularly intercepted needy Indians as they crossed the village plaza and attempted to convince them to accept a loan, saying: "Here man, take some money, you have lots of time to find a way to repay it during the five years of the

corregimiento" (the *alcalde*'s tenure). The priest lamented that the Indians, even when they declined such offers, ultimately had to return to the
alcalde mayor to request funds, exposing themselves to his harsh and
violent methods of debt collection. What the priest of Ixtlán describes
resembles more the persuasion of a fast-talking salesman than the outright
naked force more often attributed to the *alcalde mayor* and his band of
tyrants. Furthermore, Perez stated that the peasants often refused the
repartimientos, at least initially. In short, if the peasants described by
Perez were being forced to accept the money, it is an economic force. They
accepted the *repartimientos* out of economic necessity, not owing to political coercion. The *teniente* was merely exploiting this economic need.[79]

The second letter submitted by the Bishop is even more suggestive. In
1784 the priest of Ayoquesco, Antonio Porley, reported on the *repartimiento* of the current *alcalde mayor*, whom he condemned for employing
much violence in the collection of his debts. Priest Porley, however, admitted that in his district, the *repartimientos* were not distributed forcefully,
although he did note that the *alcalde mayor* always let the Indians know
that it would please him greatly if they took *repartimientos* from him. He
continued by naming a number of Indians who had been convinced to
accept funds to produce cochineal, including the Indians of San Pedro el
Alto, who did not "need the *repartimiento* because they all, or at least the
majority of them, were well-off [*acomodados*]." Whether or not he was
correct about the economic condition of these particular Indians, Porley
revealed several important points about the *repartimiento*. First, he admitted that the Indians were not forced to accept loans, even if there might
have been benefits to keeping the *alcalde mayor* pleased.[80] Second, he
suggests clearly that the *repartimiento* offered financing, which at least
some peasants needed. Porley's point was that the Indians of San Pedro
Alto were well-off and thus had no need for the *repartimientos*. This
implies unambiguously that poorer Indians did need the *repartimientos*,
that the loans offered by the *repartimiento* provided funds without which
they would not have been able to afford certain things. Like the priest of
Ixtlán, Porley disapproved of the way in which the Indians spent their
money. As the priest lamented: "The Indian does not reflect on the future,
but only attends to the present, they take as much as is offered to them,
although they know that they will have to repay it very expensively and
with a thousand aggravations." Badly spent or not, the peasants desired
the loans, and they requested them.[81]

The testimonies of the two Oaxacan priests are illuminating. Both opposed the *repartimiento* vehemently because they attributed to it signifi-

87

cant suffering among the Indians in their districts, especially resulting from the often violent manner in which the *alcaldes mayores* attempted to collect debts from delinquent debtors. Upon reading these testimonies, one is convinced by the sincerity of the authors; these are impassioned pleas for help from clergymen who seem to care deeply about their parishioners. Nevertheless, their interpretations are strongly biased. For example, from the Church's standpoint, the *repartimiento* was usury; the implicit interest rate of *repartimiento* transactions always exceeded 5 percent. Usury perhaps, but nobody, not even the Church, was willing to lend funds to the Indians at the rate of 5 percent. If the Church's guidelines had truly dictated the terms of commerce, then peasants would have been denied access to credit.

In addition, both priests disapproved of the way in which the Indians spent the monies that they received from the *alcalde mayor*, suggesting that the Indians were foolish or shortsighted to take *repartimientos* from violent usurers. Even if the Indians did take the money merely to fund their drinking binges, a claim which the priests no doubt realized would magnify the evils of the system, they were acting of their free will. That the priests saw such behavior as repugnant is immaterial. In fact, it is doubtful that this type of behavior was as common as the priests claimed, if for no other reason than the *alcalde mayor* would have resisted lending funds for such a purpose, not because he objected to the debauchery, but because he needed to ensure that the activities which he funded were likely to produce income. On the other hand, it is likely that the *alcalde mayor* took advantage of the Indians' greater needs during fiesta times, lending the peasants money for the festivities and demanding repayment in cochineal at harvest time. As long as the *alcalde* made sure that he did not lend more than he could reasonably expect to collect later, this would have been an effective way to increase business. Peasants taking *repartimientos* for "drunken festivals" probably did earn the disapproval of the parish priest, yet they were freely negotiating with the *alcalde mayor*. In fact, however, peasants usually took loans to finance production or consumption of more utilitarian items, whether cochineal, draft animals, or basic consumer necessities.

It should not be surprising that poor peasants would need and seek credit, even when the cost of that credit was high and the displeasure of facing the *alcalde* and his debt collectors potentially great. When the alternative to the *repartimiento* meant forgoing needed or desired goods or even experiencing hunger, it probably required little arm-twisting to convince a peasant to borrow from the *alcalde mayor*. In fact, many eighteenth-century defenders of the *repartimiento* pointed to what they claimed was an unquenchable hunger for credit on the part of the Indians. An example is the Conde de Tepa, an *oidor* of the Audiencia de México who wrote a lengthy 1775 defense of the *repartimiento*. In one of the more interesting passages of his *dictamen*, Tepa seemed almost perplexed by what he perceived to be the Indians' addiction to credit. Implicitly recognizing that *repartimiento* credit was expensive, Tepa seemed puzzled that poor Indians were not alone in taking *repartimiento* loans.

> What is even stranger, the rich Indians, of which there are many in the province of Oaxaca, take money in the *repartimiento* depriving themselves of the profit and utility which they give to the *alcalde mayor*. The character of the Indian is incomprehensible.[82]

Tepa underlined the fact that the *repartimiento* was a desired system of credit, one which even attracted Indians with greater resources and ostensibly more limited need of credit. Incapable of understanding why wealthy Indians would borrow at high rates of interest, Tepa concluded that this "strange" behavior was due to the fact that Indians were "guided generally by superstition and are not governed by the common norms of other people." That the "rich" Indians might have had very rational reasons for borrowing funds from the *alcalde mayor* rather than risking their own wealth failed to occur to Tepa. Like other Spaniards, he was incapable of imagining that the Indians might have acted rationally in managing their economic activities.[83] The same attitude was exhibited nearly two decades later by Viceroy Revillagigedo the Younger, who was annoyed by what he perceived to be the Indians' inability to break with the custom of receiving funds and goods on credit. Because of this "custom," the Viceroy lamented, the 1786 prohibition of the *repartimiento* had led to economic depression.[84]

The perplexity of Tepa and the frustration of Revillagigedo would have been of little surprise to the *alcaldes mayores* of Oaxaca, who were quick to point to the Indians' unceasing demand for credit. When in 1784 the *alcaldes mayores* of Oaxaca defended themselves against an anonymous condemnation of their business dealings, most responded that the demand for *repartimiento* credit among the Indians was great. The officials of Teposcolula, Zimatlán, Cuatro Villas, and Villa Alta all claimed that they were constantly forced to turn down requests for *repartimientos* or to advance less than requested. *Alcalde mayor* Llano of Antequera described the Indians' demand for credit as "insatiable." *Alcalde mayor* Gonzalez de Mesa of Xicayan reported that he gave the Indians only a third of what they requested. The official of Teococuilco and Teozacualco admitted to funding between one-third and one-half of the requests, rejecting the rest for fear that the Indians would be unable to repay. The official of Teutila also denied many solicitations, believing that the borrowers were not creditworthy. As the official of Villa Alta put it, if all requests were granted, his funds "would be gone in one day."[85] When, four years later, after the introduction of *intendencias* and the adoption of Article 12 made the *repartimiento* illegal, the *alcalde mayor* of Teotitlán del Valle was accused of forcing an Indian to accept a *repartimiento*, he ridiculed the accusation, stating: "Indians are capable of requesting the cargo of a flotilla, and [so] it is a platitude [*vulgaridad*] and a misunderstanding of the *repartimiento* to say that they are forced."[86]

The *alcaldes mayores* certainly had strong reasons to exaggerate or even lie about the Indians' desire for *repartimientos*. After all, they were defending a system profitable to them which was under attack from many sectors of colonial society. Yet, the Indians described by the *alcaldes mayores* were behaving much like poor people in other societies. Economic necessities which arose from poverty and the need to smooth out consumption drove the Indians into the credit market.[87] Confronting a creditor eager to extend them credit, they borrowed voraciously. On occasion, however, they proved unable to meet their obligations promptly, and when this occurred, they had to deal with the *alcalde mayor* and his debt collectors and this was never pleasant. The officials claimed that they regularly denied requests for *repartimientos*, and this also seems credible. Like creditors in any society, the *alcaldes mayores* had to be cautious not to make bad loans, and they did so by closely screening potential borrowers. If a peasant incurred more debt then he could repay, the *alcalde mayor* lost his principal, and this was bad business.[88]

One final and important hypothesis can be formulated from the reports of Porley and Perez, the two parish priests: the *repartimiento* was a system of credit that served especially the needs of the poorest peasants, who most likely had no alternative sources of credit. Priest Porley of Ayoquesco mentioned the case in which "well-off" peasants took *repartimientos* to produce cochineal, a fact that he considered noteworthy and exceptional since, Porley reasoned, "well-off" peasants did not need the official's credit. The other priest, Perez of Ixtlán, showed how poor peasants always succumbed to the offers for money extended by the *tenientes*; even if the peasants turned down the credit initially, they always returned and took a *repartimiento*. What the observations of both priests suggest is that the *repartimiento* was a system of credit that primarily catered to (or preyed upon) the poorer Indians. Porley implied that wealthier peasants had alternatives to the *repartimiento*, perhaps by financing their own production or using their greater creditworthiness to obtain credit from alternative sources. Perez, in contrast, noted that poor peasants were most prone to borrow from the magistrate (or least able to refuse).[89] In short, *repartimiento* credit was most likely to be secured by poorer peasants. It was a credit source of last resort.

This hypothesis is further corroborated by the 1784 defense of the system by the *alcalde mayor* of Xicayan, Joseph Gonzalez de Mesa. *Alcalde mayor* Gonzalez de Mesa defended the *repartimiento* by pointing to the fact that only the officials who possessed judicial power would loan funds to the poor peasants. As he argued, "private merchants only contract with trustworthy and propertied Indians so as not to risk their money, but the unfortunate and destitute only find refuge in the *alcalde mayor*."[90]

Poor Indians borrowed from the *alcalde mayor* because only he would lend to them. And given the claim made by many *alcaldes mayores* that they regularly refused requests for loans, one must conclude that there were some peasants too poor to gain entry into even the *repartimiento*. This is further suggested by the fact that before receiving *repartimiento* loans, some peasants were required to find guarantors, fellow community members who would vouch for their creditworthiness and assume their debt if they defaulted. Apparently, there were some peasants who the official viewed as inherently not creditworthy.[91]

An *alcalde mayor* sought his political post for one reason — he hoped to grow rich from the operation of his *repartimientos* and depart from his district a wealthy man. Undoubtedly, many succeeded. Spanish officials usually enjoyed high returns but also faced the potential of total loss of their principal, for the trade in which they were engaged was highly risky. Because of the risk, the *repartimiento* often led to violence, as the royal officials were not at all reluctant to use coercive measures to collect their debts. Debtors were imprisoned, even beaten at times, and all for the magistrate's pursuit of economic returns. While despicable, such offenses were the exception, not the rule. In the overwhelming majority of *repartimientos*, loans or goods were received and debts were repaid without violence. In examining more closely than ever before how the system of *repartimiento* actually operated, this chapter has been able to show that past depictions have been simplistic. It is true that the Spanish officials employed violence in their efforts to profit, but the Indians were neither passive victims nor involuntary participants. The *repartimiento* existed for a reason less sensational, but altogether more logical, than has traditionally been claimed. It existed as an institution of credit designed to operate in a risky, colonial environment characterized by imperfect market integration. By reducing transaction costs, the costs of assessing creditworthiness and collecting the debts, the *repartimiento* made profitable (and less risky) the provision of credit.

Indians participated in the *repartimiento* voluntarily. Lack of coercion, however, is not meant to suggest that Indians enjoyed political, economic, social, or judicial equality to Spaniards. In fact, one of the arguments in this chapter has been that Indians had few alternatives but to seek credit from the *alcaldes mayores* because of their poverty and the colonialists' perceptions of Indians. Poverty was partially the consequence of Indians' disadvantaged positions in a colonial society that placed socioeconomic and legal restrictions upon them. Eighteenth-century Oaxacan peasants needed credit, just like poor people do in modern economies, and, like their modern counterparts, colonial Oaxacans had limited sources for such finances. Encountering an *alcalde mayor* who was eager to profit and willing to lend, the peasants borrowed willingly. Peasants did not need to be coerced to accept *repartimiento* credit, because the alternative was no credit at all.

Chapter Five

Informal Credit Institutions and Cross-Cultural Trade

P easants were not alone in their dependence on credit. In fact, one of the dominant features of the Spanish-American colonial economies was the heavy reliance on credit in virtually all economic and social sectors. The wealthiest miners depended on large loans to finance their explorations.[1] Agricultural properties of all sizes had large, outstanding mortgages. Enrique Florescano has argued that without ample credit, a "*hacienda* was simply not a good business."[2] Commerce also relied on credit. Powerful merchants issued *libranzas*, literally, "promissory notes," to expand their trade and to overcome their lack of liquidity.[3] The same merchants supplied goods on credit to traveling salesmen, often their own agents, who peddled the goods in remote corners of the colony. The *alcaldes mayores* relied on financing to operate their *repartimientos*, turning either to *consulado* merchants or borrowing directly from ecclesiastical sources.[4] According to David Brading, Mexico suffered from an acute shortage of minted coins, and "the inevitable result of this situation was an almost universal reliance upon credit transactions."[5]

But while most Mexicans relied on credit, peasants were limited, largely, to the credit provided by the *alcalde mayor* and his system of *repartimiento*. There were other sources of credit, but Indians did not regularly have access to these sources. Merchants and private traders did, at times, sell goods on credit or loan funds to the peasantry, but only to a limited number of known individuals. Storekeepers in small towns, able to judge the creditworthiness of their regular customers, sold inexpensive goods on credit to peasants that they knew to be trustworthy, no doubt making additional credit contingent on the prompt repayment of debts.[6] But even these stores were not always an alternative source of credit for peasants, since often they were owned and operated by the *alcalde mayor* himself.[7] *Hacienda* owners loaned funds to Indians in nearby communities, especially if the Indians were also occasional employees. *Hacendados* and

93

Indians who came into contact frequently developed relations which gave the former at least some leverage with which to collect debts and greater information with which to assess the creditworthiness of borrowers.[8] What distinguished the *alcalde mayor* from the storekeeper and *hacendado* was his ability and willingness to extend credit to a larger percentage of the inhabitants of his district, including Indians whom he might not know personally. Because the *alcalde mayor* could use the Crown's authority to collect debts, his range of potential clients was much broader.[9]

Institutional economists have long urged scholars to examine more closely the institutional framework within which business is conducted because, as Nobel laureate and economic historian Douglass North notes, institutions "determine transaction and transformation costs and hence the profitability and feasibility of engaging in economic activity."[10] Institutional economists predict that obstacles and barriers to trade (i.e., market imperfections) lead to the adaptation of institutions or the creation of new ones designed to diminish or eradicate such obstacles. Institutions aim to reduce transaction costs, the expenses associated with conducting business, and thus permit commerce to occur where otherwise it might prove uneconomical.

The *repartimiento* was such an institution. It helped compensate for weak market integration and the poor penetration of the state in rural areas, and thus permitted the widespread provision of credit to Mexico's indigenous population. Its operation by the *alcalde mayor* helped reduce risk to an economically tolerable level. The *repartimiento*, then, was a system of credit designed to function in a climate of high risk, in which most merchants were unwilling to expose their capital. As has been repeatedly argued, this was the primary reason for the *repartimiento*'s existence.[11]

The difficulties addressed by the *repartimiento* were not entirely unique to colonial Spanish America. In fact, one finds nearly identical problems in most rural credit markets in modern developing countries. During the past several decades, economists have grown increasingly aware of the obstacles to financing peasants in poorly integrated markets, and the result has been the emergence of a substantial literature addressing such issues.[12] Economists had long observed that peasants in developing regions had limited options for obtaining the credit that they so desperately needed. Nearly the only creditor in most rural areas was the local moneylender, who charged rates often exceeding 75 percent per year. Many economists attributed this to the fact that the moneylender exercised monopoly power, and they recommended the entry into the rural credit market of institutional creditors who would be able to undercut the moneylender's interest rates. The newer literature on rural credit markets has recognized and addressed the failure of most of these institutional creditors to compete with local moneylenders. Institutional creditors experienced crippling rates of default and failed to put the moneylenders out of business. As it turned out, the moneylenders performed a necessary economic function and cannot be so easily dismissed as the economic parasites that they are often portrayed.[13]

Learning from past mistakes, economists have begun to develop more sophisticated models for understanding the operation of informal credit markets. Specifically, economists have identified three difficulties which are especially acute in the rural credit markets of developing economies; these are termed the screening problem, the incentives problem, and the enforcement problem. The screening problem refers to the fact that creditors face an enormous and costly task of determining (screening) the creditworthiness of potential borrowers, overcoming what economists term information asymmetries. Lenders must screen their potential clients carefully and wisely, and this requires access to information that is often costly to obtain. The incentives problem concerns the equally costly task assumed by lenders of ensuring that borrowers engage in activities which increase the likelihood of debt repayment. Finally, lenders face the enforcement problem, the challenging and expensive undertaking of collecting debts.

Economists now argue that the informal institutions of credit that succeed are those best able to reduce the transaction costs associated with screening, incentives, and enforcement. As Karla Hoff and Joseph E. Stiglitz maintain, "It is the markets' responses to these three problems, singly or in combination, that explain many of the observed features of rural credit markets."[14] In other words, the village moneylenders monopolize the provision of credit because they have a comparative advantage at reducing the costs related to screening, incentives, and enforcement.

Employing the perspectives of this new literature on informal credit institutions, one observes that the *repartimiento* of the Spanish *alcalde mayor* developed mechanisms to reduce the transaction costs associated with these three obstacles. Screening essentially entails the acquisition of information about the creditworthiness of potential borrowers, such as a credit check in a developed economy. Economists have discovered that one of the primary reasons why moneylenders so often enjoy a monopoly over a local area is that their greater familiarity with an area and its people provides them with access to cheap information. Their monopoly, then, is geographical and informational. Other creditors cannot bid the cost of

95

credit downward, because they lack information about credit risks and to obtain such knowledge is prohibitively expensive. If they try to enter the market without information, they experience crippling levels of loan default.[15] To a certain degree, such a spatial monopoly existed in rural colonial Oaxaca. Spaniards living in the city of Oaxaca, who might have desired to compete with the *alcalde mayor*, had little ability to obtain dependable and affordable information about borrowers. In contrast, the *alcalde mayor* and his *tenientes* knew the villages and the populations well. In selecting *tenientes*, the Spanish official and his financial backers sought individuals who were both trustworthy and experienced in the district. In addition, the *alcalde mayor* enjoyed access to the civil records of previous government officials, which might have been useful in obtaining additional information about the character of individuals or specific villages. Most important, as the near monopoly provider of credit in the countryside, the *alcalde mayor* knew a peasant's total debt burden and could assess whether or not a peasant had the capacity to meet additional obligations. Clearly, the official did not want a debtor to get in over his or her head, for this nearly guaranteed default. Control over better information gave the *alcalde mayor* a decided advantage because without such data potential creditors could not safely compete. The *repartimiento*, then, helped to reduce the high cost of screening and thus made the provision of credit both less risky and more profitable.

The incentives problem is slightly more difficult to document in the *repartimiento* system of informal credit. Often the incentives problem is dealt with indirectly by lenders who might incorporate into the contract stipulations that will reward borrowers who repay promptly. By doing so, the creditor provides an incentive to the borrower to behave responsibly. In the *repartimiento*, however, there were no such stipulations regularly included in the oral contract. Lenders can also use more direct incentives, most notably the threat to deny additional credit to delinquent borrowers. By making new loans contingent on the responsible actions of debtors, the creditor can induce better compliance.[16] The official of Teotitlán del Valle managed his *repartimientos* in such a manner. A peasant by the name of Mateo Mendez of the village of Santiago Matatlán testified in 1792 that his *alcalde mayor* had denied his request for a *repartimiento* loan until he first repaid fully an earlier obligation.[17] This Teotitlán official was employing incentives to induce more favorable borrower behavior.

While the moneylending practices of the *alcalde mayor* addressed the problems associated with screening and incentives, it was his greater ability to counter the enforcement problem which gave him the decided advantage over potential competitors. The *alcalde mayor* could use the judicial power with which he was vested to help enforce repayment of debts. This point, of course, has been emphasized throughout this book. It is only repeated here to show that the problems faced by creditors during Mexico's colonial era were not unique to those times. Lenders, and especially those operating in less well integrated markets, always encounter difficulties collecting debts and enforcing contracts. Financial arrangements such as the *repartimiento* aim to reduce the costs associated with such problems and risks.

Loan Contracts and Cross-Cultural Trade

Risk was not the only obstacle that the *repartimiento* succeeded in overcoming. Exchange between the *alcaldes mayores* and Oaxaca's cochineal producers was further burdened by two additional factors. First, the *alcalde* and the producers came from two very different worlds and did not share a common language and culture, and this complicated the process of transacting and increased the potential for conflict and uncertainty. Second, the nature of the business required the Spanish officials to make a tremendously large number of very small loans, which had the potential of making the cost of conducting business uneconomical. An examination of the *repartimiento* transaction for the production of *grana* cochineal illustrates how features of the cochineal *repartimiento* served to overcome these potential barriers to trade and to permit the system to function more efficiently and economically by reducing transaction costs and the uncertainties of cross-cultural trade.

Trade between Indians and Spaniards involved trade between people of distinct cultures, languages, and economic strategies, all of which increased uncertainty and the potential for conflict. In his extensive study of cross-cultural trade in many different regions and at many different times in history, Philip Curtin concluded that three elements made cross-cultural trade problematic. First, lack of a common language made communication between parties difficult, and this, among other factors, necessarily increased the costs of contracting, agreeing on the terms of exchange. Second, the differing lifestyle and cultural practices of the "other" appeared strange and unpredictable, introducing greater uncertainty and wariness into the transaction. Last, outsiders, people foreign to the local community, were viewed as less trustworthy than people of the same cultural group. According to Curtin, such cultural and lingual differences

97

were formidable barriers to commerce, and had to be eliminated or diminished if trade were to thrive. As Curtin argued, "These problems in cross-cultural understanding in general have meant that cross-trade has almost always been carried out through special institutional arrangements to help guarantee the mutual security of the two sides."[18]

In *repartimiento* transactions, the need for "special institutional arrangements" was even greater than in the cases discovered and examined by Curtin. Because the *repartimiento* always involved the extension of credit, the need for understanding, trust, and predictability was especially profound. Unlike a simple sale or barter transaction, credit transactions necessarily take a long time to complete. Months or years might pass between the loan and its repayment. This "long transaction time" expanded the potential for uncertainty and conflict, and thus increased the need for understanding and predictability. Features of the *repartimiento*, what Curtin might term "special institutional arrangements," served to reduce the difficulties created by lack of a common language and to make more predictable the behavior of trading partners, thus simplifying this cross-cultural trade, diminishing the potential for dispute, and reducing the costs of transacting business.

In the cochineal *repartimiento*, for example, the terms of loans extended to producers were fixed, unaffected by changing market conditions. Documents referencing thousands of loans were located in the surviving archival records and with only occasional exceptions, the terms were identical. In virtually every case, Indian producers received twelve reales (1.5 pesos) for each pound of dried cochineal that they promised to deliver in the future. Frequently, borrowers repaid their twelve-real loans in cash, at sixteen reales (2 pesos) rather than delivering a pound of finished dyestuff. This seems to have especially been the practice when debtors failed to produce the cochineal, due to harvest failure or some other cause.[19]

Typical of such cochineal *repartimiento* contracts was the one described in 1798 by Gabriel Cristobal, the forty-year-old governor of Miahuatlán, who noted that his *alcalde mayor*, don Fausto Corres, regularly advanced twelve reales in coin to villagers, expecting a payment of one pound of cochineal in the future, and demanding sixteen reales instead when the cochineal itself was not delivered at harvest time.[20] Antonio Porley, the parish priest of Ayoquesco, described the same system in 1784. Cochineal producers there received advances of twelve reales per pound, repaying sixteen reales when their harvests failed.[21] In the words of the *alcalde mayor* of Zimatlán-Chichicapa, "If on the completion of the term for the delivery of the cochineal [the debtors] do not have it nor can they be made to pay it in specie, then they do it at the rate of two pesos per pound; which is the regular price for this fruit at harvest time."[22]

The standard twelve-reales-per-pound loan was stable over a very extended time period as well. While its origins are obscure,[23] by the mid–eighteenth century this price was already universal. When in 1752 the Viceroy asked the *alcaldes mayores* to discuss the ways in which *repartimientos* operated in their districts, all ten of the Oaxacan officials who responded wrote that advances were made for cochineal at the rate of twelve reales per pound.[24] Throughout the remainder of the century, only infrequently were there exceptions to what John Chance termed the "twelve-real standard."[25] This standardization of the credit price was not unique to the cochineal *repartimiento* either; Arij Ouweneel discovered that the *alcalde mayor* of Zacatlán, Puebla, had been advancing the fixed rate of twelve pesos per half-"*carga*" of eggs "since time immemorial."[26]

This seemingly uneconomic practice makes some sense when viewed as a response, in part, to the conditions of cross-cultural trade. The fixed rate at which cochineal was contracted reduced the potential for future disputes and made simpler the process of transacting. Each *alcalde mayor* made hundreds or even thousands of loans to individuals he barely knew who spoke a language different from his own. Furthermore, these loans were always made orally, without any form of written contract. The absence of a *lingua franca* proved less of an obstacle since both parties were fully aware of the "customary" contract terms. It was a simple transaction, in which the producer delivered 1 pound of cochineal for each 1.5 pesos he or she was advanced. Both parties understood the unambiguous terms.

In addition, most *repartimiento* advances for cochineal were for very small amounts. An analysis of surviving records shows that the average-sized loan (the mean) was for fewer than ten pesos, and that the median loan was even smaller. Many advances were for just one or two pesos.[27] A good example of the number and size of loans extended in a typical season is provided by the portfolio of cochineal *repartimientos* of don Luis Frejomil, who was the *alcalde mayor* in 1765 of the district of Teotitlán del Camino. In anticipation of the upcoming cochineal harvest, Frejomil contracted with 791 different individuals from ten separate towns to deliver a total of 4,991 pounds of cochineal at the forthcoming harvest in exchange for cash advances, an average *repartimiento* of only 6.3 pounds. Even at its market price, the average value of each *repartimiento* was just 14.5 pesos. It is difficult to assess the transaction costs incurred for each of the

99

791 separate transactions, but they must have been significant. Not only did Frejomil need to reach an agreement with and disburse funds to each of the 791 individuals, but he had to record the loans, keep track of them, and most likely and wisely visit each of the ten towns at least once over the course of the production cycle to ensure that the contracted producers were in fact using the funds as agreed. Finally, *alcalde mayor* Frejomil, or his *teniente*, had to return to each town at harvest time and collect the cochineal due from each producer.[28] Because the potential profit of each loan was small, the *alcalde* earned worthwhile gross profits only by making hundreds or thousands of loans. While the marginal cost of contracting any single loan was not great, the total cost of negotiating thousands of individual loans would have been prohibitive. One needs to keep in mind that the cost of reaching an agreement on the terms of a loan depends little on the size of the loan. Thus, it costs a creditor the same amount to negotiate a loan for ten pesos as it would for a thousand-peso loan. Unquestionably, it would have been costly (and would not have been worthwhile) for the *alcalde mayor* to negotiate (and perhaps haggle over) each and every individual loan, and so he reduced significantly the transaction costs by always advancing the same price to all borrowers—a price, no doubt, at which he nearly always earned good returns. This stability was economically necessary because the profitability of his loans depended on keeping the cost of doing business low. The fixed *repartimiento* price eliminated the need for constant negotiation and replaced it with stability. The *alcalde mayor* saved the time and effort that would have otherwise been devoted to haggling over the terms of every *repartimiento* loan. The cost of conducting business was reduced, and the Spanish official's potential profits rose. The stability of the *repartimiento* contract for the production of cochineal, then, made solid economic sense. It was an economically efficient solution to a number of potentially crippling barriers to trade.

One obvious consequence of this price stability was that the *alcalde mayor* earned a varying rate of return on his advances from year to year, depending on the existing market price. Peasants, likewise, borrowed at a rate which differed from year to year. While the advance price was fixed, the market price of cochineal, of course, fluctuated, as would any commodity. Figure 5.1 shows market prices in Oaxaca for the years 1758–1821, as recorded by the Registro de Grana, the office set up in 1758 at the Crown's order to oversee and regulate the trade.[29] The median price of cochineal in Oaxaca for this period was eighteen reales per pound. In a

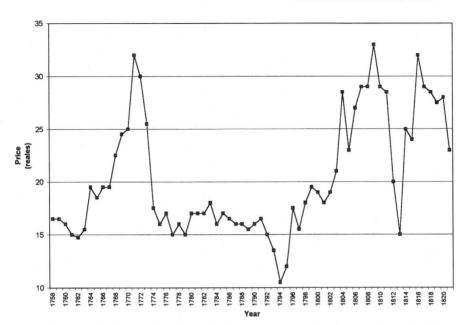

FIGURE 5.1. Registro price of *grana* in Oaxaca, 1758–1821. Source: Appendix B.

"typical year," then, the *alcalde* earned a simple gross return of 50 percent, a good return, no doubt, even after accounting for expenses and loan defaults. In some years, the *alcalde* earned more, and in other years, less. Certainly, the customary lending rate of 1.5 pesos per pound yielded a good return for the official in all but a few catastrophic years. Even when the market price dropped and the *alcalde*'s expected return fell correspondingly, it was probably not worth the added hassle or expense to adjust downward the *repartimiento* advance. And, as will be shown below, Indians came to view this as the "fair" rate and exercised considerable resistance when *alcaldes mayores* attempted to reduce it. Reducing the *repartimiento* rate to earn an extra real per pound was probably not worth the headaches that the peasant producers could (and would) have caused the *alcalde mayor* had he tried it, and so he rarely bothered.[30]

Things looked very different from the other end of the transaction, from the perspective of the indigenous dye producer. Whereas the profit realized by the Spanish *alcalde mayor* rose or fell in direct relation with the world price of cochineal, the Indian producer's gain remained constant. He or she received twelve reales for the labor involved in producing a pound of dye, regardless of local supply or the strength of demand in

101

Europe. The indigenous economy was thus insulated to a degree from the vicissitudes of the market economy. Income remained dependable and predictable, at least for that portion of the cochineal contracted for delivery to the Spanish official.[31] In addition, the price stability complemented the economic rationale or strategy of the indigenous cochineal producer, which differed from that of the Spaniard. The *alcalde* and his merchant backer sought to maximize the return on their investments. In contrast, the cochineal producer was largely a self-sufficient peasant who entered into the market mainly to cover those few essential expenses requiring money or outside income: tribute to the Crown, an expenditure for the village fiesta, payment to the priest for religious rites, legal fees for a land dispute, purchase of some item in the local store, or acquisition of some staple goods to smooth out consumption during the low times of the agricultural cycle. Furthermore, the peasant lived in a world where the cost of living in all but extraordinary years remained fairly regular and constant. The cost of tribute, for instance, stayed virtually the same for the entire colonial period. The potential wage from a day's work on a *hacienda* was almost invariably 1.5 to 2 reales. Thus, the stability of the *repartimiento* price was not unique. From year to year, the income needed to meet regular expenses remained fairly stable and the labor employed to obtain this level of income also remained relatively constant. Each twelve reales of income required the labor necessary to produce one pound of cochineal.

This is not to suggest that peasants were economically irrational and eschewed opportunities to earn a better deal. By accepting twelve reales as an advance payment, peasants did relinquish what was in many years significant future value in exchange for immediate liquidity. Given a more competitive business atmosphere, Indians would surely have chosen to borrow from whomever offered the most favorable terms. Barriers to entry into the credit-provision business in rural Spanish America, however, guaranteed that there was little or no competition. The *alcalde mayor* could offer "take-it-or-leave-it" terms, and most credit-hungry peasants would have no choice but to "take."

The stability of the contract price and terms may seem peculiar to modern readers, but the nature of the cochineal *repartimiento*, including the large number of low-value transactions between individuals largely "foreign" to one another, put a premium on stability and predictability. The potential for cheating diminished to the extent that the terms of exchange remained invariant. Stability of terms kept transaction costs at a minimum and diminished the potential for cheating.[32]

The "Customary" Price

The stability of the *repartimiento* contract was, in part, a reflection of the need of the *alcalde mayor* to keep transaction costs at a minimum. For the Indian cochineal producer, in contrast, negotiating a loan was at most a yearly (or semi-yearly) task. Yet the stability of the *repartimiento* contract also benefited the recipient, even if this was never its intention. The universality of the transaction gave loan recipients some recourse in the event of a disagreement with the *alcalde mayor* or his *tenientes*, since terms were known by everyone. The very standardization also reduced the potential for disputes since neither party could too easily claim that the loan terms differed from the norm. While it was clearly unintended, then, the "twelve-real standard" gave some protection and security to cochineal producers against the potential arbitrariness of the *alcalde mayor* and his *tenientes*.

Ample evidence exists to suggest that producers saw twelve reales as a fair and just contract price and resisted any tampering with it, at least downward. The language used by peasants to describe the cochineal *repartimiento* suggests that they saw the "twelve-real standard" as legitimate. Typical was Juan José Benítes, from the town of San Mateo Sindihui, jurisdiction of Teozacoalco in the Mixteca Alta, who testified in 1808 that he had approached his *alcalde mayor* two years earlier when he learned that the official was distributing *grana* cochineal loans at the rate of twelve reales per pound, "as has always been customary." The reference to the price as "customary" and Benítes's willingness to receive a loan at this rate suggests strong acceptance of its legitimacy.[33] Similarly, in reference to his cochineal *repartimientos*, don Fausto de Corres, the official of Miahuatlán, noted in 1798 that the rate of twelve reales per pound was "stipulated and agreed upon by immemorial custom."[34]

Additional evidence for the legitimacy of the "twelve-real standard" *repartimiento* contract rate is provided in a 1798 case in which the *alcalde mayor* of Nexapa, Nicolás Larumbe, convinced the villagers of his district to accept just ten reales per pound because of the depressed price of the dye at that time.[35] A number of Indian producers testified later that they also had received production loans, at the lower-than-normal rate of ten reales per pound, from a prominent local merchant named don Antonio de la Cantolla Santelizes. The peasants had grudgingly accepted a mere ten reales initially because market prices were so low that the lenders refused to give them anything greater. When at harvest time the market price of cochineal had recovered, however, producers felt that they deserved the difference between the contracted price of ten reales and the customary price of twelve reales per pound, since the depressed market conditions that had required them to deviate from the customary price in the first place no longer existed. Cantolla Santelizes, the merchant, apparently agreed, either voluntarily or under pressure, because several Indians attested that they were given an additional two reales in payment upon delivery of the dye to Cantolla. In contrast, Larumbe refused to adjust the payback price, which led some aggrieved producers to file a protest against Larumbe with the Oaxacan *intendente*. Evidently, the communities felt cheated by the loss of these "customarily paid" extra two reales and were sufficiently incensed to appeal for justice, though in other years they were perfectly willing to contract to deliver cochineal at twelve reales per pound, even when market prices were much higher. This demonstrates quite unambiguously that the customary *repartimiento* price of twelve reales held great legitimacy and was considered just and fair. The Nexapans took less than the customary twelve reales per pound in 1798 because they were given a choice to either "take it or leave it" by their *subdelegado* Larumbe and the merchant Cantolla Santelizes, and their own personal needs left them no real alternative but to grudgingly "take" just ten reales per pound. Nonetheless, when the price recovered and the reasons for which they accepted the lower-than-normal cash advance were no longer valid, they felt it their moral right to demand recompense.[36]

In a similar circumstance, the inhabitants of the jurisdiction of Papalo, subject to the *alcaldía mayor* of Teotitlán del Camino, requested and received a royal order from the Real Audiencia stipulating that their *alcalde* should allow them to pay back their cochineal debts at the "customary" payback rate of one pound for each twelve reales advanced. The *alcalde mayor*, don Luis Frejomil, had made loans at the rate of just nine reales per pound, owing to the disruption of commerce resulting from war with Portugal during the late 1760s and the belief that the "*guerrilla*" would be lengthy. The producers accepted the loans but subsequently refused to repay them at less than twelve reales. A local Spaniard explained that this was owing to the rapid resumption of trade with Spain at the war's conclusion. In a rare exhibition of regional solidarity, the indigenous governors, *alcaldes*, and elders from the entire district met and drafted a complaint against the magistrate to present to the Real Audiencia, for which they were granted the royal order. Not only did the communities of Teotitlán del Camino view the customary twelve-real rate as inviolable, but the members of the Audiencia also recognized it as the accepted and just contract price.[37]

A final example is provided from a case involving an intracommunal dispute which arose when the village *alcalde* (not the Spanish *alcalde mayor*)[38] was accused of having misused communal funds. In 1786 the people of Tepuxtepec, a Mixe-speaking town in the jurisdiction of Villa Alta, demanded that José Vasquez, who had served as village *alcalde* in 1782 and 1783, produce an account of his expenditures during his tenure. Specifically, the *"común"* claimed that Vasquez had collected cochineal from the community for village expenditures which he never made. Consequently, the community members demanded compensation for the cochineal, which weighed a total of eighty-six pounds. In their account, they valued the cochineal at 12 reales per pound, despite the fact that in 1782 the Oaxacan market price had been 17 reales per pound, and in 1783, 18 reales, and was 16.5 reales in 1786. Presumably, Vasquez sold the cochineal at the market rate, yet the community assessed the "value" of cochineal at the rate of 12 *reales* per pound; the community had come to internalize the value of a pound of cochineal at 12 reales, regardless of the world price.[39]

That the peasants viewed as legitimate the twelve-real *repartimiento* advance shows that this was a price at which they received at least limited monetary reward. This contradicts the allegation made by Oaxaca's *intendente corregidor*, Antonio de Mora y Peysal. Mora, the staunchest opponent of the system of *repartimiento*, went to considerable pains to demonstrate that the indigenous cochineal growers actually lost funds through the *repartimiento*. In 1793 Mora outlined the many expenses incurred by the growers in order to prove that the twelve reales paid to them through the *repartimiento* failed even to cover their costs.[40]

But the most convincing evidence that twelve reales afforded significant gain to the cultivators comes from the era following independence. In the 1830s, the price of cochineal in Oaxaca dropped below 12 reales and never afterward reached that earlier level. Despite the low prices, indigenous growers continued to produce large quantities of cochineal. In fact, in 1850 production climbed to 970,800 pounds, the largest quantity produced since the glorious years of the 1770s and early 1780s, despite the prevailing Oaxacan price of 5.5 reales per pound. That peasants continued to produce large quantities despite the low prices might be explained by increases in productivity or improvements in technology. There is no evidence, however, for either. Nor can this phenomenon be attributed to an increase in the coercive capacity of the financiers, who might thus have been able to extract more from the Indians. Instead, it seems rather clear that despite the depressed prices, peasants continued to bene-

105

fit from cochineal production, albeit more modestly. In the years after independence, peasants probably dreamed about the "good old days" when they received twelve reales per pound.

The Price of Exploitation

Market prices varied from year to year and even from month to month. Indian cochineal producers, however, regularly accepted a constant twelve reales as advanced payment for the future delivery of a pound of cochineal. When market prices rose, the price differential (i.e., market price minus *repartimiento* price) increased, and, consequently, so did the *alcalde mayor*'s potential profits. The peasant's income, however, remained the same. The stability of the *repartimiento* price, then, largely insulated the peasant producer from the effects of changing market conditions. Except for the rare instance when the world price fell to levels too low to permit the Spanish official to make loans at twelve reales, or when warfare blocked transatlantic shipping routes and discouraged any investment in export products altogether, the indigenous dye producer could rely on a constant rate of income for work performed. This dependability provided some security to the peasant household economy. Income from the production of cochineal was predictable, and because the dyestuff was sold in advance to the *alcalde mayor*, the peasant did not need to be concerned with the possibility of prices plummeting or face the risk that low demand would make its sale impossible. Producers were paid in advance, greatly reducing the risk of unforeseen occurrences.

Producers, however, were generally well informed about market prices and were thus aware that the pound of cochineal for which they received twelve reales was worth, at times, considerably more in the market. While occasionally peasants complained about prices, what appears to have mattered more was the continued availability of the loans at a cost considered just and fair. Most Indians needed *repartimiento* credit in order to participate in the market at significant levels. As small-scale producers, peasants also needed credit to carry them from the leaner agricultural months to the harvest. Thus, that the terms of the loans were often costly was not of the utmost importance. What mattered instead was the continued availability of the credit.

This phenomenon presents an interesting perspective on the level of "exploitation" of the *repartimiento*, in general, and of the *repartimiento* of money for the production of cochineal, specifically. By comparing the

12-real *repartimiento* price with the Oaxacan market price of cochineal in any given year, we can measure the "cost" to the producer of selling his or her cochineal in advance. Thus, in 1771, a year in which the price-per-pound of the dyestuff in Oaxaca reached a high level of 32 reales, the sale in advance to the *alcalde mayor* cost the producer 20 reales (32 − 12 = 20). At the other extreme, in 1794 the market price of cochineal dipped to a mere 10.5 reales per pound, which meant that for each pound he had contracted to receive, the *alcalde mayor* would have actually lost 1.5 reales, plus the interest he was paying on his principal.[41]

The initial conclusion seems straightforward—the *repartimiento* in 1771 was more exploitative than in 1794 because the income forgone by selling in advance was greater in 1771. Producers sold their production in 1771 for only 37.5 percent of its market value. In 1794, in contrast, Indian cochineal producers received in advance amounts greater than their output was actually worth when they repaid the Spanish official. Thus, in 1794 the *repartimiento* was not at all "exploitative."

Such a conclusion, however, oversimplifies. From the perspective of the indigenous producer, the labor employed in both years to produce a pound of cochineal was equivalent, and so was the advance price. In effect, the peasant received an equal advance for equal work. In both years, the labor required to produce one pound of cochineal earned twelve reales.

But another factor needs to be considered. In those years when the market price of dyestuff was elevated, producers realized an additional material benefit that was not immediately apparent. Producers contracted to deliver cochineal in the future to the Spanish official in exchange for a cash payment in advance. With part of this advance, peasants had to purchase the inputs needed to produce the cochineal owed to the *alcalde mayor*, but they could also, if they chose, buy additional inputs to produce additional dye, output in excess of what was contracted and owed to the Spanish official. As will be discussed below, peasants often did this, producing surplus cochineal which they sold at market prices in an "open market" parallel to the *repartimiento*. The recipient of a *repartimiento* was required to first repay the *alcalde mayor* but could then sell at the market price, often to the *alcalde mayor* himself, whatever surplus remained.

This fact complicates the discussion of relative levels of exploitation, for when the market price was high, the indigenous cochineal producer benefited by selling his or her surplus at elevated prices. Thus, in 1771 surplus dyestuff could be sold for 32 reales per pound, in comparison to

1794 when it was worth only 10.5 reales. In both years, the recipient of a *repartimiento* agreed to deliver cochineal at the rate of 12 reales per pound. The previously contracted portion of production earned the same amount, regardless of the market price. In 1771, however, each pound of surplus production earned 32 reales, much more than a surplus pound in 1794. This suggests, then, that the peasant dye producer benefited most when prices were high, in the very years when the *repartimiento* appeared most exploitative, owing to the price differential between the customary *repartimiento* rate and the actual market price.

Indians viewed the customary cochineal *repartimiento* rate of twelve reales as fair, just, and inviolable. Even when the market price per pound rose much higher, 12 reales was still accepted as the "going rate" for advance payments against future dye production. Indeed, when the price was high, many Indian producers benefited. In effect, the "twelve-real standard" rate became the regular entrance price into the credit market. Producers knew that they could receive an advance against future production, but only if they accepted the rate of twelve reales per pound.

Numerous obstacles limited trade between Indians and Spaniards, especially owing to the heavy dependence on credit of most Indians. The difficult tasks of gauging the creditworthiness of borrowers and then later collecting debts discouraged merchants from entering the market. The small size of most loans also made the trade unattractive, since one needed to secure a large number of borrowers to realize earnings sufficient to make the effort worthwhile. In addition, there was a real risk that the transaction costs of loans of such small value would consume any profitability. Finally, the cross-cultural trade of Indians and Spaniards introduced a host of uncertainties which threatened to further increase the costs of conducting business

As suggested, institutional economics urges historians to examine the institutional framework in which business is conducted. Institutions are designed to overcome obstacles to trade and to reduce the costs of transacting, doing business. The *repartimiento* was such an institution, one which helped to overcome each of the obstacles mentioned above. The *alcalde mayor* provided credit to Indians, where merchants would not, because he was in a better position to collect reliable information about potential borrowers and because he could more easily collect debts. His ability to make loans that others would not meant that the *alcalde* was assured a market size sufficient to compensate for the small profitability of each of the individual small-valued loans. He profited because of the volume of his trade. In addition, his monopoly of the credit market, a monopoly which resulted from the barriers of entry that other merchants faced, enabled him to reduce transaction costs by offering a "take-it-or-leave-it" rate of twelve reales per pound in the cochineal *repartimiento*. Contracting always at the "twelve-real standard" reduced the potentially crippling expense of negotiating thousands of small-valued loans. Finally, the "twelve-real standard" reduced the levels of uncertainty which were inherent in this cross-cultural trade and diminished the potential for costly and annoying disputes.

The cochineal *repartimiento* was designed with the intention of reducing the risks and transaction costs faced by the *alcalde mayor*. It had, however, the unintended effect of reducing the uncertainties faced by the cochineal producers as well. Producers came to see the "twelve-real standard" as the customary price and fought to guarantee that price when officials attempted to pay less. Even the Real Audiencia came to view this rate as the legitimate price for cochineal *repartimientos*.

Chapter Six

A Risky Business:
Credit and Default in the Dye Trade

T he rate of interest charged on borrowed funds in any credit market is a function of the real or perceived level of risk, among other factors. In colonial Spanish America, interest rates were artificially controlled, to a considerable extent, by the usury laws of the Catholic Church, which for all intents and purposes prohibited creditors from charging more than 5 percent. While it might have been economically rational for creditors to loan funds at the rate of 5 percent to the wealthy owner of a *hacienda* who could offer his property as collateral security, a poor peasant unable to guarantee a loan found that nobody was willing to extend credit at this bargain rate. Indians were generally perceived to be poor credit risks, and, consequently, credit at the Church-sanctioned rate of 5 percent was not made available to them.[1] Ironically, while the Church condemned as usury the business practices of the *alcaldes mayores*, the ecclesiastical bodies were far too fiscally conservative to risk their own funds in loans to the peasantry. One scholar found that some Church entities were so risk-averse that they preferred to hold their capital inactive rather than to expose themselves to even an inkling of risk.[2]

Lenders, nonetheless, succeeded in circumventing Church regulations by including the interest charge in the sale price of goods, an implicit interest charge. This practice was not new to colonial Spanish America; such transactions were commonplace in medieval and early modern Europe.[3] Peasants received their credit, but at a far higher interest rate, a rate which more accurately reflected the risk to which the lenders exposed their money.

In the conventional historiography of Spanish-American economic relations, this important risk factor is usually ignored. That *repartimiento* prices were so unfavorable to indigenous Americans is explained simply as the extortion of the Spanish authorities. Numerous examples are provided to illustrate that the *repartimiento* permitted the Spanish official to capture the output of indigenous labor at confiscatorily low prices, or to sell products from Spain, from the Spanish *haciendas*, or from other indigenous regions at ridiculously inflated prices. As John Chance put it, the *repartimiento* "more nearly resembled robbery than commerce." According to Nancy Farriss, "only the loosest definition of trade, to the point of being meaningless, could include the *repartimiento* system."[4]

That historians should so roundly condemn the system is hardly surprising. Moneylenders are often at the receiving end of harsh criticism, owing to the misperceived nature of their business activities. As a recent study of informal finance observed, "the popular view of informal finance is of powerful moneylenders who exploit the poor through usurious interest and unfair seizure of collateral." Economists now resoundingly reject such simplistic depictions and see the activities of moneylenders as far more complex and beneficial.[5] Employing some of the same criteria considered by developmental economists, this chapter will further challenge the conventional condemnation of the *repartimiento* by first explaining why the implicit interest charges collected in the *repartimiento* were so high and then demonstrating that the actual profits reaped by the *alcaldes mayores* were far lower than the high interest charges would suggest. In general, the reason that Indians paid dearly to borrow was because they were less likely to repay on time and more likely to default entirely. Given the high level of risk, Indians enjoyed few sources of credit and paid a premium to borrow. Most peasants had only the *alcalde mayor* from whom to borrow, and the *alcalde* considered such loans warranted only because he charged a high implicit rate of interest. After accounting for losses, the profitability of the *alcaldes mayores' repartimientos* was not so excessive.[6] As the study of informal finance cited above shows, "the higher rates that moneylenders and pawnbrokers charge are in large part due to the higher costs and risks associated with informal loans."[7]

Historians of colonial Spanish America have long pointed to the significant disparity between *repartimiento* prices and market prices. Charles Gibson claimed that through the *repartimiento*, "in the seventeenth century cows and mules were sold in Indian communities at profits of several hundred per cent."[8] Horst Pietschmann found the markup of *repartimiento* goods in Puebla to be 70–80 percent for livestock and 100 percent or more for other goods.[9] Robert W. Patch deduces from prices that he collected that "profits were between 68 and 132 percent of invested capital for patíes, between 44 and 122 percent for mantas, and between 33 and 100 percent for thread."[10] Such unfavorable prices, historians have

111

TABLE 6.1

Simple Gross Rate of Return on Cochineal Loans

Year	Rate of return	Year	Rate of return	Year	Rate of return	Year	Rate of return
1758	37.50%	1774	45.83%	1790	33.33%	1806	125.00%
1759	37.50%	1775	33.33%	1791	37.50%	1807	141.67%
1760	33.33%	1776	41.67%	1792	25.00%	1808	141.67%
1761	25.00%	1777	25.00%	1793	12.50%	1809	175.00%
1762	22.92%	1778	33.33%	1794	−12.50%	1810	141.67%
1763	29.17%	1779	25.00%	1795	0.00%	1811	137.50%
1764	62.50%	1780	41.67%	1796	45.83%	1812	66.67%
1765	54.17%	1781	41.67%	1797	29.17%	1813	25.00%
1766	62.50%	1782	41.67%	1798	50.00%	1814	108.33%
1767	62.50%	1783	50.00%	1799	62.50%	1815	100.00%
1768	87.50%	1784	33.33%	1800	58.33%	1816	166.67%
1769	104.17%	1785	41.67%	1801	50.00%	1817	141.67%
1770	108.33%	1786	37.50%	1802	58.33%	1818	137.50%
1771	166.67%	1787	33.33%	1803	75.00%	1819	129.17%
1772	150.00%	1788	33.33%	1804	137.50%	1820	133.33%
1773	112.50%	1789	29.17%	1805	91.67%	1821	91.67%

SOURCE: Calculated from data in Appendix A.

argued, yielded enormous profits to officials and served to further impoverish the peasantry.

Undoubtedly, a cursory look at the *repartimiento* for the production of cochineal would also suggest enormous "profits." *Alcaldes mayores*, in partnership with their merchant backers, did buy cochineal from Indian producers at prices which were nearly always well below the market price. By subtracting twelve reales, the normal advance received by Indian dye producers, from the market price of cochineal in Oaxaca for each year, one can calculate the simple gross rate of return realized on the *alcalde*'s investment, his decision to extend a loan.[11] The results of this calculation are presented in Table 6.1 for the period 1758–1821.

Several major trends are observable from the data. During the ten-year period running from 1764 to 1773, the simple returns accruing to the *alcalde mayor* and his partners in the cochineal *repartimiento* rose sharply relative to the years directly before and after. Between 1792 and 1795 profits in the cochineal *repartimiento* plummeted, and the trade ceased to produce returns in the last two years. Finally, at the turn of the century, potential simple gross rates of return rebounded sharply, reaching an apex in 1809. Over the entire period 1759–1821, the average simple gross rate of return per pound of cochineal contracted by the *alcaldes mayores* through the *repartimiento* was 70 percent, or 8.36 reales. Perhaps more instructive, the median simple return was 50 percent, or 6 reales.

At first glance, the profitability of the dye *repartimiento* seems abundant. Such a conclusion, however, is hasty. As will be demonstrated, the net profits and annual rate of return enjoyed by the company of the *alcalde mayor* and his financiers were much lower than the data in Table 6.1 might lead one to suspect. The reason that the profitability of the *repartimientos* have been exaggerated is simple: historians have typically pointed to the gross profits reaped on only one or two individual transactions and have incorrectly jumped to conclusions from there. For example, when Gibson noted that "in the seventeenth century cows and mules were sold in Indian communities at profits of several hundred per cent," he was confusing the markup of this merchandise with net profit.[12] Gibson neither considered the expenses that the *alcalde* and his partners incurred, nor the possibility that some of the debts went uncollected. To gauge more accurately the returns realized, operating costs as well as the interest due on borrowed capital (or interest income forgone, if using personal funds) would have to be taken into account. In addition, one would have to account for losses, especially in the cochineal industry in which an extremely high proportion of the loans proved uncollectible and the collection of the many loans that were eventually repaid involved long delays and much effort. When one considers these expenses, the result is a return on total investment far below the return on many of the more profitable transactions.[13]

The *repartimiento* existed, in part, because only the justice-wielding *alcaldes mayores* felt sufficiently secure to extend loans to the general Indian population. It was to take advantage of this political power that Mexico's powerful merchants joined forces with the *alcaldes mayores* for the joint exploitation of a region. Yet, even the *alcalde*'s ability to employ judicial authority was not sufficient to eradicate risk and guarantee debt collection. While the officials could reduce risk to what was usually a profitable level, they too proved unable to collect many debts. The sheer number of surviving references to unpaid or uncollectible loans leaves no doubt that the *cobranza*, the collection of the contracted debts, was extremely difficult. In fact, it is partially owing to the large number of defaults on *repartimiento* loans that so much information about *repartimientos* can be reconstructed.[14] Unpaid debts eroded sharply the net returns, the actual profits, that the functionaries and their partners enjoyed on their overall investments.

Risk was further inherent in the production of cochineal, which was particularly vulnerable to unfavorable weather. A sudden, unexpected rainfall or an unusually windy afternoon were often sufficient to destroy an entire harvest of cochineal fattening in a peasant's *nopalera*. As a result, producers frequently found themselves without any dyestuff when the *alcalde mayor* or his *teniente* circulated to collect the outstanding debts. Bad weather, however, was the least of the *alcalde*'s concerns. Much more troublesome was the frequent evasion of payment by debtors, and this extended to non-cochineal *repartimientos* as well. Often peasants contracted *repartimientos* and then used the entire loan for purposes other than cochineal production. Alternatively, they concealed their output from the *alcalde mayor* with the intention of selling it later at a higher price.

The Spanish officials could and did use their judicial authority to try and collect debts, but they still failed to collect much of what was owed to them. Imprisoning a debtor in hope of forcing the debtor's family to find some way of meeting an outstanding debt was not uncommon, but the large percentage of cases in which debtors spent extended periods in jail would suggest that this had only limited effect. Prison probably served more as a stimulus to others to pay promptly. The *alcalde mayor* sometimes also confiscated the delinquent borrower's personal goods, hoping to recover his funds, but this too produced limited results since most peasants possessed little of marketable value.[15]

When the *alcalde mayor* believed that a peasant in default was sincere in his or her attempts to pay, two realistic options were available to the unpaid official. Either he could simply write off the loan as a loss, or he could extend another production loan to the cochineal producer in the hope of collecting both the original and the new debt at the next harvest. This second option was common, according to the Oaxacan *alcaldes mayores* who responded to the questionnaire about the *repartimiento* circulated by the Viceroy in 1752. The *alcaldes* from Ixtepeji, Zimatlán-Chichicapa, Miahuatlán, Teotitlán del Camino, and Tehuantepec all reported that when harvests failed and they were unable to collect the *grana* owed to them, they were usually forced to risk still more capital in order to refinance the producers, hoping to recoup the entire debt at the following harvest.[16] The Conde de Tepa referred to this practice among Mexican officials who made *repartimiento* loans for the production of cotton as well as cochineal.[17] No matter how hard an *alcalde mayor* tried, however, some loans were never collected, often because his term in office ended before all of his debts could be collected. The official of Nexapa estimated that in his district the *alcalde mayor* usually had in the neighborhood of twenty thousand pesos still outstanding at the termination of his five-year term.[18] And while outgoing officials were sometimes able to strike deals with their successors to help collect debts still outstanding, they did so at a steep discount.

While the *alcaldes mayores* were much better equipped to collect debts than private merchants were, at times they too were overmatched. The desperate request for help in collecting cochineal debts written in October 1769 by don José Molina, the *alcalde mayor* of Villa Alta, to the Viceroy of New Spain, don Carlos Francisco de Croix, provides insight into the *alcalde*'s difficult task of managing his loans. Molina complained that it was common for him and fellow officials to have to wait for two to three years to collect a debt, and that when a producer's cochineal harvest failed, they were frequently left with no option but to provide a new loan in the hope that the entire amount would be repaid in the following harvest. The shrewd *alcalde*, wrote Molina, had to be vigilant in his loan distribution and debt collection or face bankruptcy. This, Molina noted, involved choosing carefully to whom to lend funds, assuring that the loan recipient truly had a *nopalera*, a cactus grove, ready for introduction of the "*semilla*," the pregnant cochineal insects, and confirming that the funds were actually employed in the production of the dyestuff. It was not uncommon, wrote Molina, for producers to use the loans for other purposes, only to hide when the debt collector circulated at harvest time. Finally, stated Molina, collecting debts had become especially difficult as of late, due to the high market price of three pesos (24 reales) per pound of cochineal. The high price, claimed the *alcalde mayor*, encouraged many producers to sell their cochineal in Oaxaca or to traveling merchants, rather than to deliver it to him as contracted.[19] The Viceroy responded sympathetically to Molina's request for help by sending an envoy to Villa Alta; the envoy visited each of the twenty-three towns in which Molina's borrowers lived and obtained pledges from them that the loans would be repaid in the following May 1770 cochineal harvest. The case ended with these promises, and the issue does not reappear in other documents, which may suggest that Molina eventually did collect most of what was owed to him. Nonetheless, by then payment had been delayed an additional year, further reducing Molina's rate of return on the funds he had loaned. The official's principal had also ceased to circulate for another year. It had failed to produce additional revenues and had cut into his profits.[20] Despite his considerable efforts to screen and monitor his borrowers, Molina still faced considerable difficulties collecting his debts.

Doña Eugenia García de Najera was also forced to request the Viceroy's help in collecting debts outstanding from the cochineal *repartimientos* made by her husband, don Juan Benito de Muedra, who died while serving as *alcalde mayor* in the district of Zimatlán. Doña Eugenia complained that the Indians who had received the loans were using the death of her husband as an excuse not to complete their contracts.[21]

One receives an almost comical impression of the peasants' *repartimiento* debt evasion from the anti-*repartimiento* testimony presented in 1784 by Antonio Porley, the parish priest of Ayoquesco. Porley condemned the Spanish official of his district, the *corregimiento* of Oaxaca, for employing great violence in the collection of debts. According to the priest, many of the indebted Indians were fearful of being arrested by the *teniente* and, consequently, fled the village and hid in the mountains whenever there was news of the official's pending arrival in the village. This had worked, apparently, until the *alcalde mayor* appeared on Ash Wednesday without any prior warning, rounding up some of the debtors before they could flee. Another new trick of the debt collectors was to arrive unannounced at night when, as Porley noted, many debtors returned to the village believing that the cover of darkness would provide them safety. In the past, the *teniente* would visit the village to collect debts only on Monday, Tuesday, and Wednesday, and this provided the debtors relief from their concealment between Thursday and Sunday. Now, however, the *alcalde* had stationed a permanent collector in the village, and so debtors had no alternative than to remain hidden until the *alcalde*'s term in office expired. Of course, another alternative would have been to pay the *alcalde mayor*. Why the peasants of Ayoquesco went to such great extremes not to pay is unclear. Perhaps they lacked the cochineal; yet one cannot help but wonder whether they resisted repayment because they knew that they could get away with it. What is certain, however, is that their evasion was expensive and a nuisance for the official. His frequent visits to the village cost him time and money.[22]

Even when debts were collected, it was often only after great investment of time and effort on the part of the Spanish official. In 1788, for example, Bernardo Antonio, an Indian and ex-governor of Santa María Tepoxco in the jurisdiction of Teotitlán del Camino, issued a complaint

116

against his *alcalde mayor*, don Manuel José López, who he said had ordered his arrest for a *repartimiento* debt contracted five years earlier. Beginning in 1782, Antonio, on behalf of his village, had secured a cash loan to produce 155 pounds of cochineal. Of this amount, Antonio had already repaid his *alcalde mayor* for 142 pounds, 4 ounces, leaving an outstanding debt of just 12 pounds, 12 ounces. According to the account supplied by *alcalde mayor* López, however, Antonio had repaid him in eighteen separate installments, spread over the course of six years from 1782 to 1787. López had waited six years and still had not succeeded in collecting the entire outstanding debt. Furthermore, the amount he did receive came in eighteen separate payments, which required the same number of transactions and probably many more visits to the village and house of Bernardo Antonio, very costly in both time and effort. *Alcalde mayor* López loaned Antonio a total of 232.5 pesos to deliver 155 pounds of cochineal. Had Bernardo paid promptly, the *alcalde* would have enjoyed a gross profit of 33 percent, given that the Oaxacan market price of cochineal in that year was 16 reales per pound. Thus, the 232.5 pesos invested would have produced 310 pesos. In reality, however, López had to wait over six years for at least a portion of the repayment, making his real return on the investment much lower. If one were to assess and deduct the transaction costs of the eighteen separate payments, the net return would be lower still. Had *repartimiento* interest been charged explicitly (at a fixed interest rate), then the loan to Antonio would have continued to accrue interest. This was not the case, however, and no additional interest was collected by the *alcalde mayor*. Instead, part of *alcalde mayor* López's principal was out of circulation, failing to earn any return at all and costing him at least 5 percent to carry.[23]

The practice of repaying debts little by little was not unique to Bernardo Antonio. Father Porley of Ayoquesco reported that *repartimiento* debts were often repaid a bit at a time. According to the priest, the debtor who failed to pay at least half a pound or one peso each week risked being tossed in prison. Evidently, the *alcalde mayor* was content to be repaid in installments. It was better than default.[24]

A less detailed yet potentially more persuasive picture is presented by a 1765 case involving the *alcalde mayor* of Nexapa, don Faustino Manero. In March of that year Manero paid ten thousand pesos to the incoming *alcalde mayor*, don Gabriel Gutierrez de Ruvalcava, who agreed in return to delay his scheduled assumption of the position of *alcalde mayor* of Nexapa until late July. In the contract, Manero wrote that he needed the extra months to collect cochineal and other debts owed to him by the inhabitants of his jurisdiction, some of whom were presently incarcerated for their debts. Unfortunately, the contract did not specify the total value of Manero's outstanding debts, but obviously it must have been a very sizeable amount. Certainly Manero would not have agreed to pay Gutierrez ten thousand pesos unless the outstanding debts were significantly higher, especially since Manero was having difficulty collecting the funds and would probably never recover some portion of them. The clear conclusion from this evidence is that Manero had loaned a considerable amount, incurred tremendous risks, and would fail to collect some of his outstanding capital. Whether he realized any net return at all is unclear, but certainly the ten-thousand-peso payment greatly reduced the profit that the *alcalde mayor* had hoped to receive.[25]

Manero's successor, don Gabriel Gutierrez de Ruvalcava, also was owed a large amount at the close of his tenure. On 6 October 1770, Gutierrez wrote to the Viceroy, the Marques de Croix, advising him that because of a severe crisis in Nexapa, he had been unable to collect many of his cochineal debts, which he estimated to total five hundred arrobas (12,500 pounds). The *alcalde mayor* placed the value of these debts at nineteen thousand pesos since all but a few of the loans had been extended at the customary rate of twelve reales. Fearful that he would lose much of his principal, Gutierrez proposed to split evenly with the royal treasury both the nineteen thousand pesos and whatever net profit could be obtained from the sale of the cochineal in Veracruz. Gutierrez requested only that the Viceroy allow him to prolong his authority in Nexapa so that he could collect his outstanding receivables in the following harvest. The Viceroy rejected the scheme, intimating that the king did not accept bribes, and told Gutierrez that he would have to depend on the benevolence of his successor, an honest man, who would collect for Gutierrez whatever he could.[26]

Lending funds for the production of cochineal was a risky business. The potential gross profit on any individual transaction could be large, but the real overall profit on *repartimiento* loans was much lower. Twelve reales advanced might double in six months, or it might be lost forever, joining the many loans classified by the *alcaldes mayores* as *incobrables*, "uncollectible." Only by considering the combined outcome of all of these individual transactions, from the easily collected, to the delayed, to the uncollectible, can the real rate of return be calculated on the credit-providing activities of an *alcalde mayor*.

Unfortunately for the historian attempting to reconstruct the business dealings of the *alcaldes mayores*, the personal account books of these Spanish officials entered rarely into the public domain. Individual unpaid debts frequently resulted in imprisonment, and subsequent public investigations shed light on these *repartimiento* transactions. The *alcalde*'s complete records, however, remained in his private and personal possession. Nonetheless, several such detailed account books were located, and one set of these records can be used to approximate the real return enjoyed by *alcaldes mayores* from *repartimientos* for the production of cochineal dye.

The book used for the estimated calculations below, which dates from the early 1780s, belonged to the *alcalde mayor* of the cochineal-rich district of Teposcolula in the Mixteca Alta, Francisco Rojas y Rocha.[27] It was chosen over others because the *alcalde mayor* of Teposcolula kept more detailed records of his loans, including both the dates on which many of the loans were made and repaid. Most of the loans recorded in the ledger were extended by the magistrate himself, but some portion of the debts were owed to his predecessor, José Mariano de Cardenas, and passed onto Rojas for possible collection upon the termination of Cardenas's tenure. In all, Rojas's records indicate loans of approximately 3,951.72 pesos against the future delivery of 2,723.13 pounds of cochineal, for an average advance payment of 11.6 reales per pound.[28] As of 13 February 1784, the last date on which an entry in the book was made, *alcalde mayor* Rojas had collected 32.55 percent of the contracted debts, or 886.39 pounds (or equivalent payments in coin) possessing a market value of approximately 1,877.34 pesos, based on the corresponding annual price per pound recorded at the Oaxacan cochineal Registry. After 13 February 1784, no further entries were made, suggesting that this ledger was probably a copy of the magistrate's records made shortly thereafter.

Of the 2,723.13 pounds contracted to be produced, the entries in the account book include dates on 67.47 percent, or 1,837.19 pounds. These dated entries can be used to approximate the potential rate of gross return on the *alcalde*'s commercial dealings. So as not to bias the results downward, the loans which were passed to *alcalde mayor* Rojas by his predecessor were omitted. Many of these loans, all of which had been outstanding for more than 3.5 years, would probably never be collected, but, in any event, they would not have impacted the profitability of Rojas's money-lending since these uncollected debts were his predecessor's losses, not his. Excluding his predecessor's loans, then, the official of Teposcolula's loans totaled 1,551.78 pesos against 1,074.50 pounds of dyestuff (an average of 11.55 reales per pound). By 13 February 1784, he had already collected 352.55 pounds, or just under 16 percent of the cochineal due. Of the

TABLE 6.2
Length of Time *Repartimiento* Loans Outstanding
(Teposcolula, 1781–1784)

Length of time outstanding	Number of loans	Pounds out- standing	As percentage of total outstanding		Sum	Years outstanding
0–6 months	7	42.00	4.6%	↘		
6–9 months	8	148.56	16.4%	→	29.4%	0–1.0
9 months–1 year	2	75.75	8.4%	↗		
1–1.5 years	0	0	0%			
1.5–2 years	4	244.63	27.0%	↘		
2–2.5 years	7	138.50	15.3%	→	50.7%	1.5–3.0
2.5–3 years	6	76.31	8.4%	↗		
More than 3 years	13	179.78	19.9%	→	19.9%	3+ years
TOTALS	50	905.53	100.00%		100.00%	

SOURCE: Derived from AGN, Archivo Histórico de Hacienda, Real Administración de Alcabalas, cajita no. 43.

loans still outstanding, several were recent advances, three of which were made on that very day. The overwhelming majority, however, were debts long overdue.

In Table 6.2 these outstanding debts (the 84 percent yet to be collected, for which we have the loan date) are broken down by the length of time outstanding. Of these debts, 70.6 percent had been contracted more than 1.5 years earlier and had been uncollectible at the harvests in which they were due. Nearly 20 percent were debts contracted more than three years earlier. While it is impossible to know what percentage of these cochineal debts were ultimately collected by the *alcalde mayor*, certainly some were uncollectible. This, at least, was the opinion of *alcalde mayor* Rojas. Beneath some of the book's entries, comments were added, presumably by the *alcalde* or his *teniente*, and they reveal their opinion of the likelihood of collection. Some of these comments are reproduced in Table 6.3. These debts were probably never collected. The tone of the comments suggests that the *alcalde mayor* had resolved not even to bother pressuring for them, despite the fact that two were for large amounts, far in excess of the average cochineal loan.

TABLE 6.3
Alcalde Mayor's Assessment of Outstanding Debts

Name of debtor	Comment	Amount of debt
María Alvarez	Deceased, lost.	4 lbs.
María Vizente	Claims to have already paid.	1 lb.
J. Cruz y común	Denied. Alcalde's records not believed.	53 lbs., 3 oz.
Felipe Bernave	Denied. Claims he paid.	0.5 lbs.
Juan Cayetano	Difficult as debtor is a real swindler.	74 lbs.

SOURCE: AGN, Archivo Histórico de Hacienda, Real Administración de Alcabalas, cajita no. 43.

In order to more accurately assess the profitability of *repartimiento* moneylending, both an upper- and a lower-bound estimate[29] of this *alcalde mayor*'s gross profits will be calculated. For the upper-bound estimate, it will be assumed that the *alcalde* succeeded in collecting every debt, the entire 1,074.5 pounds. This assumption is made so that the maximum possible rate of gross return on the official's commercial dealings can be calculated. In contrast, the lower-bound estimate will assume that some portion of the overdue debts went uncollected. These two calculations will provide a rough estimate of the minimum and maximum gross profits realized by this *alcalde mayor* in these particular years.

To compute the upper-bound rate of gross return on the total of all the debts for which dates were available, an imaginary date was chosen for ultimate repayment of all outstanding debts. For this procedure, it was optimistically assumed that *alcalde mayor* Rojas succeeded in collecting all the outstanding cochineal in the upcoming harvest of May 1784, which was three months after his account book ends. Thus, 1 May 1784 was used as the collection date for all debts still outstanding when the account book was prepared. The dates used for all other debts were the actual dates upon which these debts were paid. All of the data corresponding to these loans are reproduced in Appendixes C.1 and C.2, including the name of the borrower, the dates, the time outstanding, the contract terms, the repayment data, and the computed annual[30] gross return of the individual transactions.[31]

Using 1 May 1784 as the closing date for these transactions, the annualized gross returns on the individual transactions range from a high of 237.63 percent on a debt repaid in just two months to a low of just over 10 percent for debts outstanding in excess of three years.[32] The aggregate annualized gross rate of return on all of these *repartimiento* transactions was 22.51 percent. In simpler terms, this meant that on average for each 100 pesos the *alcalde mayor* loaned, he collected in money or cochineal a total of 122.51 pesos one year later.[33]

A lower-bound estimate can be calculated by predicting that some percentage of the outstanding debts proved uncollectible, not unreasonable given both the length that some debts were overdue and the opinions of the *alcalde mayor* as to the likelihood of collection. For this purpose, let us suppose that all debts not yet overdue,[34] and 75 percent of the debts already past due were collected on 1 May 1784, and that the remaining 25 percent of delinquent debts were never collected.[35] Under these revised conditions, the annualized gross return of the Spanish official dropped to 11 percent, indicating that *alcalde mayor* Rojas's moneylending business was only marginally profitable after he paid the interest due on the principal he had borrowed in order to enter the business (see Appendix C.2 for detailed data).

The gross returns calculated for the *alcalde mayor* of Teposcolula were in line with claims made by eighteenth-century defenders of the *repartimiento*. In 1790, for instance, the *subdelegado* of Villa Alta estimated that prior to his tenure the average return on capital invested by Spanish officials in his wealthy district was approximately 24 percent, before accounting for losses due to uncollectible debts.[36] Similarly, the deputies of commerce of Oaxaca placed the return on *repartimientos* at 15–20 percent, losses included.[37] Brading reported similar results. He calculated the return on the capital invested by the *alcalde mayor* of the Oaxacan coastal province of Xicayan for the years 1781 to 1784 at around 20 percent.[38] Finally, Ouweneel estimated the returns of the *alcalde mayor* of Zacatlán to be 8–13 percent on his *repartimiento* of bulls.[39]

It is essential to understand that the rates of return estimated for the Teposcolulan magistrate are gross returns. They fail to account for the many other expenses he incurred. These estimated gross rates of return merely indicate that in the period 1780–1784, *alcalde mayor* Rojas on average collected yearly in revenues between 11 and 22.5 percent more than he loaned. Net profits (revenues minus expenses) were clearly lower.

When one deducts, for example, the cost of carrying the principal, the typical 5 percent interest payments on borrowed loans, the rate of return earned annually by the *alcalde mayor* for these years drops to 6 percent and 17.5 percent, depending on the level of default assumed. In addition, these returns fail to account for the salaries paid to the *tenientes* charged with collecting debts, nor do they include the costs incurred in setting up his offices and business. Including such costs would reduce further the return on the *alcalde mayor*'s *repartimiento* loans.[40]

By employing basic accounting procedures to measure the economic returns accruing to *alcalde mayor* Rojas of Teposcolula, we have shown that the profits typically attributed to the Spanish officials are grossly exaggerated. In the case of this official's *repartimientos*, estimated returns ranged from 11 to 22.5 percent per year before deducting administrative costs and the payment of interest on borrowed funds. Such returns were not excessive. Given the extreme riskiness of his investments, they were surprisingly modest. Certainly, *alcaldes mayores* and their financial backers who earned such returns must usually have considered their efforts well compensated or they would not have invested and exposed their capital in the first place. These rates are far lower, however, than those typically attributed to these Spanish officials.

Risk is a crucial element that must be considered when studying any credit system. In the *repartimiento*, risks were high. Consequently, rates of return on some of the individual transactions needed also to be high to warrant exposing funds to possible loss. The delays (and defaults) involved with the *repartimiento* loans made for the production of cochineal were sufficiently common to erode dramatically the average rates of return enjoyed by the *alcalde mayor*.

Nonetheless, returns on capital of the magnitude realized by the *alcalde mayor* of Teposcolula were considerably higher than those enjoyed in many colonial Mexican enterprises. David Brading estimated the profit rates on a number of different ventures, none of which exceeded 10 percent. Two *haciendas*, Chapingo and Ojo de Agua, generated returns of 5.6 and 7 percent, respectively, for the years 1800–1805. According to the 1866 work of Francisco Pimentel, which Brading cites, *haciendas* in Mexico normally earned less than 6 percent per year on capital invested. This is further corroborated by the performance of Jesuit properties in Mexico, which while known for their efficient operation, enjoyed returns of less than 4 percent.[41] Nor were Jesuit estates in other parts of Spanish America much more profitable. Nicholas P. Cushner estimated the profit rate on a Jesuit *hacienda* in Peru to have averaged around 5.8 percent for the period 1691–1766.[42]

The merchant house of the wealthy Fagoaga family, the same family who, Brading wrote, "could lay claim to the leadership of the Mexican

123

silver industry,"[43] was not able to earn even as much as the typical *hacienda* on many of its investments. In 1758, for example, the family invested more than 317,000 pesos to purchase, pay taxes on, and transport supplies from that year's *flota*. The merchandise took three years to sell and generated revenues of 346,771 pesos, a return over the period of 9.3 percent, or an average of only 3.1 percent per year.[44]

Periodic inventories of the Fagoaga family's investments indicated that the return on the investment of their capital was not great; it was modest to poor. For the period December 1736 to January 1757, the net return on investment was 5.6 percent. Between February 1762 and January 1770, the net profit rate was only 4.4 percent. Finally, the family enjoyed net returns on investments for the period January 1770 to March 1781 of a paltry 2.1 percent.[45]

In comparison to the experiences of the wealthy and politically connected Fagoaga family, then, the returns enjoyed by *alcalde mayor* Rojas of Teposcolula were fairly good. The Spanish official's *repartimiento* dealings yielded gross profits of 22.5 percent before defaults. Even after deduction of costs, debt service, and the almost certain default by some borrowers, the official realized returns on principal greater than would have been possible in many other ventures. His profits were not, however, phenomenal, especially when one considers the high level of risk to which he exposed his capital.

Oaxacan officials arrived at their posts well financed by wealthy merchants or hefty Church loans. With these funds, they had five years to benefit from the dye trade, to use these funds to purchase cochineal at low prices and sell it for a gain. Undoubtedly, most found their new positions to be lucrative. The post of *alcalde mayor* in a cochineal-producing region of Oaxaca was by far the most sought after in New Spain, and for good reason: large profits were obtainable by the vigilant and cautious investor.[46] It is, however, incorrect to suggest that the *alcaldes'* business dealings were "robbery" or that they earned inordinately large returns on their investments. If the implicit interest rates on *repartimiento* transactions were high, it was because only high interest rates could justify the risks of these loans. This was probably best described by the Tribunal del Consulado in its 1794 defense of the *repartimiento*. In response to those who condemned the system, the *consulado* argued that the system was only "unjust" to those who paid their debts promptly, because on these transactions the *alcalde mayor* realized very high returns. As the merchant guild noted, however, another large percentage of *repartimiento* recipients paid late or defaulted, and on these loans the *alcalde mayor* earned little and lost much. The *alcalde mayor* offered the same price (and charged the same implicit interest rate) to both in order to cancel out the bad debts with good ones.[47] While many of the transactions were very profitable to the *alcalde*, average rates of return were much lower, because of loans that proved uncollectible and the long delays involved with collecting many others.

There is additional evidence to suggest that the profitability of *repartimientos* was not so exceptionally high. We have the surviving records of Sebastian de Labayru, an *alcalde mayor* of Miahuatlán who died in office during the mid-1770s. His records indicate that in addition to the *repartimiento*, through which normally he advanced twelve reales against the future delivery of each pound of cochineal,[48] Labayru and his agents also purchased cochineal in the local Miahuatlán markets at "*precios corrientes*," the going market prices. In most harvests, some producers inevitably harvested more cochineal than they were required to deliver to the *alcalde* in payment of their contracted debts, and this surplus was sold in local markets, just like any other surplus production. In addition, some wealthier peasants financed their own production of cochineal, selling their entire output in the "free market." During his years as *alcalde mayor*, 1772–1776, Labayru's *tenientes* bought large quantities of this additional *grana*, paying prices that ranged from sixteen to twenty-eight reales per pound, well above the standard *repartimiento* price of twelve reales per pound. In total, Labayru's ledger indicates that during these five years he invested outside of the *repartimiento* roughly 138,837 pesos to purchase 54,092 pounds, an average of 2.57 pesos (20.5 reales) per pound. *Repartimiento* acquisitions during the same years delivered another 96,610 pounds and cost Labayru 145,303 pesos, an average price of twelve reales per pound. These data are summarized in Table 6.4. By employing individuals to purchase cochineal in the Miahuatlán markets, Labayru perhaps hoped to make a few reales per pound reselling the dye in Oaxaca, although this proved less than profitable during the final three years, in two of which Labayru's agents evidently bought much of the dye during months in which the price was high and, consequently, paid more than the year's average price at the Oaxacan registry. At the very least, Labayru increased the quantity that he could send to Veracruz for export. Labayru probably hoped that the prices would return to the levels reached in 1772 and before. And the fact that *grana* did not spoil permitted merchants to wait out periods of depressed prices. Regardless, one cannot help but conclude that the dye trade was highly speculative.[49]

125

TABLE 6.4

Cochineal Purchased by the *Alcalde Mayor* of Miahuatlán, 1772–1776

Year	Pounds bought in market	Pesos paid in market	Pesos per pound paid in market	Average Oaxaca price per pound	Pounds bought in repartimiento	Pesos paid in repartimiento	Pesos per pound repartimiento
1772	8,157	25,872	3.17	3.75	21,792	32,908	1.51
1773	7,110	21,191	2.98	3.19	22,074	33,110	1.50
1774	11,549	29,993	2.60	2.19	23,547	35,444	1.51
1775	11,281	28,332	2.51	2.00	16,621	24,977	1.50
1776	15,995	33,449	2.09	2.13	12,576	18,864	1.50
TOTALS	54,092	138,837	2.57	2.65	96,610	145,303	1.50

SOURCE: AGN, Tierras, vol. 1037, exp. 2, pp. 81, 85, 88v, 95v, 102; Appendix A, this volume.

Why, though, would Labayru pay as much as twenty-eight reales for a pound of cochineal when he could obtain the same one pound for just twelve reales through the *repartimiento?* The answer is simple. The purchase of cochineal at the market price required no prolonged outlay of funds but was a transaction started and completed quickly. Labayru faced much less risk with his capital, enjoyed greater liquidity, and was nearly guaranteed a rapid, albeit modest, return if he chose to sell in Oaxaca. In contrast, had he loaned twelve reales for the future delivery of a pound of cochineal, he might have had to wait two, three, or more years for repayment and might never have been repaid. The *alcalde mayor* of Zimatlán, Yldefonso María Sanchez Solache, made this very argument in 1784. Buying cochineal at harvest time at the *precios corrientes*, Solache suggested, was often more profitable than the *repartimiento*, since one avoided the risks of exposing money to lengthy and difficult collections or even total loss.[50]

Perhaps Solache was exaggerating. Yet one cannot help but conclude that there must have been years in which the risk of exposing funds exceeded much of the potential benefit of extending *repartimiento* loans. Why, then, did the officials and their merchant backers continue to expose their principal to such great risks rather than simply buy the finished cochineal at market prices? In all likelihood, the *repartimiento* was usually profitable and produced windfall profits in certain years. Regardless, by contracting to receive cochineal from the indigenous producers, the *alcalde mayor* guaranteed himself a regular supply of dyestuff. Had he supplied himself solely through purchases at harvest time, he would have had to compete with itinerant peddlers, who might have been able to undercut him because of their lower administrative costs. Furthermore, without the financing of the *repartimiento*, total production of dye would have been much lower. After all, many peasants needed the financing to permit them to produce cochineal, and other peasants only produced it because in doing so they gained access to credit. In short, extending loans through the *repartimiento* guaranteed the *alcalde mayor* a dependable, large supply of cochineal.[51]

Chapter Seven

Indians and Markets

Because moneylending was risky and repayment often delayed, don Sebastian de Labayru, the *alcalde mayor* of Miahuatlán, considered it a worthy investment to purchase dye at the *precio corriente*. Far from extraordinary, this seems to have been a normal practice for the Spanish officials. In the Viceroy's 1752 investigation into the *repartimiento*, several *alcaldes mayores* from cochineal-producing districts of Oaxaca responded that they not only purchased *grana* from the indigenous producers through loans against future production, the *repartimiento*, but they also bought very significant quantities in the local markets at current market prices. Table 7.1 shows the quantities purchased by a number of *alcaldes mayores* through both the *repartimiento* and at the market price.[1]

Between 23 and 42 percent of the cochineal by weight that the *alcaldes mayores* purchased was bought in local markets at the existing market price. While some of this was undoubtedly cochineal that *repartimiento* recipients produced in excess of their obligations and then sold on the "open market," it also suggests rather strongly that a significant percentage of Indian producers were sufficiently well off to be able to produce dyestuff without relying on the financing of the *repartimiento*. These latter individuals were able to purchase necessary inputs without credit from the *alcalde mayor*. Without obligations to the Spanish official, they could sell their finished product entirely on the "open market." That many chose to sell directly to the *alcalde mayor* need not be viewed as suspicious. There were advantages of convenience and economy in selling to the largest and most local consumer. In fact, much additional cochineal did circumvent the *alcalde mayor*, to be sold in local markets or to itinerant merchants who were either independent peddlers or the agents of Oaxacan merchants. Joaquín Vasco, a friar from Santa María Ecatepec in the district of Nexapa, estimated in 1776 that in his district half of the cochineal was

TABLE 7.1

Cochineal Bought in Market versus *Repartimiento* by Year

Alcaldía mayor	In repartimiento	*In market*	Percentage bought in market
Ixtepeji in 1752	4,000 pesos	2,000 pesos	varied
Nexapa in 1752	700–800 arrobas	400–500 arrobas	33–42%
Teotitlán del Camino in 1752	400–500 arrobas	150–200 arrobas	23–33%
Miahuatlán–Labayru in 1770s	773 arrobas	433 arrobas	36%

SOURCE: AGN, Subdelegados, vol. 34; AGN, Tierras, vol. 1037, exp. 2, pp. 78–81.

bought by the *alcalde* through the *repartimiento* and the rest was pur-chased by merchants at the market price.[2]

Self-financed peasants were not the only producers who sold cochineal on the open market. Some indigenous producers who received *reparti-miento* loans harvested sufficient cochineal not only to deliver their con-tracted quantities to the *alcalde mayor*, but also to sell surplus production on the open market. While production was certainly risky, in most years, cochineal was harvested, *repartimiento* debts were repaid, and producers were left with additional dye which they could market on their own. This last point is important because it suggests that at least some producers benefited from cochineal production beyond what they earned through the receipt of *repartimiento* loans. Potentially, producers who sold surplus dye in the market could enjoy substantial profits.

A brief review of the production process is instructive. The cochineal insect is parasitic to the *nopal* cactus. By inserting its proboscis through the cactus wall, the insect feeds on nutrients inside the *nopal*. Cochineal dye producers built small "nests," usually made of corn husks or palm leaves, into each of which they placed around twenty-five pregnant fe-males. One nest was then attached to each cactus leaf. Upon hatching, the insects left the nest and spread out over the entire leaf, inserting their feed-ing devices into the cactus. Over the next four or five months, the insects fattened while the producer attempted to protect them from natural ene-mies. Next, the producer harvested the cochineal by carefully brushing the

129

insects off the cactus and into a container. Finally, the cochineal insects were killed by drowning, heating, or suffocation, and then dried for sale.[3]

The yield of cochineal harvested for each pound of cochineal "seeded," placed in nests on the cactus, differed depending on area, climate, soil quality, and irrigation. José Antonio Alzate, the eighteenth-century scientist, noted that in Nexapa one pound of "seed" could produce forty-eight pounds of cochineal insects when conditions were favorable, but that the yield in Zimapán and other parts of the Mixteca was lower.[4] Another source placed the output produced by one pound of seed at twenty-five pounds.[5] A present-day producer of cochineal in Oaxaca reports that thirty females produce nine grams of harvested insects, which computes to approximately forty-seven pounds yielded per pound of seed, in line with the eighteenth-century estimates.[6]

The standard contract made with the *alcalde mayor* required that for each twelve reales advanced, the producer had to deliver 1 pound of *grana seca*, dried cochineal. After being killed, the insects were dried in the sun or by application of heat. During this process the weight of the cochineal decreased by one-third to two-thirds.[7] Acting conservatively, if we accept 66 percent, two-thirds, as the amount of shrinkage, then 1 pound of pregnant females placed in a *nopalera* produced between 8 and 16 pounds of dried cochineal, based on the above biological yields.[8] A bit more conservative, Thomas Carillo, a priest in Miahuatlán, estimated in 1752 that 1 arroba of seed placed in the *nopalera* produced 4 arrobas of *grana seca*, a ratio of 1:4.[9] In short, available estimates suggest that 1 pound introduced could yield between 4 and 16 pounds of finished dye.[10]

Returning to the producer in colonial Oaxaca, once he or she had received the *repartimiento* loan from the *alcalde mayor*, it was necessary to purchase cochineal "seed" to place in the *nopalera*. If, for example, the producer had received a loan of 120 reales (15 pesos) for the future delivery of 10 pounds, then enough cochineal "seed" would have to be purchased to produce at least 10 pounds of dried cochineal. Assuming, again, 66 percent shrinkage, then it was necessary to produce 30 pounds of live cochineal to end up with 10 pounds dried. Production of 30 pounds live required the introduction of between 0.625 and 2.5 pounds of seed, depending on the expected yield.[11] The cochineal seed cost about the same per pound as *grana seca*, dried cochineal.[12] Thus, assuming the producer purchased 2.5 pounds of seed (the minimum necessary introduction, based on the lowest estimated yield) and paid the median price during the colonial period of 18 reales per pound, he or she had to spend only 45 of the 120 reales purchasing cochineal to place in the *nopalera*. This left the producer with a 75-real surplus to be spent as desired.[13] Some producers used the extra reales for immediate needs, as did Pedro de Vera, the Indian *alcalde* of San Andres in Teposcolula, who along with other community members took out a cochineal loan for 2.5 arroba (62.5 pounds) in October 1781 to pay tribute.[14] In contrast, other producers undoubtedly purchased as much cochineal seed as their loans would allow. The recipient of a 120-real loan could buy 6.67 pounds of seed at 18 reales per pound and produce, if all went well, 26.68 pounds of dried cochineal, assuming the low-end yield of 1 pound seed per 4 pounds dried. After delivering to the *alcalde mayor* the 10 pounds owed, the producer still had 16.68 pounds, which could be sold at the current market price. At the median market rate in Oaxaca of 18 reales, this 16.68 pounds generated 300.25 reales, or 37.5 pesos. To place this figure in perspective, it was equivalent to 150 to 200 days' work on a *hacienda*, based on the typical daily wage of 1.5 to 2 reales. In short, with each 1-pound loan that the producer received from the *alcalde mayor*, 2.6 pounds could, theoretically, be harvested. After repaying the loan, the producer still had 1.6 pounds of his own. The *alcalde mayor* paid 12 reales for his 1 pound, while the producer received 1.6 pounds, expending only the labor of his or her own family members.

Of course, most of the above discussion is theoretical; it provides no evidence to show that indigenous cochineal producers actually enjoyed such benefits. One archival reference, however, shows that they sometimes did. When, in 1752, the Miahuatlán priest Thomas Carillo estimated that 1 pound of cochineal seed yielded 4 pounds of finished dye, he also noted that a peasant receiving a 150-peso *repartimiento* to produce 4 arrobas of dye would normally spend about 75 pesos purchasing seed. The rest of the loan was the peasant's to use as he wished.[15]

A question logically arises; if cochineal production was potentially so profitable, then why did producers continually request loans rather than finance production themselves out of their own earnings? The likely answer is multifaceted. First, most Oaxacans were too poor to afford the luxury of spending the entire loan on cochineal production. Therefore, at least part of the loan was spent for immediate needs, and this reduced directly the surplus dye produced. Second, in many years the harvest failed. This meant that in the following year the producer had to request an additional loan and then repay the current and the past year's debts, which left little or no surplus. Finally, since production was risky, the producer preferred to jeopardize another's capital rather than his or her own slim resources. When harvests failed, the *alcalde mayor* lost money, while the producer had already spent the funds. True, the *alcalde* and his *tenientes*

131

demanded payment of the debts, and at times even placed the debtor in prison, but if the delinquent borrower appeared honest and had made a good-faith effort to produce the cochineal that he had contracted to deliver, the risk of prison was probably low (and the effectiveness of imprisonment even lower). Taking a *repartimiento* loan, then, served to reduce the risk to which a peasant exposed himself.

No matter how they financed it, many producers were able to market their own cochineal on the open market — to traveling merchants, at local *tianguis*, or down in Antequera. It was common for wealthy Oaxacan merchants to supply itinerant peddlers with money to travel to cochineal-producing villages at harvest time to purchase dye directly from producers. At least some of these agents were owners of small stores specializing in the purchase and sale of cochineal dye. Many such shops were found on Calle de la Cochinilla,[16] located one block from Antequera's central plaza. These storekeepers journeyed to the nearby markets of Ejutla and Ocotlán to buy cochineal on the account of the merchants who financed them. As compensation for their services, the storekeepers were paid a fee of one peso per arroba of twenty-five pounds.[17]

A stream of itinerant merchants also regularly visited the cochineal-producing towns near Teposcolula, where indigenous producers often had surplus dye which they marketed themselves. In September 1771, for example, don Esteban García, a wealthy Teposcolulan merchant and mill owner, advanced Juan Pérez, a mestizo peddler, four hundred pesos to buy *grana* cochineal. Pérez agreed to deliver the dyestuff to García in December at a rate two reales below the market price current in Teposcolula. According to Pérez, he bought the cochineal at the weekly *tianguis* of Yanhuitlán, Tamazulapán, and the Chocho-speaking towns around Coixtlahuaca at the going rate in these *grana*-producing villages.[18] Lucas Pimentel also served as a purchasing agent for Esteban García. In 1771 Pimentel received from García 1,166.25 pesos to use in the purchase of cochineal from indigenous producers. Like Juan Pérez, Pimentel contracted to deliver the dyestuff at two reales below the market price in the plaza of Teposcolula. García was not Pimentel's only financier. The *alcalde mayor* of Teposcolula, José Mariano de Cardenas, also employed him to buy surplus cochineal from Indian producers at market prices.[19] Twenty-five years later, in 1796, Mariano Ayala received three thousand pesos from don Pedro Otero, a merchant of Nochistlán, to purchase *grana*. Ayala received one real per pound as compensation for his labor.[20] Evidently, Indians also purchased cochineal in local *tianguis*. In 1784, for example, the parish priest of Ayoquesco referred to indigenous cochineal producers who sold their output to other Indians in the markets of Ocotlán.[21]

In contrast, John K. Chance found that market sales by indigenous producers of cochineal were uncommon in Villa Alta, where the *alcalde mayor* was the only purchaser at least into the 1770s. Chance does not indicate, however, whether the *alcalde* bought any of the dye at market prices, outside of the *repartimiento*.[22] In fact, the 1770 petition filed by *alcalde mayor* Molina of Villa Alta suggested that merchants did, at least at times, pass through Villa Alta. Molina claimed that it was common for Indians to default on their *repartimiento* debts when the price of cochineal was high, choosing to sell to traveling merchants instead at the higher market rates. Molina also complained that many Villa Alta producers took advantage of high prices by transporting their *grana seca* to sell in the weekly market of Antequera.[23]

This was certainly common by the final years of colonial rule. At each of the city's entrances, a customs official was placed to issue *pases*, literally, declarations of the merchandise carried into or out of the city, for the purpose of ensuring collection of the *alcabala* sales tax. While sale by Indians of their own production was exempted from the *alcabala*, in 1810, 1811, and 1812 customs officials nonetheless kept records of the products Indians introduced into the city for sale. Some of these records survive and give an indication of the volume of cochineal brought by indigenous producers for sale in Antequera.[24]

In the months for which data survive, 1,586 *pases* were issued to indigenous people transporting cochineal into Antequera for sale. In total, 73,040 pounds of cochineal were introduced, for an average entry of 46.05 pounds. The median amount per shipment was one arroba of 25 pounds. Significantly, there were 140 entries of fewer than 10 pounds.

The image presented by these customs *pases* is striking. Hundreds of producers descended from their pueblos carrying their cochineal, which they sold for a few pesos in Oaxaca. Cochineal prices in the city were always slightly higher than those in the producing towns, and an extra real per pound was often sufficient incentive for peasants to make the journey. The dates included in the records reveal that each week, beginning on Thursday, dozens of Indians passed through the customs checkpoints at the city's entrances. On Friday, still more arrived, and a few stragglers arrived on Saturday. All undoubtedly were heading for Oaxaca's large Saturday market, intending to sell their surplus dyestuff, at times just a couple of pounds and at other times large amounts.

The average amount of cochineal introduced into Oaxaca and recorded

TABLE 7.2
Cochineal Marketed by the Quero Family

Family member	Date	Pounds	Pesos per pound	Value (pesos)
Andrés Quero	March 9, 1810	350.0	3.63	1,270.50
Domingo Quero	March 9, 1810	175.0	3.63	635.25
Vicente Quero	March 15, 1810	600.0	3.63	2,178.00
Faustino Quero	April 13, 1810	62.5	3.63	226.88
Andrés Quero	April 26, 1810	375.0	3.63	1,361.25
Andrés Quero	June 8, 1810	450.0	3.63	1,633.50
Domingo Quero	June 8, 1810	1,175.0	3.63	4,265.25
Vicente Quero	June 8, 1810	1,125.0	3.63	4,083.75
Faustino Quero	June 8, 1810	50.0	3.63	181.50
Andrés Quero	May 10, 1811	250.0	3.56	890.00
Faustino Quero	May 17, 1811	75.0	3.56	267.00
Domingo Quero	May 24, 1811	575.0	3.56	2,047.00
Fabián Quero	May 24, 1811	575.0	3.56	2,047.00
Vicente Quero	May 24, 1811	800.0	3.56	2,848.00
Faustino Quero	May 31, 1811	12.5	3.56	44.50
Faustino Quero	February 12, 1812	100.0	2.50	250.00
Andrés Quero	February 28, 1812	100.0	2.50	250.00
Vicente Quero	March 5, 1812	75.0	2.50	187.50
Domingo Quero	April 3, 1812	150.0	2.50	375.00
Faustino Quero	April 24, 1812	25.0	2.50	62.50
Andrés Quero	June 19, 1812	200.0	2.50	500.00
Vicente Quero	June 26, 1812	75.0	2.50	187.50
Andrés Quero	August 28, 1812	200.0	2.50	500.00
Domingo Quero	August 28, 1812	312.5	2.50	781.25
Fabián Quero	September 11, 1812	200.0	2.50	500.00
Vicente Quero	September 11, 1812	175.0	2.50	437.50
TOTALS		8,262.5		28,010.63

SOURCE: Derived from AGEO, *Cuadernos donde constan las introducciones de indios que no causan alcabalas*, legajos 7 and 8, various expedientes, 1810–1812.

by the customs officials, 46.05 pounds, was quite high, especially given the extremely high market price of *grana*, which was valued at 29 reales per pound in 1810 and 28.5 reales in 1811, making the average shipment in 1810 worth 167 pesos. Several possibilities exist to account for the high average. Most likely, some individuals brought the *grana* of their relatives or friends to sell in the city. In other cases, several community members may have taken to market the entire community's output. Since Indians traveling to Oaxaca did incur some costs, certainly there was a minimum quantity of *grana* worth marketing and anything below this amount was not worth the bother. This would have encouraged peasants to pool their output and send only one individual to market.

Evidence, however, suggests yet another possibility — that some Indians produced large amounts of cochineal, large enough to raise dramatically the overall average. While some producers struggled to bring a couple of pounds to market and others proved unable to even repay their outstanding debts, a few wealthy Indians produced large quantities, perhaps employing poorer Indians to do some or all of the labor.

Numerous entries showed Indians introducing amounts in excess of one hundred pounds, a notable quantity. For example, five individuals, all with the surname Quero and all from the Oaxacan valley town of Mitla, traded heavily in cochineal. Almost certainly related, Andres, Domingo, Fabiano, Faustino, and Vicente Quero brought over four tons of *grana* to Oaxaca during these three years alone. Table 7.2 shows the amounts brought by the Quero group as well as the dates that they passed through customs.[25]

In total, the Queros introduced 8,262.5 pounds of cochineal into Oaxaca during these years, an amount worth in excess of twenty-eight thousand pesos. There is no conclusive evidence that the Queros were trading in cochineal produced in their own *nopaleras*. They may instead have purchased it in and around Mitla on behalf of a Oaxacan merchant, or they may have been delivering their village's cochineal to the *alcalde mayor* or to market to sell.

Regardless, some cochineal producers had larger operations than the typical cochineal producer, who produced small quantities in a backyard *nopalera*. The *alcalde mayor* of Ixtepeji commented in 1752 that some producers hired *peones* at harvest time, especially women and children, to harvest the *grana* from the cacti. Since most producers used family labor, those who hired additional workers were undoubtedly harvesting larger quantities.[26]

Some Indians grew wealthy dealing in cochineal, such as Juan de Aguilar, a tribute-paying Indian from San Pablo Mitla. In 1791 Aguilar petitioned his *alcalde mayor* for permission to travel to Spain to sell his cochineal because the existing price was so depressed in Mexico that no profit could be made by selling it and he feared that instead he would suffer a loss. According to Aguilar, he had been producing and trading cochineal since childhood, and through his hard work had amassed "a modest principal." At that moment, he had twelve *zurrones* of cochineal ready for shipment to Spain, where he hoped they would fetch a higher price. Given the existing Oaxacan price of cochineal in 1791, these twelve *zurrones* were worth approximately 4,950 pesos. This was not Aguilar's entire fortune, either. Before requesting permission to go to Spain, he prepared a will, in which he placed his net worth at fifteen thousand pesos.[27] Of course, Juan de Aguilar was unusual; the benefits most Indians obtained from the dye trade were much more limited. Some, however, did grow rich.

Cochineal was colonial Mexico's second largest export, and in many years, its annual production was valued in Oaxaca at several million pesos.[28] Production was almost exclusively in the hands of Indians, and so it should not be surprising that some grew wealthy from the trade, even though Spaniards did, obviously, take most of the profit. The existence of wealthy Indians like the Quero family and Juan de Aguilar suggests the possibility that in late-colonial Oaxaca there had developed significant levels of economic differentiation within at least some peasant communities. Furthermore, it is likely that the prohibition of the *repartimiento* increased this differentiation in the last decades of the colonial era.

In 1786 *repartimiento* financing of cochineal production was made illegal, and, as a result, most Spanish merchants withdrew their investment capital. As financing became less available, the quantities of dyestuff produced fell sharply.[29] That production did not disappear entirely was the result of two factors. First, some *subdelegados* provided illegal loans to producers despite the prohibition. Second, wealthier peasants were able to finance their own production. Producers dependent upon loans from the *alcalde mayor*, however, curtailed production, owing to the absence of *repartimientos*. Those able to finance production themselves, however, continued to do so, and, in fact, benefited from the 1786 ban. They continued to produce cochineal but received better prices for their output because the overall production had declined. These "wealthier" peasants faced less competition, and prices rose accordingly. They enjoyed a windfall from the high prices after 1800.

This suggests the possibility that in the last two decades of colonial rule the economic differentiation within the Indian communities of Oaxaca increased. Poorer peasants received fewer loans to produce cochineal, and, consequently, the price rose once the depressed demand of the early 1790s recovered.[30] Wealthier peasants grew wealthier still as they received higher prices for their cochineal production. On the eve of independence, the economic gap between the rich and poor within the indigenous communities increased.

Oaxaca to London: A Balance Sheet

Every document has to be checked and re-checked. The full accounts of an affair cannot be called complete until it has been carried through to a conclusion from A to Z. How can one be satisfied for instance with the presentation of the accounts of the French India Company, which simply says without further details that from 1725 to 1736, the difference between purchases in the Indies and sales in France showed an 'average profit of 96.12%'? When a series of transactions is linked together like a multi-stage rocket, the last capsule cannot stand for the whole. The historian needs to know the initial outlay, the expenses of the voyage and the laying-up of the ship, the value of the merchandise and cash taken on the outward leg, the series of deals and profits made in the Far East and so on. Only then would it be possible to calculate or even try to calculate the real profit.[1]

In the cochineal-producing districts of Oaxaca, the spring and early summer were particularly busy times of the year. Not only did peasants labor long hours on their *milpas* tilling and planting, they also harvested their cochineal and prepared it for delivery to the *alcalde mayor* or for sale in a local *tianguis*. For the Spanish official and his assistants, the months April to June were consumed with the *cobranza*, the collection of *grana seca* in payment of *repartimiento* debts. Upon delivery of their cochineal harvest, *repartimiento* recipients completed their financial obligations to the *alcalde mayor*. Payment represented the final step from the perspective of the Indian debtors, but for the Spanish officials collection of the cochineal was but an intermediate step. As the principal operator of the *repartimiento*, the *alcalde mayor* was essentially a moneylender who, in partnership with his financial backers, sought to profit from the interest on loans that he made to indigenous *grana* producers. By colonial standards, he and his partners were rather successful, realizing estimated annualized net profits of from 6 to 17.5 percent (in at least one case) on invested capital.[2] Whereas (unlike other merchants) the *alcalde mayor* could obtain cochineal cheaply by making risky *repartimiento* loans, once he had the finished dye in hand, a Spanish official was largely indistinguishable from any other merchant trading in cochineal. He faced comparable risks, incurred the same costs, paid identical taxes, and competed in similar markets.[3]

Merchants sought to profit by buying cochineal cheaply in one place and selling it dearly elsewhere. Many expenses, however, were incurred along the way, and, as Fernand Braudel correctly argues, the task of the historian is to evaluate the entire vertical process, from the initial purchase to the final sale. This chapter will reconstruct, step by step, the "multi-stage rocket" of the cochineal trade. Beginning at the end of the process, it looks first at the price of cochineal in Europe, which fluctuated sharply during the period under investigation, reflecting both changing conditions of supply and demand and rising costs incurred by merchants and passed on to consumers.[4] Next, this chapter examines the great number of expenses incurred by cochineal merchants, and demonstrates that the cost of conducting business in the cochineal trade rose sharply over the period under examination. War increased the dangers of transatlantic commerce, causing the cost of maritime insurance and ocean freight to skyrocket. War also inflated the cost of running an empire, and the imperial states of the time resorted to increasing taxes to finance these wars. Cochineal, one of the most valuable and highly demanded colonial products, was an easy target for tax collectors in Spain as well as other European ports.

The War on Prices

The profitability of the cochineal trade naturally depended on the price merchants could obtain for their dyestuff in Europe, and so it would be nearly impossible to even attempt to estimate the trade's profitability without reliable price data. Fortunately, the market for cochineal in England and Holland was sufficiently important that cochineal was regularly traded at the commodities exchanges of London and Amsterdam, and prices were closely recorded. For the London exchange, prices are available in published sources for each year after 1782. Dutch prices begin much earlier, in 1589, and continue, with only occasional interruptions, until 1802.[5] By combining the English and Dutch prices, it is possible to construct a "European" price series for the entire period 1758–1821.[6]

This European price series was constructed as follows: for the years 1758–1781, the Dutch price was used. Between 1782 and 1802, prices are available for both Amsterdam and London, and the average of these two quotations was adopted. Finally, the prices used for the years 1803–1821 are those of the London exchange. Such a methodology appears sound, for the individual Dutch and English price series are highly correlated. Regression analysis performed for the twenty-one years in which quotations were available on both exchanges reveals a very high correlation, indicated by an *r* value of .94.[7] This suggests that information flowed regularly between the two exchanges and that cochineal prices thus tended to fluctuate similarly in the two cities. This conclusion is supported by Braudel's description of the trading practices in the Amsterdam and London exchanges. According to Braudel, brokers sought and received on a regular basis information on market prices in the other exchange.[8]

A comparison of the European price data with that of the series recorded by the Oaxacan cochineal registry suggests a surprisingly regular and dependable flow of information across the Atlantic as well, at least during times of international peace. Several different regression analyses were performed to measure the level of correlation between the two series. First, for the entire period 1760–1821,[9] *r* was computed to be .64, indicating a fairly strong positive correlation. Next, the period was divided into two parts, 1760–1792 and 1793–1815, and a regression was run on each. For the first, prices were very strongly correlated (*r* = .82), but only a weak correlation was discernible for the latter years (*r* = .46). The weaker correlation after 1793 clearly reflects the frequent interruptions in transatlantic trade, owing to the nearly constant state of warfare associated with the wars of the French Revolution and Napoleon.

Figure 8.1 shows the Oaxacan and European price series. The years in which Spain was at war are identified on the figure by the rectangular blocks labeled A through E. War disrupted transatlantic trade, which tended to reduce the supply of American goods in Europe and increase prices correspondingly. War had the opposite effect on the prices of these same commodities in Mexico. When shipping lanes closed or threatened to close, Mexican merchants found themselves stuck, at times for prolonged periods, with unmarketable merchandise which they desperately sought to unload even at low prices.

This phenomenon is observable in Figure 8.1. In rectangle C, which outlines the first phase of the Napoleonic Wars, one notes a rise in the price of cochineal in Europe starting in 1797, a rise so steep that by 1798 the price had doubled relative to 1796. While the European price of *grana* skyrocketed, the price in Mexico remained stagnant. This occurred, in part, because in these years, especially 1797, Great Britain imposed a successful blockade of Spanish shipping.[10] In the entire year 1797 a mere 20,950 pounds of *grana* were exported from Mexico, representing only 4 percent of the year's registered production.[11] This naturally reduced the available stock of cochineal in Europe, causing the price to rise. No corresponding price increase occurred in Mexico because the prospects of ex-

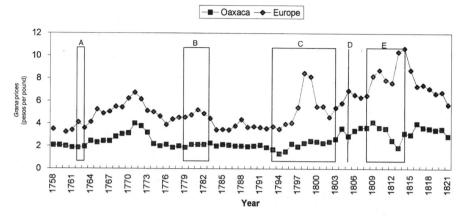

FIGURE 8.1. Cochineal prices in Europe and Oaxaca, 1758–1821. Sources: Appendix B; Tooke and Newmarch, 2:400; and Posthumus, 1:420–23.

porting dye were dismal. With the weakening of the trade embargo, the supply of cochineal in Europe was once again replenished, causing the price to return to more normal levels. In 1799, 1,015,050 pounds of cochineal were shipped from Veracruz to Cádiz,[12] and the price on the London exchange fell 34 percent, from a 1799 average of 7.88 pesos per pound to just 5.19 pesos per pound in 1800.[13]

European prices for cochineal returned to and remained at more modest levels until they were once again shocked by war in 1805, when Spain and France allied against Great Britain in what has come to be called the War of the Third Coalition. The war proved disastrous for Spain, as the British again succeeded in virtually halting Spanish imperial commerce.[14] Reduced supply in Europe, as well as the rising cost of freight and insurance, caused the price of cochineal in London to once again rise to the high level of 6.94 pesos per pound, as the export of cochineal from Mexico shrank in 1805 to just 21,200 pounds.[15] At the same time, the price of *grana* in Mexico dropped (see section D on Figure 8.1). Beginning with the peace of Amiens in 1802, the price of cochineal in Europe rose for three years, despite the arrival of large shipments from Mexico. High prices and open shipping lanes also pushed up the price in Mexico. When Spain once again entered the war in 1805, however, shipping decreased, causing prices to rise even more steeply in Europe and to drop in Mexico. European merchants, expecting available supplies to prove inadequate, bid the price of cochineal up. Merchants in Mexico, in contrast, sought to sell their dye rapidly, fearing that a lengthy war might once again strand in

141

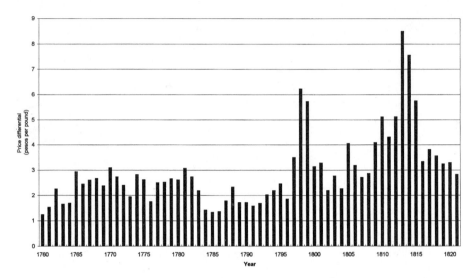

FIGURE 8.2. Price difference for *grana* between Oaxaca and Europe, 1760–1821. Sources: Appendix B; Tooke and Newmarch, 2:400; and Posthumus, 1:420–23.

Veracruz the cochineal into which they had invested their capital. As a result, the many sellers and few buyers for cochineal in Mexico forced prices down. The result of war, then, was to increase prices in Europe and decrease them in Mexico.[16]

While Spain's involvement in the War of the Third Coalition lasted only ten months before Great Britain's victory at the battle of Trafalgar in October 1805, Figure 8.1 clearly shows the war's effect on the price of cochineal. The brevity of the interruption of transatlantic commerce suggests that European merchants may not have been responding to actual reductions in supply but rather were speculating that the war would last longer. The price was bid up because merchants hoped they could earn large speculative profits if the war continued.

With the return of peace in late 1805, the dye price in Europe began a several-year's-long retreat, matched in Mexico by a corresponding price increase. This convergence would be expected, as prices on both sides of the Atlantic readjusted to the end of hostilities and the reopening of commerce.

The price decrease in Europe, however, was neither profound nor lasting. Prices remained fairly high after the return of peace and then skyrocketed with Napoleon's 1808 invasion and six-year occupation of Spain. In

142

Oaxaca, the drop in the price of cochineal was almost as severe (see rectangle E on Figure 8.1). In 1813, a year in which the price differential between the two markets reached an all-time high of 8.5 pesos per pound, the European price was 5.5 times greater than the Oaxacan price. Not only did the price reflect conditions in Spain, it also was influenced by the chaos in Oaxaca, where the insurgent army of Morelos had captured the city in November 1812 and retained control until early 1814. Registered production in Oaxaca dropped to record low annual levels, averaging only 189,337.5 pounds in 1812 and 1813. Low levels of production in Oaxaca certainly account for the continuance in 1815 of high prices in London, even after the defeat of Napoleon.

The defeat of Napoleon, the restoration of Ferdinand VII to the Spanish throne, and the royalist reconquest of Oaxaca all contributed to the normalization of trade in cochineal. Between 1814 and 1816, the price differential between Mexico and Europe narrowed, as prices in the former rose and those in the latter fell. After 1816, prices once again moved in tandem — the war-induced distortions had subsided. The yearly price differentials for the entire period 1760–1821 are shown in Figure 8-2.

Cost Accounting from the Nopalera *to Europe*

The sale of cochineal in Europe was the ultimate objective of a merchant, and the sale price largely determined whether the venture succeeded or failed. Not only did this price need to be sufficiently high to cover the many costs that the merchant incurred, it also had to provide him with his mercantile profit. Cochineal might change hands several times before reaching its final consumer, or a merchant might retain ownership of the commodity from its place of production in rural Oaxaca until its sale in Spain or beyond. Its arrival in London, Amsterdam, or Marseilles might only be a temporary stopping point before its re-export to even more distant markets such as St. Petersburg or India.[17] *Grana cochinilla* nearly always fetched high prices in Europe, and merchants specializing in it could profit handsomely if their commerce proceeded smoothly. As was the case with any eighteenth-century transoceanic trade, however, cochineal merchants had to remain patient, because the length of time between the purchase of dye in Oaxaca and its resale in Northern Europe could be significant. Not only did considerable time elapse, but merchants incurred many expenses en route. Dye had to be packaged, registered, transported to Veracruz,

143

TABLE 8.1
Cost in Pesos to Construct One Zurrón

Year	Cost	Year	Cost	Year	Cost
1752	2.56	1788	3.28	1792	3.25
1752	2.00	1789	3.75	1793	3.25
1752	2.75	1790	5.50	1794	4.31
1772	3.00	1791	3.13		

SOURCES: AGN, Subdelegados, vol. 34, f. 105; f. 119; f. 135; AGN, Civil, vol. 302, *primera parte*, p. 51; AGN, Industria y Comercio, vol. 22, exp. 2, pp. 9, 34, 67, 84, 149; AFY, 2.3.3; AGN, Consulado, vol. 93, exp. 11.

insured, and then shipped overseas. At several points along the way, taxes were assessed. The analysis that follows tracks the course of cochineal exports, estimating many of the expenses that merchants incurred.

PACKAGING THE COCHINEAL

Before it could be shipped, cochineal had to be packaged carefully to guard against damage. Cochineal came in various grades of which *grana fina*, top-quality dye, fetched by far the highest prices. The dried cochineal insect body resembled a gray-colored seed, and this is why it was called *grana*, which means grain or seed. For the *grana* to be classified as *fina*, it was essential that it retain this shape.[18] As a result, the packaging of the dye was a critical task.

Special containers, variously referred to as *zurrones, sobornales, costales, sacos*, or *tercios*, were constructed to transport the *grana*, and these contained from 7 to 9 arrobas each, the equivalent of between 175 and 225 pounds total. A *zurrón*, as the package was most commonly called, was constructed of two layers of leather, one cured and one raw, and a straw lining called a *petate*. These were sewn together with leather cord. While the cost of packaging was not exorbitant, it was borne by the merchant. Table 8.1 shows the cost of building a cochineal *zurrón* for selected shipments in selected years from 1752 to 1794.[19] The 1752 figures were estimates presented by the *alcaldes mayores*, but the other figures in the table represent actual costs recorded in documents. Based on this small data set, the average cost of building a *zurrón* for the entire period was 3.34 pesos.

TRANSPORTING THE COCHINEAL BY LAND

Once the cochineal was packaged and labeled, it was ready for shipment to Oaxaca and then to Veracruz. In southern Mexico, roads, often little more than unimproved paths, were mountainous, rugged, and poorly maintained, which made transport by wagon impossible. Instead, goods were carried by human porters or, more commonly, by mules, whose maximum load of around 225 to 250 pounds was equivalent to approximately one zurrón of *grana seca*.[20] There were several possible routes from Oaxaca to Veracruz. The most direct route headed northwest out of Oaxaca through the Valley of Etla, turned north at Las Sedas, followed the Cañon of Tomellín through the town of Cuicatlán to Teotitlán del Camino, and then continued to Tehuacan, Orizaba, Cordoba, and, finally, Veracruz. A less direct route to Veracruz, but still an important Oaxacan road, turned west at Las Sedas, passed through the Mixteca districts of Nochistlán, Teposcolula, and Huajuapan, continued through the Pueblan towns of Acatlán and Izúcar, and then veered northeast to Puebla de los Angeles, where the road then connected with the main Mexico City–Veracruz road. Yet another road connected Oaxaca with the southern coast, crossing the cochineal-rich district of Miahuatlán. The road to Tehuantepec passed through Nexapa. A small road also linked Villa Alta with Oaxaca, connecting with the Oaxaca–Mitla road near Tlacolula. All of these routes and other Oaxacan roads are illustrated on Map 3. It should be noted that these were only the principal routes; most other destinations were accessible via smaller roads and paths.[21]

The freight rates charged by professional muleteers, called *arrieros*, depended on distance, terrain, and the length of time needed for the trip. A handful of records were located, permitting a rough estimate of land freight charges for cochineal in the eighteenth century. Table 8.2 displays freight rates for selected mule trips from 1752 through 1820.[22] Based on the data, the average freight charge was 1.841 reales to transport each ton of *grana* one kilometer.[23] This figure is in line with those computed by other historians. Clara Elena Suárez Argüello calculated a nearly identical figure, finding that the average freight charge for shipping tobacco from Mexico City to Oaxaca in 1800 was 1.88 reales/ton/kilometer.[24] My estimate of 1.841 reales is also in line with the highest of the figures calculated by John Coatsworth for nineteenth-century wagon-freight rates.[25] At this average rate, transporting one twenty-five-pound arroba of cochineal the 383 kilometers from Oaxaca to Veracruz cost approximately 8.82 reales, or 1.1 pesos. The *alcalde mayor* also had to transport the dye

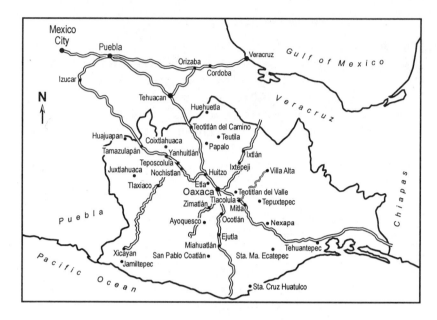

MAP 3. Eighteenth-Century Roads in Southern Mexico

between the village in which it was produced and the *cabecera*, the town in which his official residence was located, and then he had to bring the cochineal to Oaxaca. Each of these steps cost the merchant additional freight charges.

SHRINKAGE

The cochineal received by the *alcalde mayor* in repayment of debts had been recently harvested and killed. While producers dried the dye before delivering it to the *alcalde mayor*, inevitably some additional drying occurred, causing the dyestuff to lose weight before it was actually marketed.[26] Weight loss cost merchants money since the dye that they purchased weighed more than what they ultimately sold. Merchants with experience dealing in cochineal expected this and sometimes recorded the amount of *merma* ("shrinkage"). While the costs of shrinkage were not enormous, they must be tallied to accurately reflect all expenses incurred by the *alcalde mayor* and other cochineal merchants. Table 8.3 lists either actual losses sustained or expert colonial estimates of the typical amount of shrinkage, based on the data available.[27]

The average amount of shrinkage in Table 8.3 is 4.37 percent. The

146

TABLE 8.2
Freight Rates for Mule Transport of Cochineal

Year	Route	Kilometers	WEIGHT Arrobas	Tons	Freight (reales)	Freight rate (reales/ ton/km)
1752	Ixtepeji to Oaxaca	48	9.00	0.113	14	2.593
1752	Tehuantepec to Oaxaca	251	8.00	0.100	48	1.912
1752	Nexapa to Oaxaca	124	14.00	0.175	72	3.318
1752	Nexapa to Oaxaca	124	7.00	0.088	24	2.212
1752	Nexapa to Veracruz	507	8.00	0.100	108	2.130
1752	Oaxaca to Veracruz	383	8.00	0.100	72	1.880
1752	Zimatlán to Veracruz	411	8.00	0.100	64	1.557
1767	Teotitlán del Camino to Veracruz	281	8.00	0.100	48	1.708
1767	Orizaba to Veracruz	151	96.00	1.200	216	1.192
1788	Teposcolula to Veracruz	406	71.00	0.888	780	2.165
1789	Teposcolula to Veracruz	406	123.00	1.538	832	1.333
1790	Oaxaca to Puebla	363	64.00	0.800	512	1.763
1790	Puebla to Acapulco	537	64.00	0.800	1,024	2.384
1790	Teposcolula to Veracruz	406	124.72	1.559	896	1.416
1792	Teposcolula to Veracruz	406	140.00	1.750	780	1.098
1792	Teposcolula to Veracruz	406	123.48	1.544	840	1.340
1792	Teposcolula to Veracruz	406	122.00	1.525	780	1.260
1811	Miahuatlán to Oaxaca	99	120.00	1.500	180	1.212
1820	Oaxaca to Veracruz	383	1.00	0.013	12	2.507

SOURCES: Figures for 1752 come from AGN, Subdelegados, vol. 34; for 1767, see AGN, Civil, vol. 302, *tercera parte*; for the Teposcolula-to-Veracruz data, see AGN, Industria y Comercio, vol. 22, exp. 2; for 1790, see AFY, 2.3.3; for 1811, refer to AGEO, Real Intendencia II, legajo 40, exp. 23, p. 19; and for 1820, see Bustamante, *Memoria estadística de Oaxaca*, 25.

data, however, reflect shrinkage over a variety of distances. Dye trans- 147
ported to Veracruz continued to lose weight while it lay in storage awaiting shipment to Spain. Likewise, the voyage to Spain typically took three
to four months, during which time additional shrinkage occurred. Most of
the figures in the table show weight loss between the point of production
and the port of Veracruz. Assuming that some additional shrinkage oc-

TABLE 8.3
Weight Shrinkage of Cochineal

ID no.	Route	Type of observation	Original weight (pounds)	Shrinkage loss (pounds)	Per- centage lost
1	Oaxaca to Cádiz	estimate	200.00	12.50	6.25
2	Oaxaca to Veracruz	estimate	200.00	6.00	3.00
3	Veracruz to Cádiz	estimate	200.00	6.00	3.00
4	Oaxaca to Veracruz	actual	4,450.00	317.56	7.14
5	Ixtepeji to Oaxaca	estimate	25.00	0.75	3.00
6	Oaxaca to Veracruz	estimate	25.00	1.75	7.00
7	Oaxaca to Veracruz	estimate	25.00	1.50	6.00
8	Zimatlán to Veracruz–Cádiz	estimate	212.50	9.00	4.24
9	Teotitlán del Camino to Veracruz–Cádiz	estimate	1.00	0.06	6.00
10	Teposcolula to Veracruz–Cádiz	actual	1,776.03	72.28	4.07
11	Teposcolula to Veracruz–Cádiz	actual	3,000.00	60.06	2.00
12	Teposcolula to Veracruz–Cádiz	actual	3,118.00	98.25	3.15
13	Teposcolula to Veracruz–Cádiz	actual	3,087.00	61.00	1.98
14	Oaxaca to Cádiz	actual	200.00	12.00	6.00

SOURCES: ID nos. 1–4 are from AGN, Consulado, vol. 93, exp. 11, 1814; for ID nos. 5–9, see the respective "Informes" of the *alcaldes mayores* of Ixtepeji, Nexapa, Zimatlán, and Teotitlán del Camino, in AGN, Subdelegados, vol. 34, 1752; for ID nos. 10–13, see, in order, AGN, Industria y Comercio, vol. 22, exp. 2, pp. 9, 34, 35, and exp. 3, pp. 49–50; for ID no. 14, see Torales Pacheco, 2:176.

curred en route to Spain, a figure of 5 percent overall shrinkage seems reasonable. This means that each arroba harvested weighed only 23.75 pounds upon sale in Europe.

COMMISSIONS

Merchants sent their *grana* from Oaxaca to Veracruz by means of *arrieros* (muleteers), who, in turn, delivered the cochineal to an agent designated by the merchant. Called *encomenderos* or *comisionistas*, these agents registered the dye for export, obtained the necessary export papers, and secured space aboard outbound cargo ships. In exchange for their services, *encomenderos* received a fee, called either a *comisión del recibo* or an *encomienda*. *Comisionistas* also operated in Cádiz, unloading the cochineal shipped from Mexico and selling it to local merchants or dye brokers. The payment made to the Cádiz factors was termed an *encomienda de venta*, or a *comisión de venta*. Such commissions were additional expenses incurred by cochineal merchants.

According to Louisa Schell Hoberman, the rate of commission in the seventeenth century ranged from 4 to 5 percent of the value of the merchandise.[28] Javier Ortiz de la Tabla Ducasse found that *encomenderos* were charging from 3 to 5 percent before the declaration of *comercio libre* lowered rates to 2.5 percent.[29] In the cochineal trade, however, the *comisión del recibo* appears to have been about 2.5 percent for the entire period after 1750. The *alcaldes mayores* of Ixtepeji, Nexapa, Zimatlán, and Miahuatlán all reported in 1752 that 2.5 percent was the rate of the *encomienda* in Veracruz.[30] In Cádiz during the 1760s, merchants paid an *encomienda de venta* of 2.5 percent, plus an additional 0.5 percent fee called a *corretaje*, a brokerage fee.[31] The prevailing rate in Mexico in 1797 was also 2.5 percent.[32] The cost to merchants of commissions, then, was significant, about 5 percent of the value of the cochineal — 2.5 percent in Veracruz and an additional 2.5 percent in Cádiz.

REGISTERING THE COCHINEAL

Laws regulating the dye trade required merchants to present their cochineal for inspection at the Registro de Grana in Oaxaca. The registry was established in the 1750s in an attempt to guarantee the integrity of the cochineal trade after the repeated discovery of shipments of adulterated cochineal. Unscrupulous peasants and merchants mixed the cochineal with sand, dirt, ashes, corn tassels, or other foreign substances to increase its weight. Despite repeated warnings issued by the Crown, abuses continued throughout the colonial period and after.[33]

The registration of cochineal was a serious procedure. Every Wednesday the *corregidor*, the official scribe of the *cabildo*, several designated *grana* experts, two merchants, and several other lower officials all congregated at the Registro to inspect and register the cochineal. Merchants' zurrones were opened, and inspectors extracted samples of the *grana* from various parts of the zurrón using a "hollow pole resembling a syringe."[34] If the cochineal was deemed pure, the zurrón was closed, numbered, marked with a royal seal, and the owner was given an official document verifying registration and declaring the weight of the zurrón's contents. If the cochineal failed the inspection, the owner could be assessed penalties. The obligatory registration cost two pesos per zurrón, which was distributed among the officials and experts conducting the inspection.[35]

TAXES AND COCHINEAL

The fee to register the cochineal was just one of the many taxes imposed upon the trade. In the last several decades much scholarly attention has been directed to the late-colonial surge in revenues accruing to the Crown from the establishment of monopolies, the imposition of new taxes, and the more rigid collection of existing levies.[36] *Grana* cochineal was a prime target for the Crown's fiscal exactions because of its high value and low price elasticity of demand. Because *grana* was an export product, the tax could be easily collected.[37]

Much of the tax burden on cochineal was imposed during the last decades of colonial rule.[38] These new taxes contributed to the rising price of *grana* in Europe, as merchants were able to pass much of the tax burden on to final consumers. In September 1819, José María Quirós, secretary of the *consulado* of Veracruz, prepared a report arguing that excessive taxation harmed colonial trade. As evidence, he presented a chart illustrating the particularly heavy tax burden weighing on the cochineal trade.[39] Quirós's calculations are reproduced here as Table 8.4. Based on Quirós's figures, in 1819 the taxes paid for cochineal, from the time of its departure from Oaxaca to its re-export from Spain, amounted to 39.76 pesos per arroba, equivalent to 12.72 reales per pound. While the figure represents the tax burden for merely one year, it gives a good notion of the high tax burden imposed on the cochineal trade. Reconstructing the tax burden levied on cochineal or any other product over an extended period of time is a difficult process for several reasons. First, new taxes were periodically imposed and the rates of others often changed. Following every alteration is nearly impossible, owing to the lack of any single authoritative source. The tax that was imposed to subsidize the hospital of San Sebastian (no. 5 on the list), for example, was not collected during the entire period under investigation, but was imposed only in the year 1811.[40] The *alcabala* supplement (no. 3 on the list) was imposed, withdrawn, and then re-introduced. In October 1780 Viceroy Martín de Mayorga issued an edict implementing the *alcabala* supplement to help Spain in its war with Great Britain. Collection of the supplement continued until mid-1791.[41] In September 1810 the Crown again imposed a supplement, equal in amount to the prior one.[42] The Crown collected another tax called the *derecho de convoy*, but only in the years after 1810. Revenues from this emergency

TABLE 8.4

Tax Rates on Cochineal in 1819

No.	Tax description	Amount
1	Oaxacan municipal taxes[a]	6.25 pesos per arroba
2	Alcabala sales turnover tax	3.0% at 90 pesos per arroba
3	Alcabala supplement	1.0% at 90 pesos per arroba
4	Arbitrio[b]	1 peso, 7 reales per arroba
5	Hospital tax[c]	2 pesos per 7.5 arrobas
6	Export taxes from Mexico[d]	8.0% at 90 pesos per arroba
7	Consulado fees in Mexico[e]	1.5% at 90 pesos per arroba
8	Almirantazgo[f]	0.1% at 90 pesos per arroba
9	Military reinforcement[g]	3.0% at 82.8 pesos per arroba
10	Consulado fees in Spain	1.0% at 82.8 pesos per arroba
11	Armament in Spain	0.5% at 82.8 pesos per arroba
12	Guadalquivir toll	0.5% at.82.8 pesos per arroba
13	Temporary tax[b]	2.5% at 82.8 pesos per arroba
14	Export tax from Spain	15% at 82.8 pesos per arroba

SOURCE: AGN, Consulado de Veracruz, caja 252, exp. 8, 1819.

[a]This tax was collected for "the maintenance of troops" in the aftermath of Morelos's occupation of Oaxaca (see AGEO, Tesorería Principal de Oaxaca, legajo 8, exp. 12, 1816; and AGEO, Le Aduana, 1820a).

[b]The arbitrio de grana, established in 1727, was to be collected upon export from Veracruz at the rate of 15 pesos per zurrón of 8 arrobas. The funds were to be used for the construction and maintenance of the quay, the moat, and the parapet at the port of Veracruz (see Fonseca and Urrutia, 4:591). The arbitrio was sometimes referred to as the derecho de entrada.

[c]The hospital tax was first levied in 1811 to help finance the Hospital de San Sebastian in Veracruz (see Lerdo de Tejada, p. 22).

[d]Export duties were called derechos de almojarifazgo.

[e]The consulado fee was commonly known as the avería, as were certain other taxes.

[f]The almirantazgo was an "admirality duty" charged for the concession of loading and unloading cargo.

[g]Collected in Spain, this tax was called the derecho de reemplazo.

[h]I was unable to determine what this tax was for or when it was first implemented. I reluctantly decided to ignore it and not include it when calculating the total tax burden.

tax were intended to protect major trade routes from insurgents.[43] Due to the frequent introduction of new taxes and the reformulation of others, the reconstruction of the tax burden imposed on trade is complicated. Because there does not exist any single source for identifying all taxes, one cannot be sure precisely when some taxes were introduced or when the rates of others were changed.

An equally serious problem is that of determining the price at which a good was appraised for tax purposes. Customs officials in Veracruz and Cádiz were charged with determining the value of goods and assigning a price, called either an *aforo* or an *avaluo*, at which the goods were to be taxed. According to Juan Carlos Garavaglia and Juan Carlos Grosso, two historians who have worked closely with *alcabala* taxes, customs officials revised the *avaluo* every two years. Without these figures, one cannot reconstruct the tax levies.

Unfortunately, no official lists for cochineal were discovered, and its appraised value could be located for only nineteen years.[44] The data indicate that for cochineal the officials in Veracruz assigned an *aforo* close to the product's Oaxacan market price.[45] This amount differs from what other historians have found for other colonial goods. Claude Morin cites a colonial official who claimed that the *aforo* rates were typically 45 percent below the market rate. Garavaglia and Grosso found the exact opposite for Tepeaca, Puebla, where the *avaluo* assigned to merchandise was 40 percent above the market value declared by the taxpayer.[46] Viceroy Revillagigedo complained in 1793 that the *aforo* was often set artificially high to increase royal revenues, and was a burden on trade.[47] It would be useful, of course, to have a complete set of *avaluo* rates for cochineal, but the close link between the Oaxacan market price and the Veracruz *avaluo* permits at least a rough estimation of the tax burden and will be used later in this chapter to compute the estimated long-term tax burden on cochineal.

Curiously, in Spain the *avaluo* on *grana* did not change for the entire period after the 1778 promulgation of *comercio libre*. In that year, the Crown produced a new list of tariff rates, an *arancel*, to be applied to goods imported from the Indies.[48] *Grana fina*, Oaxacan cochineal, was appraised at 6,624 reales de vellón per quintal, equivalent to 82.8 pesos per arroba.[49] When Quirós, the secretary of the *consulado* of Veracruz, prepared his list of the taxes paid by cochineal in 1819, the *avaluo* on cochineal was still 6,624 reales vellón per quintal.[50] This trend is further substantiated by Javier Cuenca Esteban, who found that the tariff *avaluos* on a number of commodities listed in the *arancel* of 1816, cochineal included, were the same as those specified in the 1778 *reglamento*.[51]

The inconsistent application of taxes by colonial officials presents still another obstacle to an accurate measure of the tax burden. For instance, the *alcabala* on cochineal was usually not collected until the commodity reached Veracruz, since no taxable sale had taken place earlier.[52] When the cochineal arrived in Veracruz, however, it was automatically assessed an *alcabala*, whether a sale occurred or not.[53] In Veracruz, tax collectors were at least consistent, charging the *alcabala* as a percentage of the *avaluo*. Occasionally, however, a taxable sale was judged to have occurred in Oaxaca, which required the tax to be collected by local Oaxacan administrators. The custom in Oaxaca was to charge one peso per arroba, regardless of the *avaluo*, although even this practice was not universal.[54] In one case, a cochineal merchant from Pinotepa del Rey paid a 6 percent *alcabala* on cochineal to an administrator in Jamiltepec. The merchant later complained that the payment was "excessive," since the customary tax in Oaxaca was one peso per arroba and even the Veracruz rate was only 3 percent. As if to corroborate the confused state of royal taxation policies, the tax collector of Jamiltepec claimed that neither he nor anyone else in Jamiltepec knew the correct *alcabala* rate on cochineal.[55] Fortunately, most cochineal passed through Oaxaca without incurring an *alcabala*. As a result, the *alcabala* tax in Oaxaca can be ignored when calculating the typical tax burden on the dye trade. Normally, no tax was due.

A similar inconsistency was noted in the rate charged for the *derecho de convoy*. Theoretically the tax rate was 2 percent of the value of the goods shipped. The records for the province of Oaxaca for the year 1815, however, clearly indicate that, at least in that year, a flat rate of one-third of a peso per arroba of *grana* was regularly charged, rather than a rate based on 2 percent of the cochineal's value.[56] A document from 1816, in contrast, showed that Hijos de Bustamante y Compañía paid the *derecho de convoy* on 121.5 arrobas of dyestuff at the rate of 2 percent on the prevailing *avaluo* of 100 pesos per arroba.[57]

Changing tax rates, new taxes, and inconsistency on the part of colonial tax collectors make difficult the precise reconstruction of the tax burden on cochineal. Nonetheless, despite the obstacles, a fairly accurate estimate of the tax burden can be made for the period 1758–1821. The estimated yearly total tax burden imposed by the Spanish crown on cochineal, from its extraction from Oaxaca to its re-export from Spain, is shown

153

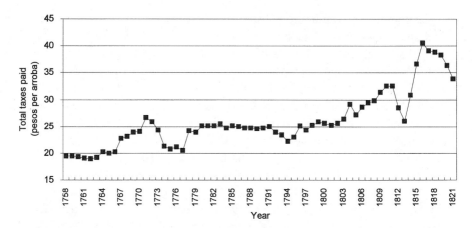

FIGURE 8.3. Estimated yearly total tax burden on cochineal, 1758–1821. Source: Appendix E.

in Figure 8.3.[58] As can clearly be seen, the tax burden increased steadily over the course of the period, especially after the turn of the nineteenth century. As it did in nearly every other branch of the colonial economy, the Crown increased dramatically its share of the cochineal industry.[59]

TRANSATLANTIC SHIPPING

When the cochineal arrived in the port of Veracruz, it was necessary for merchants to secure cargo space for the dyestuff aboard ships bound for Spain. While one would imagine this to be a simple process, the surviving documentation suggests otherwise. Transatlantic shipping was highly regulated within the Spanish empire. Goods imported into Mexico from Northern Europe were required by law to pass first through the Spanish port of Cádiz. Similarly, all goods exported from Mexico went directly to Cádiz, regardless of their ultimate destination. Furthermore, until 1778, most merchandise could only be shipped in the Crown's "annual" *flota*, the fleet system.[60] Even after *comercio libre* was extended to Mexico, however, shipping was restricted to ports within the Spanish empire and only permitted in boats granted licenses by the Crown.[61]

The 1789 commercial reforms had little effect on the trade routes of cochineal, as Cádiz retained an overwhelming dominance of the *grana* trade long after the introduction of *comercio libre*. According to data collected by John Fisher, during the years 1782–1795, Barcelona, the second most active Spanish port, received less than 6 percent of the cochineal imported into Spain; the rest went to Cádiz.[62]

In what was already a highly regimented system of imperial trade, cochineal was assigned a special status, which placed additional restrictions on its export from Mexico. According to the Laws of the Indies and reiterated in the Real Proyecto of 1720, it was mandatory that exports of cochineal, indigo, silver, and gold be transported on or escorted by warships, in order to protect this merchandise from seizure by pirates and other enemies.[63] While this afforded some protection for the merchant's cargo, space aboard such ships was limited and silver and gold were given priority. This meant that on some voyages, space was inadequate to accommodate all of the cochineal awaiting shipment in Veracruz and some was left behind, placing an additional economic burden on its unlucky owners. In the second half of the eighteenth century, this situation grew so common that some merchants, unable to get their cochineal aboard sanctioned ships, began petitioning Crown agents for special arrangements.

In 1778, for example, the *alcalde mayor* of Miahuatlán, don Francisco Javier de Corres, submitted a request for help in sending 114 zurrones of his cochineal aboard the next available ship. His request initiated an investigation, which prompted Pedro Antonio de Cosio, the Administrator of Royal Finances in Veracruz, to explain the crisis situation facing the cochineal industry at that time. In typical years merchants brought to Veracruz for shipment to Spain approximately 1,000 zurrones of Oaxacan cochineal. In 1777 alone, however, merchants introduced a record 3,632 zurrones, far beyond the legal cargo space available. As a result, much cochineal remained stranded in warehouses. In some cases, as Cosio noted, merchant ships outfitted with armament sufficient for their defense were permitted to ship surplus cochineal without an accompanying warship.[64]

This was how the Count of Reparaz, don Juan Bautista Uztariz, managed to send a large shipment of cochineal to Cádiz in 1772. In that year, he submitted a request for permission to ship 600 zurrones of cochineal aboard *El Buen Consejo*, a ship owned by his own trading company, the Casa de Uztariz. According to the Count, at least, the Crown's requirement that cochineal be sent aboard ships of the royal armada was due to the considerable freight revenues earned by the Crown. Perhaps because he also offered to pay the Crown the freight that would have been owed had the 600 zurrones been sent on a warship instead, the Count was granted permission to send the *grana* aboard his own ship.[65]

While the Crown required that cochineal be sent on or accompanied by war ships, at least in the 1770s it continually proved unable to supply sufficient space to accommodate the stock that merchants hoped to send to Cádiz. In March 1775 Viceroy Antonio María de Bucareli was forced to address this inadequacy after several *consulado* members issued complaints to his office regarding merchants who had not been able to load their cochineal aboard either of the two warships preparing to return to Spain. Captains of the two ships, the *Astuto* and the *Urca Santa Rita*, had begun accepting cargo and had rapidly filled both with a combined total of only 1,700–1,800 zurrones of cochineal, this at a time when the *grana* stock in Veracruz was approaching 4,000 zurrones. According to the *consulado*, several merchants claimed to have arrived promptly after learning that the ships had opened their registers, but the ships had stopped accepting new cargo after only two days. Such merchants, the *consulado* correctly argued, suffered economically from the lack of cargo space, for having invested large amounts of capital in the purchase of cochineal, their dye remained stranded in the port of Veracruz. Consequently, their funds were tied up in cochineal rather than earning additional interest from new investments. As a result, the *consulado* asked the Viceroy to intercede.[66] After investigating the case, Viceroy Bucareli ordered the two ship captains to redo their registrations. In addition, he authorized the use of a well-armed merchant ship to transport additional cochineal, but only on the condition that the merchandise be transferred to a warship in Havana, if one were available in port.[67]

Because of its tremendous value, cochineal was assigned a special status within what was already a highly regimented system. Warships, however, were simply inadequate to transport all available cochineal. Undoubtedly, this problem was especially severe in the 1770s, the decade in which *grana* production and exports reached record highs. All of the cases found in which this problem arose dated from that decade. While the Crown proved somewhat flexible, permitting merchants to outfit ships in extreme cases, it was certainly an additional burden on merchants, both administratively and economically.

Merchants shipping cochineal to Spain naturally had to pay ocean freight charges. Unfortunately, little evidence on ocean freight rates was found in the archives, and all of the documentation that was located specified the same rate for cochineal. Fabián de Fonseca and Carlos de Urrutia, two economic historians who wrote a massive history of royal finances in 1792, presented a Crown declaration from the beginning of the century, dated 1709, which stated that *grana* was to be charged in freight nine reales per arroba between Veracruz and Cádiz.[68] The ocean freight charge for cochineal was also nine reales per arroba, according to the Reales Proyectos of 1711, 1717, and 1720, the royal guidelines for imperial commerce.[69]

Not only did official sources place the rate at nine reales, but this was the rate in all of the documentation encountered which referred to actual charges for shipping cochineal. Between 1766 and 1768, don Rodrigo Antonio de Neyra, the wealthy financier of the *alcaldía mayor* of Teotitlán del Camino, sent to Cádiz 922 arrobas of cochineal spread out over five separate shipments. In each case, he was charged for ocean freight at the rate of nine reales per arroba.[70] Similarly, the 1760 register for a ship called the *Halcón* recorded many cochineal shipments, all of which paid ocean freight charges at nine reales per arroba.[71] Finally, this was also the rate charged for the numerous *grana* shipments aboard the *flota* of 1760.[72]

In no other documents were freight rates on cochineal specified explicitly. Several cases did, however, refer to the collection of freight on *grana* at the rates prescribed by the Real Proyecto. Contained in the documents pertaining to Neyra, for example, were ten receipts for shipment of *grana* from Veracruz to Cádiz dating from the years 1767–1770. Shipping receipts were preprinted with blank spaces for the information specific to each transaction. When a merchant loaded his merchandise aboard a ship, the blank spaces on the receipt were filled in and he was given the receipt for his records. Each receipt listed the owner of the merchandise, the quantity of the good loaded, to whom it should be delivered in Spain, and the freight charge payable upon delivery. Each of the ten receipts for the shipment of Neyra's cochineal simply specified that the freight charge for shipment would be the amount specified by the Real Proyecto.[73]

Similarly, in 1775 the captains of a ship named *Urca Peregrina* requested permission to bring back to Cádiz on their own accounts cochineal that they had purchased in Veracruz. They were granted authorization and were also informed that they would pay freight in Cádiz in the amount specified by the Real Proyecto of 1720.[74]

Finally, the same conditions were applied when in 1780 non-war ships were commissioned to help transport to Cádiz the large stock of cochineal stored in Veracruz. The ship captains were informed that one-half of the 1720 Real Proyecto freight rate would be paid to them if they shipped the cochineal only so far as Havana, and the entire amount if they continued on to Spain.[75]

All of the evidence located suggested that the freight charge to transport cochineal from Veracruz to Cádiz was nine reales per arroba. It seems difficult, however, to accept that the rate remained constant during the entire century, that fluctuation did not occur in response to supply and demand or conditions of risk. For example, when in the 1770s cargo space for cochineal was particularly inadequate, one would have expected merchants to offer a premium fee to ensure that their *grana* found space aboard a ship. It is possible, of course, that "supplements" were paid to ship captains to win cargo space when it was scarce. This would have had the effect of raising the freight rate closer to its real market value. No evidence of this practice was uncovered, however.

Another factor that must have influenced the real cost of transatlantic shipping was risk. During times of war, for instance, transatlantic shipping was more dangerous because of the risk of capture or destruction by enemies. This increased risk was naturally reflected in higher insurance premiums (discussed below), and ships operating in a free market would have demanded higher freight rates to compensate for the greater cost of insurance.

This conclusion is supported by the findings of Douglass North, who conducted an extensive study of ocean freight rates. After 1750, North contends, "ocean freight rates tended to move in like fashion on all of the major commodity routes of the world which were competitive." As an example of an uncompetitive route, North pointed to the monopoly of the East India Company, in which freight rates were not parallel to free-market rates. Because the East India Company enjoyed a monopoly on its route, one cannot expect that it responded as rapidly, or in the same manner, to conditions shaping the market as did shippers forced to compete.[76] Certainly, the monopolistic Spanish fleet system also served to artificially control freight prices, at least until it was disbanded by *comercio libre*. Insulation from market forces, then, helps explain how freight rates might not have fluctuated before 1778.

With the passage of commercial reforms in 1778, the stability of monopoly fleet freight rates gave way to the fluctuations of a freer market. Article 46 of the declaration of *comercio libre* granted freedom for ship captains and merchants to negotiate sea freight charges.[77]

According to the *consulado* of Seville, Spanish imperial ocean freight rates were high, at least until *comercio libre* broke the monopoly of the *flota*. In 1788 the *consulado* reported that the transatlantic exports of Peninsulars had benefited from the opening of trade because the cost of shipping, insurance, and taxes had fallen. Before *comercio libre*, the *consulado* remarked, an arroba of cooking oil cost twenty-four to twenty-five reales to ship to America, but after *comercio libre* it could be shipped for as little as six reales.[78]

The *consulado*'s euphoria must certainly have subsided when, five years later, France declared war on Spain, sending freight rates spiraling upward, at least according to the data collected by Douglass North. When

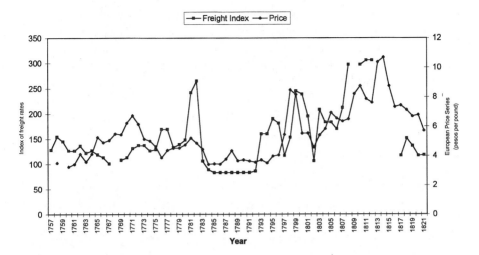

FIGURE 8.4. Ocean freight rates and European *grana* prices, 1757–1821.
Sources: North, "Role of Transportation," Appendix Table 1 (p. 235); Tooke and
Newmarch, 2:400; and Posthumus, 1:420–23.

the *consulado* prepared its 1788 report, freight rates were, for the fifth suc-
cessive year, at the lowest they had been since at least 1757, the year
North's index begins. By 1793, however, freight rates had doubled, and
they continued to rise until peaking in 1811 at nearly four times the low
rates sustained during the 1780s. Rates did not return again to levels comparable to those of the 1780s until the middle of the nineteenth century.[79]

If the introduction of *comercio libre* truly increased competition in
Spanish shipping, the bonus of inexpensive ocean freight rates was short-
lived. Eighteenth-century wars were interpreted by enemies and pirates to
mean open season on merchant cargo ships. In fact, higher risks of seizure
caused insurance premiums to skyrocket, greatly increasing the cost of
transatlantic shipping. The twenty years of war that began in 1793 were
particularly severe. Freight rates rose sharply and, consequently, so did the
prices of commodities transported.

That much of the late-colonial surge in the European price of cochineal
was a reflection of the rising costs of transportation can be seen in Figure
8.4, which plots North's index of freight rates against the European price
series that is shown in Figure 8.1 for the years 1757–1821. In the first two
decades, the slope of the curves have opposite values. When freight costs
rose, the price of cochineal fell, and vice versa. This should not be seen as
anything but coincidence. Before 1778, freight rates between Mexico and

159

Spain were fixed and thus had no influence on the fluctuation of final prices. After 1778 approximately, we begin to see a stronger correlation between the two variables.[80] During the decade of the 1780s, both the price of *grana* and the cost of freight remained low. With the start of war in 1793, however, both rose rapidly. They fell in tandem in 1802, the year the Peace of Amiens was reached, but climbed together to great heights after Napoleon invaded Spain. Finally, Napoleon's defeat coincided with the fall in prices and in the cost of transport.

MARITIME INSURANCE

Transatlantic shipping was fraught with risk. As a result, few merchants could afford not to insure their goods against the potential for transatlantic disasters, both natural and man-made. Although the Crown required that cochineal travel on or be escorted by warships, the dyestuff was not entirely secure from danger. Even well-armed ships could be sunk by enemies or captured by pirates. In addition, inclement weather caused frequent shipwrecks during the eighteenth century, and no ship was immune to storms.

Antonio García-Baquero González identified 126 Spanish ships that were lost during the years 1717–1778 while crossing the Atlantic Ocean. Pirates captured or sank forty-one of the ships, and the other eighty-five were shipwrecked. Piracy was closely associated with war and the English. Ninety percent of the ships lost to pirates during this period were lost during times of international war, and over 90 percent of the pirates were identified as English.[81] García-Baquero's study ends in 1778, but the risk of piracy seems only to have escalated, especially after the 1793 outbreak of war and the ensuing two decades of European conflict. Estimates of the losses during the entire era of war total 186 ships and 22 million pesos.[82] While the risk of piracy escalated during wartime, shipwrecks caused by bad weather or poor navigation might occur at any time, as in July 1733 when a hurricane destroyed seventeen of the *flota*'s ships off the coast of the Bahamas.[83] Most ships completed the voyage between Veracruz and Cádiz unscathed, but the danger of catastrophe always existed. García-Baquero González found that 96 percent of the ships making the trip between 1717 and 1778 arrived without delay. Four percent, however, experienced difficulties.[84]

160

A large shipment of cochineal belonging to the prominent trading house of the Conde de Reparaz, the Casa de Uztariz, was lost in a 1772 disaster. The Count was granted permission in 1772 to outfit two ships to transport one thousand zurrones of his own cochineal to Cádiz. Both ships, *El Buen*

Consejo and *El Prusiano*, were shipwrecked off the Caribbean island of Anguilla and five hundred zurrones of cochineal, presumably the cargo aboard *El Prusiano*, were lost.[85]

Merchants and ship owners sought to protect themselves against the financial disaster of such unforeseeable catastrophes by purchasing maritime insurance. Colonial insurance policies operated much like modern ones. Merchants paid premiums based on the declared value of their cargo, and, in the event of loss, insurers paid to the merchant the amount specified by the policy. Similarly, ship owners secured coverage against the possible loss or damage to their ships.[86] The cost of insurance responded, as one would expect, to the perceived risks of transatlantic commerce.[87] Insurers earned their profits by collecting more in premiums than they paid out in losses. Naturally, when insurers determined travel to be less safe, they demanded higher premiums to compensate for the greater risk.

Surviving archival records permit a fairly intensive economic analysis of maritime insurance for colonial Spanish-American shipping, at least for the years 1784 to 1817. Data suggest that insurance premiums charged on transatlantic voyages were not onerous, except during wartime, when the risk of piracy or war-inflicted damage led many insurers to withdraw from the insurance market altogether, and drove those still willing to provide coverage to charge astoundingly high rates. Figure 8.5 shows "peacetime"[88] insurance premium rates charged to merchandise and ships for travel between Spain and Veracruz for most of the years between 1784 and 1817.[89]

For the years prior to 1784, information about the cost of insurance is more sketchy. A 1788 report on commerce produced by the *consulado* of Seville claimed that the 1778 promulgation of *comercio libre* had brought about an average reduction of 50 percent on transatlantic insurance premiums.[90] Ortiz de la Tabla cited a letter sent to Viceroy Revillagigedo in 1793 by the prominent merchant Thomas Murphy, in which Murphy also commented on the reduction of rates to Mexico, from around 6–8 percent before *comercio libre*, to just 1.25–1.5 percent afterward.[91] In addition to *comercio libre*, Antonio-Miguel Bernal credits the rate reduction to the "proliferation of insurers" during this period, as well as the general decline in premiums throughout Europe after 1770.[92] The claims made by the *consulado* and Murphy are corroborated by the sparse data uncovered for this earlier period. In the months of March and June, 1772, three ship owners insured their vessels at peacetime rates of between 5 and 5.25 percent for the one-way voyage from Cádiz to Veracruz.[93] By the mid-1780s,

161

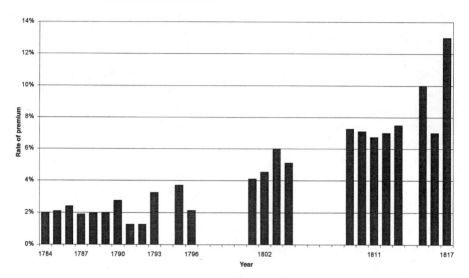

FIGURE 8.5. Average insurance rates for cargo and ships traveling between Spain and Veracruz, 1784–1817. Source: Appendix D.

peacetime rates for the identical route were less than half that rate. Presumably, *comercio libre* drove insurance rates down, owing to the increased competition in Spain among insurers who were responding, perhaps, to the rise in private shippers who were outfitting merchant boats destined for American ports. Both the *consulado* and Murphy, however, presented their reports during a brief interlude before the onset of war, a war that would raise greatly both risks and insurance rates. Neither could have possibly anticipated the 1793 outbreak of war and still less its longevity. The shock to the insurance market caused by the decades of war kept rates elevated even after the cessation of hostilities and the return to normalcy.

As Figure 8.5 indicates, the low rates of the 1780s continued until 1793, the year in which the peacetime rates began to rise gradually. At the end of the century, rates ranged between 4 and 6 percent and continued to climb, reaching around 7 percent, where they remained until 1813. Peacetime rates peaked in 1815 and 1817, at 10 and 13 percent, respectively. In short, one sees a rather significant upward trend in the peacetime rates charged during the years after 1793.

Again, and this is very important, these were peacetime rates. Insurance rates skyrocketed during times of international strife. One scholar noted that the mere rumor of war in 1793 caused insurance premiums to rise "enormously" on exports from Barcelona. He also cited a colonial merchant who claimed that in the war year of 1805 goods arriving in Veracruz were burdened by insurance rates of 40–50 percent.[94] Policies during this period often stipulated rate increases if war were to erupt during the period of coverage, and, of course, during much of this period Spain was embroiled in conflict. For example, a policy written in July 1790 provided for a rate of 1.75 percent between Veracruz and Cádiz, but on the condition that "if during these risks war or hostilities were to occur with England or any other power employing maritime forces, [the insured] will pay 20 percent [*sic*] above the stipulated premium."[95] Similarly, in February 1796 coverage for the transport of merchandise from Veracruz to Cádiz aboard a warship was secured at the rate of 1.75 percent of the merchandise's value, under the condition that if war were to erupt, the rate would rise to 16 percent.[96] Such a variable rate was increasingly common over the decades of war. In April 1796, merchandise was underwritten at 2.25 percent, increasing to 20 percent if war broke out within fifteen days of the ship's departure from Cádiz.[97] In February 1803, the owner of *La Fraternidad* insured his ship for 24,155 pesos at 3.75 percent on the condition that the premium would increase to 30 percent if war with France or Great Britain were to arise, and 12 percent if the war were against any other country.[98] In July of the same year, a merchant insured his goods for the voyage from Veracruz to Cádiz at 5.5 percent, agreeing to pay an additional 45 percentage points, for a total of 50.5 percent, in the event of war.[99] In September 1799, the owner of a ship called *Aguila* insured his vessel, which he valued at 12,677 pesos, at the astronomical rate of 60 percent.[100]

Extraordinarily high rates during wartime were not unique to the Spanish insurance market. Frank Spooner found that in 1782, during the War of American Independence, Dutch insurers charged 30 percent to one ship transporting cargo one way from Amsterdam to Boston. Earlier in the conflict, in 1777, some ships bound for the Dutch West Indies were unable to obtain insurance even at 30 percent. Finally, in 1777 a ship returning to Amsterdam from Jamaica paid a premium of 25 percent.[101]

One might imagine that the insurance companies earned enormous profits during the Napoleonic Wars, but this is not so obviously the case. Most insurers wanted nothing to do with insuring ships during the wars, even after seeing their more courageous competitors charge 40 or 50 percent. During certain years of conflict, it was difficult to obtain insurance at even such inflated rates. Indeed, no data whatsoever is recorded for a handful of years (1794, 1797–1798, 1800–1801, 1805–1808, and

1814), suggesting that companies did not extend any insurance policies for trade between Veracruz and Cádiz in these years (see Figure 8.5 and Appendix D).[102] These years were precisely the years in which maritime trade would have been most risky, since in most of them Spain was at war against England, the greatest naval power of Europe. War with France seems to have had some, but much less, impact on insurance rates. Another possibility for the dearth of data, at least for the years 1798–1799 and 1805–1808, is that these periods correspond to the era during which the Crown permitted the entry of neutral ships into its ports. Neutral ships acquired insurance elsewhere.[103]

Sending ships into hostile waters was extremely risky and, consequently, insurers were only willing to underwrite policies if rates were justifiably high. Rates of 30–50 percent seem not to have been uncommon during the worst of the wars, and, apparently, some companies refused to provide coverage even at these rates. These were high-risk capital ventures, and most companies preferred the safety of suspending operations until conflicts ceased. What seems astonishing is that at times merchants found it economical to pay such high rates. Certainly, the high cost of insurance drove many commodities out of the transatlantic trade, as is suggested by the export data displayed in Figure 8.6, which demonstrates the sharp decrease in exports from Spain to Spanish America after 1793. Unless the potential profitability of a commodity was spectacular, no merchant would have agreed to pay such elevated premiums. Yet, trade did not cease entirely. At least in the case of cochineal, price data suggests that exports probably remained profitable through most of the war years, even if profitability decreased. But if one considers that merchants had to pay from 20 to 50 percent above the cost of the commodity just to buy the insurance to protect their capital, then trade does not seem especially attractive, or at least it seems highly speculative.

Merchants who did incur the expenses of insurance during wartime (or who threw caution to the wind and shipped goods uninsured) hoped to reap high gross profits by taking advantage of war-induced scarcities. Merchants paid high premiums because they expected to be more than compensated when they sold their goods. Ship owners, in contrast, had less obvious incentives for paying high insurance premiums. Yet ships continued to sail the Atlantic in all but the most dangerous years. The only possible explanation is that ship owners also were more generously rewarded during wartime, undoubtedly by charging high rates themselves, rates which at the very least yielded profits equal to what they would have earned had there not been hostilities. One imagines that most ship owners

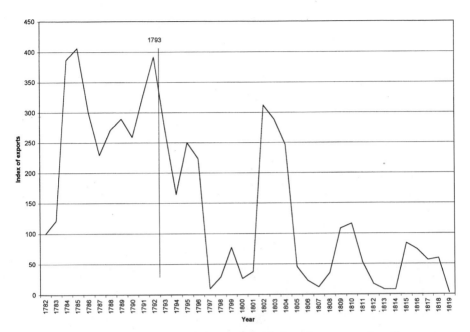

FIGURE 8.6. Total exports from Spain to Spanish America, 1782–1819. Sources: John R. Fisher, *Commercial Relations between Spain and Spanish America*, 46; and John R. Fisher, *Trade, War, and Revolution*, 80.

withdrew from these dangerous voyages, leaving the courageous with a valuable and scarce commodity — cargo space. The inevitable conclusion is that most of the increase in freight rates during wartime can be attributed to the rising cost of insurance coverage for the ships. With the exception of the compensation paid to the crews, which also rose during war, other expenses related to shipping probably remained more or less the same. Freight rates doubled between 1792 and 1793, and during several of the war years reached almost triple the 1792 rate. This was almost certainly caused by insurance premiums, which would have had to increase at a much greater rate.[104]

War increased dramatically the risk of exporting cochineal from Mexico and led to higher insurance premiums. During the 1790s and in the first fifteen years of the 1800s, insurance premiums reached extraordinarily high levels as war raged incessantly in Europe. The extremely high price of *grana* in Northern Europe during these years undoubtedly reflected the high cost of insurance. Figure 8.7 compares peacetime insurance rates from Figure 8.5 with the European price of cochineal. As is clear, the two series moved in tandem and rose sharply after 1793. There seems little

165

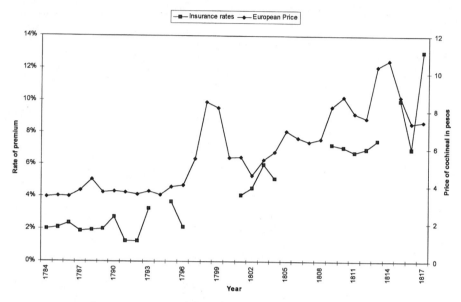

FIGURE 8.7. Insurance rates and European cochineal prices, 1784–1817.
Sources: Tooke and Newmarch, 2:400; and Posthumus, 1:420–23.

doubt that the high cost of insurance premiums pushed the price of cochineal higher and higher. These high prices did not generate greater revenues for the cochineal merchants, however. Instead, they merely served to offset premiums to insurers or losses to pirates. Merchants could at least take comfort in the fact that they were able to pass much of the increased cost of insurance on to consumers.[105]

As for previous analyses, the purpose of examining the insurance market is to estimate the cost incurred by merchants trading in cochineal. The problem with doing this for insurance is that we must decide how to deal with the fact that premium rates were often conditional on the actual outbreak of war. Also, we must decide how much to estimate for insurance during those years in which coverage was suspended, although for the most part in such years commerce probably ceased. While no perfect solution to these problems exists, it is at least reasonable to proceed with the supposition that during wartime merchants paid rates of between 20 and 50 percent, and that during peacetime, they paid the going rate as depicted in Figure 8.5.

As can be seen in Table 8.5, rates responded rapidly to the advent or even the threat of war. For the purpose of estimating insurance expenses, however, it seems prudent to designate each year as either a "war year" or

TABLE 8.5
Impact of War on Insurance Rates

Date	Event	Impact on rates
January 2, 1793	Louis XVI beheaded	Rates in January average 1.5 percent
February 1, 1793	France declares war on England and Holland	Rise in February to 6.75 percent.
March 7, 1793	France declares war on Spain	No more policies until early 1795
First half of 1795	Spain and France are negotiating peace	New policies written at rates of 3–4 percent
July 22, 1795	Peace of Basel ends Spain's war with France	Rates fall to 2 percent
August 19, 1796	Spain and France sign Treaty of Ildefonso	No policies after April 1796
October 7, 1796	Spain declares war against England	No more policies until late 1801
October 1801	England and France begin negotiations	December 1801 — policies resume at 5 percent
March 25, 1802	Peace of Amiens — official end of war	Rates fall to a still cautious 4 percent
May 16, 1803	France and England resume fighting	Rates rise in April by 50 percent and stay at this new plateau of 6–7 percent
December 14, 1804	Spain joins war against England	Last policy is November 1804; do not resume until October 1809
January–March 1808	Napoleon invades Spain	Underwriting still suspended
June 1808	English–Spanish conflict officially over	Still no new policies being written
March 1809	Spanish junta establishes military treaty with England	
October 1810		Policies resume despite French occupation

SOURCE: Derived from Artola, *Enciclopedia de historia de España*, vol. 6, *Cronología, mapas y estadísticas*. On insurance rate, see Appendix D.

a "peace year," and proceed as if all cargo in a given year paid either 167 the "war rate" or the "peace rate." Table 8.6 used the information from Table 8.5 to designate each year as either a "war" year or a "peace" year for the purpose of insurance rates.

Another potential complication relates to the Crown's concessions to neutral ships, by which neutral shipping was given permission to stop

TABLE 8.6
Spain's War Status for the Purpose of Insurance Rates

Year	Status	Year	Status	Year	Status	Year	Status
1793	war	1799	war	1805	war	1811	peace
1794	war	1800	war	1806	war	1812	peace
1795	peace	1801	war	1807	war	1813	peace
1796	peace	1802	peace	1808	war	1814–1821	peace
1797	war	1803	peace	1809	war		
1798	war	1804	peace	1810	peace		

SOURCE: Derived from Artola, *Enciclopedia de historia de España*, vol. 6, *Cronología, mapas y estadísticas*. On insurance rate, see citations in text.

NOTE: The classifications are, of course, artificial. In a number of the years classified as "peace" years, Spain was at war, as was the case for the period 1811–1814, for example, during which time Spaniards fought against Napoleon's occupation of Spain (1808–1814). These years are nevertheless considered "peace" years for our purposes, since we know that "peacetime" insurance premiums were being charged.

in Spain's peninsular and American ports between November 1797 and April 1799, and again during the years 1805–1808. Theoretically, neutral ships were free from attack by the British and thus faced far fewer risks and paid lower insurance premiums. The question arises as to how we should treat the years during which the neutral trade was legal — whether the cost of insurance should be presumed "low," as if premiums in such years were more typical of peacetime.

For the calculations that follow, the impact of neutral shipping is ignored. While it is probable that neutral ships faced fewer dangers than Spanish vessels, they certainly did not operate with impunity. Despite the concession, Spain's Minister of Finance, Francisco de Saavedra, reported in early 1798 that the British blockade was even curtailing the departure of neutral ships from Cádiz.[106] In November, the Viceroy of Mexico, Miguel Josef de Azanza, informed that trade with Spain was still at a standstill, that few vessels had managed to penetrate the British naval blockade, and, consequently, that eight thousand zurrones of cochineal remained stranded in Veracruz warehouses.[107] In short, the concession to neutral ships was no panacea. The British blockade was sufficiently menacing to dissuade most merchant vessels.

Even when neutral ships did land at Veracruz, it did not necessarily result in inexpensive, risk-free passage. The greatest beneficiary of neutral trade was the United States, which took full advantage of the war-induced opening of the Spanish trade monopoly, experiencing a commercial boom with its Spanish-American neighbors.[108] But American ships were not immune to attack by enemy warships, despite U.S. neutrality. In fact, during these years the French seized hundreds of American merchant vessels, sparking the so called "Quasi War with France."[109] Available data on maritime insurance rates contracted in the United States demonstrate unambiguously that the dangers were very real. Average premium rates for cargo and vessels traveling from ports in the United States to ports in the Spanish-American empire were 12.4 percent in 1798 and 10.3 percent in 1799, the two years during which the neutral trade was legal.[110] These rates were as much as six times greater than the average peacetime rates incurred earlier in the decade. And these were *average* rates; individual policies sometimes reached 20–25 percent for the voyage from Philadelphia to the Caribbean Islands.[111] While these rates are still below some of the higher war premium rates paid by merchants in Cádiz, one cannot help but conclude that the additional costs and inconveniences of shipping on "foreign" ships would have offset much of the advantage reaped by the lower insurance costs. For the sake of simplicity and not without some rationale, then, the impact on marketing costs associated with the concession to neutrals is ignored.

Table 8.7 shows the estimated cost of insuring one arroba of cochineal during most of the years after 1784. For each of the "peace" years, the average rates depicted in Figure 8.5 were used. For the "war" years, two estimates were calculated, one at the low-end wartime rate of 20 percent and the other at the high-end wartime rate of 50 percent. The estimates were obtained by simply multiplying the yearly premium rate by the price of cochineal per arroba in Veracruz.[112] The results are predictable. During the peaceful years 1784–1792, insurance was very affordable, costing between 0.5 and 1.5 pesos per arroba. At prices so low, few merchants would have chosen *not* to have insured their cargo. With the 1793 outbreak of hostilities against France, however, estimated insurance grew very expensive, ranging between 8 and 25 pesos per arroba, depending on the war rate assumed. Insurance premiums grew even higher when Spain went to war against England in 1797, and peaked in 1801. While premiums dropped with the return of peace, they remained above the earlier peacetime levels. Spain's return to war against England in December 1804

169

TABLE 8.7
Estimated Cost of Insuring an Arroba of Cochineal from Mexico to Spain

Year	Rate	Oaxaca price (pesos per pound)	Veracruz price (pesos per pound)	Veracruz price (pesos per arroba)	Estimated premium per arroba at 20% war-year rates	Estimated premium per arroba at 50% war-year rates
1784	2.00%	$2.00	$ 2.25	$56.25	$1.13	$1.13
1785	2.09%	2.13	2.38	59.38	1.24	1.24
1786	2.38%	2.06	2.31	57.81	1.37	1.37
1787	1.88%	2.00	2.25	56.25	1.05	1.05
1788	1.95%	2.00	2.25	56.25	1.10	1.10
1789	2.00%	1.94	2.19	54.69	1.09	1.09
1790	2.75%	2.00	2.25	56.25	1.55	1.55
1791	1.25%	2.06	2.31	57.81	.72	.72
1792	1.25%	1.88	2.13	53.13	.66	.66
1793	war year	1.69	1.94	48.44	9.69	24.22
1794	war year	1.31	1.56	39.06	7.81	19.53
1795	3.70%	1.50	1.75	43.75	1.62	1.62
1796	2.13%	2.19	2.88	71.93	1.53	1.53
1797	war year	1.94	2.60	65.00	13.00	32.50
1798	war year	2.25	2.63	65.87	13.17	32.93
1799	war year	2.44	2.66	66.58	13.32	33.29
1800	war year	2.38	2.95	73.64	14.73	36.82
1801	war year	2.25	3.10	77.51	15.50	38.75
1802	4.56%	2.38	3.05	76.33	3.48	3.48
1803	6.02%	2.63	3.22	80.42	4.84	4.84
1804	5.13%	3.56	4.16	103.96	5.33	5.33
1805	war year	2.88	4.16	103.96	20.79	51.98
1806	war year	3.38	4.00	100.00	20.00	50.00
1807	war year	3.63	4.00	100.00	20.00	50.00
1808	war year	3.63	4.00	100.00	20.00	50.00
1809	war year	4.13	4.80	119.95	23.99	59.97
1810	7.08%	3.63	4.80	120.00	8.50	8.50
1811	6.75%	3.56	4.32	108.00	7.29	7.29
1812	7.00%	2.50	4.00	100.00	7.00	7.00
1813	7.50%	1.88	4.54	113.47	8.51	8.51
1814		3.13	12.82	320.47		
1815	10.00%	3.00	4.80	120.00	12.00	12.00
1816	7.00%	4.00	5.17	129.13	9.04	9.04
1817	13.00%	3.63	5.20	130.00	16.90	16.90

SOURCE: Data are extrapolated from data in Figure 8.5. See text for descriptions.

once again drove the cost of insurance skyward. The cost of insuring an arroba of cochineal ranged between 20 and 60 pesos.

There is little doubt that many merchants refused to pay such high insurance rates. It probably seemed foolish, and simply bad business, to pay premiums of 50 percent. Doubtless, some merchants gambled and shipped their commodities uninsured. The economic rewards for such valor were potentially phenomenal. Most merchants, however, could ill afford to be so daring, for if their uninsured cargo were lost, they would be instantly bankrupted. What alternative existed to either paying high premiums or shipping goods uninsured? A merchant could wait out the war, hoping for a rapid return to peace. There is little doubt that many Spaniards chose this latter option, shipping their goods only after peace, and peacetime insurance rates, resumed.[113] This was not without significant economic cost, however, because merchants found their capital tied up in cochineal, or other export commodities, for considerable periods. A merchant who purchased dye in late 1804 might have found himself stuck with it until 1810, paying 5 percent interest on his capital investment for more than five years.

RE-EXPORT FROM SPAIN

Merchants in Mexico shipped large quantities of cochineal to Spain. While most of the dye was subsequently re-exported to final markets in Northern Europe, Spanish colonial commercial law required that it first pass through the Iberian Peninsula. Because of its importance as an *entrepôt* for colonial commodities, foreign merchants enjoyed a strong mercantile presence throughout the colonial period, first in Seville and later in Cádiz.[114] Many of the foreign merchants residing in Spain specialized in the re-export of cochineal to the important markets of Marseilles, London, or Amsterdam.[115] Frequently, then, *grana* changed hands in Cádiz, having been purchased there by non-Spanish merchants.[116]

Regardless of the owner, the export of *grana* from Spain entailed still additional costs. Export taxes, discussed above, were 15 percent of cochineal's *avaluo* rate of 82.8 pesos per arroba.[117] Re-exporting the dye also meant additional freight and insurance charges. Finally, cochineal was assessed import tariffs by the governments of the nations into which it was introduced.

171

Just like the Veracruz-to-Cádiz route, merchants purchased maritime insurance to protect their shipments from Cádiz to Northern Europe. Premium rates for these routes, which undoubtedly responded to the same risks as did the transatlantic trade, tended to be slightly less than those

TABLE 8.8

Insurance Premiums from Cádiz to Northern European Ports

Date	Route	Rate	Item
May 1788	Cádiz to London	1.25%	silver
May 1788	Cádiz to Amsterdam	1.50%	silver
August 1788	Cádiz to Marseilles	1.00%	vermillion
August 1788	Cádiz to London	1.00%	grana
October 1788	Cádiz to London	1.75%	efectos
October 1788	Cádiz to London	1.00%	grana
October 1788	Cádiz to Amsterdam	1.75%	grana
December 1788	Cádiz to London	1.50%	silver
May 1790	Cádiz to London	1.00%	grana
May 1790	Cádiz to Marseilles	1.00%	grana
June 1790	Cádiz to London	1.50%	grana
June 1790	Cádiz to Amsterdam	1.50%	anil/grana
October 1790	Cádiz to Marseilles	1.00%	grana
October 1790	Cádiz to London	1.50%	anil
March 1791	Cádiz to Marseilles	1.00%	grana
March 1791	Cádiz to Amsterdam	1.75%	cueros
June 1791	London to Cádiz	1.50%	lanas
June 1791	Amsterdam to Cádiz	1.50%	canela
June 1791	Cádiz to Marseilles	0.75%	plata
December 1791	Cádiz to London	1.00%	grana
December 1791	Cádiz to Marseilles	1.50%	cueros
December 1791	Amsterdam to Cádiz	2.00%	efectos
May 1792	Cádiz to London	1.00%	casco
June 1792	Marseilles to Cádiz	1.25%	efectos
December 1792	Cádiz to London	1.25%	grana
December 1792	Cádiz to Marseilles	1.75%	cueros
February 1802	Cádiz to London	5.00%	
February 1802	Cádiz to Marseilles	3.50%	
February 1802	Cádiz to Northern France	5.00%	
December 1809	Cádiz to London	4.75%	
January 1810	Cádiz to London	4.50%	
November 1810	Cádiz to London	5.00%	

SOURCES: AGI, Consulados, Libro 444B; AGI, Consulados, legajo 78; AGI, Consulados, legajo 518.

for the Veracruz to Cádiz voyage. Table 8.8 shows a sample of insurance rates charged to merchandise shipped from Cádiz to either London, Amsterdam, or Marseilles for a number of years, all of which were during peacetime.

In May 1788, merchants paid 2 percent to ship goods from Veracruz to Cádiz and only 1 percent from Cádiz to Marseilles, 1.25 percent to London, and 1.5 percent to Amsterdam. In February 1802, merchants were paying 5.25 percent for the transatlantic route, while the rates from Cádiz to European ports had also increased, rising to 5 percent to London and 3.5 percent to Marseilles. Finally, in December 1810, the premium rate from Veracruz was 6.5 percent, whereas one month earlier it had been 5 percent for the Cádiz-to-London trip. In short, rates were slightly lower within Europe. Unfortunately, we do not have rates reflecting wartime, although, of course, trade between warring nations was curtailed. Owing to the paucity of the European insurance data uncovered, it is not possible to estimate the costs that would be incurred by a cochineal merchant. The few data points collected, however, do suggest that insurance premiums for the shorter intra-European voyage were nearly as expensive as those for the Cádiz-to-Veracruz route.

European rulers turned to import-export taxes as a major source of government revenues. The only import tariff schedule located in which cochineal was listed applied to imports into England starting in 1782. Table 8.9 shows the import duties on cochineal for the period 1782–1821 in both English and Spanish currencies. For most of this period, England assessed modestly low import duties on cochineal. After 1798, however, and especially after 1809, the English tax burden on cochineal grew to very high levels. This tax increase coincided, in fact, with the rising tax burden on *grana* imposed by the Spanish Crown after 1800. By 1819, one arroba of cochineal was assessed 15.63 pesos in taxes upon its entry into England. When the cost of Spanish taxes is added, the total tax burden reached 55.38 Spanish pesos, an amount equal to 65 percent of the product's value that year in Oaxaca.

TOTALING THE COSTS

173

Merchants specializing in the cochineal trade incurred a great number of expenses. To be brought to market, the dye needed protective packaging, and the merchant also incurred both land and sea freight charges. Insurance was necessary to protect against risks, both natural and human. States struggling to meet expenses during an era of frequent warfare ex-

TABLE 8.9

Duties on Cochineal Imported into England

Period	Shillings per pound	Pence per pound	Pesos per pound	Pesos per arroba
1782–1787	0	2.25	.0469	1.17
1788–1794	0	3.00	.0625	1.56
1795–1797	0	0	.0000	0.00
1798–1802	0	10.00	.2083	5.21
1803	0	11.25	.2344	5.86
1804	1	0.50	.2604	6.51
1805	1	1.00	.2708	6.77
1806–1808	1	1.75	.2865	7.16
1809–1812	2	0	.5000	12.50
1813–1818	2	4.50	.5938	14.85
1819–1821	2	6.00	.6250	15.63

SOURCE: Tooke and Newmarch, 2:400.

NOTE: There were 12 pence in a shilling, and 20 shillings in 1 pound sterling. The exchange rate used to convert to pesos was £1 = 5 Spanish pesos.

acted increasingly burdensome taxes. All of these expenses served to re-duce the merchants' profits or, at the very least, required them to invest more and more capital just to maintain profits at previous levels. The rate of return on investment necessarily fell.[118] Merchants even saw some of their cochineal profits evaporate as the *grana* dried and the weight of their merchandise shrank. This chapter has attempted to impute estimated val-ues to each of these costs incurred by the cochineal merchant.

The total of all variable expenses[119] incurred by a cochineal merchant marketing a fixed amount of *grana* between Oaxaca and London in each year can be estimated by adding the sum of these expenses to the amount spent for the initial purchase of the dyestuff in Oaxaca.[120] With the excep-tion of the cost of ocean freight and intra-European maritime insurance, for which exact or complete figures are lacking, these variable costs are presented in Appendixes E.1 and E.2, and plotted in Figure 8.8.[121] Two series are shown in the figure, one that reflects "wartime" insurance pre-miums of 20 percent and another reflecting "wartime" premiums of 50 percent.[122] For non-war years, "peacetime" insurance rates are used in

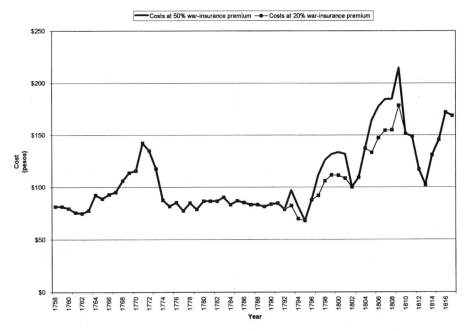

FIGURE 8.8. Costs of marketing one arroba of cochineal, Oaxaca to London, 1758–1817 (excluding ocean freight and intra-European insurance). Sources: Appendixes E.1 and E.2.

both series. Merchants are assumed to have bought their cochineal in Oaxaca at the market price prevailing in each year, according to the figures recorded by the cochineal Registry.

The figure illustrates a number of trends. With the exception of the five years from 1768 to 1773 (years in which the high value of dyestuff in Oaxaca drove costs above 100 pesos per arroba), the period until about 1797 was characterized by fairly stable costs, averaging around 85 pesos. The costs incurred to purchase in Oaxaca and market in London one arroba of cochineal increased tremendously, however, toward the end of the period under examination. After hitting its lowest point at 66.86 pesos in 1795, costs rose sharply and constantly, peaking in 1809 at 213.44 pesos. During the last quarter-century of colonial rule, costs in the cochineal trade grew steeply. Most of this late-colonial increase is attributable to two factors: (1) the increasingly predatory fiscal policies of the Spanish (and even the British) Crown, and (2) the sharp increase in insurance premiums caused by the rise in war-related risk. The variable costs of

175

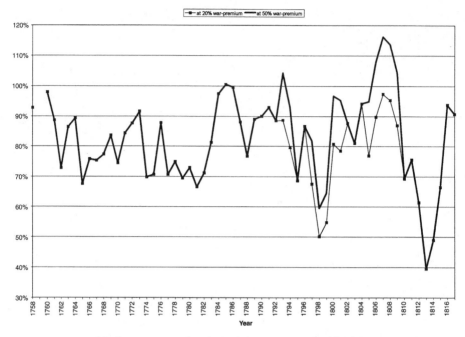

FIGURE 8.9. Marketing costs of cochineal as a percentage of final price in Europe, 1758–1817. Sources: Appendixes E.1 and E.2; Tooke and Newmarch, 2:400; and Posthumus, 1:420–23.

trading in cochineal rose sharply in the late-colonial period, and if one were to account for ocean freight and intra-European insurance, both of which were adversely affected by the wars, then the increase would have been steeper still. Dye merchants had to invest more and more money to market each arroba of cochineal.

A Final Account

That merchants had to outlay more and more capital did not, however, necessarily mean that the dye trade had become unattractive. As long as they enjoyed handsome profits, merchants would continue to invest in cochineal. There is, however, good reason to believe that the dye trade's profitability grew less stable in the second half of the period under investigation, as probably was the case for all transatlantic trade. Two additional analyses were carried out in an effort to determine (or at least estimate) the trade's profitability. First, the ratio of total variable costs per

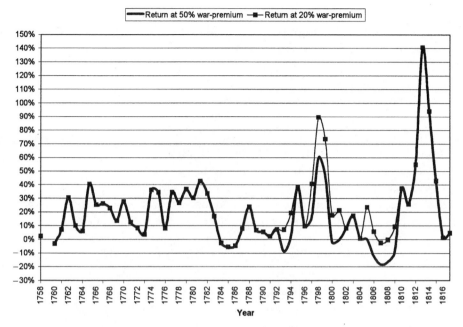

FIGURE 8.10. Estimated return to merchant on investment in cochineal, 1758–1817. Sources: Appendixes E.1 and E.2.

arroba to the European price of *grana* per arroba was computed. Since profitability is determined, in part, by the difference between costs and revenues (the final sale price), this ratio (costs ÷ revenues) reflects the evolution of the trade's potential profitability. The lower the ratio, the greater the profitability.[123] The second computation measured the merchant's return on his investment by taking the ratio of profits (revenues − costs) to costs (i.e., profits ÷ costs). As in the prior case, this calculation measures profitability, albeit from a slightly different angle.[124] The results of both calculations are shown in Figures 8.9 and 8.10, respectively.[125]

Examining Figure 8.9 first, one sees that the rising costs of the trade as earlier described translated into higher final prices, as merchants were normally able to pass along to consumers the added costs of marketing this largely price inelastic commodity. A trend that is discernible, however, is the increasing volatility that begins in the 1780s. In 1781 costs represent a mere 67 percent of gross revenues, suggesting the strong potential for profits. The ratio continues to rise until the period 1784–1787, three years in which costs and revenues are nearly identical. This indicates that cochineal traders lost money in these years after accounting for fixed costs,

177

ocean freight, and intra-European insurance premiums. During the rest of the colonial era, the ratio (costs ÷ revenues) fluctuated violently, but the general tendency in most years was for the figure to be slightly above (less profitable than) the earlier period. Costs consumed a larger and larger percentage of revenues.

Figure 8.10 shows the same trends, albeit in a slightly different way. The return on the merchant's investment was steady and rewarding until the mid-1780s, when the industry became unprofitable for several years, followed by another half-dozen years (leading up to the wars) in which profitability seems dubious. During the remainder of the colonial era, returns exhibited great instability, yielding potentially fabulous returns in a few years but nearly certain losses in many others. It should be noted that the several years of really phenomenal returns exhibited in the figure, especially the years 1798–1799 and 1813–1814, were extraordinary and probably misleading. The years 1797–1799, and especially 1797, were the years in which the British erected successful blockades of Spanish transatlantic commerce. The interruption of trade served to drive a wedge between prices in Mexico and London. Windfall profits were earned by the lucky few who held cochineal in Northern Europe during these years. Most of the dyestuff, however, had to wait out the war in Veracruz or Cádiz.[126] Similarly, the years 1813–1814[127] were the two years affected by Morelos's occupation of Oaxaca, which began in November 1812. During those two years, prices in Europe rose to unprecedented levels, driven by speculation and the near-total abandonment of cochineal production in Oaxaca. Equally as influential was the total collapse of the cochineal price in Oaxaca, the result, no doubt, of the abandonment of the city by the cochineal merchants.[128] Nonetheless, merchants fortunate enough to have found themselves possessing *grana* in Europe certainly made a killing.

As Figure 8.10 shows, the decade from approximately 1784 to 1794 marked a shift in the profitability of the dye trade. Prior to this decade, cochineal had nearly always produced significant and stable profits. After a 1781 peak during the War of American Independence, however, the potential profitability of the trade plummeted to historic lows.[129] Excluding 1788, the one very profitable year, the estimated profit rate for a merchant for the non-war years 1784–1792 averaged only 2.17 percent, clearly signifying a loss after deducting for all additional costs. During the years 1784–1786, losses were sustained even before other costs — loan-servicing, ocean freight, intra-European insurance, and overhead — were paid. Unquestionably, merchants trading in cochineal during this decade lost money.

As one would expect, the dismal returns in the cochineal trade during this decade discouraged investment in the industry. In fact, the impact was profound and immediate. In 1784 output was 46 percent lower than the previous year, and it continued to decline for several more years. Reduced profitability drove merchants to invest capital elsewhere, and, as a result, *repartimiento* loans dried up and production fell. The industry's profitability recovered somewhat during the second half of the 1790s, but the nature of the trade, and in fact all transatlantic trade, had been radically altered. Overseas trade after 1793 involved far greater risk than pre-war trade, not only because of the dangers of piracy. Merchants had to put up increasingly more capital to participate in the cochineal trade, owing to the rise in taxes, costs of insurance, and ocean freight charges. Yet the guarantee of profits was every year less certain.[130] Thus, it should be of little surprise that the abandonment of the cochineal trade, which began in 1784, should have continued into the nineteenth century. The trade, and probably all transatlantic trade, produced less profit yet entailed greater risk, an obviously unappealing combination.

This conclusion is important because it provides an alternative hypothesis to the traditional explanation for why cochineal production decreased during the 1780s. Scholars have attributed the decline in cochineal production solely to the promulgation of Article 12 of the 1786 Ordinance of Intendants, which officially banned *repartimientos*. They have argued that Indians, freed from the coercion of the *alcalde mayor*, chose to abandon the forced production of cochineal.[131] Hamnett, who examined the decline most closely, attributed it to four factors: (1) fear among Spanish cochineal growers that the Church would successfully impose an obligatory tithe on their production, a fear that was partially realized by the 1780 Edicto Sangriento, which threatened Spanish producers with excommunication if they did not pay a full 10 percent tithe; (2) concern on the part of the *alcaldes* and their backers about the Crown's growing attempts to collect *alcabala* taxes on dyestuff purchased directly from the Indians, sales of which had been traditionally exempted; (3) the great famine of 1785–1787; and (4) the introduction of the Ordenanza de Intendentes and its prohibition of *repartimientos*.[132]

While each of these factors had an impact, none caused the decline. First, cochineal was a product produced almost entirely by Indians and

179

the proposed tithe applied only to Spaniards, who controlled less than 3 percent of the production. Even if the tithe had driven all Spanish producers to abandon production, the impact on total output would have been negligible.[133] Nor does the proposed *alcabala* reform explain the depression. As Hamnett explained, the *bando* which reformed the *alcabala* was introduced in 1780 and abrogated the following year. While production in 1781 was depressed, perhaps related to the *bando*, production recovered fully in 1782 and 1783. The depression began in 1784, three years after the reversal of the *bando*.[134] Hamnett also pointed to the famine of 1785–1787, which devastated Oaxaca's indigenous communities. The famine very well might have had a negative impact on cochineal production, but the depression began before the famine and continued long after, and so the famine could not have been its cause.[135] Finally, the system of *intendencias* and the prohibition of the *repartimiento* were implemented in December 1786, significantly after the 1784 start of the depression. Furthermore, the *subdelegados* regularly disobeyed the ban. While it is indisputable that Article 12 adversely affected production, it did not initiate the downturn, which began prior to the Article's promulgation.

The low profitability of the dye trade after 1784 suggests an alternative explanation for the reduction in output. With little prospect of profiting from investments in cochineal, merchants invested in other sectors of the economy. When *repartimientos* were officially prohibited in 1786, then, output was already depressed owing to decreased profitability. It was not the ban on *repartimientos* that initiated the downturn; merchants, not Indians, abandoned the dye trade.[136]

Additional evidence is available to document the industry's depression in Europe after 1784. Comparing the figures for gross production of cochineal in Oaxaca during this period and prices per pound of cochineal in Amsterdam for the same years, one notes a significant trend.[137] In 1784 cochineal production dropped 46 percent relative to the prior year and remained at depressed levels for the remainder of the colonial period. Whereas in 1782, production exceeded 1,000,000 pounds, by 1784 output had dropped to just 535,900 pounds. One would expect a drop in production of this magnitude to stimulate a large increase in price, but none occurred. Instead, the decrease in output occurred at a time of falling prices. Table 8.10 compares five-year average output of cochineal in Oaxaca with average market prices per pound (converted to Spanish pesos) for the same periods in Amsterdam.

Average output for the first four quinquennia was large, with the period 1774–1778 posting the highest figure, in excess of 1,000,000 pounds per

TABLE 8.10

Output in Oaxaca and Dutch Prices of Cochineal

Year	Average output (pounds)	Average price (pesos)
1764–1768	876,825	4.60
1769–1773	948,011	5.50
1774–1778	1,101,258	4.15
1779–1783	943,673	4.33
1784–1788	490,662	3.43
1789–1793	451,060	3.52
1794–1798	490,575	4.75

SOURCES: For output figures, see Appendix A; for average prices, see Posthumus, 420–22.

NOTE: Posthumus gives prices in Dutch guilders per Dutch pound. These were converted to Spanish pesos and Spanish pounds according to the following rates: 1 peso = 0.45 guilders and 1 Dutch pound = 1.08 Spanish pounds.

year. The latter three periods, in contrast, averaged barely half of the earlier amounts. What is startling, however, are the prices at which cochineal was traded in Holland during these years. Before 1784, a pound of cochineal was valued at 4.15 pesos or more, topping 5.5 in the five-year period 1769–1773. During the two five-year periods following 1784, however, the average cochineal price dipped to around 3.5 pesos. Price and output of cochineal dropped sharply at the same time.

Because it was the sole producer and exporter of *grana fina* in the eighteenth century, output in Oaxaca determined entirely the world's supply.[138] If demand were constant, then a sharp drop in production would push prices up, since consumers would be bidding for scarcer supplies. In the 1780s, however, this did not happen. A steep drop in output was accompanied by a similarly significant decrease in the price. What this suggests is that demand also dropped after 1784, so much so that it more than offset the 50 percent decline in supply. This observation is evidence for an alternative explanation for the initial catalyst of the late-colonial commercial depression in Oaxaca. Production dipped in the 1780s because of an economic downturn in Europe.

The cochineal depression in Europe is further corroborated by Mar-

181

ten G. Buist's study of the European trading house of Hope and Company. Buist traces the attempt by merchant Henry Hope to corner the European cochineal market in the late 1780s. In 1787 and 1788, Hope, along with his agents in France, Holland, Great Britain, and Spain, purchased 732,540 pounds of cochineal, thought by Hope to be the entire supply in Europe at that time. Hope believed that this speculative investment, whose total value was a staggering 6,128,341 guilders (£551,109), would reap large returns if he were able to drive prices up by controlling supply and creating an artificial shortage. Instead, the venture proved disastrous, as Hope had only succeeded in selling 70 percent of the dye by 1793, and all at prices below what he himself had paid.[139]

Had demand not been depressed, Hope's monopolistic venture might have succeeded. Based on the Oaxacan registration figures, the 732,540 pounds of cochineal that Hope hoarded was equivalent to 95.3 percent of the cochineal produced in those same years, 1787–1788. The experience of Hope and Company illustrates that the sharp decline in production in Oaxaca did not result in a shortage of *grana* in Europe. Lower levels of supply did not cause a shortage, because demand decreased at a similar or greater rate. Cochineal production may have been depressed in Oaxaca, but demand in Europe was even more severely depressed.

While the abolition of the *repartimiento* certainly contributed to the decline in cochineal production in Oaxaca, the European depression of the 1780s, and the greater riskiness of the trade after 1793, were equally influential. Production of cochineal dropped sharply in 1784, two years before the 1786 prohibition of the *repartimiento* took effect. This suggests that the decline in output which began in 1784 was, at least initially, a response to economic factors of supply and demand rather than political factors, the abolition of *repartimientos*. The drop in European demand led to a fall in prices and a corresponding shift downward in supply, that is, output in Oaxaca. This depression continued into the 1790s and the trade remained unprofitable.

Chance found that in Villa Alta cochineal production declined before the ban on *repartimientos* was introduced, which, he conjectures, was in response to other factors.[140] Years later, in 1791, a wealthy Indian cochineal producer and trader from Mitla named Juan de Aguilar complained that the value of cochineal in Mexico had sunk so low that profits from its trade were minimal and the risk of losing money was great.[141] Given the reduced profitability of the trade, it is not surprising that many merchants withdrew entirely from the dye trade during this decade.

Further evidence of declining interest in the dye trade comes from a

1795 grievance filed against the *subdelegado* of Cuatro Villas del Marquesado by the community of Santo Tomás Mazaltepec in the jurisdiction of the old *alcaldía mayor* of Huexolotitlán. The Indians of this community complained that in the past when the price of *grana* was three pesos per pound, the magistrate had required repayment of cochineal *repartimiento* debts in cochineal.[142] In 1795, by contrast, the official was demanding that debts be repaid in coin at the rate of sixteen reales for every twelve reales advanced. According to the debtors, the Spanish official refused to accept payment in dyestuff, claiming that it was worthless.[143] Long a commodity highly demanded, cochineal had lost its value.

Demand for cochineal in Europe probably remained depressed until the very last years of the eighteenth century. According to the *consulado* of Veracruz, as late as March 1797 cochineal was "*sin demanda.*"[144] The decreased European demand for cochineal explains, in part, its reduced output and price in Oaxaca during this period. The Oaxacan price of cochineal reached all-time lows in the 1790s, trading for only 13.5 reales in 1793, 10.5 reales in 1794, and 12 reales in 1795. While the ban on *repartimientos* made the financing of production difficult (not to mention illegal), depressed demand in Europe made it economically unattractive, and this obviously facilitated the decision made by financiers to abandon the cochineal industry and the *repartimiento* which financed it.

Faced with greater risks, rising costs, and increasing taxes, merchants increasingly withdrew their capital from the cochineal industry and reinvested it in more attractive industries. In many ways, Article 12 probably accelerated a process already well underway, and one which would become even more permanent with the advent of war after 1793. The question arises: Where did the prominent dye traders choose to move their funds? Unfortunately, we can only speculate. Clearly, the near-constant state of warfare that began in the final decade of the century had a profoundly negative impact on all goods traded across the Atlantic. Given cochineal's highly price-inelastic demand, cochineal merchants must have been better able than others to withstand the war-induced rising costs of trade, passing additional costs onto consumers. That the profitability of cochineal was reduced during this era anyway strongly suggests that few commodities remained very profitable at the end of the colonial period.[145]

183

While certainly speculative, there is at least some evidence to suggest that merchants who withdrew their capital from the export trade invested instead in mining. Brading has shown that in the decades after Gálvez's visit to Mexico, the Crown provided increasingly generous subsidies to the mining industry in an effort to resurrect abandoned mines.[146] Building on Brading's work, Coatsworth has argued that government subsidies served to artificially resuscitate an unprofitable mining industry by encouraging a shift of capital to that industry and away from more productive enterprises, especially in agriculture.[147] At least until the mid-1780s, the cochineal industry does not seem to support Coatsworth's contention. Throughout the 1770s and early 1780s, the Spanish officials were well financed and the industry flourished. With the decline of the industry after 1784, however, dye merchants did withdraw their capital and at least some apparently invested in mining, perhaps responding to the artificially distorted profitability described by Coatsworth. Hamnett refers to the case of Juan Baptista de Echarri, the prominent cochineal merchant, who in June 1787 suddenly withdrew his capital from the cochineal-rich district of Teotitlán del Camino, where he had been the financier of the *alcalde mayor*. Just several years earlier, his two brothers, Juan Francisco and Juan Felipe, had invested funds in the resurrection of several abandoned Oaxacan mines. It seems likely that Juan Baptista took the monies he extracted from the district of Teotitlán del Camino and invested them, perhaps in partnership with his brothers, in mining. His prominence among Oaxacan miners is certain, as is evidenced by the 1790 recommendation made by the *intendente corregidor* of Oaxaca, Antonio de Mora y Peysal, for Echarri's election to the Diputados de Minería.[148] It seems likely that other wealthy merchants redirected their capital to mining, an industry that remained profitable until Napoleon's 1808 invasion and Hidalgo's 1810 rebellion forced the Crown to curtail the subsidies.[149] Mining was not the only beneficiary of the divestment of funds from transatlantic commerce. Salvucci found that Mexico's domestic textile industry boomed "after 1796, when Spanish trade with the colonies virtually ceased."[150]

The cochineal industry, meanwhile, went from bad to worse. Already depressed in the late-colonial era, Mexico's independence would usher in a much more profound crisis. Decades later, Oaxacan elites would still harken back to the glorious cochineal economy of the colonial era.

Chapter Nine

Epilogue

T he late-colonial decline of the Oaxacan dye industry initiated a process that accelerated rapidly after Mexico gained its independence in 1821.
Throughout the colonial period, Oaxaca retained a virtual monopoly on
the production of *grana fina*, which served to keep the price of this commodity relatively (and, perhaps, artificially) high. The Spanish Crown
prohibited the production of *grana fina* outside of Oaxaca, and this prohibition remained in effect until 1819, when the Crown extended permission to produce cochineal to Yucatán and Guatemala.[1] Cochineal flourished in Guatemala after 1819, so much so that it nearly completed the
economic devastation already begun in Oaxaca. Competition from Guatemala drove the price of cochineal rapidly downward, although it is not
clear whether this occurred because of overproduction or because Guatemala enjoyed comparative advantages.[2] In any event, the price of cochineal in Oaxaca fell rapidly after independence, as is shown in Figure 9.1,
and continued falling throughout the 1820s. In 1837 it dipped below 10
reales and never again entered into double digits. Despite successful efforts
in the late 1840s to increase production to levels comparable to those
sustained in the boom years of the 1770s, the value of the output was a
small fraction of what it had been in those earlier glory days. Both the total
annual output and the total value of that output per year are shown in
Figure 9.2. Production began a general upward trend in the mid-1820s, a
trend which was sustained until the mid-1850s. But despite this significant
growth in output, the overall value of production in Oaxaca fell continually. The price of cochineal was simply falling more steeply than output was growing.

Independence, then, struck a decisive blow to the Oaxacan cochineal
industry. Never again would Oaxaca enjoy its earlier opulence. For decades Oaxaca's leaders mourned the decline of this "precious fruit" and

185

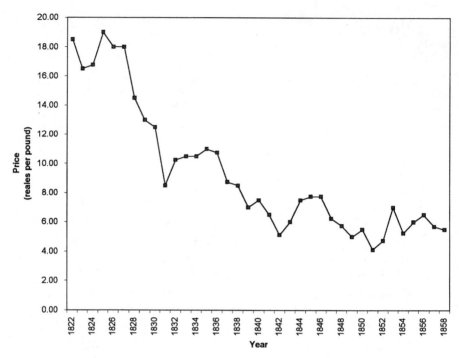

FIGURE 9.1. Oaxacan cochineal prices, 1822–1858. Source: Appendix B.

lamented their inability to find another commodity capable of producing comparable wealth. The post-independence collapse of the cochineal trade contributed to a steep decline in Oaxaca's economy, one that would continue into the twentieth century. Throughout the colonial era, Oaxaca was one of Mexico's most prosperous provinces. With the end of the colonial period, Oaxaca became one of Mexico's poorest states.

Oaxaca's transformation from a rich colonial province to a poor independent state permits an interesting hypothesis: Oaxaca's cochineal industry developed behind the protectionist walls erected by Spain's interventionist and rigid commercial restrictions. Spanish colonial economic and commercial policies entailed the erection of many barriers to and limitations on trade. The Crown prohibited specific social classes and ethnic groups from engaging in certain economic activities, and required the acquisition of Crown licenses to engage in many others. Some of the more lucrative industries—tobacco, gunpowder, and mercury, for example—were taken over by Crown monopolies. Likewise, the Spanish state often

186

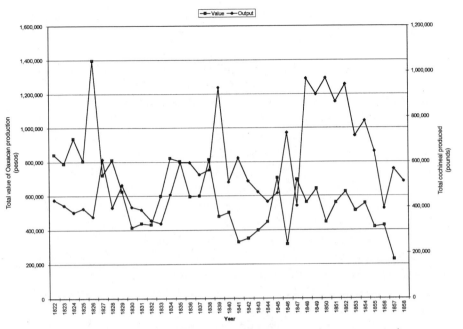

FIGURE 9.2. Total output of cochineal and its total value after Mexican independence, 1822–1858. Source: Appendix B.

designated which regions would be allowed to produce which commodities, partly in an effort to encourage the colonies' orientation toward the external sector. While such laws and restrictions distorted the allocation of economic and human resources, they also served to benefit certain groups and prejudice others.[3] The argument can be made that the Crown's meddling was largely responsible (if not purposefully) for Oaxaca's economic prosperity. At least in part, Oaxaca reaped great wealth from the production of *grana cochinilla* because government policies prejudiced other regions that might have otherwise proven to be more efficient. Most important, in prohibiting other colonies from producing cochineal, the Crown limited production and kept prices high. Independence forced Oaxaca to compete directly with more efficient producers, which it was unable to do effectively. As soon as the Crown lifted its restrictions in 1819 and granted permission to Guatemala to produce cochineal legally, the Oaxacan industry crumbled. Once the protection of colonial commercial policies was removed, the Oaxacan cochineal industry proved unable to compete with the more efficient Guatemala. In short, the Crown's endless

187

meddling in the economy served to reallocate resources and artificially protect certain industries.

The history of peasants and peasant communities in Mexico has been one of near-constant struggle to survive the economic depredations of overlords. The Aztecs were only the last of the pre-Columbian rulers to demand tribute from subjugated peasant communities. The Spanish conquerors who destroyed and then replaced the Aztec imperial government continued to collect tribute and created new mechanisms to extract wealth from indigenous Mexicans. The historiography of colonial Mexico is replete with examples of the suffering and exploitation experienced by Indians at the hands of greedy and sadistic Spaniards. Undoubtedly, much of this Black Legend history is accurate. Yet, even by the end of Spanish-colonial rule, indigenous peasants in most parts of Mexico, and especially in Oaxaca, retained sufficient land and other resources to enable them to produce for themselves the bulk of their subsistence. They survived colonial rule, having successfully defended their means of production. Proletarianization for most Mexicans occurred much later, only after the expansion of national markets and the creation of a modern state under the rule of Porfirio Diaz.

This study has illustrated one primary aspect of the "strategy of survival" employed by the indigenous population of Oaxaca during the colonial period. Oaxacan Indians turned to the colonial market as a means of obtaining valuable agricultural inputs and badly needed income, critical supplements to their subsistence agriculture. The primary economic activity of Oaxacan peasants, apart from staple crop production, was the cultivation of *grana cochinilla*, a red dye demanded in large quantities by the booming textile industries of northern Europe. Oaxacan peasants specialized in cochineal because they enjoyed a comparative advantage over competing Spanish *haciendas* in the production of the dyestuff, which was a labor-intensive process, demanding the constant attention and care that only peasant households could expend economically. In effect, Indians identified and seized an economic niche which they could exploit to their own benefit.

The physical demands of cochineal production may have ideally suited the peasant household economy, but its production required outside financing. Spanish officials, the *alcaldes mayores*, became bankers to the Indians, lending money through the *repartimiento* to be repaid in finished cochineal. For the creditor, cochineal *repartimiento* loans could be extremely lucrative, since they permitted the creditor to obtain a valuable export commodity at bargain prices. While potentially profitable, the moneylending business was also very risky. For one thing, cochineal production was highly susceptible to loss from natural causes. Birds, animals, and many insects preyed on the cochineal bugs and even slight weather extremes could destroy the harvest. More risky still, peasants often resisted, to the best of their abilities, full compliance with contracted obligations. When the price of cochineal rose, producers sometimes reneged on their *repartimiento* obligations, choosing to sell their output at market prices instead. Other peasants who took loans gambled that they could avoid the *alcalde mayor* and his debt collectors, conveniently disappearing whenever the official appeared in the village. The difficult task of collecting debts meant that most merchants refused to lend money to Indian producers for fear of losing their capital. The *alcaldes mayores* lent funds where other merchants would not because they were vested with the judicial power necessary to enforce contracted debts. Even with this authority, the Spanish officials failed to collect some debts rightfully owed to them, and many more were collected well past their due dates.

The *alcaldes mayores* responded to the high risk of late repayment of debts and the frequency of borrower default by charging high implicit rates of interest in their *repartimiento* loans. Indians contracted in advance to sell their output at prices well below what they could have received had they marketed their cochineal themselves. Poverty, however, induced many to surrender future income to obtain money immediately. At virtually any moment, the indigenous producer could approach the *alcalde* or the *teniente* and receive funds in exchange for only a promise to deliver cochineal in the future. This convenience, however, was not cheap. The *alcalde* charged high implicit interest rates because the high risk of default meant that only by doing so was he guaranteed an overall rate of return comparable to other investments. Yet despite charging high rates of implicit interest, the profitability of *repartimientos* was quite modest. Certainly officials sometimes made enormous profits, but more often, returns were good but not extraordinary.

Indians of colonial Mexico were generally poor, in part because of the socioeconomic and legal limitations placed on them by colonialism. Because they were poor, peasants depended on the credit provided by the Spanish officials to permit them to participate more widely in the marketplace. *Repartimiento* credit made high-priced livestock affordable. The *repartimiento* was also a ready source of funds when harvests failed or fell short of the household's needs, providing peasants with living expenses to tide them over until the following harvest. Entrepreneurial peasants could borrow funds and attempt to generate additional income from the production and marketing of cochineal. The *repartimiento*, then, far from a system of coercion, sometimes served to alleviate the hardships of life in rural colonial Oaxaca, even though this was not the *alcalde mayor*'s intention. When the corn or bean harvest was less than sufficient, the peasant could always turn to the *alcalde mayor* for a *repartimiento* loan that could then be used to purchase necessities, food included. Recipients of *repartimiento* loans were fortunate, for their access to credit enabled them to perform economic activities beyond the means of credit-poor peasants and served to smooth out their consumption during the agricultural cycle. Credit, however, has its opposite side: debt. Many Indians accepted too much credit and had difficulties extricating themselves from the burden of their debts. This was certainly not in the *alcaldes*' interests since excessively indebted peasants often defaulted, and default cost the magistrates dearly. When peasants failed to pay promptly, the *alcaldes mayores* could be ruthless, resorting to violent means to collect their debts. Peasants were fortunate to have access to *repartimiento* credit, but the system had a very ugly and violent side to it nonetheless.

Historians have misinterpreted such debt-collection techniques, among other factors, as evidence that the *alcaldes mayores* forced *repartimiento* loans upon Indians, concluding that market-oriented behavior on the part of indigenous Mexicans was coerced. With only one dependable source of credit, starving, indigent, or merely credit-hungry peasants had nowhere else to turn. When the alternative was no credit at all, they did not have to be coerced to accept loans, even at high interest rates. Access to credit mattered more than its price. The *alcaldes mayores* did not have to coerce Indians to participate in the market. Indians accepted *repartimientos* voluntarily.

Appendixes

APPENDIX A

Prices Paid for Oaxacan Posts as *Alcalde Mayor* by District

XICAYAN

Year	Recipient	Pesos	Comments
1780	Joséf Gonzalez de Mesa	grant	
1773	Joséf de Ayala Matamoros	grant	
1768	Francisco Dominguez de Lozada	grant	
1763	Gaspar de Morales y de los Ríos	grant	
1757	Joséf Gil de Araujo	grant	
1748	Joséf Hurtado y Benzal	17,181	
1744	Juan Baupista Clavell	8,500	
1737	Pedro Angel de Yrigoyen de Dutari	8,300	
1732	Francisco Antonio Tocano	8,300	
1730	Blas Clavigero	8,300	
1728	Miguel de Yrigoyen y de Echenique	grant	
1719	Fernando Tamayo	7,500	
1716	Nicolas Carillo de Albornoz	10,000	
1710	Gregorio de Luzena	7,300	
1709	Felipe Sánchez de Mobollan	6,000	
1708	Francisco Beaumont	7,000	
1703	Pedro Ramirez de Arellano	grant	
1699	Francisco Carillo de Albornoz	7,000	

SOURCE: AGI, Audiencia de México, 1219.

CHICHICAPA-ZIMATLÁN

Year	Recipient	Pesos	Comments
1781	Yldefonso Sánchez y Solache	grant	Replaced deceased father as AM
1780	Fran. Xavier Sánchez de Solache	grant	
1774	Bernardo Joséf Carillo	grant	
1766	Francisco de Baeza y Moncada	grant	
1760	Carlos de Velasco	grant	
1747	Francisco Ibanez de Corbera	5,060	
1744	Manuel de Amenabar	4,800	
1740	Francisco de Obregon	4,300	
1735	Juan Francisco de Puertas	4,000	
1733	Juan Antonio de Mogaguren	4,300	
1731	Pedro de Valdenebro	4,300	
1728	Juan de Yarza y Azcona	grant	
1718	Francisco Rodriguez Franco	grant	
1716	Juan de Yarza y Azcona	grant	
1708	Manuel Ruíz de Velasco	3,000	
1704	Juan Ignacio de Santillana	grant	
1695	Gabriel de Macazaga	6,500	

SOURCE: AGI, Audiencia de México, 1220.

CUICATLÁN AND PAPOLOTIPAC (Teotitlán del Camino)

Year	Recipient	Pesos	Comments
1779	Manuel Joséf Chacon	grant	
1775	Martín Joséf de Alegría	grant	
1772	Francisco Antonio de Ariz	grant	
1766	Juan Antonio de Goytia	grant	
1761	Luis Frejomil	grant	
1745	Joséf Frejomil y Figueroa	4,140	
1745	Joséf de Ustariz	4,000	
1737	Joséf Antonio Valiente	3,600	
1732	Francisco Canton Villarmea	3,600	
1731	Jacinto Fernandez de Osorio	3,600	
1728	Francisco Solanot	grant	
1718	Joséf de Llanes Robles	grant	
1707	Martín de Burgos y Salinas	3,000	
1704	Joséf Muñoz y Estrada	grant	

SOURCE: AGI, Audiencia de México, 1221.

VILLA ALTA

Year	Recipient	Pesos	Comments
1781	Pablo de Ortega	grant	
1777	Francisco Marty	grant	
1768	Sancho Pison	grant	
1761	Joséf de Molina y Sandoval	grant	
1758	Alonso Basco y Vargas	grant	
1747	Miguel Joséf de Iturbide	8,625	
1742	Manuel Valentín de Bustamante	7,500	pd. 4,000 & owes 3,500 within 2 years
1737	Juan Martinez de Yriarte	7,500	
1733	Juan Francisco de Puertas	7,500	
1728	Joachin de Padilla y Estrada	6,000	120,000 rr de vellon
1727	Antonio Blanco Sandoval	grant	
1718	Joséf Francisco de Madrigal	7,000	
1712	Gaspar de los Reyes	7,000	
1708	Juan de Santander y Rada	5,000	
1705	Ant. Andrés de la Vega y Miranda	grant	
1701	Diego de Rivera y Cotes	grant	
1700	Francisco Benitez de Maldonado	grant	

SOURCE: AGI, Audiencia de México, 1222.

NEXAPA

Year	Recipient	Pesos	Comments
1781	Juan Casimiro de Ozta	grant	
1775	Ant. Mendez Prieto y Fernandez	grant	
1770	Pantaleon Ruíz de Montoya	grant	
1763	Gabriel Gutierrez de Rubalcava	grant	
1760	Vicente Bueno de la Barbolla	grant	
1750	Juan Joséf Martinez y Aguirre	15,365	
1748	Miguel de Ybarra	1,500	partial term
1744	Francisco Benitez Murillo	9,100	182,000 rr vellon (rv)
1744	Pedro Bernardo de Yrigoyen	1,275	25,500rv.—to finish Garcia's term
1741	Nicolas de Cengotita y Ybarra	4,166	to finish Garcia's term
1737	Miguel de Yrigoyen y Echenique	9,000	
1735	Ignacio de Alvarado	11,000	
1733	Joséf Javier García	9,500	died after 6 months in office
1728	Placido de Porra	9,000	180,000 rr vellon
1722	Joséf López Zapatas	grant	
1716	Antonio Yriarte de Cortazar	5,500	Requested as Substitute for Gov. of Chile for which he pd.
1708	Joséf de Zozara	grant	
1705	Juan Saenz de Viteri	grant	
1702	Antonio Osorio	grant	

SOURCE: AGI, Audiencia de México, 1223.

TEPOSCOLULA

Year	Recipient	Pesos	Comments
1775	Francisco Rojas y Rocha	grant	
1767	Joséf Mariano de Cardenas	grant	
1762	Diego Antonio de Neira Ponce y Leon	grant	
1754	Cayetano de Tapia y Madina	grant	
1741	Juan Antonio Fernandez de Cordoa	775	supplement to García de Fuentevilla's
1738	Joséf de Ita y Salazar	3,100	
1737	Pedro de Valdenebro y Robles	1,433	2nd payment
1735	Juan Antonio García de Fuentevilla	3,100	post served by Fernandez de Cordoba
1731	Antonio de Silva	1,500	2nd payment (got sick at 1st)
1731	Pedro de Valdenebro y Robles	3,100	see additional payment above
1728	Antonio de Silva	2,250	see additional payment above
1718	Francisco Rodriquez Franco	grant	
1710	Juan de Torres	2,000	
1708	Fernando Manuel de Bustamante	2,400	600 doblones
1705	Francisco Benitez Maldonado	3,000	
1702	Alonso de Soto y Guevara	grant	

SOURCE: AGI, Audiencia De México, 1224.

TEOZACOALCO-TEOCOCUILCO

Year	Recipient	Pesos	Comments
1776	Joséf Fernandez de Molina	grant	
1770	Joséf Andrés de Prado y Ulloa	grant	
1764	Jacinto de Ledos	grant	
1755	Salvador Fernandez Pinero	grant	
1750	Joséf Melchor de Ugalde	2,800	
1744	Juan Antonio Escudero Gilón	2,500	
1736	Baltasar Montoya Maldonado	2,500	
1735	Juan Leonardo Roldán	2,500	
1728	Juan Bernardo de Mendinueta	1,875	37,500 rr vellon
1718	Fernando Ximenez de Cisneros	2,500	
1710	Matheo Ruíz Vasurto	800	
1709	Joséf Jacques Campillos	800	
1707	Antonio de Montalban y Carrion	grant	
1704	Diego Francisco de Bosque	grant	
1700	Martín de Beroiz	grant	

SOURCE: AGI, Audiencia de México, 1225.

TEOTITLÁN DEL VALLE (Mitla)

Year	Recipient	Pesos	Comments
1775	Juan Antonio de Goytia	grant	
1769	Joséf Domingo de Valdivieso	grant	
1764	Luís Bermudo Soriano	grant	
1754	Joséf Andres del Prado y Ulloa	grant	
1746	Miguel Joséf de Iturbide	2,900	
1739	Bernardo de Leza	2,500	
1735	Joséf de Arreze	2,500	
1731	Francisco de Obregon	2,500	
1729	Joséf Paulo de Ygueregui	1,875	37,500 rr vellon
1708	Juan Antonio de Hano y Escalante	4,000	1,000 doblones for this & Miahuatlán
1705	Dionisio de Abella y Mendoza	grant	
1700	Juan de Santander y Rada	2,000	
1699	Luís Francisco de Padilla		
1696	Joséf de Villa Septiem	4,000	
1693	Antonio de Somoza y Lozada	2,500	
1689	Esteban García Labrador	2,500	

SOURCE: AGI, Audiencia de México, 1225–26.

TEHUANTEPEC

Year	Recipient	Pesos	Comments
1781	Tomás de Mollinedo	grant	
1776	Juan Bauptista de Ugarte	grant	
1768	Juan Antonio Lardizabal	grant	
1762	Juan Bauptista Martiniena y Echarri	grant	
1756	Antonio del Frago	grant	served elsewhere instead
1750	Manuel Fernandez de Figueroa	6,842	
1741	Juan Calero Bohorquez	3,500	
1738	Miguel de Calero y Bohorquez	3,500	
1734	Joséf Antonio Izquierdo	grant	
1727	Felipe Conde y Calbo	grant	
1717	Pedro Sarabia Cortes	grant	
1712	Marques de Villa Puente	3,500	
1700	Joséf de Cuellar y Ocon	grant	
1700	Martín de Benoiz	grant	

SOURCE: AGI, Audiencia de México, 1225.

MIAHUATLÁN

Year	Recipient	Pesos	Comments
1774	Francisco Xavier de Corres	grant	
1768	Sebastian de Labayru	grant	
1765	Ramón de Marinelarena	grant	
1748	Joaquín Prieto Isla	5,710	
1747	Baltasar Benzaval	3,910	
1743	Joséf de Pumarejo Badmes	3,400	
1735	Juan Tomás Trujillo	3,000	
1732	Pedro Alvarez de Monjardín	3,000	
1728	Simonde Larrazaval	3,000	
1728	Juan Christosomo de Barroeta	2,250	45,000 rr vellon
1716	Juan Dongo		5,400 for this & AM of Teot. del Valle
1716	Manuel de la Fuente Rosillo		1,600 doblones for Miah. & Teot. del Valle
1708	Juan Antonio de Hano y Escalante		1,000 doblones for Miah. & Teot. del Valle
1705	Francisco de Mier y Torres	grant	
1701	Geronimo Feliz Davila Ponce de León	grant	
1700	Martín Ortiz de Velasco	grant	
1698	Francisco Antonio de Machuca	3,000	
1697	Pedro Rufel	3,000	
1695	Juan Martinez de Morentín	6,000	
1687	Diego Martinez de Cabezas	2,000	2,000 escudos
1686	Bernardo Gutierrez de Cabiedes	3,500	

SOURCE: AGI, Audiencia de México, 1226.

TEUTILA

Year	Recipient	Pesos	Comments
1774	Felipe Ordoñez	grant	
1770	Antonio Manzana Henriquez	grant	
1766	Mariano de los Ríos	grant	
1750	Lorenzo Ant. Correa y Troncoso	2,900	
1747	Francisco Antonio Bermudez	2,875	
1742	Pedro Osorio	2,500	
1736	Francisco Antonio Baquero	2,500	
1732	Juan Bauptista de Pagaolerdi	2,500	
1730	Francisco Antonio de Azcarate	2,500	
1726	Francisco de Obregon	grant	
1719	Martin de Carranza	2,400	600 doblones
1713	Pedro de Mendival y Lazcano	grant	
1708	Francisco de Algara	1,600	400 doblones
1706	Ignacio Gil de Rosas	1,600	400 doblones
1705	Francisco Gutierrez de la Carrada		5,000 pesos for this & AM of Guaxapa
1702	Tomás Ponce de León	grant	
1700	Manuel de Bingara	grant	

SOURCE: AGI, Audiencia de México, 1225.

CORREGIMIENTO DE OAXACA and CUATRO VILLAS

Year	Recipient	Pesos	Comments
1728	Blas Martinez del Campo	2,250	45,000 rv for Corr. De Oax
1716	Joséf Antonio Gonzalez	5,000	for 4 Villas
1711	Thomas Francisco Zabalza	3,000	for 4 Villas
1710	Marques de Villa Puente	3,000	for 4 Villas

SOURCE: AGI, Audiencia de México, 1223.

IXTEPEJI

Year	Recipient	Pesos	Comments
1709	Ignacio Gonzalez de la Sarte	grant	
1709	Simón Pérez de Pavia	grant	
1705	Pedro Damaso de Ampuero	grant	
1695	Francisco de Alvarado	4,000	
1695	Fernando de Saavedra	2,000	
1691	Francisco Davila y Medina	3,500	
1687	Pedro de Bohorquez	grant	
1686	Santiago Martinez de Concha	5,500	

SOURCE: AGI, Audiencia de México, 1227.

APPENDIX B

Annual Output, Price, and Value of Cochineal in Oaxaca, 1758–1858

Year	Pounds cochineal registered	Reales per pound	Pesos per pound	Total value (pesos)
1758	675,562.0	16.50	$2.060	$1,393,347
1759	686,812.0	16.50	2.060	1,416,550
1760	1,067,625.0	16.00	2.000	2,135,250
1761	788,625.0	15.00	1.880	1,478,672
1762	832,500.0	14.75	1.840	1,534,922
1763	599,625.0	15.50	1.940	1,161,773
1764	898,875.0	19.50	2.440	2,191,008
1765	1,082,250.0	18.50	2.310	2,502,753
1766	932,625.0	19.50	2.440	2,073,273
1767	849,375.0	19.50	2.440	2,070,352
1768	621,000.0	22.50	2.810	1,746,563
1769	1,024,312.5	24.50	3.060	3,136,957
1770	1,043,437.5	25.00	3.130	3,260,742
1771	1,050,187.5	32.00	4.000	4,200,750
1772	839,677.5	30.00	3.750	3,148,791
1773	782,437.5	25.50	3.190	2,494,020
1774	1,558,125.0	17.50	2.190	3,408,398
1775	837,000.0	16.00	2.000	1,674,000
1776	808,550.0	17.00	2.130	1,718,169
1777	1,244,812.5	15.00	1.880	2,334,023
1778	1,057,800.0	16.00	2.000	2,115,600
1779	842,625.0	15.00	1.880	1,579,922
1780	1,385,437.5	17.00	2.130	2,944,055
1781	464,625.0	17.00	2.130	987,328
1782	1,035,675.0	17.00	2.130	2,265,539
1783	990,000.0	18.00	2.250	2,227,500
1784	535,900.0	16.00	2.000	1,171,800
1785	537,750.0	17.00	2.130	1,142,719
1786	610,875.0	16.50	2.060	1,259,930
1787	451,125.0	16.00	2.000	902,250
1788	317,662.0	16.00	2.000	635,324
1789	478,125.0	15.50	1.940	926,367
1790	471,150.0	16.00	2.000	942,300
1791	538,650.0	16.50	2.060	1,410,341
1792	433,125.0	15.00	1.880	839,086

Year	Pounds cochineal registered	Reales per pound	Pesos per pound	Total value (pesos)
1793	334,250.0	13.50	1.690	564,047
1794	655,550.0	10.50	1.310	860,409
1795	584,125.0	12.00	1.500	876,188
1796	207,450.0	17.50	2.190	453,797
1797	493,425.0	15.50	1.940	956,011
1798	512,325.0	18.00	2.250	1,152,731
1799	452,675.0	19.50	2.440	1,103,395
1800	374,400.0	19.00	2.380	889,200
1801	406,012.5	18.00	2.250	913,528
1802	433,550.0	19.00	2.380	1,029,681
1803	559,350.0	21.00	2.630	1,468,230
1804	346,500.0	28.50	3.560	1,134,406
1805	191,250.0	23.00	2.875	549,844
1806	251,550.0	27.00	3.375	848,981
1807	341,550.0	29.00	3.625	1,143,119
1808	358,200.0	29.00	3.625	1,298,475
1809	343,350.0	33.00	4.125	1,416,319
1810	545,727.5	29.00	3.625	1,978,262
1811	478,912.5	28.50	3.563	1,706,070
1812	199,800.0	20.00	2.500	449,500
1813	178,875.0	15.00	1.875	335,391
1814	327,937.5	25.00	3.125	1,024,805
1815	283,275.0	24.00	3.000	849,825
1816	358,687.0	32.00	4.000	1,410,748
1817	315,000.0	29.00	3.625	1,141,875
1818	250,412.0	28.50	3.563	892,093
1819	493,200.0	27.50	3.438	1,695,375
1820	375,662.5	28.00	3.500	1,314,775
1821	311,787.5	23.00	2.875	896,389
1822	432,062.5	18.50	2.313	1,001,457
1823	408,150.0	16.50	2.063	841,809
1824	377,412.5	16.75	2.094	790,207
1825	394,037.5	19.00	2.375	935,839
1826	357,617.5	18.00	2.250	804,628
1827	610,187.5	18.00	2.250	1,395,421
1828	398,187.5	14.50	1.813	721,715

Year	Pounds cochineal registered	Reales per pound	Pesos per pound	Total value (pesos)
1829	498,862.5	13.00	1.625	810,652
1830	400,437.5	12.50	1.563	625,684
1831	389,000.0	8.50	1.063	413,313
1832	342,050.0	10.25	1.281	438,252
1833	328,925.0	10.50	1.313	431,714
1834	455,825.0	10.50	1.313	598,270
1835	597,400.0	11.00	1.375	821,425
1836	597,400.0	10.75	1.344	802,756
1837	544,400.0	8.75	1.094	595,438
1838	564,600.0	8.50	1.063	599,888
1839	928,800.0	7.00	0.875	812,700
1840	511,400.0	7.50	0.938	479,438
1841	618,000.0	6.50	0.813	502,125
1842	516,200.0	5.13	0.641	330,610
1843	468,000.0	6.00	0.750	351,000
1844	424,600.0	7.50	0.938	398,063
1845	462,700.0	7.75	0.969	448,241
1846	729,200.0	7.75	0.969	706,413
1847	406,400.0	6.25	0.781	317,500
1848	968,800.0	5.75	0.719	696,325
1849	899,200.0	5.00	0.625	562,000
1850	970,800.0	5.50	0.688	642,425
1851	866,400.0	4.13	0.516	446,738
1852	943,600.0	4.75	0.594	560,263
1853	715,400.0	7.00	0.875	625,975
1854	782,800.0	5.25	0.656	513,713
1855	647,125.0	6.00	0.750	556,247
1856	395,200.0	6.50	0.813	418,006
1857	569,072.0	5.70	0.713	427,020
1858	514,537.0	5.50	0.688	228,339

SOURCES: The most complete sets of figures (1758–1858) are in the 1858 "Memoria del gobierno del estado de Oaxaca," AGEO; the *Boletín de la sociedad Mexicana de geografía y estadística* 7 (1859); Hamnett, *Politics and Trade*, Appendix 1 (for the years 1758–1821); and Dahlgren, appendix 2 (for the years 1758–1854). None of these sources include data for 1820. For that year, see Bustamante, *Memoria estadística de Oaxaca*.

Returns to the *Alcalde Mayor* of Teposcolula, 1781–1784 (assuming no defaults)

Daily interest rate = 0.06%; annual interest rate = 22.51%.

Debtor	Date of loan	Date paid (see text)	No. days due	Percentage of total days due	Pounds contracted
Diego Hernandez	31-Jan-1781	01-May-1784	1,186	3.49%	50.00
Domingo de Santiago	01-Feb-81	01-May-84	1,185	3.49%	20.00
Gregorio Peralta	01-Feb-81	01-May-84	1,185	3.49%	12.50
Bentura Bega	01-Feb-81	01-May-84	1,185	3.49%	1.13
Joséf de la Cruz y común	01-Feb-81	01-May-84	1,185	3.49%	53.19
Marzelo Seria	01-Feb-81	01-May-84	1,185	3.49%	13.25
Salvadór López	01-Feb-81	01-May-84	1,185	3.49%	2.53
Domingo Quiros	01-Feb-81	01-May-84	1,185	3.49%	25.00
Juan Tadeo Tiburcio	03-Feb-81	01-May-84	1,183	3.48%	2.19
Salvadór López	15-Feb-81	20-Apr-81	64	0.19%	2.97
Salvadór López	15-Feb-81	16-Apr-82	425	1.25%	10.00
Bernardo Hernandez y común	25-Feb-81	01-May-84	1,161	3.42%	12.00
Juan Pedro	15-Mar-81	01-May-84	1,143	3.36%	4.00
Antonio Benito	19-Jun-81	01-May-84	1,047	3.08%	25.00
Pedro de Silva	30-Jun-81	01-May-84	1,036	3.05%	25.00
Vicente Barrio	16-Jul-81	01-May-84	1,020	3.00%	4.00
Domingo de la Cruz	16-Jul-81	01-May-84	1,020	3.00%	6.31
Pedro de Vera y común	22-Sep-81	01-May-84	952	2.80%	12.50
Ysidro Salazár	05-Oct-81	31-Jul-82	299	0.88%	1.00
Ysidro Salazár	05-Oct-81	03-May-83	575	1.69%	3.00
Vicente Montesinos	05-Oct-81	01-May-84	939	2.76%	6.00
Pedro de Vera y común	09-Oct-81	01-May-84	935	2.75%	62.50
Lorenzo López	10-Oct-81	01-May-84	934	2.75%	25.00
Marcos López	30-Nov-81	01-May-84	883	2.60%	5.00
Matías de la Cruz y común	01-Dec-81	26-Jun-82	207	0.61%	100.00
Matías de la Cruz y común	01-Dec-81	01-May-84	882	2.60%	15.50
Domingo de la Cruz	09-Feb-82	01-May-84	812	2.39%	12.00
Nicolás Rodriguez	06-Jun-82	08-May-83	336	0.99%	4.00
Miguel Sánchez y común	07-Jun-82	01-May-84	694	2.04%	25.00
Fulgencio Joséf	15-Jun-82	01-May-84	686	2.02%	6.00
José Hernandez y común	30-Jun-82	01-May-84	671	1.98%	211.63

Contract rate (reales)	Pesos loaned	Payback type (dye or $)	Pounds paid	Payback price (reales)	Pesos paid	Days × loan $ ($ days)	Annual return
10	62.50		50.00	16	100.00	74,125	18.47%
12	30.00		20.00	16	40.00	35,550	10.27%
12	18.75		12.50	16	25.00	22,219	10.27%
12	1.69		1.13	16	2.25	2,000	10.27%
12	79.78		53.19	16	106.38	94,541	10.27%
12	19.88		13.25	16	26.50	23,552	10.27%
12	3.80		2.53	16	5.06	4,499	10.27%
10	31.25		25.00	16	50.00	37,031	18.48%
8	2.19		2.19	16	4.38	2,588	30.85%
12	4.45	dye	2.97	17	6.31	285	237.63%
12	15.00	dye	10.00	17	21.25	6,375	35.78%
10	15.00		12.00	16	24.00	17,415	18.86%
12	6.00		4.00	16	8.00	6,858	10.64%
10	31.25		25.00	16	50.00	32,719	20.92%
12	37.50		25.00	16	50.00	38,850	11.74%
12	6.00		4.00	16	8.00	6,120	11.93%
12	9.47		6.31	16	12.63	9,658	11.93%
12	18.75		12.50	16	25.00	17,850	12.78%
12	1.50	dye	1.00	17	2.13	449	50.86%
12	4.50	dye	3.00	18	6.75	2,588	31.74%
11	8.25		6.00	16	12.00	7,747	17.67%
12	93.75		62.50	16	125.00	87,656	13.01%
12	37.50		25.00	16	50.00	35,025	13.03%
10	6.25		5.00	16	10.00	5,519	24.80%
10	125.00	dye	100.00	17	212.50	25,875	123.43%
10	19.38		15.50	16	31.00	17,089	24.83%
12	18.00		12.00	16	24.00	14,616	14.98%
12	6.00	dye	4.00	18	9.00	2,016	54.32%
12	37.50		25.00	16	50.00	26,025	17.53%
12	9.00		6.00	16	12.00	6,174	17.74%
12	317.44		211.63	16	423.25	213,001	18.13%

Daily interest rate = 0.06%; annual interest rate = 22.51%.

Debtor	Date of loan	Date paid (see text)	No. days due	Percentage of total days due	Pounds contracted
Juan Tadeo Tiburcio	02-Jul-82	01-May-84	669	1.97%	2.00
Benito Juárez	21-Aug-82	05-Mar-83	196	0.58%	6.00
Antonio Velasco	26-Sep-82	17-Jul-83	294	0.87%	12.00
Toribio Velasco	26-Sep-82	17-Jul-83	294	0.87%	6.00
Fernando Vasquez	26-Sep-82	17-Jul-83	294	0.87%	6.00
Gregorio Marcial y común	11-Nov-82	16-May-83	186	0.55%	6.00
Mateo Ortiz	28-Dec-82	29-Oct-83	305	0.90%	12.00
Benito Juárez	05-Mar-83	01-May-84	423	1.25%	6.00
Juan Mendoza	10-Apr-83	01-May-84	387	1.14%	69.75
Simon Pérez	21-May-83	01-May-84	346	1.02%	12.00
Antonio Ramirez	26-Jun-83	01-May-84	310	0.91%	3.00
Juan Manuel	28-Jun-83	01-May-84	308	0.91%	18.00
Antonio Espinoza	06-Jul-83	01-May-84	300	0.88%	12.00
Blas José	11-Jul-83	01-May-84	295	0.87%	0.50
Manuel Velasco	17-Jul-83	01-May-84	289	0.85%	37.50
Toribio Velasco	31-Jul-83	01-May-84	275	0.81%	37.56
Felipe de la Cruz	07-Aug-83	01-May-84	268	0.79%	3.00
Felipe Aguilar	03-Sep-83	01-May-84	241	0.71%	25.00
Mateo Marcial	16-Sep-83	01-May-84	228	0.67%	2.00
Tomás de Aquino	22-Sep-83	01-May-84	222	0.65%	8.00
Pablo Pérez	25-Sep-83	01-May-84	219	0.64%	6.00
Mateo Ortiz	13-Feb-84	01-May-84	78	0.23%	12.00
Nicolás de Santiago	13-Feb-84	01-May-84	78	0.23%	10.00
Antonio Coronel	13-Feb-84	01-May-84	78	0.23%	4.00
TOTALS			33,968	100.00%	1,074.50

SOURCE: AGN, Real Hacienda, Administración de Alcabalas, caja no. 43

Contract rate (reales)	Pesos loaned	Payback type (dye or $)	Pounds paid	Payback price (reales)	Pesos paid	Days × loan $ ($ days)	Annual return
12	3.00		2.00	16	4.00	2,007	18.19%
12	9.00	dye	6.00	18	13.50	1,764	93.11%
12	18.00	dye	12.00	18	27.00	5,292	62.07%
12	9.00	dye	6.00	18	13.50	2,646	62.07%
12	9.00	dye	6.00	18	13.50	2,646	62.07%
12	9.00	dye	6.00	18	13.50	1,674	98.12%
12	18.00	dye	12.00	18	27.00	5,490	59.84%
12	9.00		6.00	16	12.00	3,807	28.76%
12	104.63		69.75	16	139.50	40,490	31.44%
12	18.00		12.00	16	24.00	6,228	35.16%
12	4.50		3.00	16	6.00	1,395	39.25%
12	27.00		18.00	16	36.00	8,316	39.50%
12	18.00		12.00	16	24.00	5,400	40.56%
12	0.75		0.50	16	1.00	221	41.24%
12	56.25		37.50	16	75.00	16,256	42.10%
12	56.34		37.56	16	75.13	15,495	44.24%
12	4.50		3.00	16	6.00	1,206	45.40%
12	37.50		25.00	16	50.00	9,038	50.48%
12	3.00		2.00	16	4.00	684	53.36%
12	12.00		8.00	16	16.00	2,664	54.80%
12	9.00		6.00	16	12.00	1,971	55.56%
12	18.00		12.00	16	24.00	1,404	155.98%
12	15.00		10.00	16	20.00	1,170	155.98%
12	6.00		4.00	16	8.00	468	155.98%
	1,551.78		1074.50		2,177.00	1,013,744	

APPENDIX C.2

Returns to *Alcalde Mayor* of Teposcolula, 1781–1784 (assuming 25 percent default)

Daily interest rate = 0.03%; annual interest rate = 11.00%.

Debtor	Date of loan	Date paid (see text)	No. days due	Percentage of total days due	Pounds contracted
Diego Hernandez	31-Jan-1781	01-May-1784	1186	3.49%	50.00
Domingo de Santiago	01-Feb-81	01-May-84	1185	3.49%	20.00
Gregorio Peralta	01-Feb-81	01-May-84	1185	3.49%	12.50
Bentura Bega	01-Feb-81	01-May-84	1185	3.49%	1.13
Joséf de la Cruz y común	01-Feb-81	01-May-84	1185	3.49%	53.19
Marzelo Seria	01-Feb-81	01-May-84	1185	3.49%	13.25
Salvadór López	01-Feb-81	01-May-84	1185	3.49%	2.53
Domingo Quiros	01-Feb-81	01-May-84	1185	3.49%	25.00
Juan Tadeo Tiburcio	03-Feb-81	01-May-84	1183	3.48%	2.19
Salvadór López	15-Feb-81	20-Apr-81	64	0.19%	2.97
Salvadór López	15-Feb-81	16-Apr-82	425	1.25%	10.00
Bernardo Hernandez y común	25-Feb-81	01-May-84	1161	3.42%	12.00
Juan Pedro	15-Mar-81	01-May-84	1143	3.36%	4.00
Antonio Benito	19-Jun-81	01-May-84	1047	3.08%	25.00
Pedro de Silva	30-Jun-81	01-May-84	1036	3.05%	25.00
Vicente Barrio	16-Jul-81	01-May-84	1020	3.00%	4.00
Domingo de la Cruz	16-Jul-81	01-May-84	1020	3.00%	6.31
Pedro de Vera y común	22-Sep-81	01-May-84	952	2.80%	12.50
Ysidro Salazár	05-Oct-81	31-Jul-82	299	0.88%	1.00
Ysidro Salazár	05-Oct-81	03-May-83	575	1.69%	3.00
Vicente Montesinos	05-Oct-81	01-May-84	939	2.76%	6.00
Pedro de Vera y común	09-Oct-81	01-May-84	935	2.75%	62.50
Lorenzo López	10-Oct-81	01-May-84	934	2.75%	25.00
Marcos López	30-Nov-81	01-May-84	883	2.60%	5.00
Matías de la Cruz y común	01-Dec-81	26-Jun-82	207	0.61%	100.00
Matóas de la Cruz y común	01-Dec-81	01-May-84	882	2.60%	15.50
Domingo de la Cruz	09-Feb-82	01-May-84	812	2.39%	12.00
Nicolás Rodriguez	06-Jun-82	08-May-83	336	0.99%	4.00
Miguel Sanchez y común	07-Jun-82	01-May-84	694	2.04%	25.00
Fulgencio Joséf	15-Jun-82	01-May-84	686	2.02%	6.00
José Hernandez y común	30-Jun-82	01-May-84	671	1.98%	211.63

Contract rate (reales)	Pesos loaned	Payback type (dye or $)	Pounds paid	Payback price (reales)	Pesos paid	Days × loan $ ($ days)	Annual return
10	62.50		50.00	12	75.00	74,125	6.16%
12	30.00		20.00	12	30.00	35,550	0.00%
12	18.75		12.50	12	18.75	22,219	0.00%
12	1.69		1.13	12	1.69	2,000	0.00%
12	79.78		53.19	12	79.78	94,541	0.00%
12	19.88		13.25	12	19.88	23,552	0.00%
12	3.80		2.53	12	3.80	4,499	0.00%
10	31.25		25.00	12	37.50	37,031	6.16%
8	2.19		2.19	12	3.28	2,588	15.43%
12	4.45	dye	2.97	17	6.31	285	237.63%
12	15.00	dye	10.00	17	21.25	6,375	35.78%
10	15.00		12.00	12	18.00	17,415	6.29%
12	6.00		4.00	12	6.00	6,858	0.00%
10	31.25		25.00	12	37.50	32,719	6.97%
12	37.50		25.00	12	37.50	38,850	0.00%
12	6.00		4.00	12	6.00	6,120	0.00%
12	9.47		6.31	12	9.47	9,658	0.00%
12	18.75		12.50	12	18.75	17,850	0.00%
12	1.50	dye	1.00	17	2.13	449	50.86%
12	4.50	dye	3.00	18	6.75	2,588	31.74%
11	8.25		6.00	12	9.00	7,747	3.53%
12	93.75		62.50	12	93.75	87,656	0.00%
12	37.50		25.00	12	37.50	35,025	0.00%
10	6.25		5.00	12	7.50	5,519	8.27%
10	125.00	dye	100.00	17	212.50	25,875	123.43%
10	19.38		15.50	12	23.25	17,089	8.28%
12	18.00		12.00	12	18.00	14,616	0.00%
12	6.00	dye	4.00	18	9.00	2,016	54.32%
12	37.50		25.00	12	37.50	26,025	0.00%
12	9.00		6.00	12	9.00	6,174	0.00%
12	317.44		211.63	12	317.44	213,001	0.00%

Daily interest rate = 0.03%; annual interest rate = 11.00%.

Debtor	Date of loan	Date paid (see text)	No. days due	Percentage of total days due	Pounds contracted
Juan Tadeo Tiburcio	02-Jul-82	01-May-84	669	1.97%	2.00
Benito Juárez	21-Aug-82	05-Mar-83	196	0.58%	6.00
Antonio Velasco	26-Sep-82	17-Jul-83	294	0.87%	12.00
Toribio Velasco	26-Sep-82	17-Jul-83	294	0.87%	6.00
Fernando Vasquez	26-Sep-82	17-Jul-83	294	0.87%	6.00
Gregorio Marcial y común	11-Nov-82	16-May-83	186	0.55%	6.00
Mateo Ortiz	28-Dec-82	29-Oct-83	305	0.90%	12.00
Benito Juárez	05-Mar-83	01-May-84	423	1.25%	6.00
Juan Mendoza	10-Apr-83	01-May-84	387	1.14%	69.75
Simán Pérez	21-May-83	01-May-84	346	1.02%	12.00
Antonio Ramirez	26-Jun-83	01-May-84	310	0.91%	3.00
Juan Manuel	28-Jun-83	01-May-84	308	0.91%	18.00
Antonio Espinoza	06-Jul-83	01-May-84	300	0.88%	12.00
Blas José	11-Jul-83	01-May-84	295	0.87%	0.50
Manuel Velasco	17-Jul-83	01-May-84	289	0.85%	37.50
Toribio Velasco	31-Jul-83	01-May-84	275	0.81%	37.56
Felipe de la Cruz	07-Aug-83	01-May-84	268	0.79%	3.00
Felipe Aguilar	03-Sep-83	01-May-84	241	0.71%	25.00
Mateo Marcial	16-Sep-83	01-May-84	228	0.67%	2.00
Tomás de Aquino	22-Sep-83	01-May-84	222	0.65%	8.00
Pablo Pérez	25-Sep-83	01-May-84	219	0.64%	6.00
Mateo Ortiz	13-Feb-84	01-May-84	78	0.23%	12.00
Nicolás de Santiago	13-Feb-84	01-May-84	78	0.23%	10.00
Antonio Coronel	13-Feb-84	01-May-84	78	0.23%	4.00
TOTALS			33968	100.00%	1074.50

SOURCE: AGN, Real Hacienda, Administración de Alcabalas, caja no. 43.

Contract rate (reales)	Pesos loaned	Payback type (dye or $)	Pounds paid	Payback price (reales)	Pesos paid	Days × loan $ ($ days)	Annual return
12	3.00		2.00	12	3.00	2,007	0.00%
12	9.00	dye	6.00	18	13.50	1,764	93.11%
12	18.00	dye	12.00	18	27.00	5,292	62.07%
12	9.00	dye	6.00	18	13.50	2,646	62.07%
12	9.00	dye	6.00	18	13.50	2,646	62.07%
12	9.00	dye	6.00	18	13.50	1,674	98.12%
12	18.00	dye	12.00	18	27.00	5,490	59.84%
12	9.00		6.00	16	12.00	3,807	28.76%
12	104.63		69.75	16	139.50	40,490	31.44%
12	18.00		12.00	16	24.00	6,228	35.16%
12	4.50		3.00	16	6.00	1,395	39.25%
12	27.00		18.00	16	36.00	8,316	39.50%
12	18.00		12.00	16	24.00	5,400	40.56%
12	0.75		0.50	16	1.00	221	41.24%
12	56.25		37.50	16	75.00	16,256	42.10%
12	56.34		37.56	16	75.13	15,495	44.24%
12	4.50		3.00	16	6.00	1,206	45.40%
12	37.50		25.00	16	50.00	9,038	50.48%
12	3.00		2.00	16	4.00	684	53.36%
12	12.00		8.00	16	16.00	2,664	54.80%
12	9.00		6.00	16	12.00	1,971	55.56%
12	18.00		12.00	16	24.00	1,404	155.98%
12	15.00		10.00	16	20.00	1,170	155.98%
12	6.00		4.00	16	8.00	468	155.98%
	1551.78		1074.50		1857.39	1,013,744	

APPENDIX D
Insurance Rates for Selected Transatlantic Routes

Date	Route	Rate	Source No.	Notes
Aug-1759	Cádiz–Veracruz	6.75%	11	24% additional if war erupts
Aug-1759	Cádiz–Veracruz	6.75%	11	20% additional if war erupts
Apr-1760	Veracruz–Cádiz	6.75%	11	24% additional if war erupts
Sep-1760	Veracruz–Cádiz	6.75%	11	20% additional if war erupts
Nov-1768	Cádiz–Veracruz	6.25%	10	coverage for 23,525 p. on ship
Jun-1772	Cádiz–Veracruz	5.25%	5	coverage for 61,000 p. on ship plus 60 days in Veracruz
Jun-1772	Cádiz–Veracruz	5.00%	5	coverage for 30,000 p. on ship plus 50 days in Veracruz
Mar-1772	Cádiz–Veracruz	5.25%	5	coverage for 50,000 p. on ship plus 24 hours in port
Jan-1776	Cádiz–Veracruz	4.75%	9	coverage for 51,000 p. on ship
Jan-1776	Cádiz–Veracruz	4.75%	9	coverage for 50,000 p. on ship
May-1776	Cádiz–Veracruz	6.00%	9	coverage for 15,000 p. on ship
Apr-1784	Cádiz–Veracruz	2.00%	8	coverage for merchandise — excluding averia ordinaria
Jan-1785	Cádiz–Veracruz	1.88%	8	coverage for merchandise — excluding averia ordinaria
Mar-1785	Cádiz–Veracruz	2.25%	8	coverage for merchandise — excluding averia ordinaria
Aug-1785	Cádiz–Veracruz	2.00%	8	coverage for merchandise — excluding averia ordinaria
Dec-1785	Cádiz–Veracruz	2.25%	8	coverage for merchandise — excluding averia ordinaria
Mar-1786	Barcelona–Veracruz	2.50%	8	coverage for merchandise — excluding averia ordinaria
Jul-1786	Cádiz–Veracruz	2.25%	8	coverage for merchandise — excluding averia ordinaria
Aug-1787	Barcelona–Veracruz	2.00%	8	coverage for merchandise — excluding averia ordinaria
Oct-1787	Cádiz–Veracruz	1.75%	8	coverage for merchandise — excluding averia ordinaria
May-1788	Cádiz–Veracruz	2.00%	1	
Jun-1788	Veracruz–Barcelona	2.00%	8	coverage for merchandise excluding averia ordinaria
Sep-1788	Veracruz–Cádiz	2.00%	8	1.5% on plata y oro & 2% on frutas — exc. Averia ord.
Sep-1788	Cádiz–Veracruz	1.50%	1	

Date	Route	Rate	Source No.	Notes
Dec-1788	Cádiz–Veracruz	2.25%	1	
Apr-1789	Veracruz–Cádiz	2.00%	8	addendum to Sept-1788 policy
Sep-1789	Veracruz–Cádiz	2.00%	8	coverage for 7 zurrones de grana addendum to Sept-1788 policy
Mar-1790	Veracruz–Cádiz	1.25%	8	coverage for silver
May-1790	Veracruz–Malaga	1.50%	1	
Jun-1790	Cádiz–Veracruz	5.00%	1	
Jul-1790	Veracruz–Cádiz	1.75%	8	adds that if war w/ England or others, premium is 20%
Sep-1790	Cádiz–Veracruz	1.75%	8	no mention of war premium
Nov-1790	Cádiz–Veracruz–Cádiz	5.25%	1	roundtrip coverage
Mar-1791	Veracruz–Cádiz	1.00%	1	
Apr-1791	Veracruz–Cádiz	1.50%	8	on 6 zurrones grana worth 4037.5 pesos — no averia ordin.
Jul-1791	Cádiz–Veracruz	1.25%	1	
Nov-1791	Cádiz–Veracruz	1.25%	1	
Mar-1792	Cádiz–Veracruz	1.25%	1	
Jul-1792	Cádiz–Veracruz	1.25%	1	
Nov-1792	Cádiz–Veracruz	1.25%	1	
Jan-1793	Veracruz–Cádiz	1.25%	8	
Jan-1793	Cádiz–Veracruz	1.75%	1	
Feb-1793	Cádiz–Veracruz	6.75%	8	insured paid in advance & also insured the premium he paid
Mar-1795	Veracruz–Cádiz	3.25%	8	on condition that it's war ship with war crew
Mar-1795	Veracruz–Cádiz	3.00%	8	on condition that it's war ship with war crew
Apr-1795	Veracruz–Cádiz	8.00%	8	but only 4% if cargo arrives safely on war ship
Dec-1795	Veracruz–Cádiz	2.00%	8	war ship w/ 3 zurrones Grana worth 1500 p. from Bustamante y parientes
Dec-1795	Veracruz–Cádiz	2.25%	8	war ship w/19 zurrones Grana from Juan de Castillo y Bustamante
Feb-1796	Veracruz–Cádiz	2.00%	8	1.75% if war ship but 16% if war erupts & captured or 8% if it arrives

Date	Route	Rate	Source No.	Notes
Apr-1796	Cádiz–Veracruz	2.25%	8	if war within 15 days of depart, 20% captured & 10% arriving safe
Sep-1799	Cádiz–Veracruz	60.00%	2	rate is 60% if seized but 40% or 50% if it arrives safely (mult. Insurers)
???-1801	Cádiz–Veracruz	3.50%	6	from List of proposed Rates—post-war
Dec-1801	Cádiz–Veracruz	3.50%	7	from List of proposed Rates—post-war
Dec-1801	Veracruz–Cádiz	3.75%	7	from List of proposed Rates—post-war
Dec-1801	Cádiz–Veracruz	5.00%	2	coverage of 10,089 pesos for ship
Dec-1801	Cádiz–Veracruz	4.75%	2	coverage of 19,000 p. for ship
Jan-1802	Cádiz–Veracruz	4.75%	2	coverage of 33,142 p. for ship
Feb-1802	Cádiz–Veracruz	3.50%	7	from List of proposed Rates
Feb-1802	Cádiz–Veracruz	5.25%	2	coverage of 16,000 p. for ship
Feb-1802	Cádiz–Veracruz	3.50%	7	from List of proposed Rates
Apr-1802	Cádiz–Veracruz	5.00%	2	coverage of 7500 p. for ship
Apr-1802	Cádiz–Veracruz	5.25%	2	coverage of 32,161 p. for ship
Apr-1802	Cádiz–Veracruz	5.25%	2	coverage of 12,000 p. for ship
Apr-1802	Cádiz–Veracruz	5.00%	2	coverage of 11,520 p. for ship
Apr-1802	Cádiz–Veracruz	5.00%	2	coverage of 20,000 pesos for ship
Aug-1802	Cádiz–Veracruz	4.50%	2	coverage of 28,801 pesos for ship
Sep-1802	Cádiz–Veracruz	4.00%	2	coverage of 32,782 p. for ship
Nov-1802	Cádiz–Veracruz	4.25%	2	coverage of 24,081 pesos for ship
Nov-1802	Cádiz–Veracruz	4.00%	2	coverage of 25,000 pesos for ship
Feb-1803	Cádiz–Veracruz	3.75%	3	30% if war w/ Fr or GB & 12% if war w/ other—24,155 p. on ship
Feb-1803	Cádiz–Veracruz	4.00%	3	coverage of 16,335 pesos on ship
Mar-1803	Cádiz–Veracruz	3.75%	8	on merchandise, but not covered for losses owing to war

Date	Route	Rate	Source No.	Notes
Apr-1803	Cádiz–Veracruz	6.50%	3	coverage of 20,205 pesos for ship
Jul-1803	Veracruz–Cádiz	5.50%	8	45% above the 5.5% if war erupts—no rebate for safe arrival
Aug-1803	Cádiz–Veracruz	7.50%	3	coverage of 30,888 pesos on ship
Aug-1803	Cádiz–Veracruz	6.00%	3	coverage of 20,282 pesos on ship
Oct-1803	Cádiz–Veracruz	6.25%	3	coverage of 16,606 pesos on ship
Nov-1803	Cádiz–Veracruz	14.00%	3	coverage of 32,593 pesos on ship
Dec-1803	Cádiz–Veracruz	6.00%	3	coverage of 42,462 pesos on ship
Dec-1803	Cádiz–Veracruz	5.00%	3	coverage of 17,700 pesos on ship
Dec-1803	Cádiz–Veracruz	4.00%	3	coverage of 24,851 pesos on ship
Jul-1803 to Jun-1804	Cádiz–Veracruz	4.25%	4	coverage for merchandise
Feb-1804	Cádiz–Veracruz	5.75%	3	coverage of 24,891 pesos on ship
May-1804	Cádiz–Veracruz	4.75%	3	coverage of 27,752 pesos on ship
Oct-1804	Cádiz–Veracruz	5.75%	3	coverage of 20,617 pesos on ship
Nov-1804	Cádiz–Veracruz	1% per month	3	coverage of 19,000 pesos on ship
Oct-1809	Cádiz–Veracruz	7.25%	8	covers 80% of the ship's value for total covered of 8,000 pesos
Apr-1810	Cádiz–Veracruz	8.00%	3	coverage of 10,566 pesos for ship
May-1810	Cádiz–Veracruz	6.75%	8	coverage of 8,000 pesos for ship
Dec-1810	Cádiz–Veracruz	6.50%	8	coverage for merchandise
Jan-1811	Cádiz–Veracruz	6.75%	8	coverage for ship & merchandise
Apr-1811	Cádiz–Veracruz	6.75%	8	coverage for merchandise

Date	Route	Rate	Source No.	Notes
Jun-1812	Cádiz–Vigo–Veracruz	7.00%	3	coverage of 27,000 p. for ship with stop in Vigo
Nov-1813	Cádiz–Veracruz	7.50%	3	coverage of 16,000 p. for ship
Oct-1815	Cádiz–Veracruz	10.00%	3	coverage of 28,000 p. for ship
Oct-1816	Santander–Veracruz	7.00%	8	increased 25% (to 32%) in case of total loss
Jan-1817	Cádiz–Veracruz	13.00%	3	coverage of 20,500 p. on ship

SOURCES: Doc. no. 1: "Libro de operaciones de la compania de seguros por Don Antonio Ramirez desde 9 de Maio 1788 a 12 de Agosto de 1795," AGI, Consulados, libro 444B.

Doc. no. 2: "Varias tomas de razon de Polizas de Seguros de embarcaciones que no tienen pliegos," AGI, Consulados, legajo 889.

Doc. no. 3: "Varias tomas de razon de Polizas de Seguros de embarcaciones a indias," AGI, Consulados, legajo 889.

Doc. no. 4: "Libro de registro de escrituras de riesgo extendidas sobre mercancias con destino a America—1803–1805," AGI, Consulados, libro 444A.

Doc. no. 5: "Libro de Toma de razon de escrituras de riesgo de flota de Luis de Cordoba jefe de la escuadra 1774," AGI, Consulados, libro 440.

Doc. no. 6: "Compania de Seguros y expedientes sobre estas companias (1793–1837)," AGI, Consulados, legajo 78, doc. 42.

Doc. no. 7: "Compania de Seguros y expedientes sobre estas companias," AGI, Consulados, legajo 78.

Doc. no. 8: "Polizas de seguros del concurso de don Antonio de Artechea," AGI, Consulados, legajo 518.

Doc. no. 9: AGI, Consulados, libro 441.

Doc. no. 10: AGI, Consulados, libro 439.

Doc. no. 11: AGI, Consulados, legajo 772.

Estimated Cost of Marketing One Arroba of Cochineal from Oaxaca to London (assuming 20 percent wartime insurance premiums and excluding ocean freight and intra-European insurance)

A	B	C	D	E	F	G	H	I
Year	Avaluo price/@ in Spain; actual value to 1778; post-1778 fixed	Average price in Europe (pesos/ lb.)	Average price in Europe (pesos/ @) [C × 25]	Value after 5% shrinkage (pesos/@) [D × 95%]	Purchase price in Oaxaca (pesos/ @) [see text]	Approx. total taxes paid to Crown (pesos/ @) [see text]	Zurrón construction (pesos/@) [see text]	Land freight Oaxaca to Veracruz (pesos/ @) [see text]
1758	70.40	3.51	87.64	83.26	51.56	19.43	.4175	1.10
1759	70.40				51.56	19.43	.4175	1.10
1760	64.90	3.24	81.00	76.95	50.00	19.30	.4175	1.10
1761	64.90	3.42	85.39	81.12	46.88	19.03	.4175	1.10
1762		4.11	102.71	97.58	46.09	18.96	.4175	1.10
1763	66.25	3.59	89.78	85.29	48.44	19.17	.4175	1.10
1764	66.00	4.13	103.16	98.00	60.94	20.24	.4175	1.10
1765	74.90	5.26	131.40	124.83	57.81	19.97	.4175	1.10
1766	86.90	4.90	122.40	116.28	60.94	20.24	.4175	1.10
1767	83.30	5.05	126.34	120.02	60.94	22.68	.4175	1.10
1768	96.50	5.49	137.25	130.39	70.31	23.16	.4175	1.10
1769	103.50	5.45	136.13	129.32	76.56	23.88	.4175	1.10
1770	106.90	6.22	155.59	147.81	78.13	24.06	.4175	1.10
1771		6.75	168.64	160.21	100.00	26.60	.4175	1.10
1772	119.00	6.16	153.90	146.21	93.75	25.88	.4175	1.10
1773	103.50	5.13	128.36	121.94	79.69	24.24	.4175	1.10
1774	102.80	5.01	125.33	119.06	54.69	21.34	.4175	1.10
1775	98.30	4.63	115.65	109.87	50.00	20.80	.4175	1.10
1776	87.00	3.88	96.98	92.13	53.13	21.16	.4175	1.10
1777	78.40	4.38	109.58	104.10	46.88	20.44	.4175	1.10
1778	82.80	4.53	113.18	107.52	50.00	24.24	.4175	1.10
1779	82.80	4.54	113.40	107.73	46.88	23.87	.4175	1.10
1780	82.80	4.75	118.69	112.75	53.13	25.13	.4175	1.10
1781	82.80	5.20	130.05	123.55	53.13	25.13	.4175	1.10

J	K	L	M	N	O	P	Q	R
Registro de grana 2p/8@ (pesos/@) [see text]	Ocean freight rate [see text]	Insurance at war rate of 20% (pesos/@) [see text]	Comisión de recibo; 2.5% in Mexico (pesos/@) [C × 2.5%]	Comisión de venta; 2.5% in Spain (pesos/@) [B × 2.5%]	Customs duties in England (pesos/@) [see text]	Total costs to merchant including purchase [columns F thru O]	Profit (pesos/@) [E − P]	Rate of return [Q/P]
.25	?	3.22	1.29	1.76	1.17	80.21	1.92	2.40%
.25	?	3.22	1.29	1.76	1.17	80.21		
.25	?	3.13	1.25	1.62	1.17	78.24	−2.41	−3.08%
.25	?	2.93	1.17	1.62	1.17	74.57	5.43	7.28%
.25	?	2.88	1.15	1.64	1.17	73.67	22.78	30.93%
.25	?	3.03	1.21	1.66	1.17	76.44	7.73	10.11%
.25	?	3.81	1.52	1.65	1.17	91.10	5.78	6.35%
.25	?	3.61	1.45	1.87	1.17	87.65	36.05	41.13%
.25	?	3.81	1.52	2.17	1.17	91.62	23.53	25.69%
.25	?	3.81	1.52	2.08	1.17	93.97	24.93	26.53%
.25	?	4.39	1.76	2.41	1.17	104.97	24.29	23.14%
.25	?	4.79	1.91	2.59	1.17	112.67	15.53	13.78%
.25	?	4.88	1.95	2.67	1.17	114.63	32.05	27.96%
.25	?	6.25	2.50	2.82	1.17	141.11	17.97	12.73%
.25	?	5.86	2.34	2.98	1.17	133.74	11.34	8.48%
.25	?	4.98	1.99	2.59	1.17	116.43	4.39	3.77%
.25	?	3.42	1.37	2.57	1.17	86.32	31.61	36.62%
.25	?	3.13	1.25	2.46	1.17	80.57	28.17	34.97%
.25	?	3.32	1.33	2.18	1.17	84.05	6.95	8.27%
.25	?	2.93	1.17	1.96	1.17	76.31	26.66	34.94%
.25	?	3.13	1.25	2.07	1.17	83.62	22.77	27.24%
.25	?	0.73	1.17	2.07	1.17	77.66	28.95	37.27%
.25	?	0.83	1.33	2.07	1.17	85.42	26.21	30.68%
.25	?	0.83	1.33	2.07	1.17	85.42	37.00	43.32%

A	B	C	D	E	F	G	H	I
Year	Avaluo price/@ in Spain; actual value to 1778; post-1778 fixed	Average price in Europe (pesos/lb.)	Average price in Europe (pesos/@) [C × 25]	Value after 5% shrinkage (pesos/@) [D × 95%]	Purchase price in Oaxaca (pesos/@) [see text]	Approx. total taxes paid to Crown (pesos/@) [see text]	Zurrón construction (pesos/@) [see text]	Land freight Oaxaca to Veracruz (pesos/@) [see text]
1782	82.80	4.87	121.63	115.54	53.13	25.13	.4175	1.10
1783	82.80	4.44	110.97	105.43	56.25	25.52	.4175	1.10
1784	82.80	3.42	85.44	81.17	50.00	24.74	.4175	1.10
1785	82.80	3.46	86.57	82.24	53.13	25.13	.4175	1.10
1786	82.80	3.43	85.64	81.36	51.56	24.93	.4175	1.10
1787	82.80	3.78	94.46	89.74	50.00	24.74	.4175	1.10
1788	82.80	4.34	108.50	103.08	50.00	24.74	.4175	1.10
1789	82.80	3.66	91.49	86.91	48.44	24.54	.4175	1.10
1790	82.80	3.72	92.98	88.33	50.00	24.74	.4175	1.10
1791	82.80	3.64	91.11	86.55	51.56	24.93	.4175	1.10
1792	82.80	3.56	88.98	84.54	46.88	23.87	.4175	1.10
1793	82.80	3.72	92.94	88.29	42.19	23.33	.4175	1.10
1794	82.80	3.51	87.68	83.30	32.81	22.24	.4175	1.10
1795	82.80	3.97	99.15	94.19	37.50	22.97	.4175	1.10
1796	82.80	4.05	101.14	96.08	54.69	25.05	.4175	1.10
1797	82.80	5.45	136.19	129.38	48.44	24.30	.4175	1.10
1798	82.80	8.48	211.94	201.34	56.25	25.24	.4175	1.10
1799	82.80	8.17	204.19	193.98	60.94	25.81	.4175	1.10
1800	82.80	5.52	137.97	131.07	59.38	25.62	.4175	1.10
1801	82.80	5.54	138.41	131.49	56.25	25.24	.4175	1.10
1802	82.80	4.57	114.22	108.51	59.38	25.62	.4175	1.10
1803	82.80	5.40	134.90	128.15	65.63	26.38	.4175	1.10
1804	82.80	5.83	145.83	138.54	89.06	29.21	.4175	1.10
1805	82.80	6.94	173.44	164.77	71.88	27.13	.4175	1.10
1806	82.80	6.56	164.06	155.86	84.38	28.64	.4175	1.10
1807	82.80	6.34	158.59	150.66	90.63	29.40	.4175	1.10
1808	82.80	6.50	162.50	154.38	90.63	29.85	.4175	1.10
1809	82.80	8.22	205.47	195.20	103.13	31.43	.4175	1.10

J	K	L	M	N	O	P	Q	R
Registro de grana 2p/8@ (pesos/ @) [see text]	Ocean freight rate [see text]	Insurance at war rate of 20% (pesos/@) [see text]	Comisión de recibo; 2.5% in Mexico (pesos/@) [C × 2.5%]	Comisión de venta; 2.5% in Spain (pesos/@) [B × 2.5%]	Customs duties in England (pesos/ @) [see text]	Total costs to merchant including purchase [columns F thru O]	Profit (pesos/ @) [E − P]	Rate of return [Q/P]
.25	?	0.83	1.33	2.07	1.17	85.42	29.00	33.95%
.25	?	0.88	1.41	2.07	1.17	89.07	15.23	17.10%
.25	?	1.13	1.25	2.07	1.17	82.12	−2.08	−2.53%
.25	?	1.24	1.33	2.07	1.17	85.83	−4.72	−5.49%
.25	?	1.37	1.29	2.07	1.17	84.17	−3.93	−4.67%
.25	?	1.05	1.25	2.07	1.17	82.05	6.56	8.00%
.25	?	1.10	1.25	2.07	1.17	82.09	19.86	24.20%
.25	?	1.09	1.21	2.07	1.17	80.29	5.50	6.85%
.25	?	1.55	1.25	2.07	1.17	82.54	4.66	5.65%
.25	?	0.72	1.29	2.07	1.17	83.52	1.91	2.29%
.25	?	0.66	1.17	2.07	1.17	77.59	5.82	7.50%
.25	?	9.69	1.05	2.07	1.17	81.27	5.90	7.26%
.25	?	7.81	0.82	2.07	1.17	68.70	13.47	19.62%
.25	?	1.62	0.94	2.07	0.00	66.87	26.20	39.18%
.25	?	1.53	1.37	2.07	0.00	86.48	8.48	9.81%
.25	?	13.00	1.21	2.07	0.00	90.78	37.47	41.28%
.25	?	13.17	1.41	2.07	5.21	105.12	95.10	90.47%
.25	?	13.32	1.52	2.07	5.21	110.63	82.22	74.32%
.25	?	14.73	1.48	2.07	5.21	110.25	19.69	17.86%
.25	?	15.50	1.41	2.07	5.21	107.45	22.92	21.33%
.25	?	3.48	1.48	2.07	5.21	99.00	8.38	8.46%
.25	?	4.84	1.64	2.07	5.86	108.18	18.85	17.42%
.25	?	5.33	2.23	2.07	6.51	136.18	1.24	0.91%
.25	?	20.79	1.80	2.07	6.77	132.20	31.44	23.78%
.25	?	20.00	2.11	2.07	7.16	146.13	8.61	5.89%
.25	?	20.00	2.27	2.07	7.16	153.29	−3.75	−2.45%
.25	?	20.00	2.27	2.07	7.16	153.74	−0.49	−0.32%
.25	?	23.99	2.58	2.07	12.50	177.46	16.61	9.36%

A	B	C	D	E	F	G	H	I
	Avaluo price/@ in Spain; actual value to 1778; post-1778		*Average price in Europe (pesos/*		*Purchase price in Oaxaca*	*Approx. total taxes paid to Crown*		*Land freight Oaxaca to Veracruz*
Year	*fixed*	*Average price in Europe (pesos/ lb.)*	*@) [C × 25]*	*Value after 5% shrinkage (pesos/@) [D × 95%]*	*(pesos/ @) [see text]*	*(pesos/ @) [see text]*	*Zurrón construction (pesos/@) [see text]*	*(pesos/ @) [see text]*
1810	82.80	8.75	218.75	207.81	90.63	32.57	.4175	1.10
1811	82.80	7.88	196.88	187.03	89.06	32.60	.4175	1.10
1812	82.80	7.63	190.63	181.09	62.50	28.45	.4175	1.10
1813	82.80	10.38	259.38	246.41	46.88	26.01	.4175	1.10
1814	82.80	10.69	267.19	253.83	78.13	30.89	.4175	1.10
1815	82.80	8.75	218.75	207.81	75.00	36.65	.4175	1.10
1816	82.80	7.33	183.33	174.17	100.00	40.55	.4175	1.10
1817	82.80	7.44	185.94	176.64	90.63	39.09	.4175	1.10

SOURCE: See text for Chapter 8.

NOTE: The symbol "@" signifies arrobas.

J	K	L	M	N	O	P	Q	R
Registro de grana 2p/8@ (pesos/ @) [see text]	*Ocean freight rate [see text]*	*Insurance at war rate of 20% (pesos/@) [see text]*	*Comisión de recibo; 2.5% in Mexico (pesos/@) [C × 2.5%]*	*Comisión de venta; 2.5% in Spain (pesos/@) [B × 2.5%]*	*Customs duties in England (pesos/ @) [see text]*	*Total costs to merchant including purchase [columns F thru O]*	*Profit (pesos/ @) [E − P]*	*Rate of return [Q/P]*
.25	?	8.50	2.27	2.07	12.50	150.30	56.39	37.52%
.25	?	7.29	2.23	2.07	12.50	147.51	38.39	26.03%
.25	?	7.00	1.56	2.07	12.50	115.85	64.12	55.34%
.25	?	8.51	1.17	2.07	14.84	101.25	144.03	142.25%
.25	?		1.95	2.07	14.84	129.65	123.05	94.91%
.25	?	12.00	1.88	2.07	14.84	144.21	62.48	43.33%
.25	?	9.04	2.50	2.07	14.84	170.77	2.27	1.33%
.25	?	16.90	2.27	2.07	14.84	167.56	7.95	4.75%

APPENDIX E.2

Estimated Cost of Marketing One Arroba of Cochineal from Oaxaca to London
(assuming 50 percent wartime insurance premiums and excluding ocean freight
and intra-European insurance)

A	B	C	D	E	F	G	H	I
Year	Avaluo price/@ in Spain; actual value to 1778; post-1778 fixed	Average price in Europe (pesos/ lb.)	Average price in Europe (pesos/ @) [C × 25]	Value after 5% shrinkage (pesos/@) [D × 95%]	Purchase price in Oaxaca (pesos/ @) [see text]	Approx. total taxes paid to Crown (pesos/ @) [see text]	Zurrón construction (pesos/@) [see text]	Land freight Oaxaca to Veracruz (pesos/ @) [see text]
1758	70.40	3.51	87.64	83.26	51.56	19.43	.4175	1.10
1759	70.40				51.56	19.43	.4175	1.10
1760	64.90	3.24	81.00	76.95	50.00	19.30	.4175	1.10
1761	64.90	3.42	85.39	81.12	46.88	19.03	.4175	1.10
1762		4.11	102.71	97.58	46.09	18.96	.4175	1.10
1763	66.25	3.59	89.78	85.29	48.44	19.17	.4175	1.10
1764	66.00	4.13	103.16	98.00	60.94	20.24	.4175	1.10
1765	74.90	5.26	131.40	124.83	57.81	19.97	.4175	1.10
1766	86.90	4.90	122.40	116.28	60.94	20.24	.4175	1.10
1767	83.30	5.05	126.34	120.02	60.94	22.68	.4175	1.10
1768	96.50	5.49	137.25	130.39	70.31	23.16	.4175	1.10
1769	103.50	5.45	136.13	129.32	76.56	23.88	.4175	1.10
1770	106.90	6.22	155.59	147.81	78.13	24.06	.4175	1.10
1771		6.75	168.64	160.21	100.00	26.60	.4175	1.10
1772	119.00	6.16	153.90	146.21	93.75	25.88	.4175	1.10
1773	103.50	5.13	128.36	121.94	79.69	24.24	.4175	1.10
1774	102.80	5.01	125.33	119.06	54.69	21.34	.4175	1.10
1775	98.30	4.63	115.65	109.87	50.00	20.80	.4175	1.10
1776	87.00	3.88	96.98	92.13	53.13	21.16	.4175	1.10
1777	78.40	4.38	109.58	104.10	46.88	20.44	.4175	1.10
1778	82.80	4.53	113.18	107.52	50.00	24.24	.4175	1.10
1779	82.80	4.54	113.40	107.73	46.88	23.87	.4175	1.10
1780	82.80	4.75	118.69	112.75	53.13	25.13	.4175	1.10
1781	82.80	5.20	130.05	123.55	53.13	25.13	.4175	1.10

J	K	L	M	N	O	P	Q	R
Registro de grana 2p/8@ (pesos/@) [see text]	Ocean freight rate [see text]	Insurance at war rate of 20% (pesos/@) [see text]	Comisión de recibo; 2.5% in Mexico (pesos/@) [C × 2.5%]	Comisión de venta; 2.5% in Spain (pesos/@) [B × 2.5%]	Customs duties in England (pesos/ @) [see text]	Total costs to merchant including purchase [columns F thru O]	Profit (pesos/ @) [E − P]	Rate of return [Q/P]
.25	?	3.22	1.29	1.76	1.17	80.21	1.92	2.40%
.25	?	3.22	1.29	1.76	1.17	80.21		
.25	?	3.13	1.25	1.62	1.17	78.24	−2.41	−3.08%
.25	?	2.93	1.17	1.62	1.17	74.57	5.43	7.28%
.25	?	2.88	1.15	1.64	1.17	73.67	22.78	30.93%
.25	?	3.03	1.21	1.66	1.17	76.44	7.73	10.11%
.25	?	3.81	1.52	1.65	1.17	91.10	5.78	6.35%
.25	?	3.61	1.45	1.87	1.17	87.65	36.05	41.13%
.25	?	3.81	1.52	2.17	1.17	91.62	23.53	25.69%
.25	?	3.81	1.52	2.08	1.17	93.97	24.93	26.53%
.25	?	4.39	1.76	2.41	1.17	104.97	24.29	23.14%
.25	?	4.79	1.91	2.59	1.17	112.67	15.53	13.78%
.25	?	4.88	1.95	2.67	1.17	114.63	32.05	27.96%
.25	?	6.25	2.50	2.82	1.17	141.11	17.97	12.73%
.25	?	5.86	2.34	2.98	1.17	133.74	11.34	8.48%
.25	?	4.98	1.99	2.59	1.17	116.43	4.39	3.77%
.25	?	3.42	1.37	2.57	1.17	86.32	31.61	36.62%
.25	?	3.13	1.25	2.46	1.17	80.57	28.17	34.97%
.25	?	3.32	1.33	2.18	1.17	84.05	6.95	8.27%
.25	?	2.93	1.17	1.96	1.17	76.31	26.66	34.94%
.25	?	3.13	1.25	2.07	1.17	83.62	22.77	27.24%
.25	?	0.73	1.17	2.07	1.17	77.66	28.95	37.27%
.25	?	0.83	1.33	2.07	1.17	85.42	26.21	30.68%
.25	?	0.83	1.33	2.07	1.17	85.42	37.00	43.32%

A	B	C	D	E	F	G	H	I
Year	Avaluo price/@ in Spain; actual value to 1778; post-1778 fixed	Average price in Europe (pesos/lb.)	Average price in Europe (pesos/@) [C × 25]	Value after 5% shrinkage (pesos/@) [D × 95%]	Purchase price in Oaxaca (pesos/@) [see text]	Approx. total taxes paid to Crown (pesos/@) [see text]	Zurrón construction (pesos/@) [see text]	Land freight Oaxaca to Veracruz (pesos/@) [see text]
1782	82.80	4.87	121.63	115.54	53.13	25.13	.4175	1.10
1783	82.80	4.44	110.97	105.43	56.25	25.52	.4175	1.10
1784	82.80	3.42	85.44	81.17	50.00	24.74	.4175	1.10
1785	82.80	3.46	86.57	82.24	53.13	25.13	.4175	1.10
1786	82.80	3.43	85.64	81.36	51.56	24.93	.4175	1.10
1787	82.80	3.78	94.46	89.74	50.00	24.74	.4175	1.10
1788	82.80	4.34	108.50	103.08	50.00	24.74	.4175	1.10
1789	82.80	3.66	91.49	86.91	48.44	24.54	.4175	1.10
1790	82.80	3.72	92.98	88.33	50.00	24.74	.4175	1.10
1791	82.80	3.64	91.11	86.55	51.56	24.93	.4175	1.10
1792	82.80	3.56	88.98	84.54	46.88	23.87	.4175	1.10
1793	82.80	3.72	92.94	88.29	42.19	23.33	.4175	1.10
1794	82.80	3.51	87.68	83.30	32.81	22.24	.4175	1.10
1795	82.80	3.97	99.15	94.19	37.50	22.97	.4175	1.10
1796	82.80	4.05	101.14	96.08	54.69	25.05	.4175	1.10
1797	82.80	5.45	136.19	129.38	48.44	24.30	.4175	1.10
1798	82.80	8.48	211.94	201.34	56.25	25.24	.4175	1.10
1799	82.80	8.17	204.19	193.98	60.94	25.81	.4175	1.10
1800	82.80	5.52	137.97	131.07	59.38	25.62	.4175	1.10
1801	82.80	5.54	138.41	131.49	56.25	25.24	.4175	1.10
1802	82.80	4.57	114.22	108.51	59.38	25.62	.4175	1.10
1803	82.80	5.40	134.90	128.15	65.63	26.38	.4175	1.10
1804	82.80	5.83	145.83	138.54	89.06	29.21	.4175	1.10
1805	82.80	6.94	173.44	164.77	71.88	27.13	.4175	1.10
1806	82.80	6.56	164.06	155.86	84.38	28.64	.4175	1.10
1807	82.80	6.34	158.59	150.66	90.63	29.40	.4175	1.10
1808	82.80	6.50	162.50	154.38	90.63	29.85	.4175	1.10
1809	82.80	8.22	205.47	195.20	103.13	31.43	.4175	1.10

J	K	L	M	N	O	P	Q	R
Registro de grana 2p/8@ (pesos/ @) [see text]	*Ocean freight rate [see text]*	*Insurance at war rate of 20% (pesos/@) [see text]*	*Comisión de recibo; 2.5% in Mexico (pesos/@) [C × 2.5%]*	*Comisión de venta; 2.5% in Spain (pesos/@) [B × 2.5%]*	*Customs duties in England (pesos/ @) [see text]*	*Total costs to merchant including purchase [columns F thru O]*	*Profit (pesos/ @) [E − P]*	*Rate of return [Q/P]*
.25	?	0.83	1.33	2.07	1.17	85.42	29.00	33.95%
.25	?	0.88	1.41	2.07	1.17	89.07	15.23	17.10%
.25	?	1.13	1.25	2.07	1.17	82.12	−2.08	−2.53%
.25	?	1.24	1.33	2.07	1.17	85.83	−4.72	−5.49%
.25	?	1.37	1.29	2.07	1.17	84.17	−3.93	−4.67%
.25	?	1.05	1.25	2.07	1.17	82.05	6.56	8.00%
.25	?	1.10	1.25	2.07	1.17	82.09	19.86	24.20%
.25	?	1.09	1.21	2.07	1.17	80.29	5.50	6.85%
.25	?	1.55	1.25	2.07	1.17	82.54	4.66	5.65%
.25	?	0.72	1.29	2.07	1.17	83.52	1.91	2.29%
.25	?	0.66	1.17	2.07	1.17	77.59	5.82	7.50%
.25	?	24.22	1.05	2.07	1.17	95.80	5.90	6.16%
.25	?	19.53	0.82	2.07	1.17	80.41	13.47	16.76%
.25	?	1.62	0.94	2.07	0.00	66.87	26.20	39.18%
.25	?	1.53	1.37	2.07	0.00	86.48	8.48	9.81%
.25	?	32.50	1.21	2.07	0.00	110.28	37.47	33.98%
.25	?	32.93	1.41	2.07	5.21	124.88	95.10	76.15%
.25	?	33.29	1.52	2.07	5.21	130.61	82.22	62.95%
.25	?	36.82	1.48	2.07	5.21	132.35	19.69	14.88%
.25	?	38.75	1.41	2.07	5.21	130.70	22.92	17.53%
.25	?	3.48	1.48	2.07	5.21	99.00	8.38	8.46%
.25	?	4.84	1.64	2.07	5.86	108.18	18.85	17.42%
.25	?	5.33	2.23	2.07	6.51	136.18	1.24	0.91%
.25	?	51.98	1.80	2.07	6.77	163.39	31.44	19.24%
.25	?	50.00	2.11	2.07	7.16	176.13	8.61	4.89%
.25	?	50.00	2.27	2.07	7.16	183.29	−3.75	−2.05%
.25	?	50.00	2.27	2.07	7.16	183.74	−0.49	−0.27%
.25	?	59.97	2.58	2.07	12.50	213.44	16.61	7.78%

A	B	C	D	E	F	G	H	I
	Avaluo price/@ in Spain; actual value to 1778; post- 1778		*Average price in Europe (pesos/*		*Purchase price in Oaxaca (pesos/*	*Approx. total taxes paid to Crown (pesos/*		*Land freight Oaxaca to Veracruz (pesos/*
Year	*fixed*	*Average price in Europe (pesos/ lb.)*	*@) [C × 25]*	*Value after 5% shrinkage (pesos/@) [D × 95%]*	*@) [see text]*	*@) [see text]*	*Zurrón construction (pesos/@) [see text]*	*@) [see text]*
1810	82.80	8.75	218.75	207.81	90.63	32.57	.4175	1.10
1811	82.80	7.88	196.88	187.03	89.06	32.60	.4175	1.10
1812	82.80	7.63	190.63	181.09	62.50	28.45	.4175	1.10
1813	82.80	10.38	259.38	246.41	46.88	26.01	.4175	1.10
1814	82.80	10.69	267.19	253.83	78.13	30.89	.4175	1.10
1815	82.80	8.75	218.75	207.81	75.00	36.65	.4175	1.10
1816	82.80	7.33	183.33	174.17	100.00	40.55	.4175	1.10
1817	82.80	7.44	185.94	176.64	90.63	39.09	.4175	1.10

SOURCES: See text for Chapter 8.

NOTE: The symbol "@" signifies arrobas.

J	K	L	M	N	O	P	Q	R
Registro de grana 2p/8@ (pesos/ @) [see text]	Ocean freight rate [see text]	Insurance at war rate of 20% (pesos/@) [see text]	Comisión de recibo; 2.5% in Mexico (pesos/@) [C × 2.5%]	Comisión de venta; 2.5% in Spain (pesos/@) [B × 2.5%]	Customs duties in England (pesos/ @) [see text]	Total costs to merchant including purchase [columns F thru O]	Profit (pesos/ @) [E − P]	Rate of return [Q/P]
.25	?	8.50	2.27	2.07	12.50	150.30	56.39	37.52%
.25	?	7.29	2.23	2.07	12.50	147.51	38.39	26.03%
.25	?	7.00	1.56	2.07	12.50	115.85	64.12	55.34%
.25	?	8.51	1.17	2.07	14.84	101.25	144.03	142.25%
.25	?		1.95	2.07	14.84	129.65	123.05	94.91%
.25	?	12.00	1.88	2.07	14.84	144.21	62.48	43.33%
.25	?	9.04	2.50	2.07	14.84	170.77	2.27	1.33%
.25	?	16.90	2.27	2.07	14.84	167.56	7.95	4.75%

Notes

Chapter 1. Introduction

1. In the literature on colonial Spanish America, the *repartimiento* is sometimes called *repartimiento de comercio*, *repartimiento de mercancías*, *repartimiento de bienes*, or the *reparto*. In colonial documents, it is almost always referred to simply as *repartimiento*. This book adopts the latter convention.

2. The Black Legend refers to the anti-Spanish view of the conquest and colonial era, which was propagated by traditional histories over the centuries. This "legend" criticized Spain's role and attributed it to the alleged cruelty of the Spanish people. Some historians believe that the entire genre began with the sixteenth-century writings of Bartolomé de las Casas, and then was continued by anti-Catholic Protestants of Northern Europe in the years that followed. See Gibson, *Black Legend*.

3. Lockhart and Schwartz, 356.

4. The classic work on the *repartimiento* is Hamnett, *Politics and Trade*; on the Bourbon Reforms and the *repartimiento*, see also Brading, *Miners and Merchants*; Stein, "Bureaucracy and Business"; John R. Fisher, *Government and Society*; Moreno Cebrián, *El corregidor de indios*; and MacLachlan. On the Bourbon Reforms in general and the Plan of Intendancies for Spanish America, see Lynch, *Spanish Colonial Administration*; Lillian Fisher; and Brading, "Bourbon Spain."

5. On Mexico, see Pastor, "El repartimiento"; Carmagnani, *El regreso de los dioses*; Pietschmann; Dehouve; Patch, *Maya and Spaniard*; Romero Frizzi, "El poder de las mercaderes"; Romero Frizzi, *Economía y vida*; Chance, *Conquest of the Sierra*; Chance, "Social Stratification"; Chance, "Capitalismo y desigualidad"; Gosner; and Ouweneel, *Shadows Over Anáhuac*. For a comparison between Mexico and the Andes, see Larson and Wasserstrom. For the Andes, see Golte; O'Phelan Godoy; Moreno Cebrián, *El corregidor de indios*; Spalding, *Huarochirí*; Spalding, "Tratos mercantiles"; Tord Nicolini, "El corregidor"; Tord Nicolini, "Los repartos legalizados"; and Sinclair Thomson. For Central America, see Patch, "Imperial Politics."

6. These debates provided the bulk of the materials used by Hamnett in *Politics and Trade*, and Brading in *Miners and Merchants*.

7. Hamnett, *Politics and Trade,* and Brading, *Miners and Merchants.*

8. Pietschmann, and Romero Frizzi, "El Poder."

9. Ouweneel, *Shadows Over Anáhuac,* 169.

10. Ibid., 208.

11. For additional comments on Ouweneel, *Shadows Over Anáhuac,* see Patch, "The Cultural, the Material, and the Spiritual" 236–39.

12. The paragraphs that follow focus only on two works: Taylor, *Landlord and Peasant,* and Hamnett, *Politics and Trade.* The historiography on colonial Oaxaca is much deeper than these, of course. Some of the other classic monographs on colonial Oaxaca that have helped to shape this book are Romero Frizzi, *Economía y vida*; Carmagnani, *El regreso de los dioses*; Pastor, *Campesinos y reformas*; Chance, *Race and Class*; and Chance, *Conquest of the Sierra.*

13. See Taylor, *Landlord and Peasant,* and Taylor, "Landed Society in New Spain."

14. See, e.g., Pastor, *Campesinos y reformas,* 264–80; Pastor, "El repartimiento," 224–26; Chance, *Conquest of the Sierra,* 103–8; and to a lesser extent, Hamnett, *Politics and Trade,* 7.

15. The notion that the Bourbon state was weak is most clearly and directly expressed by Coatsworth, "Limits of Colonial Absolutism," but this notion is implicit in the works of many colonial scholars. Van Young warns historians that to conceive of the state at all in late-colonial Mexico is "ahistorical," and he urges "taking the state back out" ("The Raw and the Cooked," 94). Taylor, in his book *Drinking, Homicide, and Rebellion,* shows how the Crown, of limited strength, responded to rebellion through a policy of appeasement rather than direct confrontation, giving in to peasant demands in most cases. Deans-Smith shows that even in sectors where the state did concentrate its economic and political resources, Bourbon rule was marked by negotiation, not absolutism. Hamnett, in *Politics and Trade,* demonstrates how the Crown even proved largely unable to force its own functionaries to abide by Article 12 of the Ordinance of Intendancies, the key piece of legislation which sought to outlaw *repartimientos.* A weak crown was not new in the eighteenth century. Weakness was institutionalized in the reign of the Hapsburgs, who sold or farmed out most Crown responsibilities, creating what many scholars have termed Spain's "indirect rule" over its colonies. The Bourbon Reforms were the Crown's attempts to address its weak, "indirect rule" and "reconquer" the colonies. But, as MacLachlan put it, "the reformers failed to achieve a perceptual revision of the colonial reality" (quotation is on p. 128, but see chaps. 5–7, in general). Many historians now agree that the Bourbon Reforms did not markedly strengthen the Crown. On the origins of Spain's "indirect rule," see Borah, *El gobierno provincial,* especially 18–27. For a different perspective and an excellent discussion of the state's role in colonial society and economy, see Andrien and Johnson, *Political Economy of Spanish America,* 3–16, 243–54; and Guardino and Walker, 14–17.

16. On the Crown's interventionist role in the economy, see Coatsworth,

"Obstacles to Economic Growth," and Andrien and Johnson, *Political Economy of Spanish America*, 3–16, 243–54.

17. On the use of courts, see Borah, *Justice by Insurance*, and Stern, *Peru's Indian People*.

18. The classic work on colonial rebellions is Taylor, *Drinking, Homicide, and Rebellion*.

19. The major exceptions to the depictions of indigenous passivity are the several works which suggest that the Tehuantepec and Túpac Amaru rebellions were anti-*repartimiento* movements. While these are significant exceptions, one must recall that the *repartimiento* was an institution that daily affected peasants' lives. Thus, these two exceptions seem too few. Both rebellions are discussed in Chapter 4.

20. For the risks of cross-cultural trade, see Curtin.

21. The New Institutional Economics and its application to historical questions is associated with the work of Douglass North. See, for example, *Institutions, Institutional Change, and Economic Performance*.

Chapter 2. The Repartimiento *and the Production of Cochineal*

1. Cited in Braudel, 2:169.

2. The most thorough discussions of the cochineal insect are Donkin, and "Memoria sobre la naturaleza, cultivo y beneficio de la grana dedicada al rey nuestro señor," AGN, Correspondencia de Virreyes, vol. 90, *primera serie*, 1794, pp. 126–230. (This latter work was prepared for Viceroy Revillagigedo by the respected scientist José Antonio Alzate y Ramirez, and hereafter will be cited as Alzate y Ramirez, "Memoria sobre la naturaleza.") See also, Dahlgren.

3. Donkin, 9–10.

4. Ibid., 14–15; and Dahlgren, 53–55, 80–81.

5. Coatsworth argues that peasant producers enjoyed a comparative advantage in the production of items demanding "close supervision," cochineal being one such commodity ("Obstacles to Economic Growth," 87).

6. For references to large-scale production of cochineal, see Donkin, 13; and Hamnett, *Politics and Trade*, 57–61. As Hamnett noted, a 4 percent tithe on cochineal produced a total of only 2,832 pesos during the six years 1784–1789. On the cochineal tithe, see also "Real provisión para que los cosecheros de grana paguen el diezmo a la santa iglesia," AGEO, Real Intendencia de Oaxaca I, legajo 4, exp. 43, 1784.

7. The production of *nopaleras* and cochineal is described well in several works. See, e.g., Alzate y Ramirez, "Memoria sobre la naturaleza," AGN, Correspondencia de Virreyes, vol. 90, *primera serie*, 1794, pp. 126–230; Dahlgren; Donkin; and "Descripción de la cochinilla mixteca." The biweekly newspaper *Gazeta de México* produced a special description of how *grana* was produced and harvested, published in three parts between 2 June and 30 June 1784 (a copy is in the AGI).

8. Alzate y Ramirez, "Memoria sobre la naturaleza," AGN, Correspondencia de Virreyes, vol. 90, *primera serie*, 1794, pp. 126–230; Donkin.

9. Ibid.

10. Díaz del Castillo, 233.

11. Lee, "Cochineal Production," 452–53. Lee further noted that the payment of cochineal as tribute was adopted by the Spaniards after the conquest.

12. Gibson, *Tlaxcala*, 149–50. According to Lockhart, in *The Nahuas after
the Conquest* (178), commoners from Tlaxcala found cochineal production so
profitable that they abandoned the production of traditional crops, which earned
them the censure of the local Indian *cabildo* in 1553. The document cited by
Lockhart is reproduced in its entirety in Mills and Taylor, 90–93.

13. Posthumus, 420–23.

14. Lee, "Cochineal Production," 459–60; but Phillips places the export
figures at between 6,000 and 8,000 arrobas, considerably lower than Lee's figures
(see "Growth and Composition of Trade," 80–81).

15. On references to cochineal in Chiapas, see Larson and Wasserstrom; on
Peru, see Ovando-Sanz.

16. AGN, Historia, vol. 75, exp. 8, p. 8v.

17. For large-scale production, see p. 17 and n. 6, this chapter.

18. Prior to the revisionist literature spearheaded by Taylor in his book,
Landlord and Peasant in Colonial Oaxaca, historians wrongly assumed that the
large estate dominated all of Mexico. The classic starting point for this earlier
work is Chevalier.

19. For the central valley of Mexico, see Florescano, *Precios del maiz y
crisis agrícolas*. For Morelos, see Martin. Patch, *Maya and Spaniard*, argues that
haciendas in Yucatan grew to be critically important by the late-colonial era. For
the Guadalajara region, see Van Young, *Hacienda and Market*.

20. The dominance of the Oaxacan countryside by peasants was demonstrated by Taylor in *Landlord and Peasant*. See also his "Landed Society in New
Spain."

21. Population data are reproduced in Reina, 188–90.

22. The following discussion about the languages and geography of Oaxaca was pieced together from a variety of sources. See Gerhard; Reina, 29–
32, 184–91; Chance, *Conquest of the Sierra*, 3–10; Whitecotton, 9–18; Romero
Frizzi, *Economía y vida*, 27–37; Chance, *Race and Class*, 10–13; and Taylor,
Landlord and Peasant, 9–34.

23. Estimates of output in each of the districts of the province of Oaxaca
were made in 1793 by the Intendant of Oaxaca, Antonio de Mora y Peysal, and are
contained in "Notas sobre grana," AGN, Historia, vol. 75, exp. 8, p. 7. Population
figures come from the census conducted by the Viceroy of Mexico, the Second
Count Revillagigedo, in 1793, the same year as Mora's data (see Reina, 188–90).
The estimates of cochineal output per thousand Indians were computed from these
two data series.

24. Intendant Mora y Peysal presented a figure for the Chontales, which was a region rather than a political district. All of the other places he noted were actual subdelegations. The Chontales region included portions of Nexapa, Huamelula, and Tehuantepec. It is not clear how Mora y Peysal disassociated the Chontal production from the separately listed districts.

25. See Hamnett, *Politics and Trade*; and Chance, *Conquest of the Sierra*.

26. These figures are presented, for they are the best available. It should be understood, however, that Mora y Peysal was simply making educated estimates.

27. AGN, Tributos, vol. 14, exp. 23.

28. For references to women and children performing the bulk of the day-to-day labor, see "Informes de curas y alcaldes mayores sobre repartimientos: Santa Catarina Ixtepeji," AGN, Subdelegados, vol. 34, p. 6. The report of Josef Victoriano de Baños, "Pedimento de oficio del señor fiscal de lo civil sobre la decadencia del cultivo de la grana," AGN, Industria y Comercio, vol. 20, ff. 165–236, also points to their dominance in the upkeep of the *nopaleras*. Finally, in his report to the Bishop of Oaxaca, Manuel Eduardo Pérez Bonilla, parish priest of Santo Tomás de Ixtlán, complained that children often failed to attend school because they were too busy working the cochineal *nopaleras* (see "Cordillera cuarta: Providencias de visita del obispado de Oaxaca—Informes de dos curas sobre repartimientos de Alcaldes Mayores," AGI, Audiencia de México, 2588).

29. Pastor makes a similar argument about cochineal (see "El repartimiento," 224–26).

30. Traditionally, the *repartimiento* is viewed as a forced system of production and consumption in which peasants were coerced into selling their output in advance at low, non-market prices, not, as I suggest, a means for producers to finance production. In Chapter 4 I address this issue, arguing that the *repartimiento* should be understood primarily as a non-coercive system of credit.

31. Pastor, "El repartimiento," 210.

32. Romero Frizzi, *Economía y vida*, 73. While Romero Frizzi does not specifically refer to these transactions as *repartimientos*, they did possess all of the salient characteristics of that institution.

33. Hoekstra, 149; Ouweneel, *Shadows Over Anáhuac*, 164–65.

34. Rowe, 163.

35. Phillips and Phillips, 172–90.

36. For a description of the *Verlagssystem*, see Braudel, 2:316–21.

37. Kohn, "Finance, Business, and Government," 13.

38. Farriss, 43; Guardino, 19–20.

39. Pietschmann, 78.

40. A third type of *repartimiento* common in other regions of Spanish America was the advance of goods repayable in indigenous output. This type of *repartimiento*, however, was not common in Oaxaca, where goods provided on credit were normally paid for in cash.

41. Hamnett, *Politics and Trade*, 6. See also "Contrato celebrado entre Don Manuel José López, alcalde mayor de Teotitlán del Camino y Don Juan Bautista Echarri de esta ciudad y comercio sobre fianza otorgada," AGEO, Real Intendencia de Oaxaca II, legajo 9, exp. 9, 1781; AGN, Subdelegados, vol. 35, p. 183, 1792; "Compañía establecida por el manejo de repartimientos por Don Ildefonso Maria Sanchez Colache, electo alcalde mayor de Chichicapa y Zimatlán, y Don Manuel Ramón de Goya del comercio de México," BNM, Manuscritos, 58, pp. 147–49. Further discussion of the financial arrangements made with the *tenientes* can be found in the numerous "Informes de alcaldes mayores y curas sobre repartimientos," in AGN, Subdelegados, vols. 34 and 45. The *alcalde mayor* of Miahuatlán in the mid-1770s paid his two *tenientes* 300 and 500 pesos per year plus living expenses. He also employed several storekeepers who were paid 100 to 150 pesos per year plus expenses (see "Inventario de los bienes que quedaron por muerte de Sebastian de Labayru, alcalde mayor que fue de Miahuatlán," AGN, Tierras, vol. 1037, exp. 2, pp. 80–80v).

42. "Informe de curas y alcaldes mayores sobre el repartimiento: Miahuatlán," AGN, Subdelegados, vol. 34, p. 141, 1752. For the same *repartimiento* schedule, see also the following "Informes" of other *alcaldes mayores* in the same volume: Nexapa, p. 119; Chichicapa y Zimatlán, p. 135; Teotitlán del Camino Real, p. 154; and Tlacolula, p. 313. These "Informes," used extensively in this study, were produced by priests and *alcaldes mayores* from districts throughout Mexico in 1752 at the request of the Viceroy, the First Count Revillagigedo, who was considering the legalization of the *repartimiento*. The *alcaldes mayores* clearly had reason to fabricate their reports, yet one is struck by the similarity of issues addressed by all who responded, officials and clergy alike. While it is important to read such reports critically, one would need to accept a broader conspiracy, for which there is no evidence, to discount them entirely.

43. "Informes de curas y alcaldes mayores sobre el repartimiento: Nexapa," AGN, Subdelegados, vol. 34, p. 119, 1752; Pietschmann, 77, and Dehouve, 87, found that the officials of Puebla and Tlapa (in modern Guerrero), respectively, also purchased their mules for the *repartimiento* at the annual fairs in Puebla.

44. On Papalo, see AGN, Civil, vol. 302, *primera parte, cuaderno de las cuentas*, pp. 21–46; for Huehuetla and Huautla, see AGN, Civil, vol. 284, exp. 6, pp. 19v–24; for Coatlán, Miahuatlán, see AGN, Tierras, vol. 1038, exp. 1, pp. 212–13; for Teposcolula, consult AGN, Real Hacienda, Administración general de alcabalas, caja 43, pp. 1–37; and for Miahuatlán in 1811, see AGEO, Real Intendencia de Oaxaca, legajo 40, exp. 24. Carmagnani (*El regreso de los dioses*, 169–70) presents a table showing the breakdown of *repartimientos* in Huehuetla and Huautla made to individuals. As best as I can figure, his numbers are incorrect. It appears that he mistakenly added together the records for *repartimiento* debts owed in pesos with others owed in cochineal, giving the sum total in pesos for each town. I note that it "appears" he did this, because adding together the two figures accounts for only some of the deviation from the correct figures. Other deviations I

cannot explain. Finally, Carmagnani incorrectly cites the document as AGN, Civil 217, exp. 6; the correct citation is AGN, Civil 284, exp. 6.

45. Dehouve argues for Tlapa, Guerrero, that one cannot discuss the household economy as separate from the communal economy since little production at the household level occurred without communal support (96). This is not the impression one receives from the Oaxacan *repartimiento*, which seems overwhelmingly organized at the household level.

46. AGN, Real Hacienda, Administración general de alcabalas, caja 43, pp. 1–37.

47. Carmagnani, *El regreso de los dioses*, 110–11.

48. For examples, see "Natural de Teotitlán del Camino contra su alcalde mayor sobre cuentas del repartimiento," AGEO, Real Intendencia de Oaxaca II, legajo 1, exp. 7, 1788; and "Don Antonio de la Cantolla Santelizes, dueño de hacienda en Nexapa se queja de los agravios cometidos por el subdelegado," AGEO, Real Intendencia de Oaxaca I, legajo 11, exp. 24.

49. Only those *repartimientos* made to *alcaldes, gobernadores, caciques*, and individuals referred to as *principales* were included. Several others, which were not counted, were made to *escribanos* and *regidores*. Data taken from AGN, Civil, vol. 302, *primera parte, cuaderno de las cuentas*, pp. 21–46; AGN, Civil 284, exp. 6, pp. 19v–24; AGN, Tierras, vol. 1038, exp. 1, pp. 212–13; AGN, Real Hacienda, Administration general de alcabalas, caja 43, pp. 1–37; and AGEO, Real Intendencia de Oaxaca, legajo 40, exp. 24.

50. For a detailed discussion of *repartimiento* default, see Chapter 6. Ouweneel (*Shadows Over Anáhuac*, 182, 200–201) also refers to the high degree of delay and default experienced by the district magistrates.

51. The *repartimiento* price of mules is illustrative. Numerous archival references to the *repartimiento* sale of mules suggest mules typically sold at a price from 28 to 50 pesos apiece, depending on quality. Even at 28 pesos, the cost of a mule represented 112 workdays at the typical colonial wage of 2 reales per day. Mules could be obtained less expensively for individuals paying with cash. The *repartimiento*, however, provided mules on credit. For more on *repartimiento* prices, see Chapters 4–6, this volume.

52. "Informes de curas y alcaldes mayores sobre el repartimiento," AGN, Subdelegados, vol. 34. For Nexapa, see p. 119; and for Chichicapa-Zimatlán, see p. 135.

53. "Testimonio de expediente reservado sobre abusos de los alcaldes mayores del obispado de Oaxaca," AGI, Audiencia de México, 1872.

54. "Informes de curas y alcaldes mayores sobre el repartimiento," AGN, Subdelegados, vol. 34.

55. For more on the sale of colonial posts, see Parry. See also Andrien, "The Sale of Fiscal Offices" (reprinted in Andrien, *Crisis and Decline*, as chap. 5). For Central America, see Patch, "Imperial Politics"; and for Oaxaca, see Hamnett, *Politics and Trade*, 16–18.

56. AGI, Audiencia de México, 1219. This legajo contains names of the officials who were granted posts and the prices they paid for the entire eighteenth century in Xicayan.

57. AGI, Audiencia de México, 1223. This legajo contains names of the officials who were granted posts and the prices they paid for the entire eighteenth century in Nexapa.

58. AGI, Audiencia de México, 1222. This legajo contains names of the officials who were granted posts and the prices they paid for the entire eighteenth century in Villa Alta.

59. Moreno Cebrián (*El corregidor de indios*, 86–96) provides an extensive sample of sale prices for the Andean *corregimientos*. Tord Nicolini ("El Corregidor," 189) also cites a number of Andean purchase prices, but I am nearly certain that his data are wrong. He claims that certain posts sold for as much as 30,000 to 100,000 pesos, amounts far in excess of any discovered for Oaxaca or cited by Moreno Cebrián in *El corregidor de indios*. It is likely that Tord Nicolini's source referred not to pesos but to reales vellon, of which there are twenty per peso; 100,000 reales vellon, then, would equal 5,000 pesos. For Central American posts, see Patch, "Imperial Politics," 86.

60. Parry, 60–61.

61. Because one paid long before one actually assumed office, the bids were lower than they would have been had the position begun immediately. Aspirants bid the assumed present value of holding the post in what was often the distant future. There was also an element of risk incorporated in such a bidding process, since one could never be certain that the conditions that made the post attractive at the time of bidding would still be relevant years later. This risk would tend to reduce the prices bid somewhat, further blurring the result. Much could change between the time that the bid was made and the moment one assumed office.

62. For Miahuatlán, consult AGI, Audiencia de México, 1226.

63. For Teposcolula, see AGI, Audiencia de México, 1224.

64. Telephone conversation with Patch, 1996. Patch has written about the purchase of the post of *alcalde mayor* in *Maya and Spaniard* and in "Imperial Politics."

65. Hamnett, *Politics and Trade*, 4.

66. The links between merchants and colonial officials is most clearly and effectively shown in Hamnett, *Politics and Trade*, 4–6 and passim.

67. "Contrato celebrado entre Don Manuel José López, Alcalde Mayor de Teotitlán del Camino y Don Juan Bautista Echarri de esta ciudad y comercio sobre fianza otorgada," AGEO, Tesorería Principal, legajo 9, exp. 9, 1781.

68. "Compañia establecida por el manejo de repartimientos por D. Ildefonso Ma. Sanchez Colache, electo A.M. de la jurisdiccion de Chichicapa y Zimatlán, y D. Manuel Ramón de Goya del comercio de México," BNM, Manuscritos, MS no. 58, p. 147–49, 1782.

69. AGN, Subdelegados, vol. 35, p. 183. See also Hamnett, *Politics and Trade*, 81–83.

70. Hamnett, *Politics and Trade*, 39–40.

71. "Contrato celebrado entre Don Manuel José López, Alcalde Mayor de Teotitlán del Camino y Don Juan Bautista Echarri de esta ciudad y comercio sobre fianza otorgada," AGEO, Tesorería Principal, legajo 9, exp. 9, 1781.

72. Kicza, *Colonial Entrepreneurs*, 192–93, 222–23.

73. "Informes de los alcaldes mayores," AGN, Subdelegados, vol. 34, 1752. See also Carmagnani, *El regreso de los dioses*.

74. In 1786, as part of the Real Ordenanza de Intendentes, a large body of legislation designed to restructure the Crown's political control over its colonies, *alcaldes mayores* were replaced by subdelegates (see Chapter 4). Despite Crown intentions that the new functionaries would remain more autonomous from local elites and refrain from trading with the Indians, the new officials continued the practices of their predecessors, although with fewer finances. For this reason, the terms *"alcalde mayor"* and *"subdelegado"* are used largely interchangeably in this study, much as they were in Mexico during the last years of Spanish rule.

75. "Don Juan José Ruiz, subdelegado del partido de Nexapa, solicita en el obispado cantidad de dinero a rédito," AGEO, Real Intendencia de Oaxaca I, legajo 10, exp. 4, 1798.

76. AGEO, Real Intendencia de Oaxaca II, legajo 6, exp. 17.

77. Hamnett, *Politics and Trade*, 108–9.

78. Not only Spanish officials but private merchants sought loans from the Church to finance their trade in cochineal dye. Such was the case of the Oaxacan trader Juan Rivero, who in 1793 received 20,000 pesos at 5 percent interest from the Oaxacan Church of Soledad for the expressed purpose of financing his dealings in the cochineal trade (see "Juan Rivero del comercio de Antequera solicita prestamo para adelantar su comercio con el de grana," AGEO, Real Intendencia de Oaxaca I, legajo 5, exp. 1, 1793).

79. See Gibson, *The Aztecs Under Spanish Rule*, 205–10. For Oaxaca, see Hamnett, *Politics and Trade*, 64–67.

80. AGN, Subdelegados, vol. 35, p. 217, 1790.

81. Taylor, *Magistrates of the Sacred*, 402; and Larson, *Cochabamba*, 124.

82. In the following case, the *alcalde mayor* of Teococuilco failed to deliver the tribute monies, and the investigation into his delinquency determined that he had employed them in the cochineal *repartimiento* ("Testimonio de pesos presentado por el contador general de reales tributos," AGEO, Tesorería Principal, legajo 4, exp. 9, 1788–1789).

83. On the Mexican Valley, see Gibson, *The Aztecs Under Spanish Rule*, 198–200.

84. For Bonavia, see AGN, Subdelegados, vol. 35, p. 197, 1790. For Conejares, see "Autos sobre los repartimientos hechos por el Subdelegado de Villa

Alta," AGEO, Real Intendencia de Oaxaca II, legajo 7, exp. 6, 1801. For a copy of the circular distributed in the latter case, see AGEO, Real Intendencia de Oaxaca II, legajo 6, exp. 19, 1801.

85. See, e.g., Gosner, 52; and Patch, *Maya and Spaniard*, 156.

86. See, e.g., "Expediente por el Ministro tesorero de Caja de Oaxaca don Francisco Antonio Villarrasa Rivera acerca de la decadencia de aquella provincia," AGI, Audiencia de México, 1780, Expedientes diarios, 1796–1797; "Representación del fiscal de lo civil que fue Manuel Martin Merino sobre el comercio y los repartimientos de los corregidores y alcaldes mayores," AGI, Audiencia de México, 1868; and "Informes de curas y alcaldes mayores sobre el repartimiento," Miahuatlán and Teotitlán del Camino, AGN, Subdelegados, vol. 34, pp. 141 and 154, 1752.

87. AGN, Real Hacienda-Alcabalas, cajita 43, p. 21.

88. Patch, *Maya and Spaniard*, 85.

89. Patch, *Maya and Spaniard*, 85, and Patch, "Imperial Politics," 105. Patch found that tribute payments and *repartimientos* occurred on the Feast of St. John (June 24) and Christmas Day. The coincidence of dates might have been a matter of convenience for the *alcalde mayor*, since these were days in which many Indians would have congregated in the village, perhaps to celebrate the holidays. They also might have been times when the peasants found themselves in need of additional funds for celebration.

90. Dehouve, 97.

Chapter 3. The Repartimiento and Crown Politics

1. Until 1751, *repartimientos* were theoretically illegal, as the Law of the Indies strictly forbade officials from conducting any form of trade with the Indians under their charge. In reality, this law was regularly disobeyed (Hamnett, *Politics and Trade*, chap. 1). Evidently, the Council of Indies opposed the sale of public offices, but their arguments were ignored by a Crown more bent on receiving the income (see Parry).

2. Libro 2, Titulo 16, Ley 54 of the Laws of the Indies specifically prohibited colonial officials from owning property or conducting commerce. The prohibition was extended specifically to the *alcaldes mayores* by Libro 5, Titulo 2, Ley 47, which stated "Que la prohibición de tratar, y contratar comprehende a los governadores, Corregidores, Alcaldes mayores, y sus tenientes" (see *Recopilación de leyes de los reynos de las indias*).

3. On the sale of offices, see Chapter 2.

4. The vehement attacks leveled against the *repartimiento* leading to the adoption of Article 12, as well as the equally passionate defenses of the system, are discussed later in this chapter.

5. The Crown issued regulations for the Cochineal Registry in 1756. These rules were reissued in 1760, 1773, and 1817, owing to continued abuses. A reproduction of this ordinance, entitled "Ordenanzas, método, o regla que se ha de

observar de efecto de cerrar la puerta á la perpetración de fraudes en la grana cochinilla," can be found in the appendix of Dahlgren. An original copy is also deposited at the Newberry Library in Chicago. These regulations are summarized in AGN, Industria y Comercio, vol. 9, pp. 135–39, 1782.

6. Throughout the colonial period and after, sacks of cochineal were often adulterated with other substances by producers and merchants in order to increase their weight and value.

7. Several documents noted that not all cochineal passed through Oaxaca for registration. For example, AGN, Civil, vol. 302, *primera parte*, p. 75, says that *grana* from Teotitlán del Camino was shipped directly to Veracruz for export. Mora y Peysal's data, used above, estimated that 15,000 arrobas were registered in Oaxaca and an additional 8,600 arrobas were collected elsewhere, suggesting that only 63.5 percent of total output was recorded by the registry. Likewise, the subdelegate of Teococuilco informed that the production of *grana* in that town was not destined for the city of Oaxaca for registration (see AGEO, Tesorería Principal, legajo 8, exp. 8, 1815). Finally, in "Memoria del gobierno del estado de Oaxaca . . . 1829" (located in the library of the AGEO), Governor Jose Maria de Murguía y Gallardi refers to the production figures recorded by the registry but adds that these figures were low since they failed to capture all production in Jamiltepec, Tehuantepec, Teotitlán del Camino, and Teposcolula, much of which never passed through Oaxaca for registry. Despite the potential incompleteness of the data, one can be fairly confident that the unrecorded amount of cochineal increased and decreased in proportions similar to that reported for *grana* recorded by the Registro, since there do not appear to have been major regional shifts in the areas of production over the course of the period under study. The only exception would be in the occasional years when weather destructive to cochineal affected one region but not others.

8. The most complete set of registry figures (1758–1858) are published in the 1858 "Memoria del gobierno del estado de Oaxaca," located at the library of the AGEO, and in *Boletín de la sociedad Mexicana de geografía y estadística*, vol. 7, 1859. See also Hamnett, *Politics and Trade*, appendix 1; and Dahlgren, appendix 2. None of these sources include prices or output for the year 1820, a year in which, for reasons unknown, no data were available. I was able to find a reference to production and prices, however, for that year (see Bustamante), and these are included with the otherwise complete series. The figures for the entire period 1758–1858 are presented in Appendix B of this volume.

9. I noted earlier that the 1786 ban coincided with but did not cause the depression, because as I show, especially in Chapter 8, the late-colonial downturn was more directly caused by a sharp decline in European demand, which occurred several years before the advent of Article 12, and this was coupled with sharply rising transaction costs associated with the nearly constant state of warfare beginning in 1793.

10. For a brief discussion of royal policy regarding the *repartimiento* be-

243

fore the 1750s, see Hamnett, *Politics and Trade*, 11–20. Hamnett found that the Crown occasionally attempted to halt the illegal trade, but that it regularly failed, at least in part owing to its less than determined efforts.

11. Hamnett noted that the *arancel* was intended to serve as a "tariff of legal prices, which the justices would then be expected to observe" (*Politics and Trade*, 20–21). The reports filed by the *alcaldes mayores* and priests of Oaxaca, however, show unambiguously that, at least in the cochineal *repartimiento*, a standard loan of 12 reales for each pound was already well established. For a detailed discussion of this "customary" loan term, see Chapter 5.

12. See Hamnett, *Politics and Trade*, 19–23.

13. The Peruvian junta did meet and prepared a list of goods, stipulating prices and typical quantities of goods to be sold on credit by the Spanish officials. For the Peruvian *arancel*, see Golte; see also Moreno Cebrián, *El corregidor de indios*, 317–58.

14. Various copies of the Cedula are in AGN, Subdelegados, vol. 34; Golte reproduced much of the original Cedula (84–85).

15. The reasons for default are dealt with at length in Chapters 4–6.

16. The responses are located in AGN, Subdelegados, vols. 34 and 45. These "Informes" provided valuable information about the operation of the *repartimiento* and the cochineal trade and are used throughout this study.

17. Numerous studies of the Bourbon Reforms exist. See, for example, Brading, "Bourbon Spain"; Hamnett, *Politics and Trade*; Stein, "Bureaucracy and Business"; Coatsworth, "Limits of Colonial Absolutism"; John R. Fisher, *Government and Society*; Lynch, *The Spanish American Revolutions*; Lynch, *Spanish Colonial Administration*; Lillian Fisher; and MacLachlan.

18. On Gálvez, see Priestly.

19. Gálvez's "Informe y Plan de Intendencias para el reino de Nueva España" can be consulted in AGI, Indiferente General, 1713. A copy was also published in Navarro García as appendix 2, 164–81.

20. According to MacLachlan, Gálvez arrived in New Spain already convinced that the colony was in desperate need of "rationalization," a position that, MacLachlan suggests, was unfounded (94–96). MacLachlan depicts Gálvez as an ideologue so convinced by his Enlightenment ideology that he was utterly incapable of making objective observations.

21. AGI, Indiferente General, 1713; and Navarro García, 168.

22. AGI, Indiferente General, 1713; and Navarro García, 167.

23. On Bucareli's opposition, see Brading, *Miners and Merchants*, 45–46; Hamnett, *Politics and Trade*, 42; Priestly, 289–92; and Calderón Quijano, 1:495–502.

24. These pre-1786 testimonies, both in favor and against the Ordenanza, provided the bulk of the resources used by Hamnett in chapter 3 of *Politics and Trade*.

25. Lillian Fisher, 49, 189. The 5 percent would ultimately produce only

paltry sums and the result was that few qualified individuals were willing to serve as subdelegates (see discussion later in this chapter, and Hamnett *Politics and Trade*, 64–71 and passim).

26. Lillian Fisher, 108.

27. AGI, Indiferente General, 1713; and Navarro García, 174.

28. Hamnett, *Politics and Trade*, 12, 41–42; MacLachlan, 114. As Gálvez probably knew, however, Indians were exempt from the *alcabala* tax on all goods that they produced. This meant that goods such as cochineal obtained by the Spanish official through *repartimiento* advances were also exempt until resold by the *alcalde mayor*. As the sale, however, was rarely, if ever, made within the district of his authority, the Spanish official was not responsible for collecting the tax on such transactions. In short, Gálvez was engaging in the politics of hyperbole.

29. AGI, Indiferente General, 1713; and Navarro García, 173.

30. MacLachlan discusses the importance of the free-trade ideology to Gálvez and his followers (114). See also Brading, *Miners and Merchants*, 114–15.

31. AGI, Indiferente General, 1713; and Navarro García, 175.

32. This is the general argument made by Brading in "Bourbon Spain" (405–6), and Lynch in *The Spanish American Revolutions* (8–9). See also Hamnett, *Politics and Trade*, chap. 3.

33. See especially Hamnett, *Politics and Trade*; and Brading, *Miners and Merchants*.

34. Ibid.

35. For examples of the pro-*repartimiento* testimonies, see the 1775 report submitted by the Oidor of the Audiencia de México, El Conde de Tepa ("Dictamen dado reservadamente al virrey de Nueva España, Don Antonio Bucareli, por el Conde de Tepa sobre el establecimiento de las intendencias," AGI, Audiencia de México, 1973); or the 1779 report by an ex-Fiscal of the Audiencia, Manuel Martin Merino ("Representación del fiscal de lo civil que fue Manuel Martin Merino sobre el comercio y los repartimientos de los corregidores y alcaldes mayores," AGI, Audiencia de México, 1868); and the 1784 defenses of the system presented by the *alcaldes mayores* of Oaxaca themselves ("Testimonio de expediente reservado sobre abusos de los alcaldes mayores del obispado de Oaxaca," AGI, Audiencia de México, 1872). These are all discussed at length in Hamnett, *Politics and Trade*, chap. 3, as well as in Brading, *Miners and Merchants*, 46–51.

36. See the 1777 anonymous condemnation of the *repartimiento* and a 1778 response by the Bishop of Oaxaca, José Gregorio Ortigoza, both in AGI, Audiencia de México, 1872. Likewise, see Bishop Ortigoza's report, "El Obispo de Oaxaca pone las providencias de su santa visita" (AGI, Audiencia de México, 2587); and see also the detailed reports of the parish priests of Ixtlán and Ayoquesco ("Cordillera segunda providencias de visita del obispado de Oaxaca," AGI, Audiencia de México, 2588). Each of these reports is discussed in Hamnett, *Politics and Trade*, chap. 3, as well as in Brading, *Miners and Merchants*, 49–50.

37. Brading, *Miners and Merchants*, 51; and MacLachlan, 113.

38. On the issue of salaries, see Hamnett, *Politics and Trade*, 64–71; Brading, *Miners and Merchants*, 84–85; John R. Fisher, *Government and Society*, 34, 85–86, 93–96; and Lillian Fisher, 81, 89. This is the argument universally presented by scholars. I am a bit skeptical, however, whether good salaries alone could have halted the illegal trade. The salaries could never have matched the potential profits of the *repartimiento*, and corruption was deeply ingrained in colonial society. Colonial offices were viewed as a means to enrich the officeholder. Furthermore, the Crown had limited ability to enforce laws in remote regions of the colonies, especially when the laws were flouted by those empowered with enforcing laws in the first place. In short, generous salaries would probably not have sufficed in eradicating *repartimientos*.

39. On the impossibility of finding *fiadores* for the new subdelegates, see Hamnett, *Politics and Trade*, 67–71. See also the report of the Fiscal Protector Borbon (AGN, Subdelegados, vol. 51, pp. 80–86).

40. Hamnett, *Politics and Trade*. Much of Hamnett's book is devoted to a presentation of the post-1786 debate over the *repartimiento*. As he argued, the prohibition of the *repartimiento* incensed the established merchants of Mexico City and Oaxaca, who had benefited from the trade with the Indians. The mounting opposition to the ban was an early indication of the societal cleavage between Creoles and Peninsulars that would eventually lead to independence. See also Stein, "Bureaucracy and Business"; and MacLachlan.

41. See Hamnett, *Politics and Trade*, chaps. 4–5; and Brading, *Miners and Merchants*, part 1.

42. See Hamnett, *Politics and Trade*, chaps. 4–5; and Brading, *Miners and Merchants*, part 1.

43. "Orden para que los intendentes informen sobre los repartimientos que prohibe el artículo 12 de la Real Ordenanza de 4 de diciembre de 1786: Mora y Peysal a Revillagigedo," AGN, Subdelegados, vol. 35, p. 28, 1790. Hamnett viewed the same documentation (*Politics and Trade*, 73–75).

44. Bonavia to Revillagigedo, AGN, Subdelegados, vol. 35, p. 197. See also Hamnett, *Politics and Trade*, 77–79.

45. Bonavia to Revillagigedo, AGN, Subdelegados, vol. 35, 208–11. See also Hamnett, *Politics and Trade*, 77–79. According to Hamnett, Bonavia was arguing that since the prohibition, the profits of the trade were going to the Indians. I understood Bonavia to be stating that the Indians had been profiting from their *repartimiento* production of the mantles but that with its prohibition, they had lost this income.

46. Mora y Peysal to Revillagigedo, AGN, Subdelegados, vol. 35, p. 217, 1790. See also Hamnett, *Politics and Trade*, 79–81.

47. MacLachlan, 113.

48. "Pedimento de oficio del Sr. Fiscal de lo civil sobre la decadencia del cultivo de la grana," AGN, Industria y Comercio, vol. 20, pp. 165–236, 1810–1811. See also Hamnett, *Politics and Trade*, 76.

49. On Mexico, see Hamnett, *Politics and Trade*; Chance, *Conquest of the Sierra*, 111; Pastor, "El repartimiento," 232–33; Pastor, *Campesinos y reformas*, 274–75; and Stein, "Bureaucracy and Business," 15, 18–19. Nancy Farriss found that in Yucatan the abolition was obeyed with little resistance (359, 370). The *repartimiento* also re-emerged in the Andes (see John R. Fisher, *Government and Society*, 88–99; Moreno Cebrián, *El corregidor de indios*, 733–35; and Lynch, *The Spanish American Revolutions*, 9).

50. "Un natural de Tlacolula contra el alcalde Mayor de Teotitlán del Valle," AGEO, Real Intendencia de Oaxaca II, legajo 2, exp. 20, 1789. This was the earliest case in which a *repartimiento* loan was found to have been made in the period after Article 12's promulgation. In the years following, however, many other cases emerged in which illegal *repartimientos* were issued. Melgar was the *alcalde mayor* in Teotitlán del Valle before the Intendancy Plan and remained as subdelegate after 1786.

51. Hamnett, *Politics and Trade*, 86–94.

52. Zamora y Coronado, 5:350–51.

53. First quotation is from Hamnett, *Politics and Trade*, 86–94; second quotation is MacLachlan, 117–18.

54. Brading, *Miners and Merchants*, 115.

55. Pastor et al., *Fluctuaciones económicas*; and Pastor, *Campesinos y reformas*, 223–30. Tithe collections reflect the general trend of the economy since, theoretically, their value fluctuates directly with the total value of production, except that they fail to capture the output of Indians who did not normally tithe. "Tithes" of 4 percent were collected from non-Indian cochineal producers. These were largely Spanish *hacendados* in the central valley of Oaxaca who tried, with little success, to compete with indigenous producers. According to Taylor, of the forty-nine *haciendas* he studied, only three had *nopaleras* and only one of these was large, with around 6,000 cacti (Taylor, "Town and Country," 79). The amount collected was very small, only 2,831 pesos, 5.75 reales in the entire six years from 1784 to 1789 (see Dahlgren, appendixes 1–4).

56. Taylor, *Landlord and Peasant*; Hamnett, "Dye Production."

57. AGI, Audiencia de México, 1675, pp. 416–20.

58. "El Virrey Conde de Revillagigedo informa sobre la decadencia del comercio," BNM, Manuscritos, MS no. 1398, pp. 324–402. Hamnett used another copy of this report, which he found in AGN, Correspondencia de Virreyes, legajo 26.

59. "Expediente por el Ministro tesorero de Caja de Oaxaca don Francisco Antonio Villarrasa Rivera acerca de la decadencia de aquella provincia," AGI, Audiencia de México, 1780, Expedientes diarios, 1796–1797. Hamnett, suggests that Villarrasa enjoyed "a reputation for impartiality" (*Politics and Trade*, 83–84).

60. "Pedimento de oficio del Sr. Fiscal de lo civil sobre la decadencia del cultivo de la grana," AGN, Industria y Comercio, vol. 20, pp. 165–236, 1810–1811. See also Hamnett, *Politics and Trade*, 129. Bishop Bergoza's position dif-

fered drastically from that of Bishop Ortigoza, who during his tenure (1775–1792) was one of the staunchest opponents of the *alcaldes mayores*. This suggests that the clergy acted as less than a unified body in regard to the *repartimiento*. In fact, a number of parish priests defended the system. Many of them are discussed throughout this work.

61. "Pedimento de oficio del Sr. Fiscal de lo civil sobre la decadencia del cultivo de la grana," AGN, Industria y Comercio, vol. 20, pp. 165–236, 1810–1811. See also Hamnett, *Politics and Trade*, 129.

62. For a detailed discussion of such expenses, see Chapter 8.

63. "Pedimento de oficio del Sr. Fiscal de lo civil sobre la decadencia del cultivo de la grana," AGN, Industria y Comercio, vol. 20, pp. 165–236, 1810–1811. See also Hamnett, *Politics and Trade*, 129.

64. See Coatsworth, "Obstacles to Economic Growth," 94. On state intervention in the colonial economy, also see Andrien and Johnson, 246–53.

Chapter 4. Coerced or Voluntary? Market Participation of Indians

Much of this chapter originally appeared in the *Journal of Latin American Studies* as "Coerced or Voluntary? The Repartimiento and Market Participation of Peasants" (vol. 28, no. 1). It is reprinted here with the permission of Cambridge University Press.

1. Don Manuel Josef Lopez, *alcalde mayor* of Teotitlán del Camino, responding to the accusation that he forced an Indian to accept a *repartimiento* ("Natural de Teotitlán del Camino contra su alcalde mayor sobre cuentas del repartimiento," AGEO, Real Intendencia de Oaxaca II, legajo. 1, exp. 7, 1788).

2. The views of Gálvez, Mora y Peysal, and others were discussed in detail in Chapter 3. Also see Hamnett, *Politics and Trade*.

3. The institution of *repartimiento* is usually used as the prime example of the barbarity and exploitation of late-colonial society. Yet few studies move beyond the mere mention (and condemnation) of the institution. Ouweneel suggests that this interpretation is an outgrowth of the Black Legend (*Shadows Over Anáhuac*, 159–64).

4. Chance, *Conquest of the Sierra*, 97.

5. On preconquest Mexican trade, see Hassig, chaps. 2–7; Berdan, "Markets in the Economy of Aztec Mexico"; and Berdan, "Trade and Markets." The immediate postconquest economy is well documented. For the economy in general, see Gibson, *The Aztecs Under Spanish Rule*, especially chap. 12. For close analysis of how Indians reacted to the goods brought by Spanish conquerors to the Mixteca Alta region of Oaxaca, see Romero Frizzi, *Economía y vida*.

6. The only exception to the tendency of historians to depict Indians as passive to the *repartimiento* is the suggestion that the Andean rebellions of Tupac Amaru and the 1660 rebellion of Tehuantepec were a response to the *repartimiento*. Both of these cases are discussed later in this chapter.

7. Regarding a weak state, see Chapter 1, note 15, this volume.

8. On the contentious relations between the *alcaldes mayores* and the priesthood, see Taylor, *Magistrates of the Sacred*, 396–423.

9. A number of leading Latin American scholars have recently employed Antonio Gramsci's concept of hegemony to help advance our understanding of state power. While little agreement exists to date, even on the term's definition, hegemonists generally argue that the dominant class uses its monopolization of the ideological tools of society to construct an ideology that reinforces its class domination. The subordinate class ultimately accepts (or is blinded by) the hegemonic ideology and sees the economic and political system as legitimate. They accept their positions in society, and rule is henceforth through consensus. Coercion and force are employed only in extraordinary cases when the system threatens to break down. Hegemonists might argue that the Crown did not need to employ coercion in the operation of the *repartimiento* because it exercised a degree of hegemony that served to co-opt peasant resistance. While logical, hegemony lacks measurability; theorists are unable to establish the degree of hegemony exercised by the state and certainly not all states are equally hegemonic. The late-colonial state did enjoy legitimacy even among the indigenous populations of Mexico, but it was a legitimacy predicated on the Crown's inability to step beyond certain boundaries, what scholars have called "the unwritten constitution," or "the colonial compact." The Crown exercised hegemony but it was a weak hegemony, one which was characterized by a limited capacity in rural, indigenous regions. The Bourbon Reforms, an attempt to address this very weakness, failed to increase significantly the state's hegemony. On hegemony's application to Latin America, see Joseph and Nugent; and Mallon, *Peasant and Nation*. For a critique of hegemony not dissimilar to the one provided above, see Scott, chap. 8.

10. Pastor, "El repartimiento," 204; Dehouve, 87, 92–93; Pietschmann, 77; Carmagnani, *El regreso de los dioses*, 172; Chance, "Capitalismo y desigualidad"; Larson and Wasserstrom, 365; Golte, 115; Spalding, "Tratos mercantiles," 605.

11. Chance, "Capitalismo y desigualidad." Spalding suggests that Andean *caciques* who did not ally themselves with their *alcaldes mayores* risked losing their posts ("Tratos mercantiles," 605).

12. Romero Frizzi, "El poder de las mercaderes," 56–57.

13. Other historians have recognized the importance to the rural economy of the work animals provided through the *repartimiento*. See, for example, Dehouve, 98; Pietschmann, 77; and especially Ouweneel, *Shadows Over Anáhuac*, chap. 4. As Dehouve notes, the Spanish officials of Tlapa purchased the animals wholesale on Spanish *haciendas*, purchases from which most Indians were excluded because sales were made only in volume. These animals were then sold on credit to peasants and *gente de razón*. Ouweneel found that with the end of the *repartimiento* in the 1780s, the number of *arrieros* decreased substantially, to the detriment of commerce. The decrease resulted because peasant *arrieros* depended on *repartimiento* mules to replenish their herds.

14. Gibson claims the *alcaldes mayores* "disposed of" silk stockings and

249

other luxury goods in the *repartimiento* (see *The Aztecs Under Spanish Rule*, 94). Stein suggests that the Peruvian *corregidores* forced Indians to buy "velvets . . . linens, baizes of Castile, fine beaver hats, mirrors, playing cards, [and] gilded paper" (see "Bureaucracy and Business," 6). These "worthless items" and others (paddocks, buttons, combs, buckles, hooks, etc.) allegedly were forced upon Andeans, according to Jorge Juan and Antonio de Ulloa, two Spaniards who were sent to the Andes by Philip V and whose 1749 report soundly condemned the *repartimiento* (see Juan y Ulloa, *Discourse and Political Reflections on the Kingdoms of Peru*, 84–86; the report is best known under the title *Noticias secretas de América*, which was the name given it by an Englishman named David Barry in 1826). Kenneth J. Andrien argues convincingly that the work of Juan and Ulloa must not be accepted as a reliable primary source since the authors failed to visit many of the regions about which they reported, basing their conclusions instead on discussions with prominent Peruvians and their Enlightenment-inspired ideologies. Andrien argues that the Juan and Ulloa piece should be viewed as propaganda, part of the emerging Bourbon project to reassert Crown control (see Andrien, "The *Noticias secretas de América* and the Construction of a Governing Ideology"). Patch claims that religious indulgences were regularly sold in the *repartimiento* in Yucatan (see *Maya and Spaniard*, 82, 91, and 158). In contrast, Lockhart and Schwartz express doubt that such worthless items really were sold in the *repartimiento* (356).

15. Ouweneel suggests that the animals helped pay for themselves over the course of the first year alone (*Shadows Over Anáhuac*, 194–95).

16. Nothing in the documentation suggests that the losses were considered abnormally high (see "Inventario de los bienes que quedaron por muerte del alcalde mayor que fue de Miahuatlán, Don Sebastian de Labayru," AGN, Tierras, vol. 1037, exp. 2, pp. 84–84v.).

17. "Borrador de cartas de Villa Alta," BNM, Manuscritos, MS no. 84 [1553], 1776–1777, p. 119v. That the *alcalde mayor* found these mules to be too sickly to distribute casts additional skepticism on other historians' claims that the Spanish officials often dealt in sickly animals.

18. Patch, "Imperial Politics," 104–5.

19. In informal systems of credit, peer pressure from other borrowers within the community often helps to reduce default. Borrowers recognize that when one of their community members defaults, they all bear some cost through less favorable terms. In some cases, failure to fulfill a contract results in village sanctions and even in total ostracism of the perpetrator (see Hoff and Stiglitz, 241).

20. Guardino, in *Peasants* (19) makes a similar point.

21. Romero Frizzi, in "El poder de las mercaderes," also suggests that *repartimiento* credit was a crucial incentive for market participation by colonial peasants.

22. Carmagnani notes the importance of the *repartimiento* in peasants' "economic strategies" as a source of income and goods, yet he stops short of

arguing that peasants voluntarily sought *repartimientos* (see *El regreso de los dioses*, 173). Peasants rarely revealed how they invested cash obtained in the *repartimiento*, although clearly much went as intended, toward financing the production needed to repay the loan. Occasionally, however, documents revealed additional peasant strategies. One woman, Bernarda Gonzalez, requested a *repartimiento* to tide her over when her harvest failed and she and her children faced starvation (see AGEO, Real Intendencia de Oaxaca II, legajo 14, exp. 5, 1811). In other cases, peasants without funds when tribute was due borrowed from the *alcalde mayor*. Since the official collected tribute, there was probably no actual exchange of money in such cases (see several entries in the ledger of the *alcalde mayor* of Teposcolula: "Libro en que consta las dependencias líquidas," AGN, Archivo Histórico de Hacienda, Real Administración de Alcabalas, cajita no. 43).

23. Carmagnani refers to the practice of Indians borrowing from the *cofradía* at an interest rate of 20 to 25 percent (see *El regreso de los dioses*, 157). Lavrin (227) found that several Oaxacan *cofradías* "invested" small amounts of fewer than 100 pesos in cochineal, presumably financing its production among the members. In fact, Lavrin, concludes, "It is unlikely that they [*cofradías*] will emerge as strong elements of the local credit market" (237). I uncovered a case in which peasants who were unable to pay their *repartimiento* debts succeeded in repaying the *alcalde mayor* by borrowing the funds from their parish *cofradía* (see "Proceso que se sigue a Nicolás Larumbe subdelegado de Nexapa por fraude en repartimiento," AGEO, Real Intendencia de Oaxaca II, vol. 6, exp. 17, ff. 105). In his 1779 *visita* of the parishes of Oaxaca, Bishop Ortigoza observed the practice in San Ildefonso de Villa Alta of the *cofradía* issuing *repartimientos* to the villagers to help pay for their religious festivities. The Bishop condemned such practices as usury (see "Cordillera segunda providencias de visita del obispado de Oaxaca. San Yldefonso de Villa Alta," AGI, Audiencia de México, 2588, Jan. 7, 1779).

24. AGI, Audiencia de México, 1872. Ortigoza, a fierce opponent of the *repartimiento*, was quick to accuse the *alcaldes mayores* and other creditors of usury.

25. "Pedimento de oficio del Sr. Fiscal de lo civil sobre la decadencia del cultivo de la grana," AGN, Industria y Comercio, vol. 20, ff. 165–236, 1810–1811. One real per month yields an annual interest rate of 150 percent (12 reales paid on an 8-real loan), higher than the rates paid to the *alcalde mayor* in all but the most extraordinary years. One real per week yields an annual interest rate of 650 percent. According to a modern study of informal finance, such local lending practices are universal. "The so-called five-six arrangement under which the borrower receives $5 in the morning and repays $6 to the lender in the evening is common" (see World Bank, "Issues," 113).

26. Taylor, *Magistrates of the Sacred*, 147.

27. "Juicio criminal contra Don Fausto Corres, subdelegado de Miahuatlán, sobre injustos repartimientos y otros excesos," AHMO, Criminal, Antequera, 1798.

28. There exists some evidence to suggest that "wealthier" (or more creditworthy) peasants had access to these alternative sources of credit that were not available to the more general (less creditworthy) Indian population. The *repartimiento*, then, would have been the source of credit for those who did not qualify for these private sources—in effect, a source of last resort. Even the *alcalde mayor*, however, refused to loan funds to some Indians, for he, too, had to worry about collecting his debts. This hypothesis is more fully developed later in this chapter.

29. In fact, the executors of Trujillo's will managed to collect only 6 pesos of the 1,270 outstanding (see "Testamento otorgado por la albacea de Francisco Trujillo vecino de Ixtlán en la división de los bienes que quedaron por su fallecimiento," AGEO, Alcaldías Mayores, legajo 35, exp. 19, 1776–1778).

30. Hoff and Stiglitz, 236.

31. *Hacendados* extended credit to workers on their *haciendas* yet proved unable to force even them to fully repay their debts before they departed, nor did the *hacendados* even try. Instead, credit was an incentive to attract workers in the first place, and peasants sought to maximize their indebtedness, that is, their advanced wages. The more privileged rural workers were often the most indebted. For a review of this literature, see Bauer, "Rural Workers"; see also Knight.

32. "José de Bal contra Francisco Herrera del pueblo de Villa Alta por deuda de pesos," AJVA, Civil, no. 269, 1759–1764.

33. See the viceroy's questionnaire accompanying the "Informes de curas y alcaldes mayores," AGN, Subdelegados, vol. 34, 1752.

34. According to Douglass North, the degree of institutional organization "determine[s] transaction and transformation costs and hence the profitability and feasibility of engaging in economic activity" (see *Institutions, Institutional Change, and Economic Performance*, 118). Hegemony theories suggest that institutions reflect and disseminate the values, laws, and customs that reinforce the rule of the dominant class and bring about subaltern compliance. Scott points out, however, that the underdevelopment of the elites' (the colonials') institutions in most peasant societies reduces the plausibility that they truly exercise hegemony. "Living outside the cities where agencies of hegemony are quartered . . . and having its own shadow institutions . . . the peasantry is simply less accessible to hegemonic practice" (Scott, 321). Rural colonial Oaxaca would be a classic case where the weakness of dominant-class institutions would greatly reduce the hegemonic power.

35. That the *alcalde mayor* was unique in his ability to loan funds extensively to Indians is recognized by several other scholars. See, for example, Pietschmann, 77–79; and Spalding, "Tratos mercantiles," 598.

36. Carmagnani, "Un movimiento político indio." See also Rojas; Díaz-Polanco; and Manso de Contreras. A published, 1662 version of the events is contained in Manso de Contreras. An authoritative history of the 1660 movement remains to be written.

37. Golte (176–83) subtracted the sum of per capita *repartimiento* debts

and annual tribute burdens from his estimates of per capita income per province. He then argued that the provinces whose net incomes (income after payment of *repartimiento* debts and tribute) were 20 pesos or lower were those with the greatest participation in the rebellion. This proved, he claimed, that *repartimientos* were the primary cause of the rebellion's outbreak.

38. O'Phelan Godoy, 118–26.

39. Stern, *Resistance, Rebellion, and Consciousness,* 39–42.

40. Stavig.

41. Sinclair Thomson, 147, 171.

42. While rebellions were rare in southern Mexico, protests or riots were common. Several involved conflicts over the *repartimiento,* especially the way in which debts were collected (see Taylor, *Drinking, Homicide, and Rebellion,* 120, 134).

43. See, for example, Pastor, *Campesinos y reformas,* 417–18.

44. Hamnett makes the astute observation that while the popular uprising of 1810 was largely sparked by economic grievances against mercantile interests, such tensions were neither new nor did they disappear after the rebels were defeated (*Roots of Insurgency,* 29–30).

45. See "Queja de Don Ramon Garces vecino de Guadalcazar de la jurisdicción de Tehuantepec sobre que el alcalde mayor le embaraza comprar grana," AGN, Marina, vol. 38, exp. 4, pp. 46–49, 1771; "Real Provision para que la justicia de Villa Alta no embaraze el comercio de Don Gabriel Roldán de Oaxaca," AGN, Tierras, vol. 2962, exp. 106, 1772; and the testimony of Juan de Izurquisa, in "Proceso que se sigue a Nicolás Larumbe subdelegado de Nexapa por fraude en repartimiento," AGEO, Real Intendencia de Oaxaca II, vol. 6, exp. 17, 1801. See also "Notas sobre grana," AGN, Historia, vol. 75, exp. 8, pp. 7–9.

46. See bishop's report labeled No. 3 and dated Oaxaca, 20 July 1778, in AGI, Audiencia de México, 1872. Bishop Ortigoza also condemns the *alcaldes* for usury, in "El Obispo de Oaxaca pone las providencias de su santa visita," AGI, Audiencia de México, 2587. In the same case, he reproaches the Indians for usury in their dealings with one another. And in his *visita* of San Yldefonso de Villa Alta on 17 January 1779, he condemned the indigenous *cofradía* for alleged usury (see "Cordillera segunda providencias de visita del obispado de Oaxaca," AGI, Audiencia de México, 2588).

47. For this perspective, see Larson and Wasserstrom, 365; Pastor, "El repartimiento," 201, 206; Golte, 114; and Farriss, 44.

48. Farriss, 44.

49. That interest rates charged to recipients of *repartimiento* loans were so high was a reflection of the high levels of risk to which the *alcaldes mayores* exposed their funds. Debtor default and delay were extremely common. High rates of interest charged on individual *repartimiento* transactions merely produced normal rates of return on the overall funds loaned. For a more detailed examination of returns on *repartimiento* loans, see Chapter 6.

50. Charging an implicit interest charge rather than an explicitly usurious rate protected merchants from the condemnation of the Church. Charging interest in this way dated from the medieval era, when the power of the Church and its sensitivity to usury were high (see Kohn, "Merchant Banking," 15).

51. The issue of risk is discussed in great detail in Chapters 5 and 6 of this volume.

52. For a nice description of clerical accusations of usury directed against fifteenth-century Spanish merchants involved in the advancing of money to sheep owners against the future delivery of wool, see Phillips and Phillips, 175.

53. See, for example, "Inventario y aprecios de bienes del difunto Capitán Manuel Maria de Ortega, subdelegado que fue de Miahuatlán," AGEO, Real Intendencia de Oaxaca II, legajo 40, exp. 24, 1811. Ortega, the Spanish official of Miahuatlán, purchased cochineal both through the *repartimiento* at 12 reales per pound and directly in cash at the considerably higher market price.

54. AGEO, Alcaldías Mayores, legajo 34, exp. 14, 1774.

55. The best sources on the debate over the *repartimiento* in Mexico are Hamnett, *Politics and Trade*; Brading, *Miners and Merchants*; and MacLachlan, chap. 6. The 1786 abolition of the *repartimiento* did not stimulate a trade boom as its authors predicted. Instead, in the 1780s the cochineal industry declined by 50 percent, as the financiers for the *alcaldes mayores* withdrew their investment funds from rural Oaxaca. See also the lengthy discussion in Chapter 3, this volume.

56. "Informes de curas y alcaldes mayores sobre el repartimiento, Nexapa," AGN, Subdelegados, vol. 34, p. 119, 1752; "Superior Despacho para que los vecinos de Villa Alta paguen a Don José Molina lo que le adeudan de la grana," AJVA, Civil, legajo 328, 1770; "Testimonio de expediente reservado sobre abusos de los alcaldes mayores del obispado de Oaxaca," AGI, Audiencia de México, 1872; and Ouweneel, 177.

57. O'Phelan Godoy, 99–102.

58. According to the Conde de Tepa, an Oidor of the Audiencia of Mexico who wrote an impassioned defense of the *repartimiento* in 1775, it was common for Indians to take loans and then complain about the *alcalde mayor* when he came to collect the debts (see "Dictamen dado reservadamente al virrey de Nueva España, Don Antonio Bucareli, por el Conde de Tepa sobre el establecimiento de las intendencias," AGI, Audiencia de México, 1973). Hamnett discusses Tepa's testimony in *Politics and Trade* (42–44). See also Brading, *Miners and Merchants*, 46–47.

59. Vidal is referred to as subdelegate since this is after the introduction of intendancies. Colonialists used the terms subdelegate and *alcalde mayor* interchangeably.

60. Perhaps it was not "sensible," but this was their obligation according to the *repartimiento* that they had accepted. This suggests an indigenous view of debt obligations distinct from that which the *alcalde mayor* certainly possessed.

61. In 1799 Izquierdo took his post as advisor to the Oaxacan Intendant, Antonio de Mora y Peysal. Mora, who became Intendant in 1787 and served until

his death in 1808, was probably the individual most adamantly opposed to the *repartimiento* in all of New Spain. For a lengthy and detailed discussion of Mora's attempts to restrict the *repartimiento*, see Hamnett, *Politics and Trade.*

62. "Los naturales de Huitzo contra el subdelegado por repartimientos ilegales," AGEO, Real Intendencia de Oaxaca II, legajo 14, exp. 5, 1811.

63. Morelos captured Oaxaca a month later, in November 1812.

64. This case had several parts, documents for which have been deposited in different archives. See "Los oficiales de la cavecera de San Pablo Coatlán y sus sujetos todos de la jurisdicción de Miahuatlán se quejan de los excesos cometidos por Don Juan Antonio Gutierrez, teniente de justicia," AGEO, Real Intendencia de Oaxaca I, legajo 9, exp. 23; and "Juicio contra Don Fausto Corres, subdelegado de Miahuatlán, sobre injustos repartimientos y otros excesos," AHMO, Criminal, 1798, Antequera; and "Queja del subdelegado de Miahuatlán contra el cura de San Juan Ozolotepec porque por su influencia le imputan aquellos vecinos repartimientos ilicitos y maltrato a los indios," AHMO, Criminal, 1798, Oaxaca. The case is also mentioned in AGN, Subdelegados 51, pp. 289–92.

65. Borah, *Justice by Insurance*, 151.

66. Taylor, *Magistrates of the Sacred*, chap. 16.

67. A number of readers have suggested the possibility that these notes were forged by the *alcalde mayor*. Proving their authenticity is obviously impossible, but they appear authentic, and there is no evidence that they were forged. While the letters unambiguously request that the *alcalde mayor* advance *repartimiento* money to Antonio, the amounts requested are different from those the *alcalde mayor* actually loaned. In addition, the total sum requested in all the letters combined is less than that which the *alcalde* ultimately advanced. One would imagine that had the official forged the notes, he would have sought a more perfect match between the letters and the real situation. Brief summaries of each note follow.

February 8, 1784 — letter 1 — Antonio asks López for a loan on behalf of Juan Baptista, an "hijo," to produce 6 pounds of *grana.*

March 18, 1784 — letter 2 — Antonio and three others, including two who sign as *alcaldes*, ask López for money to produce 2 arrobas of *grana.*

March 25, 1784 — letter 3 — Antonio and his wife Maria Rosa advise the *alcalde mayor* that they received the 75 pesos for the 2 arrobas, along with the demand that the cochineal be delivered by August, but say that even though they will place the *grana* on the *nopal* "ahora," it will not be harvested until October.

August 21, 1784 — letter 4 — Antonio asks for cash for 2.5 arrobas, and two dozen huipiles at 4 reales per huipil, and eight "*varas de chapanes*," which should all be put on his bill.

April 30, 1785 — letter 5 — Antonio remits six pounds of cochineal, apologizes for the delay and for missing the Semana Santa deadline. He promises to close the account by June.

68. "Natural de Teotitlán del Camino contra su alcalde mayor sobre cuentas del repartimiento," AGEO, Real Intendencia de Oaxaca II, legajo. 1, exp. 7, 1788.

69. It is extremely important to distinguish between the rare accusations of force made by peasants and the general suggestions that *repartimientos* were forced, accusations that often pervaded the reports of Crown officials.

70. "Los oficiales de la cavecera de San Pablo Coatlán y sus sujetos todos de la jurisdicción de Miahuatlán se quejan de los excesos cometidos por Don Juan Antonio Gutierrez, teniente de justicia," AGEO, Real Intendencia de Oaxaca I, legajo 9, exp. 23. See also, "Juicio contra Don Fausto Corres, subdelegado de Miahuatlán, sobre injustos repartimientos y otros excesos," AHMO, Criminal, 1798, Antequera; and "Queja del subdelegado de Miahuatlán contra el cura de San Juan Ozolotepec porque por su influencia le imputan aquellos vecinos repartimientos ilicitos y maltrato a los indios," AHMO, Criminal, 1798, Oaxaca.

71. "Los naturales de Huitzo contra el subdelegado por repartimientos ilegales," AGEO, Real Intendencia de Oaxaca II, legajo 14, exp. 5, 1811.

72. "Contra el alcalde mayor de Teozacoalco por un natural de su jurisdicción," AGEO, Real Intendencia de Oaxaca II, legajo 13, exp. 2, 1810.

73. "Un natural de Tlacolula contra el alcalde mayor de Teotitlán del Valle," AGEO, Real Intendencia de Oaxaca II, legajo 2, exp. 20, 1789.

74. Ouweneel, *Shadows Over Anáhuac*, 186.

75. "Naturales contra el alcalde mayor del Marquesado porque cobra con violencia," AGEO, Real Intendencia de Oaxaca II, legajo 4, exp. 13, 1795. Ouweneel uncovered a case in which peasants of Tlaxcala rejected a *repartimiento* of bulls owing to their sickly state (see *Shadows Over Anáhuac*, 189).

76. AGN, Alcaldes Mayores, vol. 1, MS no. 42, pp. 62–67, 1770.

77. The priest fails to disclose the principal with which the *alcalde mayor* produced these "profits," if they even were profits. His testimony suggests that he might really be referring to revenues. Without knowledge of the principal, any discussion of profits is meaningless.

78. "Cordillera cuarta providencias de visita del obispado de Oaxaca — Informes de dos curas sobre repartimientos de Alcaldes Mayores," AGI, Audiencia de México, 2588.

79. "Cordillera cuarta providencias de visita del obispado de Oaxaca — Informes de dos curas sobre repartimientos de Alcaldes Mayores," AGI, Audiencia de México, 2588.

80. I have little doubt that the *alcalde mayor* could occasionally use his political leverage to "encourage" peasants to cooperate. The *alcalde mayor* did profit from the *repartimiento*, especially when the recipients were lower risks and paid promptly. If the *alcalde mayor* sometimes struck deals with certain peasants in which he would treat them favorably if they agreed to deal with him commercially, I would not be surprised. I doubt, however, that this was the normal modus operandi of the *alcalde*. This would have been extraordinarily inefficient and would have entailed enormous transaction costs.

81. "Cordillera cuarta providencias de visita del obispado de Oaxaca —

Informes de dos curas sobre repartimientos de Alcaldes Mayores," AGI, Audiencia de México, 2588.

82. "Dictamen dado reservadamente al virrey de Nueva España, Don Antonio Bucareli, por el Conde de Tepa sobre el establecimiento de las intendencias," AGI, Audiencia de México, 1973.

83. "Dictamen dado reservadamente al virrey de Nueva España, Don Antonio Bucareli, por el Conde de Tepa sobre el establecimiento de las intendencias," AGI, Audiencia de México, 1973.

84. "El Virrey Conde de Revillagigedo informa sobre la decadencia del comercio," BNM, Manuscritos, MS no. 1398, pp. 324–402. Another copy of this report can be found in AGN, Correspondencia de Virreyes, vol. 26. In reference to Revillagigedo's "Informe," MacLachlan also notes the inability of the Viceroy "to consider the possibility that the 'ignorantes' might have developed a rational financial strategy both for managing their own resources and manipulating their creditors" (114).

85. The anonymous report of 1777 precedes in the legajo the *alcaldes'* 1784 responses (see "Testimonios de expediente reservado sobre abusos de los alcaldes mayores del obispado de Oaxaca," AGI, Audiencia de México, 1872).

86. "Natural de Teotitlán del Camino contra su alcalde mayor sobre cuentas del repartimiento," AGEO, Real Intendencia de Oaxaca II, legajo 1, exp. 7, 1788.

87. This was the point made by Bauer and other historians who revised our understanding of debt peonage two decades ago (see "Rural Workers"). Institutions like the *repartimiento* have been developed in other societies to meet the credit needs of peasants. See, for example, Scott's description of the Malaysian credit system of *padi kunka* (15). Barham and Coomes show that the ostensibly coercive debt-merchandise contract of the Amazon developed instead into the best solution to the high-risk environment in which it operated. More generally, there is an extensive literature on the practices of modern moneylenders and their credit systems. For an introduction, see Hoff and Stiglitz. Many of the problems faced by modern rural creditors in developing regions are very similar to those faced by the eighteenth-century *alcaldes mayores*. Such problems, as well as the modern informal finance literature, are discussed in Chapter 5.

88. Ouweneel found that the officials of Taxco monitored peasant debt burdens to prevent them from overextending themselves (see *Shadows Over Anáhuac*, 178).

89. "Cordillera cuarta providencias de visita del obispado de Oaxaca — Informes de dos curas sobre repartimientos de Alcaldes Mayores," AGI, Audiencia de México, 2588.

90. "Testimonio de expediente reservado sobre abusos de los alcaldes mayores del obispado de Oaxaca," AGI, Audiencia de México, 1872.

91. See the numerous references to *fiadores* in the account book of the

alcalde mayor of Teposcolula (AGN, Archivo Histórico de Hacienda, Real Administración de Alcabalas, cajita, no. 43). Antonio Porley, the parish priest of Ayoquesco, commented in 1784 that the *alcalde mayor* of that district always ensured that there was a *fiador* from whom he could collect if the original debtor defaulted (see "Cordillera cuarta providencias de visita del obispado de Oaxaca — Informes de dos curas sobre repartimientos de Alcaldes Mayores," AGI, Audiencia de México, 2588).

Chapter 5. Informal Credit Institutions and Cross-Cultural Trade

1. See, for example, Bakewell.

2. Florescano, "The Hacienda in New Spain," 279. See also Taylor, *Landlord and Peasant*, especially 140–42, 185–93; and Van Young, *Hacienda and Market*.

3. See Pérez Herrero.

4. See Chapter 2, this volume.

5. Brading, *Miners and Merchants*, 100. Romero Frizzi, emphasizes throughout her book the importance of credit in sixteenth- and seventeenth-century Mixteca (*Economía y vida*, especially 273–81).

6. Not much has been written about the rural storekeeper. A recent exception is Stein, "Tending the Store." The storekeeper who Stein examined reluctantly provided small amounts of credit to the local Spanish and mestizo mineworkers whom he believed were creditworthy. Despite such precautions, debt collection was difficult and many debts had to be written off. In fact the storekeeper sought good relations with the *alcalde mayor*, who might occasionally help in the collection of debts. On the importance of the credit provided by *pulperías*, see Kinsbruner. Mayo et al. argue that the credit supplied by the *pulperías* of Buenos Aires permitted the urban plebes to consume goods that would have otherwise been beyond their means (see Grupo Sociedad y Estado [Carlos Mayo, director], *Pulperos y Pulperías de Buenos Aries*). For rural colonial Oaxaca, see the discussion of stores and credit in Chapter 4, this volume.

7. See, for example, the arrangement made in March 1792 by Don Jose Maria de Ceballos, subdelegate of Miahuatlán, and Don Simon Gutierrez de Villegas, merchant of Oaxaca, for the financing of three stores, one in Miahuatlán, one in Santa Maria Ozoltepeque, and the last in Coatlán, all in the district of Miahuatlán. AGN, Subdelegados, vol. 35, p. 183, 1792.

8. For the literature on loans to hacienda peons, see Bauer, "Rural."

9. See discussion of alternative credit sources in chapter 4.

10. North, *Institutions, Institutional Change, and Economic Performance*, 118. On the economics of the institution, see also Williamson, especially chap. 1. For a recent and excellent discussion of the application of institutional economics to historical problems, see Jon Cohen.

11. Economic historians have discovered numerous historical examples of unorthodox institutions created to reduce the ambiguities and risks of informal

credit provision. See, e.g., the institutional solutions designed to facilitate the provision of credit and the collection of debts in the West African cattle trade described in Abner Cohen. Such economic institutions are ancient as well. Greif shows how institutional arrangements among eleventh-century Maghribi merchants reduced their exposure to losses at the hands of corrupt overseas agents (see "Contract Enforceability"). In "Microtheory," Greif discusses the state of the literature regarding the application of institutional economics to historical questions.

12. Most of the discussion that follows is derived from Hoff and Stiglitz.

13. Hoff and Stiglitz, 235.

14. Ibid., 237.

15. Christopher Udry found that in rural Nigeria credit markets were segmented into small geographical or social spaces, and that "almost no loans are observed to cross the boundaries of this space." He attributes this to the "informational advantages" possessed by locals (see Udry, 496; see also Hoff and Stiglitz, 241). Similarly, in her examination of the credit markets of fifteenth-century Tuscan villages, Botticini found that 99 percent of loans made to peasant households in 1427 were made by residents of the same village. She concludes that "institutional barriers and information costs were responsible for the local and isolated character of rural credit markets" (Botticini, "Private Credit Markets," 7–10; see also idem, "A Tale of 'Benevolent' Governments").

16. Hoff and Stiglitz, 240.

17. "Un natural de Tlacolula contra el alcalde mayor de Teotitlán del Valle," AGEO, Real Intendencia de Oaxaca II, legajo 2, exp. 20, 1789.

18. Curtin, 1.

19. This latter stipulation led in several cases to conflicts between the *alcaldes* and the cochineal producers. Producers were expected to repay a debt in cochineal and not in money, except when some extenuating circumstance prevented payment in dyestuff, in which case the debtors were to give the officials 16 reales per pound instead. When the market price rose above 16 reales per pound, however, producers sometimes claimed to have lost their crops and tried to repay their loans in coin. The *alcaldes*, however, insisted that the producers were merely hiding the dyestuff in order to sell it at a higher price. It should be noted, however, that frequently, perhaps usually, peasants who lost their crops did not have 16 reales with which they could repay the official. In such cases, the official was forced to refinance the peasant, find some alternative way to collect his debt, or merely accept the funds as lost. For references to this practice, see "Juicio criminal contra Don Fausto Corres, subdelegado de Miahuatlán, sobre injustos repartimientos y otros excesos," AHMO, Criminal, 1798; AGEO, Real Intendencia de Oaxaca II, legajo 4, exp. 13, 1795; AGEO, Real Intendencia de Oaxaca II, legajo 13, exp. 2, 1810; AGEO, Real Intendencia de Oaxaca II, legajo 2, exp. 20, 1792; and AGEO, Real Intendencia de Oaxaca II, legajo 7, exp. 6, 1801.

20. "Juicio criminal contra Don Fausto Corres, subdelegado de Miahuatlán," AHMO, Criminal, 1798, Antequera.

21. "Cordillera cuarta providencias de visita del obispado de Oaxaca — Informes de dos curas sobre repartimientos de Alcaldes Mayores," AGI, Audiencia de México, 2588.

22. "Testimonio de expediente reservado sobre abusos de los alcaldes mayores del obispado de Oaxaca," AGI, Audiencia de México, 1872.

23. Lee notes that the Viceroy of New Spain reported in 1575 to King Philip II that the Indians of Oaxaca usually sold cochineal for 12 reales per pound ("Cochineal Production," 458). The viceroy, of course, was not referring to a *repartimiento* transaction, yet the reference to 12 reales per pound is curious.

24. "Informes de los alcaldes mayores sobre repartimientos," AGN, Subdelegados, vol. 34, 1752, pp. 6–313.

25. Chance, *Conquest of the Sierra*, 106. Chance made no effort to explain the price stability. The cases in which the *alcalde mayor* advanced 12 reales are too numerous to list. Many dozens of documents referred to this practice and left little doubt that this "customary price" was universal. The only exception seems to be the occasional references to the "normal" practice of advancing 10 reales per pound in the coastal district of Xicayan. This might have been the result of its greater distance from markets, which entailed higher transport costs. See, e.g., the testimony of Francisco Joseph García, who noted that 12 reales was the normal advance in all Oaxacan districts except Xicayan, in which 10 reales was the standard ("Autos seguidos por los herederos de Don Rodrigo de Neyra con los de Don Luis Frejomil alcalde mayor que fue de Teotitlán del Camino sobre pesos del avío," AGN, Civil, vol. 302, *parte* 3, 1763–1799).

26. Ouweneel, *Shadows Over Anáhuac*, 176.

27. See Chapter 2, this volume. Garner discovered that in the late 1780s per capita *repartimiento* loans ranged from 2 to 27 pesos, depending on the Oaxacan district (197–99). These were primarily, but not exclusively, cochineal loans.

28. "Autos seguidos por los herederos de Don Rodrigo de Neyra con los de Don Luis Frejomil alcalde mayor que fue de Teotitlán del Camino sobre pesos del avío," AGN, Civil, vol. 302, *primera parte, cuaderno de las cuentas*, pp. 21–46.

29. Prices for cochineal are available for the period 1758–1858 in Oaxaca, 1782–1856 in London, and from the mid–sixteenth century until 1802 in Amsterdam. Regression analysis was computed on these price series, and they were found to be highly correlated. This suggests that the merchants in Oaxaca enjoyed a fairly good knowledge of the conditions of the trade in Europe and that the European trading houses received reliable information about expected shipments from Mexico. See Chapter 8, this volume.

30. In several extraordinary years, market prices were so depressed that advancing the standard 12 reales would have entailed a loss for the *alcalde*. In 1798, for example, the official of the district of Nexapa, Nicolás Larumbe, refused to advance the typical 12 reales, owing to the existing low market price. At least some of the peasants agreed to a lower advance of 10 reales per pound, perhaps realizing that they had no alternative source of credit. When the market improved

later in the year and prices recovered, the Indians refused to repay Larumbe at the lower-than-customary rate. This suggests strongly that peasants came to view the peculiar price stability as legitimate and were willing to hold the *alcalde mayor* to that rate. While never its intention, the standard rate nonetheless provided some security for peasants as well. This case and others are discussed more fully in the following section.

31. Producers of cochineal frequently produced sufficient dye to both deliver their contracted quantities to the *alcalde* and still have some surplus to sell in the plaza on market day. Surplus cochineal was sold at prevailing market prices, and thus the income, of course, did fluctuate with the world price. See Chapter 7.

32. Ouweneel notes that while the fixed price in Zacatlán's egg *repartimiento* was accepted by both parties, Indians nonetheless grumbled when market prices rose excessively above the standard rate, and the magistrates griped when the difference between the fixed rate and the market price grew too slim (*Shadows Over Anáhuac*, 176).

33. "Contra el alcalde mayor de Teozocoalco por un natural de su jurisdicción," AGEO, Real Intendencia de Oaxaca II, legajo 13, exp. 2, 1810.

34. "Queja del Subdelegado de Miahuatlán contra el cura de San Juan Ozolotepec porque por su influencia le imputan aquellos vecinos repartimientos ilicitos y maltrato a los indios," AHMO, Criminal, Oaxaca, 1798.

35. According to the registry, the Oaxacan price for cochineal in 1798 was 18 reales per pound. But as this price was a year-end average price, it is quite likely that the price at the time of the *repartimiento* was considerably lower, too low to warrant loaning at 12 reales per pound. This conclusion seems warranted since the several years preceding 1798 had witnessed some of the lowest prices ever for which data are available.

36. "Proceso que se sigue a Nicolás Larumbe subdelegado de Nexapa por fraude en repartimiento," AGEO, Real Intendencia de Oaxaca II, legajo 6, exp. 17, 1801.

37. AGN, Civil, vol. 302, *primera parte*, cuaderno 2, 1763–1799. Unfortunately, neither the actual complaint nor the royal order were located. Thus, the language of each document remains unknown.

38. The native *alcalde* should not be confused with the *alcalde mayor*. The former was a local leader elected by the indigenous community, whereas the latter was a Spaniard who had either purchased his post or been appointed by the Viceroy.

39. "El común de Tepuxtepec contra José Vasquez sobre liquidación de cuentas," AJVA, Civil, no. 428, 1786.

40. "*Notas sobre la grana*," AGN, Historia, vol. 75, exp. 8, pp. 7–9.

41. Obviously, the *alcalde mayor* would not have willingly made loans when the price dipped this low unless he felt rather certain that the price would soon recover. As mentioned, in at least several cases the Spanish officials attempted to lower the *repartimiento* rate because the world price was too low to warrant the

advance of 12 reales. In most years, the Oaxacan market price hovered in the range of 16 to 18 reales per pound.

Chapter 6. A Risky Business: Credit and Default in the Dye Trade

1. What matters is not the actual creditworthiness, but the perception. Ransom and Sutch argue that the racism of white moneylenders toward black farmers in post-emancipation United States predisposed them to believe that blacks were poorer credit risks than white farmers of similar economic status (see *One Kind of Freedom*, 13).

2. Del Valle Pavón, 231.

3. See Meir Kohn, "Merchant Banking," 15.

4. Chance, *Conquest of the Sierra*, 97; Farriss, 43.

5. World Bank, "Issues," 112.

6. Throughout this chapter I refer to the returns realized by the *alcalde mayor* on his *repartimientos*. Naturally, the returns were not entirely pocketed by the Spanish official because he usually was a partner of a wealthy merchant and the profits were divided between them based on some previously agreed upon formula. Several such contracts are discussed in Chapter 2 of this volume.

7. World Bank, "Issues," 116.

8. Gibson, *The Aztecs Under Spanish Rule*, 94.

9. Pietschmann, 78. The markup on livestock sold through the *repartimiento* in Oaxaca was also in the neighborhood of 70 to 80 percent.

10. Patch, *Maya and Spaniard*, 87.

11. The return calculated here is the simple return on the *alcalde mayor*'s loan of 12 reales for a single pound of cochineal made in each of these years. Such a figure fails to account for carrying charges and other expenses incurred by the official, such as interest on principal, administrative expenses, salaries to debt collectors, etc. In addition, this simple rate of return ignores the length that debts are outstanding. Thus, a loan of 1 peso paid back in cochineal worth 2 pesos (24 reales) would produce a simple return of 100 percent, regardless of whether the debt were paid back in one week or ten years:

$$\text{simple return} = \frac{\left(\begin{array}{c}\text{market value}\\\text{of cochineal}\end{array}\right) - \left(\begin{array}{c}\text{initial loan}\\\text{of 12 reales}\end{array}\right)}{\begin{array}{c}\text{amount of}\\\text{initial loan}\end{array}}$$

12. Gibson, *The Aztecs Under Spanish Rule*, 94.

13. Default in the *repartimiento* was extremely high, yet creditors are always faced with the inability to collect a portion of their loans, often a large percentage when the nature of the credit system is less formal. As a result, credit extensions to peasants commonly warrant high rates of interest. In James Scott's description of the Malaysian system of *padi kunca* — a twentieth-century system of credit almost identical to the *repartimiento* — peasants accepted six-month ad-

vances in cash against the following rice harvest at annualized interest rates close to 150 percent. But, as Scott warns: "There is no necessary symmetry between the gain of the moneylender and the distress of the borrower. High interest rates in rural Southeast Asia have often reflected the actual cost of money and the high risk of debtor default. Thus, while these interest terms may have been punishing to [peasants], they do not imply a fabulous return to the lender" (15 n. 44). Ransom and Sutch estimated that Georgia merchants lending to small farmers experienced default rates which reached as high as 5 percent of loaned capital (see *One Kind of Freedom*, 131; and "Credit Merchandising," 66–67). According to Goldin, a full 25 percent of debtors to these Georgia merchants defaulted on some portion of their debts (16). Furthermore, rural moneylenders in underdeveloped, poorly integrated economies always charge high rates of interest to their customers. In early-twentieth-century rural Punjab, India, moneylenders extended small amounts of credit to producers at rates ranging from 24 to 200 percent per annum (see Bhattacharya, 199). After Mexico's independence from Spain, Guatemala became a large producer of cochineal (see Chapter 9). There, informal, unsecured cash advances were made against future deliveries of dyestuff at the rate of 5 to 10 percent per month (see McCreery, 120).

14. The fact that one of our major sources of information on the *repartimiento* results from the confrontations between the *alcalde* and delinquent debtors gives historians a skewed vision of the system. The *repartimiento* most often appears in the archives when the *alcalde mayor* has arrested a debtor and pressured him, often violently, for payment. This gives a distorted view of the *repartimiento* as a whole.

15. A good example is provided by the case in which Don Mateo de la Portilla had Juan Nusique, both from Teposcolula, arrested for a debt. Nusique pleaded from prison that de la Portilla take his house in payment of the debt. De la Portilla responded, however, that the house was worthless to him, as he could never sell it and recoup his funds ("Don Mateo de la Portilla contra Juan Nusique ambos de Teposcolula por deuda de pesos," Archivo Judicial de Teposcolula, AJT, Civil, no. 1422, 1796).

16. "Informes de los alcaldes mayores sobre repartimientos," AGN, Subdelegados, vol. 34, 1752.

17. "Dictamen dado reservadamente al virrey de Nueva España, Don Antonio Bucareli, por el Conde de Tepa sobre el establecimiento de las intendencias," AGI, Audiencia de México, 1973, p. 140.

18. "Informes de los alcaldes mayores sobre repartimientos," AGN, Subdelegados, vol. 34, 1752.

19. This complaint was echoed by a number of other officials, who argued that when market prices were high collection was difficult, since many debtors would claim they had lost their harvests, preferring to repay their loans in later years after the prices had declined. See the 1752 testimony of the official of Nexapa ("Informes de curas y alcaldes mayores sobre el repartimiento, Nexapa," AGN,

Subdelegados, vol. 34, p. 119, 1752); see also the 1784 report of the *alcalde* of Zimatlán ("Testimonio de expediente reservado sobre abusos de los alcaldes mayores del obispado de Oaxaca," AGI, Audiencia de México, 1872); and the Conde de Tepa also noted this risk (see "Dictamen dado reservadamente al virrey de Nueva España, Don Antonio Bucareli, por el Conde de Tepa sobre el establecimiento de las intendencias," AGI, Audiencia de México, 1973, p. 139).

20. "Superior despacho para que los vecinos de Villa Alta paguen a Don José Molina lo que le adeudan," AJVA, Civil, legajo 328, 1770. On Nexapa, see "Informes de los alcaldes mayores sobre repartimientos," Subdelegados, vol. 34, 1752, p. 119.

21. "Doña Eugenia García de Najera viuda del difunto alcalde mayor que fue del partido de Zimatlán pide que a los naturales a los cuales su marido les dió dinero para el cultivo de la grana se lo paguen en efectivo o con grana," AGEO, Real Intendencia de Oaxaca II, legajo 23, exp. 28, 1808.

22. "Cordillera cuarta providencias de visita del obispado de Oaxaca — Informes de dos curas sobre repartimientos de Alcaldes Mayores," AGI, Audiencia de México, 2588.

23. "Natural de Teotitlán del Camino contra su alcalde mayor sobre cuentas del repartimiento," AGEO, Real Intendencia de Oaxaca II, legajo 1, exp. 7, 1788.

24. "Cordillera cuarta providencias de visita del obispado de Oaxaca — Informes de dos curas sobre repartimientos de Alcaldes Mayores," AGI, Audiencia de México, 2588.

25. AGNO, Escribano Manuel Franco de Lara, 1760, pp. 69–70.

26. AGN, Alcaldes Mayores, vol. 1, no. 42, pp. 62–67.

27. AGN, Archivo Histórico de Hacienda, Real Administración de Alcabalas, cajita, no. 43. This account book is used for all of the calculations in the next several paragraphs.

28. The ledger was probably only a part of the magistrate's total *repartimiento* portfolio. This seems probable given the low amounts it records. Certainly, it would be preferable to use a more complete account book, but unfortunately one was not discovered. Regardless, we are able to estimate the returns on at least a portion of the magistrate's loan portfolio. Since there is no reason to suspect that these loans are atypical in any way, this exercise seems instructive.

29. It is important to stress that these are estimates and are computed to give a possible range. It would be a mistake to conclude that they are precise.

30. The rate of return presented is an annualized gross "simple" (non-compounding) rate of return. Thus, a loan of 12 reales repaid in six months with a pound of cochineal worth 18 reales earns a gross return of 50 percent, but an *annual* gross return of 100 percent. Likewise, the same transaction paid back in two years earns a gross annual rate of return of only 25 percent. The formula used to calculate annual gross return is the following: $[(\$R \div \$L) \div \$L] \times (365 - D)]$, where $\$R$ = value of repayment; $\$L$ = pesos loaned; and D = Days loan outstanding.

31. The "pay-back type," either coin or dye, in which the loan was repaid, was assumed to have been dye for those loans paid on 1 May 1784. In general, the value given for each pound of cochineal repaid ("pay back price") was the price recorded by the Registry in Oaxaca. This value probably overestimates somewhat the real value, since the price of cochineal in the districts was always slightly below that in Oaxaca. In 1784 the Oaxaca price was 16 reales. The "no. days due" do *not* reflect those in Table 6.2, which calculates days from 13 February 1784, whereas the tables in the Appendixes use a date of 1 May 1784 for calculating. Finally, when no contract rate was specified, it was assumed that the *alcalde mayor* had advanced the customary 12 reales.

32. It is important to understand that the *alcalde mayor* earned an annual interest rate of 237.63 percent on the one loan for only three months. In contrast, the 5.67 percent loan was outstanding for over five years. In other words, the official received high interest for only several months, but suffered a low return for years. When calculating his overall return on his principal, then, the lower interest rate will count more heavily, since money was earning this rate much longer.

33. In order to calculate the annual gross return on the total loan portfolio, each transaction was weighted based on the value of the loan and length of time outstanding. This was accomplished by multiplying the loan value times the number of days outstanding. The product, which I termed "peso-days," revealed the number of days that each peso was outstanding. (A five-peso loan outstanding for 100 days would be weighted as 500 "peso-days," since $5 \times 100 = 500$.) The total number of "peso-days" for the *alcalde mayor*'s entire portfolio was calculated by taking the sum of each individual transaction's "peso-days." The following formula was then used to calculate the daily interest rate received by the official: Daily rate of return = ([P\$R − P\$L] ÷ P\$D), where P\$R = total pesos repaid; P\$L = total pesos loaned; and P\$D = total "peso-days." The annual rate of return = daily rate of return × 365 days.

34. Debts contracted in 1783 or 1784 were considered current, not yet delinquent.

35. In order not to prejudice the results by arbitrarily selecting which of the debts were or were not collected, I assumed that 75 percent of each individual transaction was collected and 25 percent of each one defaulted. For instance, if a debtor owed the *alcalde mayor* 10 pesos, I took 7.5 pesos as collected and assumed 2.5 to have gone uncollected.

36. Bernardino Bonavia to Virrey Revillagigedo, AGN, Subdelegados, vol. 35, p. 211–15, 1790. According to Bonavia, the *alcalde mayor* invested 100,000 pesos per year for a total of 500,000 to 600,000 pesos per five-year term. Profits over the entire period he estimated to be around 130,000 to 140,000 pesos, with uncollectible debts in the 12,000 to 14,000–peso range. See also Hamnett, *Politics and Trade*, 77–78.

37. "Pedimento de oficio del Sr. Fiscal de lo civil sobre la decadencia del cultivo de la grana," AGN, Industria y Comercio, vol. 20, 1810, ff. 165–263.

265

38. Brading, *Miners and Merchants*, 99. Brading's figures apparently included the profits realized from ultimate delivery of cochineal and cotton to final markets as well as other investments such as maintenance of several rural shops by the official.

39. Ouweneel, *Shadows Over Anáhuac*, 181.

40. The *alcalde mayor* was also a cochineal merchant. He took the cochineal that he received through the *repartimiento* and shipped it for sale in Veracruz or beyond. This involved numerous other expenses such as packaging, transporting, registering, shipping, and insuring the cochineal. Taxes also were assessed. In Chapter 8, the entire vertical process from financing and production of the dye to sale in the markets of Northern Europe will be described. The cost of each individual step — packaging, freight, taxes, etc. — will be assessed and the entire "net profit" obtainable from the cochineal trade will be estimated. In the present discussion, these are ignored. I am interested here only in the *alcalde mayor* as "moneylender" through the system of *repartimiento*. Thus, the gross profits estimated ignore what he might later earn in additional mercantile profits by shipping the *grana seca* to distant markets. The moneylending transaction between the *alcalde mayor* and cochineal producers ceases as soon as the debtor repays his debt (or when the debt is "written off" as uncollectible).

41. Brading, *Miners and Merchants*, 216–17.

42. Cushner, 122.

43. Brading, *Miners and Merchants*, 173.

44. Ibid., 120–26.

45. Ibid.

46. Hamnett shows that the purchase prices paid to the Crown for the post of *alcalde mayor* in several dye-producing districts of Oaxaca exceeded the amounts paid for other positions around Mexico (see *Politics and Trade*, 16). The anonymous author of "Productos comerciables en las alcaldías mayores," BNM, Manuscritos, MS no. 1385, pp. 208–9, claimed that the nine most lucrative jurisdictions in Mexico were all in Oaxaca — Villa Alta, Xicayan, Nexapa, Miahuatlán, Teotitlán del Valle, Zimatlán, Cuatro Villas del Marquesado, Oaxaca, and Teposcolula. Hamnett's *Politics and Trade* also cites this document (75–76). See also Chapter 2, this volume.

47. AGN, Subdelgados, vol. 51, p. 122.

48. Of the total cochineal collected through *repartimiento* advances, Labayru paid 12 reales per pound for all but a small quantity, for which he paid 16 reales per pound.

49. "Inventario de los bienes que quedaron por muerte del alcalde mayor que fue de Miahuatlán, Don Sebastian de Labayru," AGN, Tierras, vol. 1037, exp. 2, pp. 78–81. Some of the numbers had to be reconstructed owing to significant damage to the document.

50. "Testimonio de expediente reservado sobre abusos de los alcaldes mayores del obispado de Oaxaca," AGI, Audiencia de México, 1872.

51. Kicza argues in "Consumption and Control" that wealthy merchants of Mexico City used their ability to provide credit to ensure ready commodity supplies, often hoping to corner the market and reap monopoly profits on some good.

Chapter 7. Indians and Markets

1. Data extracted from AGN, Subdelegados, vol. 34, and "Inventario de los bienes que quedaron por muerte del alcalde mayor que fue de Miahuatlán, Don Sebastian de Labayru," AGN, Tierras, vol. 1037, exp. 2, pp. 78–81.

2. "Informe de Fr. Joaquín Vasco de Santa María Ecatepec," in Dahlgren, 57.

3. See Donkin; Dahlgren; Murguía y Galardi; and Alzate y Ramirez, "Memoria sobre la naturaleza," AGN, Correspondencia de Virreyes, vol. 90, *primera serie*, 1794, pp. 126–230.

4. Alzate y Ramirez, "Memoria sobre la naturaleza," AGN, Correspondencia de Virreyes, vol. 90, *primera serie*, 1794, p. 201.

5. "Instrucción declaratoria acerca del repartimiento de grana," in Dahlgren, 98.

6. Personal discussions with Ing. Ignacio del Rio, owner of Tlapanochestli, a company attempting to reintroduce cochineal production into Oaxaca, Fall 1991, Oaxaca, Mexico. Del Rio estimated that thirty females produced 9 grams, which at 70,000 insects to the pound (the estimate given by Dahlgren, 13) is a ratio of seeded to harvested live cochineal equal to about 1:47.

7. Ingeniero del Rio placed the weight shrinkage at 66 percent, as did Alzate y Ramirez, who noted that in Zimapán three pounds of "*grana verde*" produce one pound dried. In contrast, Donkin refers to Gómez de Cervantes, another eighteenth-century scientist, who found reduction to be only 33 percent (17).

8. That is, one-third of 25 pounds is about 8 pounds. And one-third of 48 pounds is 16 pounds.

9. "Informes de alcaldes mayores y curas sobre repartimientos," AGN, Subdelegados, vol. 34, 1752, p. 141.

10. The difference between 4 pounds dried *grana* and 16 pounds is, of course, very significant. The higher figure might be the biological norm, the expected output under perfect conditions, whereas the priest's lower estimate was the typical yield realized in Miahuatlán.

11. If 10 pounds dried is the goal, and each pound of seed produces 4 to 16 pounds, then an amount of seed between 10/16 of a pound (0.625 = 10 ounces) and 2.5 pounds must be introduced, since 0.625 × 16 = 10 and 2.5 × 4 = 10.

12. This conclusion is based on comparison of the prices paid for seed by a producer in 1774 and that recorded by the Registry (see "Sobre pesos de una nopalera que Vicente de la Cruz, indio de San Jacinto Amilpas, y Don Juan Nepomuceno de el Hollo, comerciante de Oaxaca, asemillaron en compañía," AGEO, Alcaldía Mayores, legajo 35, exp. 1, 1774; see also "Informe de Fr. Joaquín Vasco de Santa María Ecatepec," in Dahlgren, 55).

13. The 75 reales was the difference of 120 received and 45 spent. There

were, of course, other expenses involved since labor spent on cochineal production was diverted from other tasks and the land used for cochineal was unavailable for other crops. However, while cochineal production was quite labor intensive, it was not physically demanding. Thus, children and elders, whose opportunity costs were low, were often given the responsibilities of the *nopalera*. Furthermore, the land used for the *nopalera* could be very marginal since cacti flourish even on poor quality land.

14. AGN, Real Hacienda-Alcabalas, cajita 43, p. 21. It is possible that the community did not actually receive any money but instead cancelled its tribute debt with a promise to deliver cochineal in the future. This would have required producing funds to purchase *grana* seed from some other source. Alternatively, the community might have received only part of the money, the rest serving to cancel the tribute that they owed.

15. "Informe del cura de Miahuatlán," AGN, Subdelegados, vol. 34, 1752.

16. Calle de la Cochinilla is now named 20 de Noviembre, and is one block west of the Zócalo of Oaxaca. There is a plaque commemorating the street's earlier importance at the corner of 20 de Noviembre and Hidalgo Streets.

17. Portillo, *Oaxaca en el centenario de la independencia nacional*. A copy of this book is available at the BMLT.

18. Pérez, no doubt, hoped that the prices in these towns were more than 2 reales per pound lower than the price in Teposcolula in order to produce some profit for him after he delivered it to García, as contracted. In fact, this risky venture backfired, and Pérez was unable to repay his debt (see "El teniente de infantería Esteban García contra Juan Pérez por deuda de pesos," AJT, Civil, no. 1101, 1774).

19. "Los acreedores de Lucas Pimentel contra Pimentel sobre pesos," AJT, Civil, no. 1095, 1774.

20. "Demanda por Don Pedro Otero, comerciante de Nochistlán, contra Mariano Ayala por deuda de pesos," AJT, Civil, no. 1409, 1796. For additional examples of market transactions of cochineal, see AJT, Civil, no. 1237, 1784; AJT, Civil, no. 1155, 1767; AJT, Civil, nos. 1422, 1796; and AGN, Industria y Comercio, vol. 22, exps. 1–4, 1788–1792.

21. The priest refers specifically to the practice of certain dishonest Indians who used "*monedas falsas*" to purchase *grana* from Indian producers ("Cordillera cuarta providencias de visita del obispado de Oaxaca — Informes de dos curas sobre repartimientos de Alcaldes Mayores," AGI, Audiencia de México, 2588.)

22. Chance, *Conquest of the Sierra*, 101.

23. "Superior despacho para que los vecinos de Villa Alta paguen a Don José Molina lo que le adeudan," AJVA, Civil, no. 328, 1770.

24. "Cuadernos donde constan las introducciones de indios que no causan alcabalas," AGEO, legajos 7 and 8, various expedientes, 1810–1812. In a verbal communication of spring 1992, Dr. Juan Carlos Grosso, the historian who has probably used *alcabala* records more than anyone else, suggested that the records

collected for these years were likely done so by the Crown to estimate the cost to the royal treasury of granting exemption to Indians from this tax.

25. "Cuadernos donde constan las introducciones de indios que no causan alcabalas," AGEO, legajos 7 and 8, various expedientes, 1810–1812.

26. "Informes de curas y alcaldes mayores sobre el repartimiento: Ixtepexi," AGN, Subdelegados, vol. 34, p. 6, 1752.

27. "Sobre la licencia para pasar a España que tiene pedida Juan de Aguilar, indio tributario de San Pablo Mitla," AGN, Indios, vol. 67, exp. 278, 1791.

28. The value of output peaked in 1771 at 4,200,750 pesos. Even after the decline of the industry in the mid–1780s, the value of output came close to or exceeded 1,000,000 pesos in most years (see Appendix B, this volume).

29. Chapter 8 presents additional explanations for the late-colonial decline. For the present purpose, however, these are not important.

30. On the depressed demand of the 1790s, see Chapter 8.

Chapter 8. Oaxaca to London: A Balance Sheet

1. Braudel, 2:429.

2. See Chapter 6 for a discussion of how the Teposcolulan *alcalde*'s profits were estimated.

3. This chapter explores the cochineal trade from the point at which the officials collect their debts. Because they cease to be distinguishable from other merchants at this point, this chapter will refer to the officials, and others, merely as merchants.

4. Marginal costs in the cochineal trade were largely passed on to consumers. This was possible because the demand for cochineal had a low price elasticity. Price increases did not reduce demand dramatically; rather, consumers simply paid more. Although cochineal was an expensive dye, a small amount served to color a large quantity of cloth. Thus, the additional cost of producing textiles attributable to the rising price of cochineal was not great.

5. For the English price series, see Tooke and Newmarch, 2:400. Dutch prices for cochineal are published in Posthumus, 1:420–23. English pounds sterling were converted to Spanish pesos at the exchange rate £1 = 5 pesos. Dutch guilders were converted at the rate on 1 guilder = 0.45 pesos.

6. The year 1758 was chosen because it was the first year in which price data were also available for Oaxaca. The only year missing in the European series is 1759.

7. The standard deviation of the data was 0.5.

8. Braudel, 2:97–110.

9. The regression begins with 1760 because a Dutch price for 1759 was lacking.

10. On the effect of the Napoleonic and independence wars on Spanish imperial trade in general, see John R. Fisher, *Trade, War, and Revolution*; and John R. Fisher, *Economic Aspects of Spanish Imperialism*.

11. Export data for cochineal for various years, 1797 included, appears in Lerdo de Tejada, tables 14–35.

12. Ibid.

13. See Tooke and Newmarch, 2:400. According to the data in Tooke and Newmarch, the price of cochineal in the second quarter of 1799 averaged 11.375 pesos per pound on the London exchange. By the fourth quarter, it had fallen to 4.875. Either the dye or news of its pending arrival had obviously reached England.

14. John R. Fisher, *Trade, War, and Revolution*, 83–84.

15. For prices in London, see Tooke and Newmarch, 2:400. For cochineal exports, see Lerdo de Tejada, tables 14–35. According to Lerdo's data, the 21,200 pounds exported in 1805 were not shipped to Spain.

16. As will be argued below, much of the Oaxacan-European price differential during wartime was attributable to the sharply rising cost of insurance and ocean freight. As risks rose, so did the cost of shipping and insurance.

17. An idea of the great number of ports to which cochineal was exported between 1783 and 1786 can be seen in "Relación de la grana entrada en esta ciudad de Cádiz en embarcaciones mercantes procedentes de América bajo las reglas del libre comercio," AGI, Indiferente General, legajo 2435.

18. That the cochineal was more valuable whole had nothing to do with its potency. Whole or broken, it retained the same effectiveness as a dye. Instead, whole *grana* was valued because its purity was guaranteed. Cochineal dust, what the Oaxacans most often called *granilla*, could be easily adulterated with foreign substances. Most cochineal was *grana fina*, and in this study I have resisted entirely discussing the trade in other types. In addition to *granilla*, many other names were sometimes used to describe lower quality cochineal—*mostacilla* and *polvo*, for example.

19. The labor cost of assembling the zurrón was not given in all cases. The amount, however, tended to be very little, 2 to 4 reales a piece.

20. The typical zurrón of cochineal weighed 7 to 9 arrobas, equal to 175 to 225 pounds. For a detailed description of transportation by mule train, see Hassig, 281–83. A number of references were found to *cargas* of 2 zurrones of cochineal. This suggests that mules sometimes carried well in excess of 250 pounds. Of course, the load that an individual mule could carry depended on the size and strength of the particular beast.

21. The information for Map 3 was compiled from a variety of sources (see Borah, *Early Colonial Trade*, 25–28; Chance, *Race and Class*, 53–56; Chance, *Conquest of the Sierra*, 22; and Romero Frizzi, *Economía y vida*, 27–34). Colonial roads followed more or less the same course as do modern roads, for the obvious reason that they conform to the topography.

22. Several of the documents gave the amount of cochineal transported in zurrónes, not arrobas. In such cases, I took the weight to be 8 arrobas per zurrón. Distances were calculated using a road atlas.

23. The average was computed by simply dividing the sum of the individual freight rates by the number of samples. The median figure was found to be 1.763, not far from the average. Such a methodology naturally gives a rather rough figure. The deviation of some of the cases from the average was significant, and is probably explained by the different terrain.

24. Suárez Argüello, 183. Suárez Argüello presents a freight charge for Mexico City to Oaxaca of 24.86 granos per metric ton kilometer. This was converted to reales per ton kilometer to arrive at the figure of 1.88. There are 12 granos per real and 1 metric ton (1,000 kilograms) is equal to 2,200 pounds, or 1.1 tons. So, 24.86 ÷ 12 = 2.07 reales per metric ton per kilometer, and 2.07 ÷ 1.1 = 1.88 reales per ton kilometer.

25. Coatsworth, *El impacto económico*, 83. My rate is almost identical to the highest rates computed by Coatsworth, although it is more than double his lowest rates. This seems reasonable, however, since most of his data are for less mountainous northern Mexico. Suárez Argüello reports rates for other parts of Mexico which are sometimes 50 to 75 percent less than the Mexico City-to-Oaxaca figure (183). In fact, her Oaxacan figure is by far the highest one, attributable, no doubt, to the particularly mountainous terrain there. Another factor explaining my higher figure is that Coatsworth's figures are for wagon freight. Obviously, wagons are more efficient, since more weight can be transported per animal and per person. As a result, freight costs would be lower. Owing to its topography, wagons were never employed in Oaxaca.

26. The *alcalde mayor* of Ixtepeji claimed that the Indians frequently moistened the *grana* to increase its weight and thus its marketable value (AGN, Subdelegados, vol. 34, 1752).

27. In the last case (no. 14), a cochineal merchant expressed his delight that his zurrón of *grana* had only lost 12 pounds, when in the past, a loss of 16 to 18 pounds was common.

28. Hoberman, 44–50. Hoberman includes a nice discussion of the occupation and social origins of the *encomenderos*.

29. Ortiz de la Tabla Ducasse, 29.

30. See "Informes de curas y alcaldes mayores sobre repartimientos," AGN, Subdelegados, vol. 34, 1752.

31. AGN, Civil, vol. 302, *primera parte, cuaderno* 2, pp. 59–65. On four of the five receipts contained in these pages, a *comisión de venta* of 2.5 percent was paid, as well as an additional brokerage fee, a *corretaje*, of 0.5 percent.

32. See AGN, Intendencias, vol. 4, pp. 249–83.

33. Numerous cases were found dealing with the problem of adulterated cochineal, which indicates that this was a recurrent problem. See, for example, "Diligencias en averiguación de grana falsa que se halló vendida por Pedro Quintero Corredor," AGEO, Alcaldías Mayores, legajo 19, exp. 24, 1728; "Ejecutoria contra los reos Salvador Martín y Juan José Osorio, acusados de adulterar la grana," AGEO, Real Intendencia de Oaxaca I, legajo 4, exp. 48, 1793; "Autos

contra los vendedores de grana falsa o adulterada," AGEO, Real Intendencia de Oaxaca II, legajo 4, exp. 6, 1794; and "Las 40 arrobas que presentó en el Registro Pedro Gómez se hallaban mezclados en gran parte de grana silvestre y bodoquillo la cual fue purificada," AGEO, Real Intendencia de Oaxaca II, legajo 31, exp. 11, 1807. For a postcolonial example, see AGEO, Juzgados, legajo 8, exp. 76, 1826. For adulteration during the early-colonial period, see Lee, "Cochineal Production."

34. Joaquín Vasco, a priest serving in the parish of Santa María Ecatepec in the jursidiction of the *alcaldía mayor* of Nexapa, described this testing process in detail (see Dahlgren, 58–60).

35. The Crown issued regulations for the Cochineal Registry in 1756. These rules were reissued in 1760, 1773, and 1817, owing to continued abuses. A reproduction of this ordinance, entitled "Ordenanzas, método, o regla que se ha de observar de efecto de cerrar la puerta á la perpetración de fraudes en la grana cochinilla," can be found in Dahlgren, appendix. An original copy is deposited at the Newberry Library in Chicago. These regulations are summarized in AGN, Industria y Comercio, vol. 9, pp. 135–39, 1782.

36. For an excellent review of the literature, see Klein and Barbier. See also Coatsworth, "Limits of Colonial Absolutism"; Brading, "Bourbon Spain"; and TePaske.

37. Exports were particularly easy to tax since they all passed through Veracruz and Cádiz, which was, in fact, the reason that the Crown limited trade to these ports in the first place. In addition, items with low price elasticities of demand are ideal for assessing excise taxes since the increased price does not cause consumers to reduce demand. Thus, new taxes are guaranteed to generate increased revenues.

38. Other scholars have noted the Crown's increased fiscal extractions in the late eighteenth century. On Mexico, see, for example, Coatsworth, "Limits of Colonial Absolutism," especially 25–27. The state's increased ability to tax even reached the Kingdom of Ecuador (see Andrien, "The State and Dependency," 171–79).

39. This document was copied by Bustamante (see *Memoria estadística de Oaxaca*, 25). It was also probably seen by Lerdo de Tejada.

40. See Lerdo de Tejada, 22.

41. See Hamnett, *Politics and Trade*, 32–33; and Garavaglia and Grosso. The supplement assessed a 2 percent increase on products already taxed at 6 percent, and an increase on goods taxed at other rates in the same proportion. For cochineal, this translated into an *alcabala* supplement of 1 percent (a 33 percent increase on the earlier 3 percent rate).

42. Garavaglia and Grosso, 28–29. See also Morin, 149. According to Morin, this supplement stayed in effect until December 1816. Garavaglia and Grosso clarify the scenario: until 1816, the supplement was called a *"préstamo patriótico,"* an obligatory patriotic loan. After 1816, the rate remained at 2 per-

cent (1 percent for cochineal), but the tax was referred to as the *"aumento de alcabala,"* the *alcabala* supplement.

43. Garavaglia and Grosso, 28–29.

44. The *avaluo* for cochineal was recorded for twenty-four dates, corresponding to nineteen years. In five of the years, the *avaluo* was revised in mid-year. Naturally, in these years both records were considered.

45. The sum of all twenty-four *avaluos* collected (measured in pesos per arroba) was 1,803 pesos. The sum of all Oaxacan market prices for the same years was 1,817 pesos. The ratio of these figures (1,803/1,817) was equal to 0.992, suggesting that the customs officials attempted to appraise the cochineal at its market price. In some cases the *avaluo* exceeded the market price, and in others the opposite occurred. In fourteen cases, the two figures were within 10 percent of one another. In twenty cases, they fell within 16 percent. Regression analysis revealed a strong correlation between the set of *avaluo* prices and the set of market prices for the same years ($r = 0.87$). The correlation was much weaker when the *avaluo* rate was compared with the market price one year prior. This suggests that there was little lag — that the customs officials promptly adjusted the *avaluo* to reflect actual prices.

46. Morin, 149; Garavaglia and Grosso, 31. The case of cochineal might have been unique for several reasons. First, all *grana* was taxed in Veracruz in the same customs office. This tended to reduce the arbitrary nature of evaluating the merchandise and assigning an *aforo*. Second, the price of cochineal was well known since it was the second most valuable export and was a commodity bought and sold in large volumes in Veracruz.

47. "Sobre la decadencia del comercio," BNM, Manuscritos, MS no. 1398, pp. 324–402.

48. Torres Ramirez and Ortiz de la Tabla, *Reglamento y arranceles reales*, 85.

49. There were 20 reales de vellón (rv) in each peso, and a quintal was equal to 100 pounds, or 4 arrobas. So, 6,624 rv/quintal × 1 peso/20 rv × 1 quintal/4 arrobas = 82.8 pesos/arroba.

50. AGN, Consulado de Veracruz, caja 252, exp. 8, 1819.

51. See Cuenca Esteban, "Statistics," 390 n. 36.

52. Sales made by Indians did not incur an *alcabala* tax since Indians were exempted. Thus, the sales tax was applied in Oaxaca only when a non-Indian sold the dye. There were discussions about altering this rule in an effort to assess an *alcabala* on the *alcaldes mayores* dye purchases. In fact, a 1780 *bando* actually imposed this tax, but the *bando* was repealed the following year. During the interim, it is unclear to what degree it was actually collected (see Hamnett, *Politics and Trade*, 60–64).

53. According to Hamnett (*Politics and Trade*, 32–33), the assessment of an *alcabala* upon introduction of *grana* into Veracruz was a 1767 reform implemented by José de Gálvez, the *visitador* to Mexico. Prior to 1767, the tax had been

regularly evaded by merchants who claimed that the dye was for personal use in Veracruz. Since no sale was to take place, the merchant owed no tax. See also "Informe del consulado de México sobre varios puntos tocantes a arreglo de comercio," BNM, Manuscritos, MS no. 1304, which gives a similar explanation for the reform. Fonseca y Urrutia note that cochineal was always sold in Veracruz, making the *alcabala* payable there. Merchants evaded the tax by claiming that no sale had occurred and then sending the dye to Spain in the original owner's name (4:647). For the *bando* changing the process for assessing the tax, see "sobre el gravamen que nuevamente se ha introducido en la ciudad de Veracruz a la entrada por mar o tierra de todos los efectos cobrando 4% de alcabala," AGN, Archivo Histórico de Hacienda, legajo 502, exp. 17, 1767.

54. Many of the *alcabala* books for the *receptorías* of Oaxaca for the years after 1795 are located at the AGEO.

55. See "Don Jerónimo Estevez del comercio de Xamiltepec reclama por excessiva la alcabala que le exigió de la renta de 170 arrobas de grana," AGEO, Tesorería Principal, legajo 7, exp. 5, 1800.

56. See "Derecho de convoy," AGN, Consulado no. 740, legajo 322, exp. 6, 1815.

57. AGN, caja 175, *suelto*.

58. Figure 8.3 shows only the taxes collected by Spain. Great Britain collected customs duties on dye imports, but these are discussed later in this chapter (see the chapter section entitled "Re-export from Spain").

59. On the increasingly predatory fiscal exactions of the Real Hacienda, see TePaske.

60. While theoretically the trip was made annually, during the eighteenth century the fleet traveled far less frequently. Between 1718 and 1778, a fleet sailed from Veracruz to Spain only twenty-one times. Thirteen of these were regular "*flotas*" and eight were smaller "*azogues*," mercury fleets. Between 1739 and 1757, the fleet was replaced by *registros* — occasional boats granted permission to transport cargo to Spain. Between 1761 and 1778 only five fleets left Veracruz for Cádiz (see García-Baquero González, 1:280; see also Haring, *Spanish Empire*, 314–16).

61. Despite its age, the most comprehensive study of the Spanish fleet system is still Haring, *Trade and Navigation*. See also Haring, *The Spanish Empire*; García-Baquero González; and Walker. On Spain's declaration of free trade, see Brading, "Bourbon Spain,"; Brading, *Miners and Merchants*; John R. Fisher, *Commercial Relations between Spain and Spanish America*; John R. Fisher, *Economic Aspects of Spanish Imperialism*; and Ortiz de la Tabla Ducasse.

62. John R. Fisher, *Commercial Relations between Spain and Spanish America*, 114–17, appendix C, and tables C-1 and C-2.

63. Regarding this law, see Hamnett, *Politics and Trade*, 36. See also AGN, Marina, vol. 38, exp. 6, pp. 68–188, 1775. On early pirate attacks upon Mexico's cochineal exports, see Lee, "American Cochineal," 212–15. According to Lee

(212), attacks on cochineal shipments were so common that John Donne even mentions them in a poem, "*As Pirats which doe know / That there come weak ships fraught with Cutchannel / The men board them.*" On piracy in the eighteenth century in general, see García-Baquero González, 1:371–80.

64. AGN, Industria y Comercio, vol. 9, pp. 42–45, 75–76, and 98–99, 1778, 1779, 1780.

65. "Don Juan Bautista Uztariz, Conde de Reparaz, solicita permiso para embarcar 600 zurrones de grana en navio de su casa," AGN, Marina, vol. 38, exp. 2, 37–41. The Count had already gained permission to send 400 zurrones aboard either the same ship or another one, *El Prusiano*, also owned by his trading house. The total shipment of 1000 zurrones, approximately 200,000 pounds, was worth around 952,000 pesos in Cádiz based on the then prevailing market value of 119 pesos per arroba of *grana fina* as given in García-Baquero González, vol. 2, table no. 45, 272–275.

66. "Sobre el despacho de los navios el Astuto y Urca Santa Rita y el modo de su cargo y registros que en ellos deben hacerse," AGN, Caja 279, exp. 4, 1774. "Sobre la nulidad del embarco de granas y nombramiento de otro buque para conducir las granas sobrantes," AGN, Marina, vol. 38, exp. 6, pp. 68–188. Permission to transport cochineal to Cádiz was also extended to non-war ships in 1780. Evidently, similar circumstances existed in that year, as the stock of cochineal in Veracruz awaiting shipment was high and no war ships were available to carry it to Spain (AGN, Industria y Comercio, vol. 9, p. 108, 1780).

67. "Sobre el despacho de los navios el Astuto y Urca Santa Rita y el modo de su cargo y registros que en ellos deben hacerse," AGN, caja 279, exp. 4, 1774; "Sobre la nulidad del embarco de granas y nombramiento de otro buque para conducir las granas sobrantes," AGN, Marina, vol. 38, exp. 6, pp. 68–188.

68. Fonseca and Urrutia, 4:587.

69. Walker, 242, appendix 3, table 4.

70. AGN, Civil, vol. 302, *primera parte*, exp. 1, cuaderno 2, pp. 59–65.

71. See "Cuaderno de fletes de la carga que ha conducido el navio el Halcón," AGI, Consulados, legajo 772.

72. "Libro registro de escrituras de riesgo extendidas sobre mercancías con destino a América," AGI, Consulados. libro 443.

73. AGN, Civil, vol. 302, *primera parte*, cuaderno 2, pp. 21–23.

74. AGN, Marina, vol. 38, exp. 1, pp. 1–36, 1775.

75. "Sobre que los buques titulados la Pastora, el San Francisco, y la Carlota conduzcan el sobrante de granas y anil que no puedan abarcar los tres navios de guerra," AGN, Industria y Comercio, vol. 9, p. 108, 1780. The ships were commissioned to bring their cargo to Havana, where it was to be transferred if possible to war ships.

76. North, "Role of Transportation," 215; see also, North, "Ocean Freight Rates."

77. See *Reglamento y aranceles reales*, 21–22. According to Ortiz de la

Tabla Ducasse (28), before 1778 goods were charged freight based only on their volume, which, he claimed, benefited small, high-value items. After 1778, he added, freight charges were set at a percentage of the merchandise value. This, of course, is not entirely logical, for certainly even after 1778 volume remained an important quality determining the cost of freight. If it were not, then it would be cheaper to send a boatload of low-cost, bulky commodities than to send silver. This clearly makes no sense.

78. "Informe del consulado de Sevilla sobre el comercio libre," BNM, Manuscritos, MS no. 1397, pp. 261–308, 1788.

79. See North, "Role of Transportation," 235, appendix, and table 1.

80. The strong correlation between the two reflects the ability of merchants to unload the extra cost burden on consumers. As higher freight rates pushed up costs, the price of cochineal rose. Merchants were able to pass this cost on to consumers, owing to the low price elasticity of demand for cochineal.

81. García-Baquero González, 1:375–76. The author suggests that "English" may have come to be a generic term used to describe pirates and not an actual reflection of the nationality of the aggressors.

82. John R. Fisher, *Commercial Relations between Spain and Spanish America*, 48.

83. García-Baquero González, 1:388–94.

84. Ibid., 1:381.

85. AGN, Marina, vol. 38, exp. 5, 1776, refers to the loss by Uztariz of 500 zurrónes of *grana* aboard the shipwrecked boat *El Prusiano* but makes no reference to any other losses. However, according to García-Baquero González (1:392), *El Buen Consejo*, another boat belonging to Uztariz, which was accompanying *El Prusiano* (García-Baquero calls this ship Jesús, María y José "Prusiano") on the voyage, was also shipwrecked. Based on AGN, Marina, vol. 38, exp. 2, pp. 37–41, we know that *El Buen Consejo* also carried cochineal. No reference to lost cargo from *El Buen Consejo* suggests that its cargo might have been recovered from the shipwreck.

86. For an 1810 description of the laws regulating colonial shipping insurance, see Quirós, 286–304. See also Bernal; Garzon Pareja; and Haring, *Trade and Navigation*, 344–53 and appendix 10. For an excellent treatment of the broader eighteenth-century European market for maritime insurance, see Spooner.

87. Undoubtedly, the best economic study to date on eighteenth-century maritime insurance is Spooner. He shows how Dutch insurers responded rationally to perceived risks and how the rates that they charged reflected this. The late-century maritime insurance market in Spain was equally rational.

88. Policies often stipulated a rate but then added that an increased rate would apply if war were to erupt during the period of coverage. Thus, we have peacetime rates even for those years when Spain was at war. See below, this chapter.

89. The majority of the rates cover travel between Cádiz and Veracruz, but several were for ships arriving or departing from different Spanish ports, including

Malaga, Santander, and Barcelona. The rate displayed for each year was the average of the rates discovered for that year. The rates are displayed individually in Appendix D of this book. Data were extracted from the following sources: "Libro de operaciones de la compañía de seguros por Don Antonio Ramirez desde 9 de Maio 1788 a 12 de Agosto de 1795 con espreción de los llegados a su destino, los que han retornados, y los perdidos," AGI, Consulados, libro 444B; "Varias tomas de razon de Polizas de Seguros de embarcaciones que no tienen pliegos de escripturas," AGI, Consulados, legajo 889; "Varias tomas de razon de Polizas de Seguros de embarcaciones que van a indias," AGI, Consulados, legajo 889; "Libro de registro de escrituras de riesgo, extendidas sobre mercancías con destino a America — 1803–05," AGI, Consulados, libro 444A; "Libro de Toma de razon de escrituras de riesgo de flota de Luis de Cordoba, jefe de la escuadra, 1774," AGI, Consulados, libro 440; "Compañía de Seguros, expedientes sobre estas compañías (1793–1837)," AGI, Consulados, legajo 78; and "Polizas de seguros del concurso de don Antonio Artechea," AGI, Consulados, legajo 518.

90. "Informe del consulado de Sevilla sobre comercio libre," BNM, Manuscritos, MS no. 1397, pp. 261–308, 1788.

91. Ortiz de la Tabla Ducasse, 29 n. 50. On p. 31, Ortiz de la Tabla presented a figure of 41 pesos, 2 reales, which he claimed were the taxes, freight charges, sales commissions, and insurance on 1 arroba of cochineal. His source was an 1816 document prepared by the Secretary of the Veracruz Consulado, José Maria Quirós, and located in AGI, Audiencia de México, 2994. In the AGN, an 1819 document with Quirós's signature shows the same figure (41 pesos, 2 reales) but makes clear that freight, insurance, and commissions are *not* included (see AGN, Consulado, caja 252, exp. 8, 1819). This latter was apparently the same document that Carlos Bustamante referred to in 1820.

92. Bernal, 474.

93. "Libro de Toma de razón de escrituras de riesgo de flota de Luis de Cordoba, jefe de escuadra," AGI, Consulados, libro 440, 1774.

94. Camón Fernandez de Avila, 234–35. In fact, Camón rejects this high rate as mere exaggeration. He was wrong to dismiss it.

95. Peculiarly, the policies always stated x percent above, when they really meant x percentage points above (see "Polizas de seguros del concurso de don Antonio Artechea," AGI, Consulados, legajo 518).

96. "Polizas de seguros del concurso de don Antonio Artechea," AGI, Consulados, legajo 518.

97. Ibid.

98. "Varias tomas de razon de Polizas de Seguros de embarcaciones que van a indias," AGI, Consulados, legajo 889.

99. "Polizas de seguros del concurso de don Antonio Artechea," AGI, Consulados, legajo 518.

100. "Varias tomas de razon de Polizas de Seguros de embarcaciones que van a indias," AGI, Consulados, legajo 889. A number of different insurers under-

wrote the Aguila for varying amounts. The largest insurer covered 5,017 pesos at 60 percent, and 50 percent if it arrived safely. The rest of the coverage was secured at 60 percent if lost and 40 percent if it arrived safely.

101. Spooner, 98, 114–15.

102. The year 1799 is not included here because the one policy discovered, the policy discussed above in which a merchant paid 60 percent, seemed too much of an aberration. This "data point" was left off Figure 8.5 because it was exceptionally high and distorted the more general picture of insurance rate trends.

103. The issue of insurance on neutral ships is discussed below.

104. Let us take, for example, a hypothetical case in which freight rates were $100, and $20 of this rate (20 percent) was due to insurance. For the freight rate to increase to $200 (i.e., double), the insurance portion would have to increase to $120, holding all other costs constant. In other words, the insurance would have to increase from $20 to $120, a 500 percent rise. In fact, rates of 40 and 50 percent were ten to twenty times greater than the regular peacetime rates.

105. That most of the cost of insurance could be passed on to consumers is again a reflection of the low price elasticity of demand for cochineal, an industrial input comprising a small percentage of total costs in the booming textile industry. While the additional costs of insurance could be dumped upon the final consumer, merchants did need to put up more capital than before to market a fixed amount of cochineal. This probably resulted in a lower return on their investment.

106. John R. Fisher, *Trade, War, and Revolution*, 57.

107. Hamnett, *Politics and Trade*, 101.

108. Cuenca Esteban, "United States Balance of Payments," 32. In 1798, according to Liss, "most ships into Veracruz were North American" (20). Coatsworth, in "American Trade with European Colonies," notes the enormous expansion of U.S. exports to Spanish America in 1798–1799 (252).

109. See De Conde.

110. Cuenca Esteban, "United States Balance of Payments," 59. The rates collected by Cuenca Esteban were for ships traveling to a variety of different Spanish-American ports, not just Veracruz. A full half, however, were destined for Cuba, a relatively short trip from U.S. ports. Likely, then, the rates collected are conservatively low.

111. Adams, 729.

112. The prices of cochineal in Veracruz for 1796–1817 were calculated from the export values presented in Lerdo de Tejada, tables 14–35. The Veracruz prices for 1784–1795 were estimated as follows: The median price difference between the Oaxaca price and the Veracruz price for the years 1796–1821 was 25 percent; to estimate the Veracruz prices for the years 1784–1795, I simply added 25 percent to the Oaxaca price. This is clearly rough, but certainly gives an idea.

113. Using data from the period of the American War of Independence, the documents contained in AGN, Industria y Comercio, vol. 9, ff. 120–22, 1780,

make reference to large stocks of cochineal that were warehoused owing to the war-induced dangers of transatlantic shipping.

114. On foreign merchants in Spain during the early-colonial era, see Haring, *Trade and Navigation*, 177–79; and Elliott, 179, 184, 194, and 355.

115. On the merchandising of cochineal in Europe, see Buist, chap. 15; Braudel, 2:421–23; and Hamnett, *Politics and Trade*, 24–28.

116. I have no data which would permit me to estimate the percentage of the dye purchased by foreigners, but I would speculate that non-Spanish merchants dominated the re-export of cochineal to other European markets.

117. See, in this chapter, the above section on Spanish colonial taxes.

118. Because demand for cochineal was largely inelastic, the merchant could pass the additional costs onto consumers. It was, however, necessary for him to put up more of his capital to meet these costs without the expectation of higher net profits. Thus, his return on investment fell. He invested more and earned in profits the same.

119. All of the expenses discussed in this chapter were variable costs—they rose in direct proportion to the quantity of dye marketed. Merchants also had fixed costs—administrative overhead, salaries, etc. In addition, merchants incurred interest expenses, the costs associated with servicing loans.

120. Such an estimate is necessarily approximate owing to the numerous holes in the data. Where possible and justified, reasonable estimates have been inserted to permit a more complete picture.

121. We know that both ocean freight charges and intra-European insurance premiums rose sharply, and thus their exclusion biases the curve downwards. Freight charges recorded by Douglass North demonstrated a steep upward slope during the wars of the French Revolution and Napoleon. Likewise, the few data that we have for insurance within Europe suggest that intra-European rates followed the same course as transatlantic premiums, which should be expected. They too, then, must have skyrocketed after 1793.

122. See the section on maritime insurance earlier in this chapter.

123. The European price series can be used to give a reasonable estimate of the gross revenues (GR) obtained from the marketing of an arroba of cochineal in each year, since this is what a merchant would have received from the sale of an arroba. GR per arroba = European price per pound × 25. The profitability of this commerce also depended on how much it cost the merchant to get his dye to market, the total variable costs computed above. The ratio of these two factors (Total Costs ÷ Gross Revenue) is a reflection of the trade's profitability. In effect, it shows the percentage of revenues eaten by costs. It necessarily exaggerates profits, however, since it fails to account for fixed costs as well as the additional variable costs unaccounted for above, i.e., ocean freight and intra-European insurance.

124. For Figure 8.8, the total variable costs (intra-European insurance and ocean freight excluded) were totaled item by item based on their estimated amounts

as discussed in this chapter. The only exception was 5 percent "shrinkage," which was accounted for by reducing the gross revenues obtained in Europe by 5 percent. Thus, if 1 arroba of cochineal were exported from Oaxaca, I assumed its weight was only 0.95 arroba when it arrived in London. So, if 1 arroba were worth 100 pesos in London, then the arroba exported from Oaxaca would produce 95 pesos in revenue (100 − 5 percent = 95). Return on investment (the outlay of money for variable costs) was then calculated as follows: rate of return on investment = (Gross Revenues − Total Variable Costs) ÷ Total Variable Costs. This ratio, expressed as a percentage, is plotted for every year from 1758 to 1817 and displayed in Figure 8.10. While this calculation does not yield the actual profitability, it does give a very real indication.

125. So far in this chapter, all of the expenses discussed have been variable costs. Variable costs are expenses that rise and fall proportionally with the quantity of an item being manufactured or traded. Merchants, however, also had fixed costs, unavoidable expenses related to business in general. Startup costs, administrative overhead, and salaries were just a few of these. In addition, merchants had to pay interest on borrowed capital. An exact accounting of profits would need to consider both fixed and variable costs. It is difficult, however, to break up total fixed costs in order to assign an average fixed cost to the individual transaction of bringing a fixed amount of *grana* (1 arroba) to market. Including the cost of debt-servicing is also problematic because the length of time that money was outstanding varied greatly. Expenses were incurred throughout the voyage from Oaxaca to England. As a result, it would be necessary to estimate the length of time that each expense was outstanding. For instance, merchants paid interest (or failed to earn interest income if using personal funds) on the money used for the initial purchase price of dye much longer than that used on the funds expended to pay English import taxes. Furthermore, it is simply too difficult to estimate how long a typical shipment of cochineal was delayed between Oaxaca and England. Some cargoes undoubtedly made the entire journey much more quickly than others. Failing to account for either fixed costs or debt-servicing clearly suggests profitability higher than was really obtainable, since fixed expenses also reduced profit margins. On the other hand, the two calculations above *do* yield a figure *above* which profits certainly could not have risen, an upper-bound estimate of profitability in the cochineal trade.

126. On the impact of war on transatlantic trade, see John R. Fisher, *Trade, War, and Revolution.*

127. The return on investment for 1814 is also overstated, owing to the fact that it was the one year for which we do not have a transatlantic insurance figure. Even if we were to estimate this figure and take it into account, however, the return for this year would still be very high.

128. Registered production fell to 199,800 pounds in 1812 and 178,875 pounds in 1813, both of which were less than half the already depressed figure of

478,912.5 pounds for 1811. The price in Oaxaca fell to 15 reales per pound in 1813, barely half what it had been two years earlier.

129. It is probable that the War of American Independence drove insurance premiums skyward just as the later conflicts did, but we have no records to indicate this.

130. Even assuming the more conservative war insurance premium of 20 percent, the profit rate (see Figure 8.10) was 10 percent or lower in thirteen of the twenty-nine years from 1793 to 1821. A rate of 10 percent could not have produced much in the way of profits after deducting the additional costs not yet accounted for. (The years 1818–1821 do not appear on the graph because we do not have insurance rates for these years. Yet, even before accounting for insurance, rates of return were 10 percent or below in the period 1819–1821, and 12.86 percent in 1818, which would have almost certainly placed this year below 10 percent as well, once insurance were included.) If, instead, we use the 50 percent insurance premium, the number of years of profits of 10 percent or lower rises to seventeen, more than half the total number of years under consideration. In contrast, the period before 1783 yielded profits above 10 percent in seventeen of twenty-five years. Only one of the years from 1784 to 1792 witnessed a profit rate above 10 percent.

131. See Pastor, "El repartimiento"; Pastor, *Campesinos y reformas*; Chance, *Conquest of the Sierra*; Chance, "Social Stratification"; Chance, "Capitalismo y desigualidad"; Hamnett, *Politics and Trade*; and Reina.

132. Hamnett, *Politics and Trade*, chap. 4.

133. Dahlgren includes an appendix that lists the amounts collected from the 4 percent tithe in the years 1784–1789. Even in 1789, a year in which the amount was double that of any other year, the tithe produced only 1,003 pesos. If this was 4 percent of the total value of cochineal produced by Spaniards in that year, then Spaniards produced dye worth 25,075 pesos, representing 2.7 percent of the total value of that year's output of 926,367 pesos.

134. Low output in 1781 might have been related to the implementation of the *alcabala*, but also might have been associated with Spain's participation in the War of American Independence. In fact, Hamnett noted that the Oaxacan merchants complaining about the *bando* also noted the difficulties trade faced because of the war.

135. On the famine of the mid–1780s, see Florescano, *Precios del maiz y crisis agrícolas*. For Oaxaca, see Hamnett, *Politics and Trade*, 64–67.

136. The ban on *repartimientos* and the subsequent depression in the cochineal trade are discussed in Chapters 2 and 3.

137. For cochineal prices in Amsterdam, see Posthumus, 420–22.

138. Insignificant amounts of lower quality *grana* were produced or merely gathered wild in other parts of the Spanish dominions. Dutch and English prices referred to *grana fina* from Oaxaca.

139. Buist, 431–51. For a reference to the identical episode, see Braudel, 2:421–23.

140. Chance, *Conquest of the Sierra*, 106.

141. AGN, Indios, vol. 67, exp. 278, 1791.

142. Theoretically, the mere participation of the subdelegate in this trade was illegal, owing to Article 12.

143. "Naturales contra el alcalde mayor del Marquesado porque cobra con violencia," AGEO, Real Intendencia de Oaxaca II, legajo 4, exp. 13, 1795.

144. "Nota de los precios corrientes, fletes, comisiones y seguros que pagan los fructos de este reyno," AGN, Intendencias, vol. 4, pp. 249–83, 1797.

145. Unfortunately, detailed studies measuring the profitability of individual commodities traded overseas are lacking.

146. Brading, *Miners and Merchants*, 140–46.

147. Coatsworth, "Mexican Mining," 37–39.

148. Hamnett, *Politics and Trade*, 39–40, 159.

149. Coatsworth, "Mexican Mining," 41–42.

150. Salvucci, 152–53.

Chapter 9. Epilogue

1. Hamnett, in *Politics and Trade*, makes reference to the 1819 Reales Ordenes granting Guatemala and Yucatán permission to cultivate cochineal (144). There is some ambiguity, however, as MacLeod refers to seventeenth-century attempts, and failures, to introduce cochineal into Central America (170–75). The Crown was certainly fearful that the secrets of cochineal production would fall into the hands of its foreign rivals. In fact, a Frenchman named Thierry de Ménonville smuggled a *nopal* with live cochineal out of Oaxaca in 1777, as the French hoped to introduce its cultivation into Santo Domingo (see Hamnett, *Politics and Trade*, 2).

2. The best discussion of the nineteenth-century Guatemalan cochineal trade appears in McCreery, 113–29. Unlike Oaxaca, large non-Indian producers made a significant contribution to the overall output in Guatemala. As in Oaxaca, however, financing of cochineal producers was critical and the financiers seem to have been the greatest beneficiaries of the *grana* trade. Most interesting, the credit system operated very similarly to the *repartimiento*. Cash advances were made against future harvests and debtors often failed to repay their loans, owing both to harvest losses and deceit.

3. On the many colonial laws and commercial restrictions, see Coatsworth, "Obstacles to Economic Growth," 92–94; and Andrien and Johnson, 247–53.

Bibliography

Archives

Archivo de la Familia Yraeta, Mexico City
Archivo General del Estado de Oaxaca, Oaxaca, Mexico
Archivo General de Indias, Seville, Spain
Archivo General de la Nación, Mexico City
Archivo General de Notarias de Oaxaca, Oaxaca, Mexico
Archivo Histórico Municipal de Oaxaca, Oaxaca, Mexico
Archivo Judicial de Teposcolula, Oaxaca, Mexico
Archivo Judicial de Villa Alta, Oaxaca, Mexico
Biblioteca Miguel Lerdo de Tejada de la Secretaría de Hacienda y Crédito
    Público, Mexico City
Biblioteca Nacional de México, Mexico City

Secondary Sources

Adams, Donald R., Jr. "American Neutrality and Prosperity, 1793–1808: A
    Reconsideration." *Journal of Economic History* 40 (1980): 713–37.
Aguayo Spencer, Rafael, ed. *Obras de don Lucas Alamán: Documentos diver-
    sos (inéditos y muy raros)*. 2 vols. Mexico City: Editorial Jus, 1945–
    1948.
Andrien, Kenneth J. "The Sale of Fiscal Offices and the Decline of Royal
    Authority in the Viceroyalty of Peru, 1633–1700." *Hispanic American
    Historical Review* 62 (February 1982): 49–71.
——. *Crisis and Decline: The Viceroyalty of Peru in the Seventeenth Century.*
    Albuquerque: University of New Mexico Press, 1985.
——. "The State and Dependency in Late Colonial and Early Republican
    Ecuador." In *The Political Economy of Spanish America in the Age of
    Revolution, 1750–1850*, edited by Kenneth J. Andrien and Lyman L.
    Johnson, eds. Albuquerque: University of New Mexico Press, 1994.

———. *The Kingdom of Quito, 1690–1830: The State and Regional Development*. Cambridge: Cambridge University Press, 1995.

———. "The *Noticias secretas de América* and the Construction of a Governing Ideology for the Spanish American Empire." *Colonial Latin American Review* 7 (December 1998): 175–92.

Andrien, Kenneth J., and Lyman L. Johnson, eds. *The Political Economy of Spanish America in the Age of Revolution: 1750–1850*. Albuquerque: University of New Mexico Press, 1994.

Arellanes, Anselmo. "Grana oaxaqueña: Su decadencia y final." Paper presented at VII Seminario sobre la formación del capitalismo en Mexico, Oaxaca, 1989.

Artola, Miguel. *Enciclopedia de historia de España*. 7 vols. Madrid: Alianza Editorial, 1988–1993.

Assadourian, Carlos Sempat. *El sistema de la economía colonial: Mercado interno, regiones y espacio económico*. Lima: Instituto de Estudios Peruanos, 1982.

Bakewell, Peter J. *Silver Mining and Society in Colonial Mexico: Zacatecas, 1546–1700*. Cambridge: Cambridge University Press, 1971.

Barbier, Jacques, and Allan Kuethe, eds. *The North American Role in the Spanish Imperial Economy, 1760–1819*. Manchester, U.K.: Manchester University Press, 1984.

Barham, Bradford, and Oliver Coomes. "Wild Rubber: Industrial Organization and the Microeconomics of Extraction during the Amazon Rubber Boom (1860–1920)." *Journal of Latin American Studies* 26 (1994): 37–72.

Baskes, Jeremy. "Indians, Merchants, and Markets: Trade and *Repartimiento* Production of Cochineal Dye in Colonial Oaxaca." Ph.D. diss., University of Chicago, 1993.

———. "Coerced or Voluntary? The *Repartimiento* and Market Participation of Peasants in Late Colonial Oaxaca." *Journal of Latin American Studies* 28 (1996): 1–28.

Bauer, Arnold J. "Rural Workers in Spanish America: Problems of Peonage and Oppression." *Hispanic American Historical Review* 59 (1979): 34–63.

———. "The Church in the Economy of Spanish America: *Censos* and *Depósitos* in the Eighteenth and Nineteenth Centuries." *Hispanic American Historical Review* 63 (1983): 707–33.

Berdan, Frances F. *The Aztecs of Central Mexico: An Imperial Society*. New York: Holt, Rinehart and Winston, 1982.

———. "Trade and Markets in Precapitalist States." In *Economic Anthropology*, edited by Stuart Plattner. Stanford, Calif.: Stanford University Press, 1989.

———. "Markets in the Economy of Aztec Mexico." In *Markets and Market-*

ing, edited by Stuart Plattner, Society for Economic Anthropology. Lanham, Md.: University Press of America, 1985.

Bernal, Antonio-Miguel. *La financiación de la carrera de indias (1492–1824): Dinero y crédito en el comercio colonial español con América*. Seville: Fundación el Monte, 1992.

Bhattacharya, Neeladri. "Lenders and Debtors: Punjab Countryside, 1880–1940." In *Credit, Markets, and the Agrarian Economy of Colonial India*, edited by Sugata Bose. Cambridge: Cambridge University Press, 1994.

Borah, Woodrow, ed. *El gobierno provincial en la Nueva España, 1570–1787*. Mexico City: Universidad Nacional Autónoma de México, 1985.

———. *Early Colonial Trade and Navigation Between Mexico and Peru*. Ibero-Americana, no. 38. Berkeley: University of California Press, 1954.

———. *Justice by Insurance: The General Indian Court of Colonial Mexico and the Legal Aides of the Half-Real*. Berkeley: University of California Press, 1983.

Bose, Sugata, ed., *Credit, Markets, and the Agrarian Economy of Colonial India*. Cambridge: Cambridge University Press, 1994.

Botticini, Maristella. "Private Credit Markets and Public Finance: The Role of Jewish Lenders in Early-Fifteenth-Century Tuscany." Working paper, August 1998, in author's possession.

———. "A Tale of 'Benevolent' Governments: Private Credit Markets, Public Finance, and the Role of Jewish Lenders in Medieval and Renaissance Italy." *Journal of Economic History* 60 (2000): 164–89.

Brading, David. *Miners and Merchants in Bourbon Mexico, 1763–1810*. Cambridge: Cambridge University Press, 1971.

———. *Haciendas and Ranchos in the Mexican Bajío: León, 1700–1860*. Cambridge: Cambridge University Press, 1978.

———. "Bourbon Spain and its American Empire." In *Cambridge History of Latin America*, vol. 1, edited by Leslie Bethell. Cambridge: Cambridge University Press, 1984.

Braudel, Fernand. *Civilization and Capitalism, 15th–18th Century*. Vol. 2: *The Wheels of Commerce*. Translated by Sian Reynolds. New York: Harper and Rowe, 1982.

Buist, Marten G. *At Spes Non Fracta Hope & Co., 1770–1815: Merchant Bankers and Diplomats at Work*. The Hague: Nijhoff, 1974.

Bustamante, Carlos Maria de. *Memoria estadística de Oaxaca y descripción del valle del mismo nombre extractada de la que en grande trabajó el señor don José Murguía y Galardi*. Veracruz, 1821.

Calderón Quijano, José Antonio. *Virreyes de Nueva España*. 2 vols. Seville: Escuela Gráfica Salesiana, 1967.

Camon Fernandez de Avila, Rafael. "La emancipación y el comercio Catalán con América." *Revista de indias* 35 (1975): 229–60.

Carmagnani, Marcello. "Los recursos y los estrategias de los recursos en la reproducción de la sociedad india de Oaxaca." *Nova Americana* 4 (1981): 263–80.

———. "Local Governments and Ethnic Government in Oaxaca." In *Essays in the Political, Economic and Social History of Colonial Latin America,* edited by Karen Spalding. Newark: University of Delaware Press, 1982.

———. *El regreso de los dioses: El proceso de reconstitución de la identidad étnica en Oaxaca. Siglos XVII y XVIII.* Mexico City: Fondo de Cultura Económica, 1988.

———. "Un movimiento político indio: La "rebelión" de Tehuantepec, 1660–1661." In *El fuego de la inobediencia,* edited by Hector Diaz-Polanco. Mexico City: CIESAS, 1993.

Cassidy, Thomas J. "Haciendas and Pueblos in Nineteenth Century Oaxaca." Ph.D. diss., Cambridge University, 1981.

Chance, John K. *Race and Class in Colonial Oaxaca.* Stanford, Calif.: Stanford University Press, 1978.

———. "Social Stratification and the Civil Cargo System Among the Rincón Zapotecs of Oaxaca: The Late Colonial Period." In *Iberian Colonies, New World Societies: Essays in Memory of Charles Gibson,* edited by Richard L. Garner and William B. Taylor. Private Printing, 1986.

———. *Conquest of the Sierra: Spaniards and Indians in Colonial Oaxaca.* Norman: University of Oklahoma Press, 1989.

———. "Capitalismo y desigualidad entre los Zapotecos de Oaxaca: Una comparación entre el valle y los pueblos del rincón, época colonial." In *Lecturas históricas del estado de Oaxaca, época colonial,* vol. 1, edited by Maria de los Angeles Romero Frizzi. Mexico City: INAH, 1990.

Chevalier, François. *Land and Society in Colonial Mexico: The Great Hacienda.* Berkeley: University of California Press, 1963.

Coatsworth, John H. "American Trade with European Colonies in the Caribbean and South America, 1790–1812." *William and Mary Quarterly* 24 (1967): 243–66.

———. "Obstacles to Economic Growth in Nineteenth-Century Mexico." *American Historical Review* 83 (1978): 277–91.

———. "The Limits of Colonial Absolutism: The State in Eighteenth-Century Mexico." In *Essays in the Political, Economic and Social History of Colonial Latin America,* edited by Karen Spalding. Newark: University of Delaware Press, 1982.

———. *El impacto económico de los ferrocarriles en el Porfiriato.* Mexico City: Ediciones Era, 1984.

———. "The Mexican Mining Industry in the Eighteenth Century." In *The Economies of Mexico and Peru During the Late Colonial Period, 1760–1810,* edited by Nils Jacobsen and Hans-Jürgen Puhle. Berlin: Colloquium Verlag, 1986.

———. "La historiografía económica de Mexico." *Revista de Historia Económica* 6 (1988): 277–91.

Cohen, Abner. "The Social Organization of Credit in a West African Cattle Market." In *Friends, Followers, and Factions: A Reader in Political Clientelism*, edited by Steffen W. Schmidt. Berkeley: University of California Press, 1977.

Cohen, Jon S. "Institutions and Economic Analysis." In *Economics and the Historian*, edited by Thomas G. Rawski et al. Berkeley: University of California Press, 1996.

Costeloe, Michael P. *Church Wealth in Mexico*. Cambridge: Cambridge University Press, 1967.

Cuenca Esteban, Javier. "Statistics of Spain's Colonial Trade, 1792–1820: Consular Duties, Cargo Inventories, and Balances of Trade." *Hispanic American Historical Review* 61 (1981): 381–428.

———. "The United States Balance of Payments with Spanish America and the Philippine Islands, 1790–1819: Estimates and Analysis of Principal Components." In *The North American Role in the Spanish Imperial Economy, 1760–1819*, edited by Jacques Barbier and Allan Kuethe. Manchester, U.K.: Manchester University Press, 1984.

———. "The Markets of Latin American Exports, 1790–1820: A Comparative Analysis of International Prices." In *Essays on the Price History of Eighteenth Century Latin America*, edited by Lyman L. Johnson and Enrique Tandeter. Albuquerque: University of New Mexico Press, 1990.

Curtin, Philip D. *Cross-Cultural Trade in World History*. Cambridge: Cambridge University Press, 1984.

Cushner, Nicholas P. *Lords of the Land: Sugar, Wine, and Jesuit Estates of Coastal Peru, 1600–1767*. Albany: State University of New York Press, 1980.

Dahlgren, Barbro, ed. *La grana cochinilla*. Mexico City: Universidad Nacional Autónoma de México, 1963.

De Conde, Alexander. *The Quasi-War: Politics and Diplomacy of the Undeclared War with France, 1797–1801*. New York: Scribner, 1966.

Deans-Smith, Susan. *Bureaucrats, Planters, and Workers: The Making of the Tobacco Monopoly in Bourbon Mexico*. Austin: University of Texas Press, 1992.

Dehouve, Daniele. "El pueblo de indios y el mercado: Tlapa en el siglo XVIII." In *Empresarios, indios y estado: Perfil de la economía Mexicana* (siglo XVIII), edited by Arij Ouweneel and Cristina Torales Pacheco. Amsterdam: CEDLA, 1988.

Del Valle Pavón, Guillermina. "Las corporaciones religiosas en los emprésitos negociados por el consulado de México a fines del siglo XVIII." In *Iglesia, estado y economía: Siglos XVI al XIX*, edited by Maria del Pilar Martínez Lopez-Cano. Mexico City: Instituto Mora, 1995.

"Descripción de la cochinilla mixteca, y de su cria y beneficio," *Boletín de la sociedad Mexicana de geografía y estadísticas* 3 (1852): 82–86.

Díaz del Castillo, Bernal. *The Conquest of New Spain.* Translated by J. M. Cohen. London: Penguin, 1963.

Díaz-Polanco, Hector, ed. *El fuego de la inobediencia.* Mexico City: CIESAS, 1993.

Díaz-Polanco, Hector, and Carlos Manzo. *Documentos sobre las rebeliones de Tehuantepec y Nexapa (1660–1661).* Mexico City: CIESAS, 1992.

Donkin, R. A. "Spanish Red: An Ethnogeographical Study of Cochineal and the Opuntia Cactus." *Translations of the American Philosophical Society* 67 (September 1977): 3–84.

Elliott, J. H. *Imperial Spain: 1469–1716.* New York: Meridian, 1963.

Farriss, Nancy M. *Maya Society Under Colonial Rule: The Collective Enterprise of Survival.* Princeton: Princeton University Press, 1984.

Fisher, John R. *Government and Society in Colonial Peru: The Intendant System, 1784–1814.* London: University of London, 1970.

———. *Commercial Relations Between Spain and Spanish America in the Era of Free Trade, 1778–1796.* Liverpool: Center for Latin American Studies, University of Liverpool, 1985.

———. *Trade, War, and Revolution: Exports from Spain to Spanish America, 1797–1820.* Liverpool: Center for Latin American Studies, University of Liverpool, 1992.

———. *The Economic Aspects of Spanish Imperialism in America, 1492–1810.* Liverpool: Liverpool University Press, 1997.

Fisher, Lillian Estelle. *The Intendant System in Spanish America.* Berkeley: University of California Press, 1929.

Florescano, Enrique. *Precios del maíz y crisis agrícolas en México: 1708–1810.* Mexico City: El Colegio de México, 1969.

———. "The Hacienda in New Spain." In *Colonial Spanish America,* edited by Leslie Bethell. Cambridge: Cambridge University Press, 1987.

Fonseca, Fabián de, and Carlos de Urrutia. *Historia general de Real Hacienda.* 6 vols. Mexico City: Vicente G. Torres, 1845–1853.

Garavaglia, Juan Carlos, and Juan Carlos Grosso. *Las alcabalas novohispanos (1776–1821).* Mexico City: Archivo General de la Nación, 1987.

García Acosta, Virginia, ed., *Los precios de alimentos y manufacturas novohispanos.* Mexico City: CIESAS, 1995.

García-Baquero González, Antonio. *Cádiz y el Atlántico: 1717–1778.* 2 vols. Cádiz, Spain: Diputación Provincial de Cádiz, 1988.

Garner, Richard L. *Economic Growth and Change in Bourbon Mexico.* Gainesville: University of Florida Press, 1993.

Garzon Pareja, Manuel. "El 'riesgo' en el comercio de indias." *Revista de Indias* 35 (1975): 187–228.

Gay, Jose Antonio. *Historia de Oaxaca.* Mexico City: Editorial Porrua, 1982.

Gerhard, Peter. *A Guide to the Historical Geography of New Spain.* Cambridge: Cambridge University Press, 1972.

Gibson, Charles. *Tlaxcala in the Sixteenth Century.* Stanford, Calif.: Stanford University Press, 1952.

———. *The Aztecs Under Spanish Rule.* Stanford, Calif.: Stanford University Press, 1964.

———, ed. *The Black Legend: Anti-Spanish Attitudes in the Old World and the New.* New York: Alfred A. Knopf, 1971.

Goldin, Claudia Dale. "Credit Merchandising in the New South: The Role of Competition and Risk." In *Market Institutions and Economic Progress in the New South, 1865–1910: Essays Stimulated by One Kind of Freedom: The Economic Consequences of Emancipation,* edited by Gary M. Walton and James F. Shepherd. New York: Academic Press, 1981.

Golte, Jürgen. *Repartos y rebeliones: Túpac Amaru y las contradicciones de la economía colonial.* Lima: Instituto de Estudios Peruanos, 1980.

Gosner, Kevin. *Soldiers of the Virgin: The Moral Economy of a Colonial Maya Rebellion.* Tucson: University of Arizona Press, 1992.

Greenow, Linda L. *Credit and Socioeconomic Change in Colonial Mexico: Loans and Mortgages in Guadalajara, 1720–1820.* Boulder, Colo.: Westview Press, 1983.

Greif, Avner. "Contract Enforceability and Economic Institutions in Early Trade: The Maghribi Traders' Coalition." *American Economic Review* 83 (1993): 525–48.

———. "Microtheory and Recent Developments in the Study of Economic Institutions Through Economic History." In *Advances in Economics and Econometrics: Theory and Applications,* vol. 2, edited by David M. Kreps and Kenneth F. Wallis. Proceedings of the Seventh World Congress of the Econometric Society. Cambridge: Cambridge University Press, 1997.

Grupo Sociedad y Estado (Carlos Mayo, director). *Pulperos y pulperías de Buenos Aires, 1740–1830.* Mar del Plata: Universidad de Mar del Plata, 1997.

Guardino, Peter. *Peasants, Politics, and the Formation of Mexico's National State: Guerrero, 1800–1857.* Stanford, Calif.: Stanford University Press, 1996.

Guardino, Peter, and Charles Walker. "The State, Society, and Politics in Peru and Mexico in the Late Colonial and Early Republican Periods." *Latin American Perspectives* 19 (1992): 10–43.

Hamnett, Brian R. "Dye Production, Food Supply, and the Laboring Population of Oaxaca, 1750–1800." *Hispanic American Historical Review* 51 (1971): 51–78.

———. *Politics and Trade in Southern Mexico, 1750–1821.* Cambridge: Cambridge University Press, 1971.

———. *Roots of Insurgency: Mexican Regions, 1750–1824.* Cambridge: Cambridge University Press, 1986.

———. "Between Bourbon Reforms and Liberal Reforma: The Political Economy of a Mexican Province—Oaxaca, 1750–1850." In *The Political Economy of Spanish America in the Age of Revolution: 1750–1850,* edited by Kenneth J. Andrien and Lyman L. Johnson. Albuquerque: University of New Mexico Press, 1994.

Haring, C. H. *The Spanish Empire in America.* New York: Harcourt Brace Jovanovich, 1947.

———. *Trade and Navigation Between Spain and the Indies in the Time of the Hapsburgs.* Cambridge: Cambridge University Press, 1918.

Harris, Olivia, Brooke Larson, and Enrique Tandeter, eds. *La participación indígena en los mercados surandinos: Estrategias y reproducción social, siglos XVI a XX.* La Paz, Bolivia: CERES, 1987.

Hassig, Ross. *Trade, Tribute, and Transportation: The Sixteenth-Century Political Economy of the Valley of Mexico.* Norman: University of Oklahoma Press, 1985.

Hoberman, Louisa Schell. *Mexico's Merchant Elite, 1590–1660: Silver, State, and Society.* Durham, N.C.: Duke University Press, 1991.

Hoekstra, Rik. *Two Worlds Merging: The Transformation of Society in the Valley of Puebla, 1570–1640.* Amsterdam: CEDLA, 1993.

Hoff, Karla, and Joseph E. Stiglitz. "Introduction: Imperfect Information and Rural Credit Markets—Puzzles and Perspectives." *The World Bank Economic Review* 4 (1990): 235–50.

Jacobsen, Nils, and Hans Jürgen Puhle, eds. *The Economies of Mexico and Peru during the Late Colonial Period, 1760–1810.* Berlin: Colloqium Verlag, 1986.

Johnson, Lyman L., and Enrique Tandeter, eds. *Essays on the Price History of Eighteenth-Century Latin America.* Albuquerque: University of New Mexico Press, 1990.

Joseph, Gilbert M., and Daniel Nugent, eds. *Everyday Forms of State Formation: Revolution and the Negotiation of Rule in Modern Mexico.* Durham, N.C.: Duke University Press, 1994.

Juan, Jorge, and Antonio de Ulloa. *Discourse and Political Reflections on the Kingdoms of Peru.* Translated by John J. TePaske and Besse A. Clement. Norman: University of Oklahoma Press, 1978.

Katz, Friedrich, ed. *Riot, Rebellion, and Revolution—Rural Social Conflict in Mexico.* Princeton: Princeton University Press, 1988.

Kicza, John E. *Colonial Entrepreneurs: Families and Business in Bourbon Mexico City.* Albuquerque: University of New Mexico Press, 1983.

———. "Consumption and Control: The Mexico City Business Community and Commodity Marketing in the Eighteenth Century." *Estudios de Historia Novohispana* 12 (1992): 159–69.

Kinsbruner, Jay. *Petty Capitalism in Spanish America: The Pulperos of Puebla, Mexico City, Caracas, and Buenos Aires.* Boulder, Colo.: Westview Press, 1987.

Klein, Herbert S., and Jacques Q. Barbier. "Recent Trends in the Study of Colonial Public Finance." *Latin American Historical Review* 23 (1988): 35–62.

Knight, Alan. "Mexican Peonage: What Was It and Why Was It?" *Journal of Latin American Studies* 18 (1986): 41–74.

Kohn, Meir. "Finance before the Industrial Revolution: An Introduction." Draft chapter of manuscript entitled *Finance, Business, and Government Before the Industrial Revolution,* in possession of author.

———. "Merchant Banking in the Medieval and Early Modern Economy." Draft chapter of manuscript entitled *Finance, Business, and Government Before the Industrial Revolution,* in possession of author.

Langer, Erick D., and Gina L. Hames. "Commerce and Credit on the Periphery: Tarija Merchants, 1830–1914." *Hispanic American Historical Review* 74 (1994): 285–316.

Larson, Brooke. *Cochabamba, 1550–1900: Colonialism and Agrarian Transformation in Bolivia.* Durham, N.C.: Duke University Press, 1998.

Larson, Brooke, and Robert Wasserstrom. "Consumo forzoso en Cochabamba y Chiapa durante la época colonial." *Historia Mexicana* 12 (1982): 361–408.

Larson, Brooke, and Olivia Harris, eds. *Ethnicity, Markets, and Migration in the Andes: At the Crossroads of History and Anthropology.* Durham, N.C.: Duke University Press, 1995.

Lavrin, Asunción. "Rural Confraternities in the Local Economies of New Spain." In *The Indian Community of Colonial Mexico: Fifteen Essays on Land Tenure, Corporate Organizations, Ideology, and Village Politics,* edited by Arij Ouweneel and Simon Miller. Amsterdam: CEDLA, 1990.

Lee, Raymond L. "Cochineal Production and Trade in New Spain to 1600." *The Americas* 4 (1947–1948): 449–73.

———. "American Cochineal in European Commerce, 1526–1625." *The Journal of Modern History* 23 (1951): 205–24.

Lerdo de Tejada, Miguel. *Comercio esterior de México desde la conquista hasta hoy.* 1853. Reprint, Mexico City: Banco Nacional de México, 1967.

Liss, Peggy K. "Creoles, the North American Example, and the Spanish-American Economy, 1760–1810." In *The North American Role in the Spanish Imperial Economy, 1760–1819,* edited by Jacques Barbier and Allan Kuethe. Manchester, U.K.: Manchester University Press, 1984.

Lockhart, James. *The Nahuas after the Conquest: A Social and Cultural History of the Indians of Central Mexico, Sixteenth Through Eighteenth Centuries.* Stanford, Calif.: Stanford University Press, 1992.

Lockhart, James, and Stuart B. Schwartz. *Early Latin America: A History of Colonial Spanish America and Brazil*. Cambridge: Cambridge University Press, 1983.

Lynch, John. *Spanish Colonial Administration, 1782–1810: The Intendant System in the Viceroyalty of the Río de la Plata*. London: University of London, Athlone Press, 1958.

———. *The Spanish American Revolutions, 1808–1826*. 2d ed. New York: Norton, 1986.

MacLachlan, Colin M. *Spain's Empire in the New World: The Role of Ideas in Institutional and Social Change*. Berkeley: University of California Press, 1988.

Macleod, Murdo. *Spanish Central America: A Socioeconomic History, 1520–1720*. Berkeley: University of California Press, 1973.

Mallon, Florencia E. *The Defense of Community in Peru's Central Highlands: Peasant Struggle and Capitalist Transition, 1860–1940*. Princeton: Princeton University Press, 1983.

———. *Peasant and Nation: The Making of Postcolonial Mexico and Peru*. Berkeley: University of California Press, 1995.

Manso de Contreras, Cristóbal. *La rebelión de Tehuantepec*. Mexico City: Ediciones Toledo, 1987.

Marichal, Carlos. "La historiografía económica reciente sobre el México Borbónico: Los estudios del comercio y las finanzas virreinales, 1760–1820." Paper presented at the Coloquio Oaxtepec, Oaxtepec, Mexico, October 1988.

Martin, Cheryl English. *Rural Society in Colonial Morelos*. Albuquerque: University of New Mexico Press, 1985.

McCreery, David. *Rural Guatemala: 1760–1940*. Stanford, Calif.: Stanford University Press, 1994.

Mills, Kenneth, and William B. Taylor. *Colonial Spanish America: A Documentary History*. Wilmington, Del.: Scholarly Resources, 1998.

Moreno Cebrián, Alfredo. *El corregidor de indios y la economía peruana del siglo XVIII (Los repartos forzosos de mercancías)*. Madrid: Consejo Superior de Investigaciones Científicos, 1977.

———. "Un intento de reinstaurar los repartos de mercancias a los indios del Peru: D. Jorge de Escovedo y Alarcon." *Historia y Cultura* 10 (1978): 119–34.

Morin, Claude. *Michoacán en la Nueva España del siglo XVIII: Crecimiento de desigualdad en una economía colonial*. Mexico City: Fondo de Cultura Económica, 1979.

Murguía y Galardi, Jose Maria de. *Apuntamientos estadísticos de la provincia de Oaxaca*. 5 vols. Oaxaca: Imprenta Ignacio Rincón, 1861.

Navarro García, Luis. *Intendencias en Indias*. Seville: Escuela de Estudios Hispano-Americanos, 1959.

North, Douglass C. "Ocean Freight Rates and Economic Development, 1750–1913." *Journal of Economic History* 18 (1958): 537–55.

———. "The Role of Transportation in the Economic Development of North America." In *Les grandes voies maritimes dans le monde, XVᵉ–XIXᵉ siècles*. Paris: SEVPEN, 1965.

———. *Institutions, Institutional Change, and Economic Performance*. Cambridge: Cambridge University Press, 1990.

O'Phelan Godoy, Scarlett. *Rebellions and Revolts in Eighteenth-Century Peru and Upper Peru*. Köln: Bohlau, 1985.

Ortiz de la Tabla Ducasse, Javier. *Comercio exterior de Veracruz, 1778–1821: Crisis de dependencia*. Seville: Escuela de Estudios Hispano-Americanos, 1978.

Ouweneel, Arij. *Shadows Over Anáhuac: An Ecological Interpretation of Crisis and Development in Central Mexico, 1730–1800*. Albuquerque: University of New Mexico Press, 1996.

Ouweneel, Arij, and Simon Miller, eds. *The Indian Community of Colonial Mexico: Fifteen Essays on Land Tenure, Corporate Organizations, Ideology and Village Politics*. Amsterdam: CEDLA, 1990.

Ouweneel, Arij, and Cristina Torales Pacheco, eds. *Empresarios, indios, y estado: Perfil de la economía Mexicana* (siglo XVIII). Amsterdam: CEDLA, 1988.

Ovando-Sanz, Guillermo, ed. *Tadeo Haenke, su obra en los Andes y la selva boliviana*. La Paz, Bolivia: Editorial "Los Amigos del Libro," 1974.

Parry, J. H. *The Sale of Public Office in the Spanish Indies Under the Hapsburgs*. Berkeley: University of California Press, 1953.

Pastor, Rodolfo. "El repartimiento de mercancias y los alcaldes mayores novohispanos: Un sistema de explotación, de sus origenes a la crisis de 1810." In *El gobierno provincial en la Nueva España, 1570–1787*, edited by Woodrow Borah. Mexico City: Universidad Nacional Autónoma de México, 1985.

———. *Campesinos y reformas: La Mixteca, 1700–1856*. Mexico City: Colegio de México, 1987.

Pastor, Rodolfo, et al. *Fluctuaciones económicas en Oaxaca durante el siglo XVIII*. Mexico City: El Colegio de México, 1979.

Patch, Robert W. *Maya and Spaniard in Yucatan, 1648–1812*. Stanford, Calif.: Stanford University Press, 1993.

———. "Imperial Politics and Local Economy in Colonial Central America, 1670–1770." *Past and Present* 143 (1994): 77–107.

———. "The Cultural, the Material, and the Spiritual in New Spain." *Colonial Latin American Review* 6 (1997): 235–41.

Pérez Herrero, Pedro. *Platas y libranzas: La articulación comercial del México Borbónico*. Mexico City: Colegio de México, 1988.

Phillips, Carla Rahn. "The Growth and Composition of Trade in the Iberian

293

Empires, 1450–1750." In *The Rise of the Merchant Empires: Long-Distance Trade in the Early Modern World, 1350–1750*, edited by James D. Tracy. Cambridge: Cambridge University Press, 1990.

Phillips, Carla Rahn, and William D. Phillips. *Spain's Golden Fleece: Wool Production and the Wool Trade from the Middle Ages to the Nineteenth Century.* Baltimore: Johns Hopkins University Press, 1997.

Pietschmann, Horst. "Agricultura e industria rural indígena en el México de la segunda mitad del siglo XVIII." In *Empresarios, indios, y estado: Perfil de la economía Mexicana* (siglo XVIII), edited by Arij Ouweneel and Cristina Torales Pacheco. Amsterdam: CEDLA, 1988.

Portillo, Andres. *Oaxaca en el centenario de la independencia nacional.* Oaxaca: H. Santaella, 1910.

Posthumus, Nicholas. *Inquiry into the History of Prices in Holland.* 2 vols. Leiden: E. J. Brill, 1946, 1964.

Priestly, Herbert Ingram. *José de Gálvez: Visitor-General of New Spain (1765–1771).* Berkeley: University of California Press, 1916.

Primer censo de población de la Nueva España, 1790: Censo de Revillagigedo, "un censo condenado." Mexico City: Dirección General de Estadística, 1977.

Quirós, José María. *Guía de negociantes: Compendio de la legislación mercantil de España e Indias*, edited by Pedro Pérez Herrero. Mexico City: Universidad Nacional Autónoma de México, 1986.

Ramírez, Susan E. *Provincial Patriarchs: Land Tenure and the Economics of Power in Colonial Peru.* Albuquerque: University of New Mexico Press, 1986.

Ransom, Roger L., and Kerry Ann Odell. "Land and Credit: Some Historical Parallels Between Mexico and the American South." *Agricultural History* 60 (1986): 4–31.

Ransom, Roger L., and Richard Sutch. *One Kind of Freedom: The Economic Consequences of Emancipation.* Cambridge: Cambridge University Press, 1977.

———. "Credit Merchandising in the Post-Emancipation South: Structure, Conduct, and Performance." In *Market Institutions and Economic Progress in the New South, 1865–1900: Essays Stimulated by One Kind of Freedom: The Economic Consequences of Emancipation*, edited by Gary M. Walton and James F. Shepherd. New York: Academic Press, 1981.

Rawski, Thomas G., et al. *Economics and the Historian.* Berkeley: University of California Press, 1996.

Recopilación de leyes de los reynos de las indias. Reproducción en facsimil de la edición de Julian de Paredes de 1681. Madrid: Ediciones Cultura Hispánica, 1973.

Reina, Leticia, ed. *Historia de la cuestión agraria Mexicana: Estado de Oa-xaca, prehispánico–1924.* Mexico City: Juan Pablos Editor, 1988.

Rojas, Basilio. *La rebelión de Tehuantepec.* Mexico City: Sociedad Mexicana de Geografía y Estadísticas, 1964.

Romero Frizzi, Maria de los Angeles. *Economía y vida de los españoles en la Mixteca Alta: 1519–1720.* Mexico City: INAH, 1990.

———. *Lecturas históricas del estado de Oaxaca.* 4 vols. Mexico City: INAH, 1990.

———. "El poder de los mercaderes. La Mixteca alta: Del siglo XVI a los primeros años del XVIII." In *Familia y Poder en Nueva España*: Memoria del Tercer Simposio de Historia de las Mentalidades. Mexico City: INAH, 1991.

Rowe, John Howland. "The Incas under Spanish Colonial Institutions." *Hispanic American Historical Review* 37 (1957): 155–99.

Salvucci, Richard J. *Textiles and Capitalism in Mexico: An Economic History of the Obrajes, 1539–1840.* Princeton: Princeton University Press, 1987.

Sánchez Silva, Carlos. *Indios, comerciantes, y burocracía en la Oaxaca pos-colonial, 1786–1860.* Oaxaca: Instituto Oaxaqueño de las Culturas, Universidad Autónoma Benito Juarez de Oaxaca, 1998.

———. "Indios, Comerciantes, y Burocracía en Oaxaca, Mexico, 1786–1860." Ph.D. diss., University of California, San Diego, 1995.

Schroeder, Susan, ed. *Native Resistance and the Pax Colonial in New Spain.* Lincoln: University of Nebraska Press, 1998.

Schwaller, John Frederick. *Origins of Church Wealth in Mexico: Ecclesiastical Revenues and Church Finances, 1523–1600.* Albuquerque: University of New Mexico Press, 1985.

Scott, James C. *Weapons of the Weak: Everyday Forms of Peasant Resistance.* New Haven: Yale University Press, 1985.

Socolow, Susan Migden. *The Merchants of Buenos Aires, 1778–1810: Family and Commerce.* Cambridge: Cambridge University Press, 1978.

Spalding, Karen. "Tratos mercantiles del corregidor de Indios y la formación de la hacienda serrana en el Perú." *América Indígena* 30 (1970): 595–608.

———. "*Kurakas* and Commerce: A Chapter in the Evolution of Andean Society." *Hispanic American Historical Review* 53 (1973): 581–99.

———. *Huarochirí: An Andean Society Under Inca and Spanish Rule.* Stanford, Calif.: Stanford University Press, 1984.

Spooner, Frank. *Risks at Sea: Amsterdam Insurance and Maritime Europe, 1766–1780.* Cambridge: Cambridge University Press, 1983.

Spores, Ronald. "Differential Response to Colonial Control among the Mixtecs and Zapotecs of Oaxaca." In *Native Resistance and the Pax Colonial in New Spain*, edited by Susan Schroeder. Lincoln: University of Nebraska Press, 1998.

Stavig, Ward. "Ethnic Conflict, Moral Economy, and Population on the Eve of the Thupa Amaro II Rebellion." *Hispanic American Historical Review* 68 (1988): 737–70.

Stein, Stanley J. "Bureaucracy and Business in the Spanish Empire, 1759–1804: Failure of a Bourbon Reform in Mexico and Peru." *Hispanic American Historical Review* 61 (1981): 2–28.

———. "Tending the Store: Trade and Silver at the Real de Huautla, 1778–1781." *Hispanic American Historical Review* 77 (1997): 377–408.

Stern, Steve J. *Peru's Indian People and the Challenge of Spanish Conquest.* Madison: University of Wisconsin Press, 1982.

———. "La variedad y ambigüedad de la intervención indígena andina en los mercados coloniales europeos: Apuntes metodológicos." In *La participación indígena en los mercados surandinos: Estrategias y reproducción social siglos XVI a XX*, edited by Olivia Harris, Brooke Larson, and Enrique Tandeter. La Paz, Bolivia: CERES, 1987.

———, ed. *Resistance, Rebellion, and Consciousness in the Andean Peasant World: 18th to 20th Centuries.* Madison: University of Wisconsin Press, 1987.

Suárez Argüello, Clara Elena. *Camino real y carrera larga: La arriería en la Nueva España durante el siglo XVIII.* Mexico City: CIESA, 1997.

Taylor, William B. *Landlord and Peasant in Colonial Oaxaca.* Stanford, Calif.: Stanford University Press, 1972.

———. "Landed Society in New Spain: A View from the South." *Hispanic American Historical Review* 54 (1974): 387–413.

———. "Town and Country in the Valley of Oaxaca, 1750–1812." In *Provinces of Early Mexico: Variants of Spanish-American Regional Evolution*, edited by Ida Altman and James Lockhart. Los Angeles: UCLA Latin American Center Publications, 1976.

———. *Drinking, Homicide, and Rebellion in Colonial Mexican Villages.* Stanford, Calif.: Stanford University Press, 1979.

———. "Conflict and Balance in District Politics: Tecali and the Sierra Norte de Puebla in the Eighteenth Century." In *The Indian Community of Colonial Mexico: Fifteen Essays on Land Tenure, Corporate Organizations, Ideology, and Village Politics*, edited by Arij Ouweneel and Simon Miller. Amsterdam: CEDLA, 1990.

———. *Magistrates of the Sacred: Priests and Parishioners in Eighteenth-Century Mexico.* Stanford, Calif.: Stanford University Press, 1996.

TePaske, John J. "General Tendencies and Secular Trends in the Economies of Mexico and Peru, 1750–1810: The View from the Cajas of Mexico and Lima." In *The Economies of Mexico and Peru During the Late Colonial Period, 1760–1810*, edited by Nils Jacobsen and Hans-Jürgen Puhle. Berlin: Colloqium Verlag, 1986.

Thomson, Guy. "Traditional and Modern Manufacturing in Mexico, 1821–

1850." In *América Latina en la época de Simón Bolívar: La fomación de las economías nacionales y los intereses económicos europeos, 1800–1850*, edited by Reinhard Liehr. Berlin: Colloquium Verlag, 1989.

Thomson, Sinclair. "Colonial Crisis, Community, and Andean Self-Rule: Aymara Politics in the Age of Insurgency (Eighteenth Century La Paz)." Ph.D. diss., University of Wisconsin–Madison, 1996.

Tooke, Thomas, and William Newmarch. *A History of Prices and of the State of the Circulation from 1792 to 1856*. 6 vols. New York: Adelphi Company, 1928.

Torales Pacheco, Maria Cristina. *La compañía de comercio de Francisco Ignacio de Yraeta (1767–1797)*. 2 vols. Mexico City: Instituto Mexicano de Comercio Exterior, 1985.

Tord Nicolini, Javier. "El corregidor de indios del Peru: Comercio y tributos." *Historia y Cultura* 8 (1974): 173–214.

———. "Los repartos legalizados." *Proceso* 4 (1975): 5–10.

Torres Ramirez, Bibiano, and Javier Ortiz de la Tabla, eds. *Reglamento y aranceles reales para el comercio libre de España a Indias de 12 de octubre de 1778*. Seville: Escuela de Estudios Hispano-Americanos, 1978.

Tracy, James D., ed. *The Rise of the Merchant Empires: Long-Distance Trade in the Early Modern World, 1350–1750*. Cambridge: Cambridge University Press, 1990.

———. *The Political Economy of Merchant Empires*. Cambridge: Cambridge University Press, 1991.

Tutino, John. *From Insurrection to Revolution in Mexico: Social Bases of Agrarian Violence, 1750–1940*. Princeton: Princeton University Press, 1986.

Udry, Christopher. "Risk and Insurance in a Rural Credit Market: An Empirical Investigation in Northern Nigeria." *Review of Economic Studies* 61 (1994): 495–526.

Van Young, Eric. *Hacienda and Market in Eighteenth-Century Mexico: The Rural Economy of the Guadalajara Region, 1675–1820*. Berkeley: University of California Press, 1981.

———. "Moving Toward Revolt: Agrarian Origins of the Hidalgo Rebellion in the Guadalajara Region." In *Riot, Rebellion, and Revolution: Rural Social Conflict in Mexico*, edited by Friedrich Katz. Princeton: Princeton University Press, 1988.

———. "The Raw and the Cooked: Elite and Popular Ideology in Mexico, 1800–1821." In *The Middle Period in Latin America: Values and Attitudes in the Seventeenth and Nineteenth Centuries*, edited by Mark D. Szuchman. Boulder, Colo.: Lynne Reinner Publishers, 1989.

Walker, Geoffrey J. *Spanish Politics and Imperial Trade, 1700–1789*. Bloomington: Indiana University Press, 1979.

Walton, Gary M., and James F. Shepherd, eds. *Market Institutions and Economic Progress in the New South, 1865–1910: Essays Stimulated by One Kind of Freedom: The Economic Consequences of Emancipation.* New York: Academic Press, 1981.

Waterbury, Ronald. "Non-Revolutionary Peasants: Oaxaca Compared to Morelos in the Mexican Revolution." *Comparative Studies in Society and History* 17 (1975): 410–42.

Whitecotton, Joseph W. *The Zapotecs: Princes, Priests, and Peasants.* Norman: University of Oklahoma Press, 1977.

Wiemers, Eugene L., Jr. "Agriculture and Credit in Nineteenth-Century Mexico: Orizaba and Córdoba, 1822–1871." *Hispanic American Historical Review* 65 (1985): 519–46.

Williamson, Oliver E. *The Economic Institutions of Capitalism: Firms, Markets, Relational Contracting.* New York: The Free Press, 1985.

Woodward, Ralph Lee, Jr. *Class Privilege and Economic Development: The Consulado de Comercio of Guatemala, 1793–1871.* Chapel Hill: University of North Carolina Press, 1966.

World Bank. "Issues in Informal Finance." In *Financial Systems and Development: World Development Indicators.* New York: Oxford University Press, 1989.

Yuste Lopez, Carmen. *Comerciantes Mexicanos en el siglo XVIII: Selección de documentos e introducción.* Mexico City: Universidad Nacional Autónoma de Mexico, 1991.

Zamora y Coronado, José Maria. *Biblioteca de legislación ultramarina.* 7 vols. Madrid: Alegría y Charlain, 1844–1849.

Index